HANDBOOK OF BROADCASTING

The Fundamentals of Radio and Television

Handbook of Broadcasting

THE FUNDAMENTALS OF RADIO AND TELEVISION

Waldo Abbot

Associate Professor of Speech
Director of Broadcasting
Manager, Stations WUOM, WFUM
University of Michigan

Richard L. Rider

Supervisor, Television and Motion Pictures
Assistant Manager, WILL-TV
University of Illinois

FOURTH EDITION

McGRAW-HILL BOOK COMPANY

New York   Toronto   London   1957

PREFACE

This fourth edition of the *Handbook of Broadcasting* marks the *Handbook's* twentieth year in use as a textbook for elementary classes in the field of broadcasting. During those twenty years more than 50,000 copies have been distributed to teachers and students in this country and abroad. It is obvious that a great number of broadcasters-to-be have studied it.

In reality, the *Handbook* is more than twenty years old, for it was used for two years in mimeographed form by students in broadcasting at the University of Michigan. The *Handbook of Broadcasting* was the first textbook to cover all phases of broadcasting, and, like its author, it may be considered a "pioneer" in radio. Originally, it was concerned with only one type of microphone—the carbon—and students were warned to talk across the face of the instrument to avoid sibilation, which was emphasized by the carbon mike. This was particularly necessary in the author's classes, for his staff at that time consisted of Samuel Sylvan Simon, Grace Snyder, accompanist, Sibley Sedgewick, and Sidney Straight, soloist. They were hissed off the air in the opening announcement.

The first edition of the *Handbook* was published by McGraw-Hill Book Company in 1937. It introduced the eight-ball and the salt-shaker microphones, which names gave the broadcaster many opportunities for feeble humor. Both of these have become obsolete in this era of high fidelity. There were 689 broadcasting stations in operation in the United States, all of them amplitude-modulation.

The second edition, in 1941, ran into five impressions. It contained 18 photographic reproductions, in comparison with nearly one hundred in this edition. They showed such bygone equipment as the "machine-gun microphone attachment" for distant pickups, and crystal microphones, no longer used for broadcasting purposes. The number of stations in operation at this time had increased to 881. Only one page was devoted to frequency modulation and one page to facsimile, both of which were being introduced. Five hundred and sixty-four courses in broadcasting were being offered in American universities and colleges.

v

The third edition was published in 1950. Considerable space was devoted to frequency modulation and to facsimile; television was introduced, as well as wired wireless or closed circuit, and a section was devoted to an experimental method of color television. The section upon manual sound effects was exhaustive. Today, however, manual sound effects have largely been replaced with recorded effects.

The revision for this fourth edition is drastic. Nothing has been omitted which is of value to the student of radio. Everything that is helpful to the future televiser has been retained. Those chapters and sections of the text dealing with microphone technique, speech, pronunciation, enunciation, acting, law, etc., which are basically the same for both the radio broadcaster and the televiser, are retained, with supplementary information concerning TV. Then, despite the fact that the author of the first three editions had had two years of television programming, he recognized his own inadequacies and sought information from teachers and professionals concerning the person best able to collaborate in writing material on television. Richard Rider, Supervisor of Television and Motion Pictures at the University of Illinois, was selected. After many discussions with the publishers and others it was decided not to attempt to make two books out of the *Handbook*, but to create a combined text which would be valuable for both students of radio and of television.

The fundamentals of amplitude modulation and frequency modulation have been retained. "Fax" or facsimile has been practically eliminated except in so far as it relates to its use in the field of television. Television, both black-and-white and color, has been expanded to approximately 50 per cent of the text. McGraw-Hill Book Company has permitted a vast expansion in photographic material used to illustrate the text. The result is a textbook to be used by all beginning students in radio and/or television. All the essentials are here in one volume.

Together the four editions of the *Handbook of Broadcasting* present a history of air-borne communications in the past twenty years.

WALDO ABBOT
RICHARD RIDER

CONTENTS

CONTENTS

CHAPTER ONE

FUNDAMENTALS OF RADIO— AMPLITUDE MODULATION

This handbook is intended for the student of broadcasting, not for the radio technician. That field of instruction is in the capable hands of the physicists and electronic engineers. A broadcaster, however, should know something of the medium that makes his profession possible. Let us trace the speech of an announcer from him to his listener.

Remote Origination

The announcer will either be broadcasting a special-event program (which is called a "remote") from a dance hall, an athletic field, a church, or some other location where the event is taking place, or he will be speaking from a studio located in the broadcasting station. If the program is a remote-control program, various acoustic problems will arise. There may be an excessive period of reverberation or an echo, or there may be a great deal of background noise. If he is broadcasting from a studio, the faults which are apparent in the remote-control broadcast have been corrected by acoustic engineers.

Studio Origination

When sounds are generated in an enclosure such as a room or a studio, the impulse that reaches the ear of the listener in the room comes from several places. Some of it comes directly from the source (50 per cent or less, depending upon the distance), the source in this instance being the announcer's vocal chords. Some comes from the ceiling, the side walls, and the floor by one or more reflections from these surfaces. In a hard-plastered room, where sound waves can reflect several times without being appreciably absorbed, a note may persist from 5 to 6 seconds after it has been sounded. A condition such as this, which engineers call "liveness," is intolerable in the majority of instances for broadcasting, and even

1

conversation is difficult in such a room. To remedy this condition, sound-absorbing materials are placed on the surface of the room. There are various materials and methods for acoustically treating such studios. In many new studios additional deadening has been effected by the elimination of flat surfaces upon the walls and ceiling. A "saw-toothed" or parabolic (Fig. 1) wall breaks up the sound waves reflected from it and

Fig. 1. Studio C–WUOM. This studio has two saw-toothed walls, the third [not shown] is parabolic. The fourth wall is angled to avoid having it parallel with the opposite wall. The control room is raised above the level of the studio so that announcers or actors will not obstruct the view of the control operator. The double glass in the window is tilted toward the floor. The two panes of glass are of different thicknesses to avoid vibration. A boom mike stand is seen in the background. (*University of Michigan.*)

helps further to diffuse the waves throughout the room. In other studios the side walls are hung at an angle, slanting gradually from the floor to the ceiling.

It has been found that the most desirable period of reverberation for a radio studio is from 0.8 to 1.2 seconds. When the reverberation period is greater than this, the studio is "live" and sounds persist too long. When it is less than this, the studio is "dead" and sounds die out too soon. Singers complain that their voices seem to go into the "dead" room and do not come back. In order to create certain effects, studios are now being built with "live ends" and "dead ends." (One student in an examination stated that the "live end" was where students were presenting a play—the "dead end" held the faculty speaker.) The live end is one in which the walls are hard-surfaced and flat, built for the purpose of reflecting sounds. The deliberate purpose of this arrangement is to introduce one relatively loud reflection into the microphone and help the naturalness of the

FIG. 2. Hemihedral blisters on walls, stepped ceiling, saw-toothed walls in one of the newer N.B.C. studios. (*Johns-Manville.*)

pickup. An orchestra is placed with its back to the live end, which acts as a shell reflector. The presence of many people in a studio will tend to deaden it, since each individual's clothing absorbs the sound. An excellent studio for the broadcasting of amplitude-modulation programs is an excellent studio for frequency modulation. The AM broadcaster, unfortunately, is too frequently content with imperfect acoustics; the FM broadcaster cannot be.

Reverberation should not be confused with echo. An echo is the return of a sound by reflection after a short period of silence. Since the shortest interval of silence that the ear can detect is $\frac{1}{16}$ second, it follows that, for an echo to be present, there must be a difference of at least 70 feet between the rate length of the sound reaching the listener directly and that returning by reflection. Reverberation is the successive return of the sound by reflection at intervals too short for the ear to detect so that the sound seems to be continuous as its intensity decreases.

In an acoustically treated studio the announcer speaks to a microphone. In a perfect acoustically constructed studio, particularly for FM, the microphone is placed where it best picks up the music or speech. It may be above or some distance from the artist.

The speaker's words are carried by sound waves from his mouth to the microphone. These sound waves travel at approximately 1100 feet a second. Each note in his voice causes air vibrations or sound waves. Each sound wave has its own frequency, that is to say, the number of vibrations set in motion per second. When these notes arrive at the microphone they cause the sensitive face of that microphone to respond at like frequencies and thus change the sound wave into electrical impulses.

Microphones

There are three general types of microphones in current use in broadcasting stations today. These microphones have many trade names, but fundamentally those

FIG. 3. RCA 44BX velocity microphone. (*Radio Corporation of America.*)

used for broadcasting are velocity, dynamic, and condenser microphones.

The velocity type of microphone is frequently called the "ribbon mike," and justly so, because its operation depends upon the vibration of a very thin corrugated duralumin ribbon suspended between the poles of a strong magnet. When the ribbon is set into motion by sound vibrations, small electric currents are developed in it which are then further amplified. The ribbon microphone is equally sensitive on the two opposite sides which represent the broad faces of the ribbon, while it is comparatively insensitive on the other two edges. It is an excellent type of microphone to be used for a quartet or to be placed in the center of an orchestra. The duralumin ribbon is hung in the bottom of a V-shaped trough. The result is that speakers do not talk across this microphone, but into the trough. The velocity type of microphone (Fig. 3) is manufactured by the Radio Corporation of America and is of the standard broadcasting type.

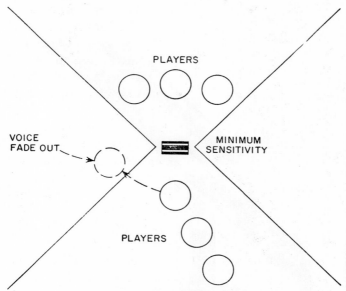

FIG. 4. Velocity mike fade-out.

The principle of the dynamic microphone is essentially that of the dynamic loud-speaker. It consists of a diaphragm on which is mounted a small coil of fine wire. This, vibrating in the field of a strong magnet, generates minute electric currents proportional to the incoming sound impulses. Its diaphragm is moved back and forth by the air or sound waves. This causes the coil to move in a powerful magnet field and electrical impulses result. The dynamic microphone may be constructed as either a directional microphone or a nondirectional microphone.

Western Electric developed the cardioid directional microphone (Fig. 6) which is really two microphones, a ribbon microphone and a dynamic microphone, each of which can be used independently or in conjunction with the other. This was the first instrument to combine not less than three pickup characteristics in one instrument. By the use of a small switch located at the base of the microphone, it is possible to convert this instrument into nondirectional, unidirectional, and cardioid or heart-shaped selectivity. Three other coverage areas designed to minimize reverberation are also possible with this microphone; Fig. 7 shows a

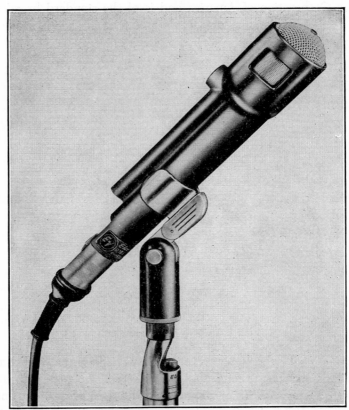

FIG. 5. Variable-D cardioid microphone 666 for television and broadcast use. (*Electro-Voice, Inc.*)

diagram of three of the pickup areas for this cardioid microphone. Radio Corporation of America makes an all-purpose microphone consisting of both ribbon-type and dynamic microphones operating in a common air-gap (Fig. 8). This microphone also has the three pickups—bidirectional, nondirectional, and cardioid. The grills or screens on all microphones are designed for protection and wind screening.

Fig. 6. The Multimike, a development of the cardioid microphone combining the features of the velocity and the dynamic microphones. (*Western Electric Company.*)

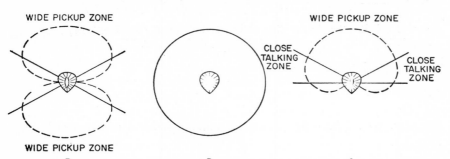

Fig. 7. Cardioid directional microphone pickup areas.

Using lightweight magnetic alloys to reduce the size of microphones, R.C.A. engineers developed a bantam-size unit which embodies the output and high fidelity of the larger types with a fraction of their weight. The Bantam is so small that it will not conceal the faces of singers and

FIG. 8   FIG. 9

FIG. 8. Polydirectional microphone Type 77-DX. (*Radio Corporation of America.*)

FIG. 9. The miniature velocity microphone, Style KB-2C. This midget microphone has a sensitivity and output level comparable to those of the larger velocity models. This Bantam is ideal for remote broadcasts, conventions, etc. The built-in swivel makes it possible to tilt the microphone forward or back. (*Radio Corporation of America.*)

speakers. It weighs only 12 ounces, making it ideal as a portable unit (Fig. 9).

The Tru-Sonic microphone system (Stephens Manufacturing Corporation, Fig. 10) is a condenser-type microphone with the auxiliary equipment in a separate unit connected to the mike by a coaxial cable. The Tru-Sonic has a very high frequency response, making it excellent for music. It is virtually blastproof. The employment of the single-microphone pickup technique so widely advocated to achieve balance can be successfully effected with this system. The uncertainty in making a new microphone setup with a strange orchestra is banished. By simply placing this mike in front of the orchestra and making a qualitative check, no

FIG. 10. Tru Sonic model C-2 microphone system, condenser type. The oscillator-demodulator (amplifier) unit is separate from the microphone. (*Stephens Manufacturing Corporation.*)

more than one or two changes are required to achieve perfect musical balance with only the single microphone.

In conventional ribbon microphone setups the recording engineer, of necessity, exercises considerable control over the character of the musical pickup. This is incidental to his prime function of maintaining levels within the limits of the equipment. Emphasis and deemphasis of certain sections of the orchestra, and the modulating of portions of the score, are more properly the responsibility of the musical director. Ordinarily these two individuals evolve a composite interpretation, which not infrequently is an unsatisfactory compromise.

Another high-fidelity condenser microphone is the Altec (Altec-Lansing, Fig. 12). This too, is a nondirectional or omnidirectional microphone of small size with tonal fidelity, full dynamic range, and negligible weight. The Altec also has its own power supply. It is greatly used upon athletic fields because of its lack of susceptibility to wind pressure.

The parabolic microphone attachment (Fig. 13) is used to directional-

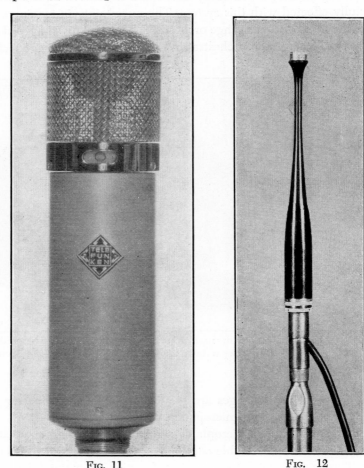

FIG. 11   FIG.   12

FIG. 11. Telefunken U-47M condenser microphone. (*American Elite, Inc.*)
FIG. 12. Altec microphone, tiny in size and omnidirectional.

ize a distant pickup. The microphone is placed in the focal point of the concave side of the bowl. The sound is reflected from the bowl to the microphone. Equipment of this type is used in convention halls and on gridirons.

Fɪɢ. 13. Parabolic attachment.

Control Console

The electric impulses that are developed in the microphone are carried to a control console (Fig. 14) adjacent to the studio in which the announcer is speaking. Here the control operator blends the output of microphones which are in use and amplifies the volume before it is sent out over special telephone lines. Special instruments calibrated in volume units (decibels), called "VU" by the technician, show the loudness of the programs at all times, and it is one of the duties of the control operator to keep the loudness within acceptable limits. The operator also checks the quality of outgoing music and speech by listening to it to see that no distortion is present. He formerly had to modulate sudden explosive sounds to avoid blasting; however, this is now accomplished automatically by equipment at the transmitter.

Fig. 14. Control console and rack, Station WUOM (*Collins Radio.*) This control
room serves two studios. WUOM has no master control. (*University of Michigan.*)

Telephone Radio Line

After the program has been amplified and monitored in the control
room, it is put onto a telephone line. The electrical impulses are carried
by this telephone line at approximately 30,000 miles per second. If the
program is a network program, it is carried by these telephone lines to
the various transmitters of the stations that compose that network throughout the country and is put into the air by the individual transmitters of
these stations. If the program is a local one, it is sent by telephone line
to the station's own transmitter.

In the early days of radio it was convenient to locate the transmitter on
the same building in which the studios were housed, but it was soon
found that this arrangement had several disadvantages, such as too much
screening of the station's signal by large steel buildings in the neighborhood and unsatisfactory ground conditions. As a result, transmitters are

now usually located several miles outside the city, where conditions are better for maximum efficiency. The Columbia Broadcasting System built an island for its transmitter off the shores of Long Island, New York.

Antenna

The straight, vertical antenna has a height equal to 0.58 of the station's wave length. The steel structure of the tower is the actual radiating system. A high-power station will radiate power that will keep electric lights in the neighborhood of the transmitter burning even after they have been turned off. One chicken raiser kept the lights on in his hen house 18 hours a day using the radio station's radiated power. A necessary part of the transmitter's radiator is the system of ground wires that is buried in the soil around the base of the antenna. Although never seen by the visitors to the stations, these bare copper wires are laid out with great care at a depth of 6 to 12 inches beneath the surface in much the same pattern as the spokes of a wheel about the hub, each wire or spoke being almost as long as the antenna itself.

Transmitter

The transmitter proper (Fig. 15) consists of a quartz-crystal oscillator which generates the radio frequency (the quartz crystal to main-

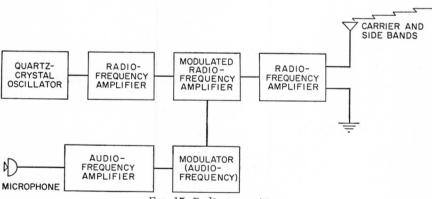

FIG. 15. Radio transmitter.

tain the exact frequency, the number of kilocycles of the station). This crystal oscillator is followed by several more stages of radio-frequency amplification which increase the power to a value suitable for modulation. The speech which comes from the microphone or incoming tele-

phone lines is amplified by a series of audio-frequency amplifiers which
terminate in a stage called the "modulator." This modulator in turn is
connected to the radio-frequency stage previously mentioned. It is at
this point that the mixing of the audio frequency and radio frequency
takes place. Further amplification follows, and the resulting power is
fed into the antenna and radiated in all directions. This modulation or
mixing process gives rise to other frequencies in addition to the carrier
frequency, which is the frequency of the quartz crystal. These other radio
frequencies, called "side bands," are located in the assigned channel on
either side of the carrier and contain the speech of the announcer whose
program we are tracing from his mouth to the radio listener. The Federal Communications Commission limits the width of this channel to
10 kilocycles.

Carrier Wave

Every station has its own carrier wave located in the center of its assigned channel. These carrier waves vary between 550 and 1600 kilocycles for the regular broadcast band. These waves travel at the speed
of light. All carrier waves travel at the same speed, but those having fewer
kilocycles do not oscillate as fast as those having more kilocycles. A station operating at 550 kilocycles has a rate of oscillation of 550,000 cycles
per second for its carrier wave.

Ground and Sky Waves

The carrier waves which are sent out by the radio station may be divided into two categories; first, the ground wave, and second, the sky
wave. During the daytime the sky waves have no effect upon the coverage of the station because they travel upward and are lost, but at night
these sky waves play a very important part because they go up and hit
the Kennelly-Heaviside layer and are reflected back to the earth. These
reflected sky waves are evident usually only after sunset and extend the
nighttime coverage of stations. The reflected sky wave is important only
to the most powerful stations in the clear-channel classification. Such
stations can be heard ordinarily during the daytime between 100 and
200 miles by means of their ground waves, but at night, through the
medium of the reflected sky wave, they are heard at great distances
because the sky waves are not absorbed by ground conditions as the
ground wave is. The sky wave is not as dependable as the ground wave of
the station, and generally this extended coverage is considered as the

secondary coverage area. It is this reflected sky wave that causes fading, inasmuch as the fading area exists where the ground wave of the station interferes with the reflected sky wave of the same station. Despite the faults and unreliability of the sky wave, a very large proportion of the radio audience depends upon sky-wave reception for its evening programs. Local and regional stations do not benefit from their reflected sky waves because they are located closer to one another than are clear-

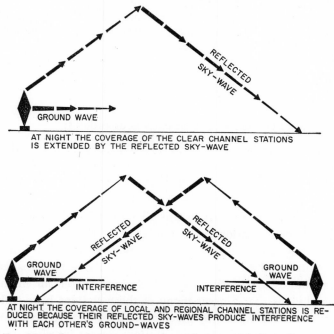

AT NIGHT THE COVERAGE OF THE CLEAR CHANNEL STATIONS IS EXTENDED BY THE REFLECTED SKY-WAVE

AT NIGHT THE COVERAGE OF LOCAL AND REGIONAL CHANNEL STATIONS IS REDUCED BECAUSE THEIR REFLECTED SKY-WAVES PRODUCE INTERFERENCE WITH EACH OTHER'S GROUND-WAVES

FIG. 16. Reflected sky waves and interference with ground waves.

channel stations and, instead of having an area cleared of interference for their sky waves, they have merely an area in which their sky waves interfere with those of another station upon the same wave length. If a listener to a regional or local station has his receiving set near the outside limits of the ground wave of a local or regional station, he will find at night that there is interference with another station because he is picking up the sky waves from one or more stations operating on the same frequency. Thus the coverage of a regional or local station is less at night than it is during the daytime, and the coverage of the clear-channel station is greater (see Fig. 16).

Clear, Regional, Local Channels

The 106 channels in the standard broadcast band are divided into three principal classes—clear, regional, and local.

1. *Clear channel.* A clear channel is one on which the dominant station or stations render service over wide areas and which is cleared of objectionable interference within its primary service areas and over all or a substantial portion of its secondary service areas.

2. *Regional channel.* A regional channel is one on which several stations may operate with powers not in excess of 5 kilowatts. The primary service area of a station operating on any such channel may be limited, as a consequence of interference, to a given field intensity contour.

3. *Local channel.* A local channel is one on which several stations may operate with powers not in excess of 250 watts. The primary service area of a station operating on any such channel may be limited, as a consequence of interference, to a given field intensity contour.

The number of channels of each class is as follows:

Clear channels	59
Regional channels	41
Local channels	6
	106

All countries are permitted to use all regional and all local channels subject to power limitations and standards for the prevention of objectionable interference. The clear channels were assigned definitely to the various countries. With only 106 channels available for broadcasting in the United States and with 2840 AM stations on the air in the fall of 1956, it is obvious that a great many of these stations have to be in the same frequencies. However, by placing them far enough apart so that the ground waves of regional and local stations do not interfere and the sky waves of clear-channel stations do not interfere, it is possible to obtain good reception from all these licensed stations. This is achieved by the Federal Communications Commission, which limits the power of the various stations and the hours in which certain stations may broadcast.

Coverage

Various stations are allotted a certain amount of power for broadcasting their programs. Those which have clear channels are generally allowed 50,000 watts; those in the regional classification do not exceed, under ordinary circumstances, 5000 watts; and those in the local category have a maximum of 250 watts. Under ordinary circumstances a station with 50,000 watts would be able to send its carrier wave approximately three times as far as a station with 250 watts. However, there are factors that determine the coverage of a station in addition to power. A station which broadcasts upon a low frequency, such as a 550-kilocycle station, will go farther with less effort than a station which is broadcasting upon a frequency of 1550 kilocycles, because the latter carrier wave has to oscillate so many more times in covering the same distance. In an article by J. M. Greene, circulation manager of the National Broadcasting Company, in *Printers' Ink*, the following illustration explains this:

To explain why one carrier wave travels farther than the other, let us compare them with two men, one tall and the other short, walking at the same speed along a soft, sandy beach. Each step absorbs energy and the result is that the taller man takes fewer steps (the radio station broadcasting upon the lower frequency) and is still going strong after the shorter man has given up (the radio station broadcasting on the higher frequency).

A second factor which determines the coverage of a radio station is the ground over which it passes. Various geological conditions affect the transmission and cut down the coverage of the station. Therefore the station which has the greatest power and the lowest number of kilocycles and broadcasts over the best ground conditions is the one that will be heard the farthest. Power is not the only factor in station coverage. It is entirely possible under certain conditions for a station operating on 250 watts to have a greater coverage than one operating on 1000 watts. Ground conductivity alone can offset the advantages of both high power and low frequency.

Interference

Not only do such things as power, the frequency, and ground conductivity affect the coverage and reception of programs, but man-made conditions may affect it. Electrical disturbances caused by X-ray machines, power lines, etc., create disturbances which affect the signal received by the broadcasting set. High steel structures surrounding the antenna of the station's transmitter will affect its coverage.

As has been pointed out, radio signals travel farther at night by their sky waves than they do during the daytime. Therefore, in order further to avoid interference, the Federal Communications Commission grants licenses to certain stations which are located close to one another to broadcast with decreased power after sunset. More stations broadcast from sunrise to sunset than are permitted to air programs after sunset.

There are other instances where stations share time, one station being permitted on the air for part of the day and another one for the balance of the day. These limitations permit the licensing of a greater number of stations.

Also in an effort to decrease interference between stations, directional antennas are sometimes installed. Under normal circumstances a vertical antenna will radiate almost equally well in all directions, but it is possible by proper modification to directionalize the radiation from an antenna. The bulk of the station's power may be sent in one direction, as is done in radio airway beacons, or it may be kept from radiating in that direction and left free to traverse all the others.

Reception

The carrier frequency and side band (sometimes called "side frequencies") come through space to be picked up by the aerial of the receiving set. Radio waves travel through the air at the speed of light, approximately 186,000 miles per second. I can remember that in the early days of radio a professor would deliver his talk to the microphone and then dash into an adjoining room to see if he could catch his closing words from a radio receiving set. He never made it. If the announcer in a prize fight is talking to a person located in the 25-cent seats 500 or 600 feet away from the ring, and to a microphone, you who are listening to the program 500 to 600 miles away will hear his voice over the radio before it will be heard by the man who has paid his quarter. These radio waves, picked up by the aerial, are changed into electrical impulses (of the same frequency as the radio waves), which are conveyed to apparatus which tunes the set to the frequency of the station. After suitable amplification, these impulses go into a detector in which the speech of the announcer, in the form of electrical impulses of the same frequency as developed by the microphone, is extracted from the carrier and side bands. Thence these impulses are further amplified and conducted to a voice coil mounted in a magnetic field. This voice coil is attached to the paper cone of the loud-speaker. The impulses cause the voice coil and hence the cone to vibrate. The vibrations of the cone result in sound waves just like those that were projected by the announcer in the studio (see Fig. 17).

The phraseology I have used in this explanation (channels, bands) is that used by technicians, specialists in electrical engineering and physics. However, it does give rise to a misconception on the part of the layman.

In reality there are no definite layers in the air. Possibly a better illustration to use in connection with broadcasting is that there are two stations, one represented by a red light and the other by a green light. When these stations are broadcasting, both lights are illuminated, and the air about them is filled with red and green rays representing their radio frequencies. Both colors are everywhere, just as their radio waves fill the air. Your receiving set is a filter which picks out only the red rays or only the green rays as you tune that filter (receiving set) to the station to which you desire to listen. The red rays do not go in a definite pathway

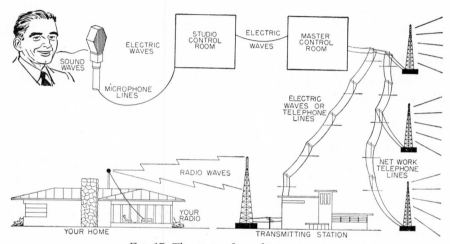

FIG. 17. The route of a radio program.

or band, but go everywhere, up and down and around the light which is the antenna of the station. If the red or green light were made brighter and dimmer according to some prearranged code, while the color was not changed, and the person watching the lights could interpret that message through the medium of a code, he would be using the light rays just as the receiving set picks up radio waves. The *intensity* of the signal is varied by the sound wave which is transmitted in the amplitude-modulated system of broadcasting.

Radio vs. TV

The unbiased radio forecaster recognizes the fact that radio will not be replaced by television. Television does not duplicate radio; it merely improves upon radio in one respect, its appeal to the eye. A new service replaces an old one only if it exactly duplicates it in every respect and then improves upon it. Radio does some things that television does not. Television requires concentration upon the screen. Radio permits you to work or play with a musical or speech background. Radio is used in 75 million automobiles. You cannot watch the TV screen and drive. In the summer. The beaches and picnic grounds are spotted with portable radios. Portable small-screen TV sets using transistors and batteries are currently available; however, reception is limited. TV will not reach all rural areas. There are thousands of miles of sparsely peopled areas where TV will never be feasible financially. The role of radio will probably be smaller and that of TV greater, but there will be more radio stations offering employment to students for many years to come.

Wired Radio

"Wired wireless," variously called "gas pipe," "carrier current," "limited-area broadcasting," and "wired radio," is not radio at all in the public conception. In "wired radio," sound waves are converted into electrical impulses which are carried over electric-power lines or gas or water pipes, instead of being transmitted through the air. The equipment used in "wired radio" is the same as that used in broadcasting through the air. A low-powered transmitter with a range not to exceed 200 feet is hooked to the power line or pipe that serves as an antenna for an ordinary radio receiving set which reconverts the electrical impulses into sound waves.

While no license is required at present for wired radio, the Federal Communications Commission has ruled that, even if a low-power radio-frequency device is exempt from licensing, it must nevertheless conform to certain technical requirements so that its emissions will not interfere with the regular radio services. Those operating such a system select a frequency not used in their locality, a frequency which will not interfere with any other station heard in the area. In other words, its emission must be measured expertly to make certain that there is no interference. The responsibility of insuring that the radiated energy does not exceed the limitations specified lies with the owner and operator of the equipment. Serious penalties, provided for in the Communications Act, include a maximum fine of $10,000 or two years imprisonment, or both. The F.C.C. regulation states specifically "while the so-called 'campus radio' of the Intercollegiate Broadcasting System, which is confined to the individual wired precincts of more than 50 schools and colleges, is not licensed, its operators see that it conforms to F.C.C. low-power rules."

These stations operate under Rule 2.102 of the Federal Communications Commission, which specifies that the maximum field strength of the radio signal must not exceed 15 microvolts per meter (inaudible on an ordinary receiver) at any point at a distance of lambda (the wave length) divided by 2 pi (6.28) from the nearest part of the transmission system. For frequencies in the lower portion of the broadcast band, such as campus stations use, this distance is around 200 feet. The transmission system may include wire lines installed by the station or leased from others, and power lines into which the signal is coupled. Since the signal is carried by these mediums to the specific locations where reception is desired, no interference is caused to distant broadcast stations on the same frequencies, and because of their compliance with the above cited rule, campus stations are exempt from many of the provisions of F.C.C. licensing procedure. For example, licensed operators are not required to operate the station, and the station itself need not be licensed by the Commission. The call letters of campus stations are assigned by the Commission, however, and all stations of the system are registered with them.

Wired radio is not a new method of transmission. It has been used by power and telephone companies. It formed the basis for Muzak, which provides music to restaurants and bars in the cities. It became a college radio at Brown University in 1936, where programs were transmitted over the heating pipes.

The wired-radio station would require approximately $350 for a transmitter; each turntable (there should be two) will cost from $150 to $750; microphones cost from $40 to $85 each; and remote pickup equipment, amplifiers, etc., must be purchased. There will be the expense of purchasing recordings, and charges for wires from the athletic buildings and fields and from remote pickup points.

CHAPTER TWO

FUNDAMENTALS OF RADIO—VERY HIGH FREQUENCIES

Frequency Modulation

The difference between AM and FM broadcasting can be visualized something like this: Think of two different lakes, each with a machine in the center creating waves which cover the surface. On one lake the waves are exactly the same distance apart but they differ in height. Some are only tiny ripples; others are great, surging whitecaps. Regardless of their height, however, the distance from one to the other is exactly the same. The waves of such a lake are comparable with the radio waves used in AM broadcasting, for these waves transmit different sounds by variations in height or amplitude instead of in distance apart or frequency.

The machine or "transmitter" in the other lake causes it to be covered with a series of waves all exactly the same height but with varying distances separating them. This second lake is comparable with waves which transmit sounds in FM broadcasting, for such waves vary in frequency instead of in height or amplitude.

Broadcasting, both AM and FM, is transmitted by electromagnetic waves which emanate from the antenna of the transmitter. Such a wave is illustrated by the peaked line in Fig. 18a. The portion above the straight line represents plus voltage, that below the line is minus voltage. The distance between the peaks depends on the frequency of the wave. This carrier wave will operate a radio receiver at the one point on the dial which corresponds with its frequency.

To transmit sound on this wave, we can modulate it by combining it with another wave which varies in accordance with the sounds to be transmitted, as in Fig. 18b. The result of such a combination is amplitude modulation, represented by Fig. 18c. The differences between the heights of the peaks are the differences of amplitude of the wave as compared to its average value, indicated by the straight line. The waves remain at the same distance apart, or at the same frequency. The receiver converts these amplitude differences back into sound.

There are serious drawbacks to this method of transmission. Lightning, street cars, electrical motors, dialing the telephone, etc., create waves which are of the identical electrical type as the amplitude-modulated wave. They tend to decrease or increase the height of the peaks, and since the height determines the sound to come from the AM receiver, these "stray" waves come through your radio set, along with the program you are attempting to hear, to cause static.

However, these unwanted waves, which affect the height of the peaks, have virtually no effect on the distance between them—their frequency

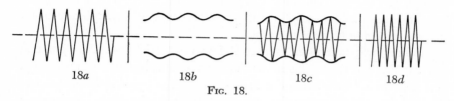

18a	18b	18c	18d

FIG. 18.

remains unchanged. This phenomenon was noticed as early as 1923 by Major Edwin H. Armstrong. He therefore began work on a new system in which the basic carrier wave is modulated, not by changing the height of the peaks, but by changing the frequency, or distance, between them (Fig. 18d).

Static can act on the FM signal just as it does on AM, but it makes no difference to you, listening to your FM receiver. The FM transmitting station modulates the carrier waves by altering the distance between them. Your FM radio converts back into sound only these differences in the frequency of the waves, and this is not changed by the stray, or static, waves. The result is reception virtually free from static.

One of the basic differences between the two types of broadcasting is the low "signal-to-noise" ratio of FM as compared to AM. As you can readily understand, there is always some background noise in any radio signal—static, electrical interference, etc. For reasonably good reception of AM signals, the signal itself must be approximately 100 times stronger than the noise. In FM, a signal only twice as strong as the noise is a satisfactory signal, because of the "limiter" effect of the FM circuit. The effect of the limiter is to dampen the silence background noise in FM reception.

Since there is no limiter in an AM circuit, the signal must be much stronger than the noise to insure satisfactory reception.

The problem of interference between stations does not exist for FM; there is virtually no limit to the number of high-power transmitters that can be operated within the frequencies assigned to FM broadcasting. For this there are a number of reasons.

One is a quality, as yet not thoroughly understood, inherent in FM. One wave will not interfere with another, even on the same band, unless the two have almost equal strength. The receiver will automatically select the stronger, and reproduce it perfectly, while blanking out the weaker completely; there is no double rendition of programs from different stations. Engineers have tested this characteristic with an FM receiver mounted on an automobile driven to a point approximately midway between two FM stations transmitting on the same frequency. The balance is so delicate that moving the car just a few feet will completely blank out one station in favor of the other.

Another important point is that FM waves tend to act like light and travel in straight lines. This limits the range of FM broadcasts, ordinarily, to a little more than twice the distance from the transmitter antenna to the horizon, which means that power stations on the same band only a few hundred miles apart do not interfere.

Additional insurance against overlapping stems from the fact that each FM channel is 200 kilocycles wide, or twenty times the width of an AM channel, and from the ruling of the Federal Communications Commission that stations serving the same area shall not operate on adjacent channels.

The idea that the range on AM is far greater than that of FM has proved to be inaccurate. FM stations have greater solid range than AM stations of the same power—particularly at night. The greater range of AM stations is a theoretical range. FM stations put out steady, unvarying signals to the limit of their primary service area. They are not interfered with by other distant stations, and they do not fade in and out as do "secondary" signals of AM stations on the wave lengths now in use.

The height of the FM antenna is more important than power. A 20-kilowatt FM station with a 500-foot radiator will get greater coverage than a 60-kilowatt station with a 300-foot radiator. In the case of frequency modulation the tower is merely a supporting unit for the radiator proper, which consists of what are known as "bays," "loops" or "rings," or in some instances, "pylons" (Figs. 19, 20, and 21).

The use of an antenna, properly constructed, installed, and directed, determines whether or not more distant FM stations will be heard, as well as the quality of signal received from near-by stations. Unlike the old type of radio waves, frequency-modulation signals are inclined to travel in a straight line like a beam of light. As with light, the distance to which these beams will reach is largely determined by the height of the sending antenna, and the position of the receiving antenna. The AM

FIG. 19. FM 12 bay ring-type antenna. (*Collins Radio Company.*)

long-wire antenna catches the long waves but confuses the ultra short waves of FM. These high-frequency short waves respond to the short span of the FM antenna, a "folded dipole," either directional or nondirectional, with or without a reflector. A dipole antenna looks something like a long paper clip. In general, and essentially with the reflector type, the antenna should be broadside to the station in order to get the strongest signal. The reflector, that is the single bar, should be back of the pickup element. The FM antenna should be mounted as high as possible. Avoid

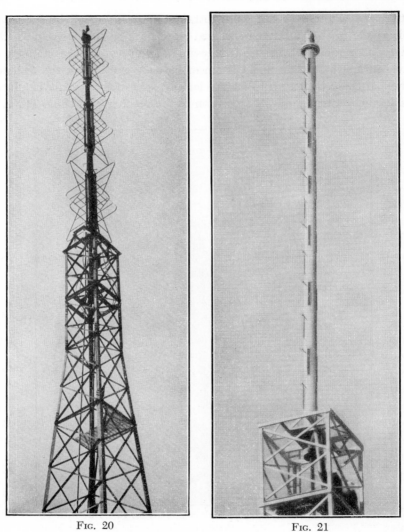

FIG. 20   FIG. 21

FIG. 20. VHF superturnstile antenna for television. (*Radio Corporation of America.*)
FIG. 21. UHF pylon antenna for television. (*Radio Corporation of America.*)

placing it near a wall, chimney, or other object which may reflect or deflect signals. A two-wire 300-ohm lead-in cable is recommended.

With the permission of the F.C.C., it is possible to transmit programs from the studios to a distant transmitter by means of a studio-to-transmitter link known as "STL." This method requires installation of a low-power, very-high-frequency transmitter and parabolic reflector, and, at the transmitter, a similar reflector to receive the beamed or transmitted signals from the station transmitter and an associated receiver which converts the received radio signal back to sound frequencies.

Telephone lines have been developed to carry up to 15,000 of these frequencies so that frequency-modulated programs may be satisfactorily broadcast over a network of stations connected by telephone lines. The relay system, however, is more economical. An alternative to wire-linked networks is a network in which a program is carried from station to station, not by wire but by radio, each succeeding station picking up the preceding station's transmission on a special relay receiver. Such a network can only operate if intermediate relaying stations are taking the program and sending out their signal. This method of network broadcasting is only practical in the case of frequency-modulation stations. A 5-microvolt signal is adequate; therefore, while the frequency-modulation program may not be received well in the home, it can be picked up with professional equipment for rebroadcasting. A 5-microvolt signal is possible for distances of 100 or more miles.

The studio control operator need not ride gain on his program as carefully as is required in the case of an AM studio production. He may permit momentarily very-high-level passages, which would be intolerable to an AM transmitter, to go on to the FM transmitter and be transmitted by it. Because the over-all background noise level of an FM signal is much lower than in the case of AM, the control operator can also permit low-volume passages of speech or music to be transmitted at the original volume level rather than to increase the level of low passages artificially, as is necessary when feeding an AM transmitter. In FM, the signal strength is always constant; changes in volume, like changes in tone, occur by changes within the wave itself. Therefore, the full orchestral range in volume, as well as in pitch and tone quality, is transmitted and received with almost perfect fidelity. The width of the new FM channels has been adjusted to permit high-fidelity transmission, making more noticeable the high frequencies in the reception, with the result that the listener has to be trained to appreciate these frequencies rather than to rely upon the lower tonal qualities of regular broadcasting.

In making available channels for frequency modulation, the government set aside exclusively for educational purposes bands which adjoin the bands for commercial purposes.

The band between 88,000 and 108,000 kilocycles is set aside to accommodate both commercial and educational FM stations. Before the end of

1956, 536 commercial FM stations were on the air, and 130 additional FM stations were owned and operated by educational institutions.

Music programs are piped over wires to various cafés, bars, and restaurants for the entertainment of their patrons. Some of these programs are now carried by frequency modulation to these places, which have sets with a set frequency that will not pick up any other station; and any other frequency-modulation receiver, not built for the reception of these programs, will get a squeal when it attempts to pick up these broadcasts. In other words, the subscribing eating place has to pay a fee for such entertainment services and no one not paying such a fee can get the programs. This is the principle of "subscription radio."

Low-power Stations

In 1948, the Federal Communications Commission made changes in its regulations, authorizing low-power frequency-modulation educational stations using transmitters of 10 watts or under (Fig. 22). This low-power type of station not only makes possible a highly desirable service in hundreds of small school systems over the country, but also provides an impetus toward the establishment of a full-power non-commercial, educational station. The low-power station operates exactly as does the frequency-modulation station except, because of its low power, it serves an area with about a 10-mile radius. It is, therefore, adequate for municipal school systems, and since the Federal Communications Commission granted the first permit for a 2½-watt station to Syracuse University, a great many boards of education, school districts, and other educational units have applied for licenses. At present, about 51 noncommercial stations are in operation. The principal reason for these low-power stations is economy. A 10-watt FM transmitter, now being offered in the school market, ranges in price from $1,500 to $3,000. The total cost for equipment and studios should not exceed $6,000 or $7,000. Applicants for the low-power FM stations are not required to submit the technical data required for a full-power station, and when the school desires to increase its power, all that it is necessary to do is to add new power stages and accessory equipment. Rules and regulations of the Federal Communications Commission permit great latitude in the number of air hours; and the station may go off the air during holidays and vacation periods.

Such low-power stations offer student and teacher the opportunity for practical experience that might be gotten in a full-power FM station.

The antenna can be placed upon the top of the school building in which the transmitter is located. Classrooms may be remodeled to be used as studios. In addition to the transmitter, the necessary equipment should include a program consolette, microphones and stands, recording equipment, playback equipment, program monitoring and talk-back equipment, control relays, wiring, etc.

FIG. 22. 10-watt transmitter for low-power station. (*General Electric Company.*)

Various manufacturers give a special price on FM receivers to school systems. These receivers may be placed in classrooms and buildings throughout the community.

Just as in the case of a full-power station, application for a license (No. 340) must be filed with the Federal Communications Commission. The manufacturer of the transmitter and the antenna to be used will give the necessary technical information. Call letters will be assigned by the F.C.C.

CHAPTER THREE

FUNDAMENTALS OF TELEVISION

The possibility of sending pictures through the air from one place to another is not a new idea. As early as 1884, Paul Nipkow patented a mechanical scanning disc. This was the first practical method of breaking pictures up into small particles that could be sent from the originating point and reassembled at a receiving point some distance away. It was a form of mechanical television. Variations of the Nipkow disc were used in further research and development until the invention of the iconoscope tube in 1923, which achievement began the era of electronic television. As is the case with most major discoveries and inventions, these developments were not isolated "finds," but rather were the inevitable results of years of study and research in physics, optics, electricity, photosensitive materials, vacuum tubes, and many other areas.

It is not possible to say that any one man invented television. There have been many men, in many different places, involved in the growth and perfection of the modern television system.

Because of its less complicated nature, sound broadcasting developed earlier than did the transmission of pictures. As early as 1920, radio station KDKA, in Pittsburgh, was broadcasting regularly. It was during that year that KDKA broadcast election returns of the Harding-Cox presidential race, and the phenomenal growth of the radio broadcasting industry was under way.

In 1923, Dr. Vladimir K. Zworykin obtained a patent for an all-electronic television camera tube which he called the "iconoscope." The iconoscope was the standard camera tube for a number of years, and is still in use at many stations for the broadcasting of films and slides. In 1929, Dr. Zworykin brought out an electronic picture tube called the "kinescope." This type of receiver tube is still in use today. Despite this major progress, it was not until 1933 to 1934 that the iconoscope was sufficiently perfected to permit the building of a practical television camera. Between 1923 and 1934 many experiments were conducted using different television systems. Experimental stations were licensed and began to broadcast. The first was operated by WGY, the General Electric radio station in Schenectady, N.Y. It went on the air in 1928. R.C.A.-N.B.C. followed in 1930, and C.B.S. in 1931. By 1939 it was clear that the all-electronic system, employing Zworykin's iconoscope and kinescope, was the method by which practical television broadcasting would be possible.

In 1940 the infant television industry thought it was ready to begin regular commercial telecasting. However, it was not until July 1, 1941, that the Federal Communications Commission licensed the first commercial television station. The first commercial license went to station WNBT, the N.B.C. station in New York. This beginning was, for all practical purposes, short-lived. The Second World War drastically arrested the development of television as a nationwide means of communication. There was continued experimentation and limited broadcasting during the war period, but it was the immediate postwar period that saw the industry grow to significant proportions. By 1947 the number of sets in use clearly showed that television was really on its way.

Frequencies and Channels

In the late 1930s and early 1940s television was considered something of a problem child. It has remained so ever since. One of the problems that has continued to plague the growth of this prodigious infant is precisely where, in the radio spectrum, it should be located. Under present United States standards a television broadcasting channel requires a band width of 6 megacycles. Since 1 megacycle is equal to 1000 kilocycles it can readily be seen that television requires some room! This is graphically brought to mind when we realize that the total AM broadcasting band runs from 550 kilocycles to 1600 kilocycles, or just 50 kilocycles over 1 megacycle!

At an early date television was moved upstairs to that portion of the radio spectrum called the "very high frequency" (VHF) range. Shortly after the earliest telecasting began, the frequencies were reshuffled to make room for FM. After this move there remained channels 1 through 13, all in the VHF range. Later channel 1 was deleted as a usable television channel. There then remained 12 VHF channels, 2–13. Channels 2–6 fell in the range of 54–88 megacycles, and channels 7–13 in the range of 174–216 megacycles. In between channels 6 and 7 space was left in which to place the FM frequencies.

With these 12 channels available the Federal Communications Commission (F.C.C.) proceeded to issue licenses. Such licensing continued until September 30, 1948. At this point the F.C.C. issued what has come to be known as the "Freeze Order." Licensing of television stations was suspended pending a complete study of all the problems involved. Of first concern was the question of how a truly national television system could be established within the existing available frequencies. There were also numerous technical questions to be answered. When the freeze occurred there were 107 stations in operation. One additional applicant held a construction permit and proceeded to complete the building of a station. So, from the issuing of the freeze order until three and a half years later there were but 108 television stations on the air.

The F.C.C. thawed the freeze on April 14, 1952, when it released its *Sixth Report and Order*. This voluminous document did several important things. It set forth a nationwide allocation plan for all available TV channels. It reserved 242 channels exclusively for use as noncommercial, educational stations. It settled the many claims and counterclaims that had been presented to the commission. And most important of all, it made available a total of 82 TV channels. The VHF channels, 2–13, remained as they were. What was added was a further shift upstairs in the radio spectrum, into the "ultra high frequency" (UHF) range. That part of the UHF range assigned to TV use runs from 470 to 890 megacycles. This permitted the assignment of channels 14–83. Early in 1956 there were 454 television stations in operation, 347 using VHF channels, and 107 using UHF.

Present TV stations operate on one of the 12 VHF or one of the 70 UHF channels. In the nationwide allocation plan, VHF and UHF channels were intermixed. That is, both kinds of channels were assigned to areas and to specific communities. For example, Chicago has assigned to it five VHF channels and five UHF. A smaller community might have only one UHF channel, but the community next to it might have a VHF. The main point is that they were not separated geographically. As we shall see, this was an important, if not entirely foreseen, aspect of the *Sixth Report and Order*.

VHF vs. UHF

Strictly speaking, there is no major difference between television broadcasting on VHF channels and on UHF channels. The same standards and procedures are used in both cases. Technically, it is not at all like the AM-FM radio situation. There are major systemic differences between AM and FM sound broadcasting.

Practically, however, there are some highly significant differences between VHF and UHF telecasting, differences which are similar to the AM-FM relationship. There are three such differences that have drastically affected the economics of the television industry.

First of all, because the UHF channels are utilizing much higher frequencies than the VHF channels, considerably more power has to be radiated to obtain a comparable coverage area. The same characteristic of radio waves is operating here that we find in AM broadcasting, where it is desirable to be as low on the dial as possible. Power and other factors being constant, an AM station broadcasting on 550 kilocycles will cover a greater area than one operating on 1550 kilocycles. The F.C.C. clearly recognizes this difference in issuing television licenses. The low VHF channels, 2–6, are authorized an effective radiated power of 100 kilowatts; the high VHF channels, 7–13, can operate with an ERP of 316 kilowatts; and UHF stations have a maximum ERP of 1000 kilowatts. So, the first problem operators of UHF stations had to face was getting a sufficiently large coverage area to enable them to compete with the VHF stations.

Secondly, since this is the highest set of frequencies ever used for public broadcasting purposes, manufacturers had done very little experimental and developmental work in the UHF range. No equipment was available that would generate the enormous amounts of power required. When the first UHF transmitters became available on the market they were of low power ratings, many as low as 1 kilowatt. Thus, in the crucial early days of station development it was impossible for the UHF stations to obtain coverage patterns equal to those of the VHF stations.

Third, and probably the most serious difficulty of all, is the fact that virtually no receivers were able to receive the UHF channels. Since all the orginal stations were VHF, there had been no need for the additional channels. Inclusion of all channels on a receiver increased the cost of the set, and this increase was naturally resisted by the buying public. To convert an existing VHF-only set costs approximatly $30, and this too, has been resisted. The early UHF stations could well wonder whether or not they actually had an audience.

The force of these three problems set in motion the proverbial vicious circle. The UHF stations did not have the coverage nor the available audience, so the networks and advertisers stayed away. Without network programs and advertising revenue the stations were well-nigh helpless in building an audience. Any effort to break this circle was almost certain to fail. The problem of power and coverage is, at least in a major degree, being solved by the broadcast-equipment manufacturers and by the F.C.C.'s approval of extremely high maximum-power standards. The problem of network affiliation, and thus increased UHF set conversion, and thus increased advertising dollars, is more thorny. The only thing that will cause people to buy all-channel sets, or to convert old ones, is a program service that they strongly desire. In most cases this means network service. The networks, on the other hand, require an audience which can be delivered for the sponsor's message. All of this left the UHF station with a nearly insoluble dilemma. Needless to say, a considerable number of UHF licenses have been returned to the F.C.C.

In areas not strongly dominated by VHF stations, UHF stations can be and are operated successfully. In strong VHF markets no real solution to the problem has been found. It is a problem of much broader concern than the economic losses of a few UHF licensees. If the United States is to have a complete national television system, with an adequate number of stations, it will be done by using the UHF range, or it will not be done at all. The answer is not yet in sight.

Despite all of this, it is too early to count UHF television as a dead issue. There are some technical advantages to the higher frequencies. It is still possible that with time, increased development, greater demand for space in the radio spectrum, and a heightened demand for more stations, UHF will be the standard frequency range for television broadcasting.

From Studio to Receiver

Most Americans see motion pictures regularly and frequently. Yet, how many of them ever stop to think just what it is they are seeing? Are they really seeing moving figures? Of course, they are not, but instead are seeing what "appear" to be moving figures. A piece of motion-picture film is simply a series of still photographs exposed in very rapid succession. When this piece of film is projected for viewing, it remains a series of still photographs projected in rapid succession. The film does not run through the projector in a continuous motion. Rather it is pulled down and projected as a series of stills, frame by frame. A "frame" is the name given to each individual still picture in a series that make up what we call motion-picture film. In sound motion pictures there are 24 of these complete frames projected each second. Actually, to avoid flicker, each frame is projected twice by use of a shutter in the projector. This means that there are 48 pictures flashed onto the screen each second.

If what we see is a series of still pictures projected in very rapid succession, why does it appear to be continuous, smooth-flowing motion? It is because of a slowness in the working of the human eye. The eye operates in such a way that when a picture is presented to it even for an extremely short period of time, an image of that picture will persist in the eye after the picture is removed. This quality of persistence of vision in the human eye makes movies possible. The eye sees only a succession of smooth-flowing pictures, whereas actually it is a series of stills with blackouts in between. Were your eyes fast enough, you would see blank spaces between the frames of a film, but since they retain an image momentarily you see moving pictures.

The same phenomenon makes it possible for us to see continuously moving television pictures. As we shall discover, television, too, operates on the basis of a certain number of frames per second. This is its first principle.

The second basic principle of television was clear to the engineers and research workers almost from the beginning. To transmit a picture from one place to another it is necessary to break the picture up into tiny pieces. Transmission of pictures by wire, or through the air, is not like mailing a package. You cannot send the whole picture at once.

Nipkow's scanning disc was a means of breaking up a picture which could later be reassembled at the receiving end. But the scanning disc was a mechanical device and was incapable of the tremendous speeds and extreme accuracies required to create a high-definition picture. So, it was clear at an early stage that the hope for picture transmission lay in some kind of electronic system.

When we are talking about pictures, or things that we see, we are really speaking about varying patterns of light intensity. As you look at this book, it is not the book itself that enters your eye and thus activates the nerves and brain. It is rather a pattern of light reflected from the book. So, in television, what we have to start with is the pattern of light reflected from the objects in the scene, or field of view of the camera. The television camera translates this pattern of light energy into a sequential pattern of electrical energy. This electrical energy is capable of being transmitted by wire or through the air. It can be amplified and controlled, and can, eventually, be brought to a receiver. The receiver translates this electrical energy back into a pattern of light energy, or as we prefer to call it, a picture. The way all this happens is the story of how television works.

The reflected light from a scene is gathered into a concentrated area by a lens. Thus far we are doing the same thing that is done in a photographic camera. In the photographic camera, the concentrated light pattern would be brought to a focus on the emulsion of a film. In the television camera, the picture is focused onto a photosensitive surface in the camera pickup tube (iconoscope, image-orthicon, or vidicon). The photosensitive surface of the pickup tube consists of thousands of elements of photosensitive material so arranged in a circuit that electrical energy can

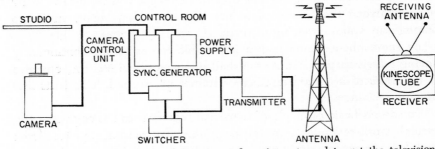

Fig. 23. Schematic drawing of the array of equipment used to get the television picture from studio to living room.

be taken off. Photosensitive material is a substance that permits the escape of electrical energy when it is activated by light. In the neck of the camera tube is an electron gun. The beam of electrons from this gun scans the photosensitive surface and restores the normal charge on it. The process is, then, that the photosensitive surface is charged by the scene which is focused upon it, and discharge, or restoration of the normal charge, results from the scanning of the electron gun. In this way, the pattern of light is changed into a corresponding electrical current. It is important to remember that the amount of electrical current resulting from this process is in direct proportion to the amount of light energy striking the photosensitive surface.

The action of the electron gun, which is called "scanning," is crucial to the functioning of the television system. It is easiest to think of scanning as resembling the way we read. Scanning is done line by line from left to right, and from top to bottom. The gun is shooting electrons only in the left-to-right movement, and by an ingenious process called "blanking" the beam is turned off in the return, or "retrace," from right to left. The electron beam traces 525 lines to form a complete picture. However, to avoid flicker, the engineers arranged the scanning so that the beam traces all of the even-numbered lines from the top to the bottom of the picture, making what is called a "field." It then jumps back to the top of the picture and traces the odd-numbered lines. This alternate system of scanning is called "interlace," and the resulting two fields form a "frame." The television frame is the same as a frame in motion pictures, that is, one complete still picture. In television, 30 frames are scanned each second. In other words, the electron beam from the gun in the neck of the pickup tube traces $262\frac{1}{2}$ lines from left to right and from top to bottom, twice, to make one complete 525-line picture, or frame—and does it in $\frac{1}{30}$ second. Try, in one of your spare moments, to figure out the speed which this process involves.

During the scanning process, as the stream of electrons strikes the charged photosensitive surface small electrical charges are permitted to escape and are collected in the circuit of the camera tube. We have done, with light, much the same thing that the microphone does to sound. The microphone changes sound waves to a sequence of electrical impulses. The camera tube changes light energy (pictures) into a sequence of electrical impulses. So, we have accomplished our main goals; we have broken the picture up into minute particles, and we have changed the light energy into electrical energy that we can control, amplify, and transmit.

For purposes of clarity I have, of course, simplified this process. Let us now add some more of the necessary information. While Zworykin's iconoscope was the first successful electronic camera tube, it has been universally replaced in studio cameras by the much more sensitive image-orthicon. Unless specifically excepted, when television cameras are mentioned in this book it is to be understood that this means image-orthicon cameras.

In broadcasting, engineers refer to a "camera chain." The camera by itself is not an independent unit. Three basic pieces of equipment comprise the camera chain; the camera proper, a power supply, and a camera-control unit. Somewhere in the system there is also included a picture monitor, and a monitor with a cathode-ray oscilloscope. All of these units are connected by cables. Different manufacturers package these units differently, but in all makes of cameras these various functions must be supplied.

When a camera chain is operating, the necessary voltages are fed to the camera from the power supply, which is usually located in the control room or some other convenient centralized point. The camera goes through the scanning process, amplifies the resulting electrical impulses, and returns them to the camera-control unit in the control room. Here the video engineer is able to make all of the necessary adjustments in picture quality. He has both a picture monitor and a wave-form monitor (cathode-ray oscilloscope) to tell him about the character and quality of the picture. He does what an audio engineer does when he is riding gain on sound, except, of course, he has many more adjustments to make.

From the camera-control unit the picture, or "signal" as it is now known, goes to the switcher. We shall have more to say about the switcher in a later chapter.

While our signal is momentarily held up in the switcher, let us add the last necessary piece of equipment in the process of producing the transmittable television signal. To insure that the scanning process is executed in time and under proper control, and that the rescanning done in the receiver at home is in time with the scanning in the camera, certain electrical impulses known as "sync pulses" are needed. These are supplied to the camera, the camera-control unit, and the switcher by the synchronizing generator, or more familiarly, "sync generator." If you have ever watched a television receiver and had the picture roll in a vertical direction you will appreciate vertical sync. When you see a weird conglomeration of lines that resemble a picture being violently pulled from the side, you can appreciate horizontal sync. If all sync is lost you get nothing but a mad scramble of lines and patterns. To be sure, sync is a very important part of the television signal.

Now we are ready to pick up our signal at the switcher. From the switcher, the signal is sent to the transmitter. There the video signal, combined with the audio, is superimposed over the carrier wave and broadcast in the same way that a radio signal is transmitted.

The television receiver must do several things. It must provide for tuning, or selection of the desired frequency or channel. It needs amplifying circuits to strengthen the incoming signal. It must provide the means for converting the audio signal back into recognizable sound, and for converting the video signal back into a recognizable picture. The audio is handled the same as in radio. More accurately, it is handled as in FM radio, because sound in television is broadcast by means of frequency modulation. The audio signal is converted into usable sound by means of the speaker.

The video signal is changed back into a picture in the receiving tube, called a "kinescope." The inner surface of the face of the kinescope is covered with a phosphorescent material. In the neck of the tube is an electron gun. Around the neck of the picture tube are deflecting coils which cause the gun to scan the inner face of the tube. The pattern scanned is identical to the pattern scanned in the pickup tube of the camera, because of the action of the sync pulses which were transmitted with the picture signal. As the stream of electrons hits the phosphorescent material it causes it to glow. This electron beam is modulated with the electric (video) currents established by the camera tube in the studio. This causes the glow of the phosphorescent material to be light or dark in a pattern similar to that in the original scene. The resulting picture is a close approximation of the original scene.

We have transferred a picture, through the air, from one place to another—from studio to home receiver.

Network Television

Network, or chain, broadcasting developed early in the history of radio. It was desirable to distribute programs from main originating points like New York, Hollywood, Chicago, and Washington. Most of the major programs are network-originated. This same development has occurred in television, and most of the high-budget TV programs are broadcast by one of the big networks.

Television signals are fed to multiple stations in one of two ways. They are carried by coaxial cable which is laid underground between two points, or they are transmitted from point to point by microwave relay stations. Coaxial cable was the first system used, and in the early days it was considered the most workable. Later experience proved that microwave systems could afford just as good service, better according to many engineers, and they were much cheaper to install than coaxial cable.

In the microwave system, the TV signals are sent by narrow-beam transmitters operating on specially assigned frequencies, are picked up by receivers, amplified, and sent on to the next station. The receiving and transmitting equipment is located on towers which are built approximately 30 to 40 miles apart. The majority of our present network television is carried by microwave relays.

It is probable that coaxial cable will continue to be installed since it serves many purposes, other than television, connected with usual tele-phone and telegraph service.

In television networking, as in radio, the distribution facilities are, for the most part, owned and operated by the American Telephone and Telegraph Company.

Pay-as-you-see TV

As television developed in the postwar period its rising costs became a serious problem. Rates for time, program production costs, and station operating costs zoomed upwards. By 1954 it was fairly common for a major network show to have a weekly production budget of $40,000 to $50,000. Class "A" time in a moderate-sized market approached a rate of $1,000 per hour. Some serious-minded men began to question whether advertising could support such an expensive medium.

One of the answers proposed is pay-as-you-see, or subscription, television. In this plan, the viewer would pay directly for certain high-cost programs which he desired to see. These premium programs would include such things as first-run movies, major-league baseball games, football games, big-time boxing matches and other costly television fare. The premise was not to replace advertising-supported television, but simply to augment it with the subscription system. For an example, let us take a world-series baseball game. If 10 million homes would be willing to pay 50 cents each for television coverage of the game, and this seems entirely possible, there would be 5 million dollars to be divided among those concerned. This is far and away more than could be extracted from even the biggest advertiser.

One of the major proponents of subscription television has been the Zenith Radio Corporation. Their system has been labeled "Phonevision." The system is simply a technical means of controlling the consumption of the programs. The signal is broadcast with a scrambling signal which distorts the picture and the sound. To get the program undistorted it is necessary to call an operator on the telephone and ask for the program. The operator then throws a switch which feeds another signal through your telephone circuit and unscrambles the picture and sound. At the end of the month you receive a bill for all of the programs that you have watched.

Two other systems have also been proposed, Skiatron's "Subscriber-Vision" and the "Telemeter" system. They are similar in purpose to Phonevision and vary only in their technical methods.

Color Television

Black-and-white television was scarcely a reality before scientists, program producers, and advertisers started to dream about transmitting pictures in color. The prospect of television in full color was breathtaking. The engineers maintained that it was simply a matter of time. So, the laboratories went to work on color TV.

As with everything in this complicated field, the answers were not easily found. Both the technical and economic aspects raised issues that were argued and fought over for years. Large companies, such as R.C.A. and C.B.S., poured millions into color television, and as one might suppose they were not working along the same lines. C.B.S. was developing its so-called sequential system, which used a mechanical color wheel in front of both the camera and the picture tube in the receiver. R.C.A. continued in the belief that only an all-electronic, instantaneous system could eventually solve all of the problems. Many other companies and interests lined up on one side of this argument or the other. But before we investigate these two systems let's go back and consider some more basic problems.

As we have seen in connection with black-and-white television, our starting point is light, or light energy. What we call the picture, or the scene, is really a pattern of reflected light. Another characteristic of light, which we have not yet discussed, is color. Because of different wave lengths in various rays of light the human eye is able to distinguish differences which we call color. Color is not a physical property alone. Color implies certain physiological and psychological effects as well as the variance of wave length. It is the response of the normal human eye to all of these attributes of light that we call color. There are three major characteristics of color with which we need to be familiar.

First of all there is "hue." Hue is the combination of factors which results in our impression of red, green, blue, orange, etc. In other words, what many people would think of as groups of similar colors can more accurately be described as hues. Secondly, a color has "saturation." Saturation determines such qualities as pale, deep, and pastel. It is the vividness or intensity of the color. Color also has "brightness." Brightness has to do with lightness or darkness exhibited by a color. Brightness is most easily understood by comparing it with a scale running from black to white, for it is the grey scale characteristic of a color.

The three primary colors of light are red, blue, and green. This means that when these three colors are combined in the proper proportion, white light will result. It also means that some combination of these primary colors will produce all of the other known colors.

With this much information about light, we are ready to consider the basic problems of color television. A color television system must be able to produce all of the many possible hues. To do this it must start with the three primary colors and blend them in the proper proportions. The color system must be able to render satisfactorily the saturation and the brightness of the color. When these things are done, true-to-life color will result.

By the time color television appeared to be a real possibility many million black-and-white receivers were in use in the United States. These represented a substantial investment on the part of the viewing public. So, the question of compatibility arose. "Compatibility" means that a television program broadcast in color can be received on ordinary black-and-white receivers, as black-and-white television, with no modification of the set. If this is not possible the color system is described as "non-compatible." It can readily be seen that compatibility was a very desirable thing to the millions of set owners, for if the system were compatible they would continue to receive programs as they had all along. In the non-compatible color systems they could receive nothing on the old set.

The Columbia Broadcasting System first achieved a method that afforded lifelike color. The C.B.S. color camera employed one image-orthicon tube and a color wheel that was segmented into the three primary colors, red, blue, and green. This wheel revolved between the orthicon tube and the camera lens. One complete frame was scanned while a single primary color was in front of the tube. So, at a precise moment a frame would be scanned while the red section of the color wheel was in front of the tube. Thus, all hues that fell within, or near, the red hue would be incorporated into the picture. At another moment it would be blue, then green, then red, etc. These single, one-color pictures were sent out in succession. Because of this fact it was called a "frame sequential" system of color television. The viewer actually saw a rapid succession of red, blue, and green pictures, but because of persistence of vision in the eye the primaries blended together into natural-looking color. The results were good enough to encourage the Federal Communications Commission to approve the C.B.S. system in 1950. The major hurdle was that the C.B.S. system was not compatible. All of the black-and-white sets would be useless for all programs broadcast in color.

R.C.A., and several other interested concerns, were not satisfied with the F.C.C. decision. They had a multimillion-dollar stake in color TV. They based their arguments on the issue of compatibility, and eventually won a modified victory.

The R.C.A. system uses a camera that contains three image-orthicon tubes (see Fig. 24). "The lens (1) collects light rays in full color from the scene being televised. The full-color image is focused into a series of mirrors. In the center are two dichroic mirrors (2) made of specially treated optical glass which has the property of reflecting one color while passing all other colors. The first of these mirrors reflects the red light, while the blue and green light passes straight through. The second dichroic mirror reflects the blue but passes the green. Thus three images, one in each primary color, are created. With the aid of regular reflecting mirrors (3) and a lens system (4), the three primary images are focused on the faces of three television camera tubes. In front of the camera tubes are color filters (5) which assure that the color quality of each primary has the precise value for the system. The electron beam in each camera tube (6) scans the image pattern which has been formed on the tube screen, thereby producing a primary color signal. The three primary color signals from the three tubes are now processed for transmission. Samples of these signals, in proper amounts in relation to each other, go to an electronic adder (7) which combines them to make the brightness, or black-and-white, signal. At the same time, samples of the three primary signals are fed to another unit (8) which encodes or combines them to produce a signal carrying the hue and saturation information. This color-representing signal is then combined with the brightness signal to form the complete color television signal."[1]

One of the great advantages of this system is that the hue, saturation, and brightness information is combined in every frame transmitted. This results in compatibility.

In an effort to achieve some workable standards as far as color TV was concerned, an industry-wide group was established, known as the National Television System Committee. This group, representing the best brains in all different branches of the broadcasting industry, finally made its recommendations to the F.C.C. These recommendations indicated that

[1] Diagram and explanation from R.C.A. pamphlet, *R.C.A. Color Television* Copyright 1953 by Radio Corporation of America.

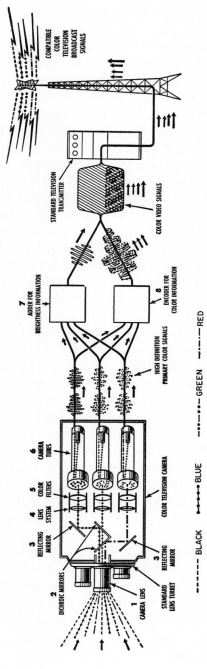

Fig. 24. Schematic diagram of the R.C.A. color television camera.

any color system approved should be compatible. They also included the technical standards for color signals. The F.C.C. adopted these standards on December 17, 1953.

As a result of this adoption, the R.C.A. system, slightly modified, was given a definite edge, and it is the system most widely employed. However, the C.B.S. system was not totally forgotten. C.B.S. and General Electric teamed together to market a compatible color system. In this system, a modified black-and-white, one-tube camera is equipped with the C.B.S. color wheel. Thus, as far as the camera is concerned, it is still a sequential system as contrasted with the R.C.A. instantaneous system. From the camera the signal is fed into a large electronic device known as a "Chromacoder." Here the signal is modified to fit all of the N.T.S.C. standards, including the making-over of the picture into one containing all of the color information. Thus, what is transmitted is a color picture of the instantaneous variety and, therefore, compatible. One advantage of this system is the avoidance of the need for the bulky, expensive, three-tube camera.

In March, 1950, R.C.A. demonstrated its tricolor kinescope tube. This important advance did away with the color wheel in the home receiver. The next step anticipated is the perfection of a tricolor camera tube. When this is available, color television will be of age.

In 1955, Du Mont introduced a radically different system of color pickup. They called it "Vitascan." This method was an almost 180-degree reversal of the traditional thinking about TV origination. In place of a pickup camera, a camera-like device is used which is really a light source. The main tube in this "Vitascan Color Studio Scanner" is a cathode-ray tube. The cathode-ray tube emits a beam of light which is directed onto the scene by a system of mirrors and lenses. This beam of light, which is in reality a flying spot, scans the scene. The pickup is accomplished by means of clusters of multiplier phototubes hung in the approximate positions where lights are normally placed in the conventional system. In other words, the pickup tubes are placed where lights normally are, and the light source is placed where the conventional camera is used.

The Vitascan system can only be used in the studio. It is essential that the cathode-ray tube scan the scene in almost total darkness. Most of the ambient light falling on the scene must be eliminated. To enable those in the studio to see, a system of stroboscopic lights is used. Earlier we discovered that blanking occurs after each field is scanned. It is during the blanking period that the scanning gun is returned to the left-hand side and top of the raster before resumption of the scanning process. By coordinating the on-off action of the stroboscopic lights with the blanking periods in the scanning process, the studio appears to be lighted. Persistence of vision makes it impossible for us to see the blanking periods in the scanning action, and this same persistence of vision gives us the impression that the lights are on at all times. Actually, of course, they are off while the beam is scanning.

The great advantage of the Vitascan system is that it can be installed and operated for a fraction of the cost of any other present method. It also has some advantages electronically since it is considerably more simple.

It may well be that the Vitascan development is another factor that will hasten the day of universal color television.

Closed-circuit Television

The term "closed circuit" implies the pickup and use of a television program without broadcasting it, at least not in the usual sense of the word. It might be used in classrooms, laboratories, theaters, or almost any place of group assembly. Closed-circuit television can be piped to the receiving points by wire, or it can be transmitted on a strictly local basis by low-power radiating devices.

In a number of medical schools, closed-circuit television is used regularly for instruction in surgery and other fields where a number of students must watch detailed and small-scale work. Television is admirably suited for this type of instruction. The University of Illinois College of Dentistry conducts several postgraduate short courses each year. Whenever appropriate, television is used on a closed-circuit basis. The dentists work and watch in the school's laboratories, while the instructor is upstairs in a television studio. The instruction is fed into the laboratories and the student dentists work right along with the instructor. All of the labs are connected to the studio by an intercom system so that at any time a student can stop the instructor and ask for a clarification of some point. In this way, as many as 200 dentists can be taught new techniques in a single session. Without TV, some of the subjects would be limited to ten students per session.

Theatre-Television (Theatre-Television Institute of New York, Inc.), which has specialized in boxing matches, operas, and other high-cost programs, is also a form of closed-circuit television. Its programs are fed around the country by A.T. & T. lines but are never transmitted publicly.

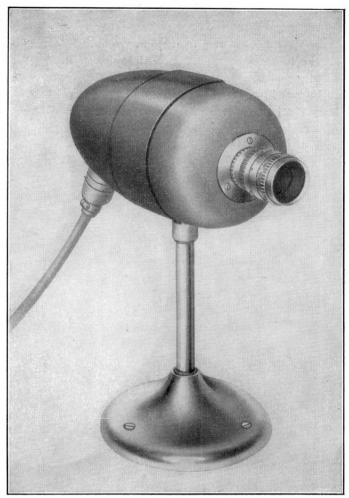

Fig. 25. G.P.L. vidicon industrial camera. (*General Precision Laboratory, Inc.*)

Industrial Television

Many industries have found that a special application of closed-circuit television allows economies, and frequently greater safety of operation. For example, in a factory, or plant, there might be a number of gauges or meters which cannot be located at a central point, but which must be continuously watched. By covering them with TV cameras and locating the receiving monitors at a central point, one man can keep track of all of the meters. In other installations it may be unsafe for anyone to be at a certain point in the operation, but visual checks are necessary. Closed-circuit television provides the answer. This kind of use has become increasingly important in operations handling radioactive materials.

Most of the industrial applications employ special cameras using the vidicon tube, rather than the more expensive image-orthicon. The vidicon requires a high light level to achieve a picture of broadcast quality, but at ordinary light levels can furnish a picture which is quite suitable for these industrial applications. Most of the manufacturers now make one or more models of industrial vidicon television cameras.

CHAPTER FOUR

RADIO AND TELEVISION PROGRAMMING

RADIO PROGRAMMING

The term "program building" in broadcasting may be applied either to the process of combining various entertainment and advertising units into an individual performance complete in itself, or to the task of arranging a series of such units into a sequence of acts for the day or the week. The problem of the program builder is to present entertainment that will hold the wavering attention of the great number of listeners; the income of his station depends ultimately upon that. To accomplish this he must consider the domestic and work habits and the attitudes, at various hours, of his listening audience. He must keep in mind the potential purchasers of the product to be advertised who will be reached during certain hours of the day. The program director of the network or of the local station, however, conforms to certain principles in the booking of the daily programs. The average radio station is on the air approximately 18 hours a day, from six o'clock in the morning until twelve o'clock at night; the director divides his day into approximately six parts of 3 hours each.

The local director should be less concerned with the quality of a single act than with the entire program for the day. In the majority of the stations associated with the various networks, the director aims to get variety and entertainment value by inserting contrasting local features between the programs received from the network. It is essential that he build up for his station a reputation for excellent programs in order to induce the listener to tune in and to stay tuned to that station automatically. To create this interest he must present a sequence of performances that are varied in character, all the time bearing in mind that different classes of people listen to programs at different times during the day.

The better practice is to avoid developing a type of listening audience.

as this discourages certain sponsors. In building programs, however, the director is conscious of the strata to which his station appeals. In larger cities, where there are a number of stations, one may appeal to the "carriage trade," using fine music and educational features for sustaining programs. Another station will feature sports broadcasts and dance selections. In many cities one station will direct its programs to foreign-speaking audiences. The result is that programs are arranged to conform to the policy of the station as established by sponsors and listeners. No hard-and-fast schedule exists for assembling the daily offering.

Morning Programs

From six o'clock until nine in the morning the program director will arrange programs to appeal to the lower and middle class in the wealth bracket. During this period there is a great deal of activity in the home. The head of the family is leaving for work, children are getting ready for school, and the mother is preparing breakfast; there is little opportunity for attentive listening. The programs for this period should be cheerful, bright, and lively to start off the day. Announcements should be short and musical selections brief and popular. Talks during this period lose their value unless they are short, and each must be a complete unit in itself to be quickly digested with the breakfast. Fifteen-minute programs are preferred at this time; they will be largely musical. There may be broadcasts of morning news. The disc jockey participation program with a lively ad-lib show is a popular early morning type.

The farmer appreciates very early morning weather forecasts and farming information. Time signals are given frequently so that the man of the house and the children may be on time to work and school.

During the second period, from nine until twelve o'clock, the audience is largely housewives. While the mother is engaged in her household tasks, she will have the radio turned on and will be listening to shopping news or cooking recipes. Announcements may be longer during this period and the programs may be largely special features arranged for the feminine listener. It is during these hours that the majority of women are heard over the radio as announcers and speakers. Women may give long commercial plugs, may describe the latest fashions, discuss interior decoration, and carry the burden of the programs. Skits that will appeal to the housewife are the types that predominate during this period. The soap operas or daytime serials follow one after another for the housewife who works as she listens. A recording or an electric-transcription library furnishes selections appealing to the women; thus the presence of the station's orchestra is not required during the forenoon.

Afternoon Programs

The noon hour is not considered a valuable hour for commercial sponsors in metropolitan areas. During this time there is generally a news broadcast or a religious program. However, the rural listener is an excellent prospect for midday programs. In examining the programs of stations we find that weather reports, market news, crop conditions, and information of interest to the farmer are broadcast around the noon hours. Between twelve and three o'clock the listener is inclined to be more leisurely, with the result that longer talks and educational programs, traffic-court programs, and others of this type are broadcast in the early afternoon hours. The housewife is a good prospect for early-afternoon programs; this is the time for intimate chats concerning the personal problems of the mother, such as those dealing with health and reading, child care, or dressmaking. A series of soap operas frequently fill all periods from 1 to 4 P.M.

The late-afternoon programs bring the children to the radio, and their value as allies in an advertising campaign is not overlooked by the sponsors. It is a general principle that the commercial plugs in daylight programs may be longer than those in the evening programs. Daylight hours reach not only the feminine and youthful audience; there is an increasing tendency upon the part of masculine workers in small shops to turn on their radios and listen as they work. Consequently these afternoon programs, while they may appeal primarily to the feminine and youthful audience, must have qualities that will interest the workers as well. Of course, during this period there are sports broadcasts.

Evening Programs

During this time the broadcasting of news seems to be a feature of nearly all stations. There may be sports résumés and dinner-music programs. With the start of the evening-program period the length of commercial copy is reduced. The whole family comprises a potential audience in both rural and urban areas, with the result that programs in the early evening are designed to appeal to all members of the family and to all wealth brackets. During the winter months this period is the most valuable of the radio day; the charge for the broadcasting facilities is highest between seven and ten o'clock in the evening, with the result that sponsors endeavor to present programs of an excellent caliber.

There is a constant search upon the part of the program director for originality and distinctiveness in program types. There have been air waves of popularity from the quiz to the "give aways." In each instance the radio showman has overworked and exhausted the popularity of the type so that new ideas must be sought. After ten o'clock in the evening, entertainment of a light nature is stressed, with dance orchestras and musical programs predominating. As the evening grows later, sustaining programs are presented by the station and must be arranged in such a way as to build up a listening audience that will attract sponsors to these hours. Delayed broadcasts from the nets, which were transcribed by the station, of programs presented earlier in the day are scheduled at this time. These consist of sustaining programs and in some instances of commercial programs which were delayed with the consent of the sponsor. In some instances where there is a time change from Eastern to Rocky Mountain time, these delayed broadcasts are an improvement in time for the advertiser.

General Requirements

All programs over radio are made up of music or talk; there are no other fundamentals than these from which to draw. The builder of programs must be ingenious in devising different arrangements. Music by itself for a long period is not advisable; it is much better to have the music interrupted by short skits or dialogues or monologues.

A radio program should be harmonious, that is, all features of the program should fit together smoothly. If the parts are not properly related, the result is discord and lack of effectiveness. In constructing the longer period for a sponsor, the builder may seek either a smooth harmony of entertainment or a contrast. As listening has been found to be an arduous occupation, there is a trend toward a contrast of component parts of the entertainment rather than a homogeneous linking of the whole. This results in a demand for variety in comedy, drama, music, and information; for unless the program contains a variety of entertainment features, certain members of its audience who demand those features will tune off. The tendency seems to be to present at least two features upon every program—an excellent orchestra and dramatics, music and a comedian, or amateurs. The feeling is that sponsors, by maintaining this formula in the building of their programs, gain a larger audience than if they presented merely a single feature. The program must start off in such a way as to attack the listener immediately and then must maintain that interest; however, the tempo of the musical numbers may be changed. The broadcaster must keep abreast of the thought, activities, and mental habits of the public. Audience interest is fickle. It is the business of the radio showman to give the public what it wants today. The program must be fresh and contain novelty from week to week. Dramatic surprises should be permitted so that the director may infuse new interest, new characters, and new entertainment ideas from time to time. As in every entertainment field, the impresario must constantly be seeking originality, ingenious combinations of old acts, new styles, unusual rhythms, or unique humorous situations, and his finger must be upon the pulse of public interest.

Radio networks and stations are at last beginning to realize that radio is an excellent advertising medium. They have preached this principle to sponsors for many years but have not practiced it themselves. The result is that various commercial programs advertise other programs, and in some instances performers upon commercial programs wander from program to program to build up the listening audience for the net or station. Station breaks and plugs are given to hold the listener to the station for programs to come. The evening hours become more coordinated instead of being individual acts in the over-all radio show.

Cyclical or block programming is used both in daytime and evening hours. An audience is created for soap operas with the result that four serials will follow each other; music, instead of running for a single 15-minute program, will run from the best in popular music through operettas, semiclassical, and classical for a full hour or two. One evening may be devoted to "who-done-its," detective and mystery shows.

Each net and station is very conscious of what its competitor is presenting and schedules programs to try to steal the audience of the more popular show. As a sponsor is hesitant in purchasing the period when another station has the big audience, every effort is put forth by the program department to originate a novel and competitive program. The weakest evening periods on the nets, 6 to 6:30 P.M. and 9:30 to 10 P.M. offer the best opportunity for competition by independent local stations. Not everyone likes an evening of mystery and murder, so the local station competes with music.

An extremely important factor in a musical program is variety. The musical director in choosing selections will avoid having series of numbers in the same key or rhythm. Such selections are generally chosen with an ear to their tempo, which is selected to fit the product being advertised. Even in the selection of musical numbers for a 15- or 30-minute program, variety is sought by the musical director in order that the appeal may be wide. Variety is essential in any program, regardless of the type. The hour at which the program is broadcast should be especially considered. The type of music played on an afternoon program should usually be different from that on the evening program. One must never forget the mood of one's audience. If the artist is a noted concert pianist, the public will listen to an entire program of his over the air, but these occasions are rare. Popular music is generally liked, but be-bop in most cases is disliked.

It is difficult for a program director to say how long a successful program should be. The broadcaster must remember that the length of the program is first of all determined by the amount of money the sponsor of the program wishes to spend. He must then try to find out which will have the greater advertising value—several short programs or fewer long programs. In determining the length of each individual program or "act" in this variety show of the air, the director must recognize the fact that, regardless of the type of performance, the radio version should be shorter than it would be if it were presented visually to an audience.

The element of timing is vital. A few seconds one way or another can, and often does, spell disaster for the program director and result in the loss of a long-time contract with a sponsor. The program builder must have a fine sense of timing or tempo, for pauses are as important as situations and gags. The listener must be given time to digest and appreciate what he hears. The pause must be accurately timed as to its location and duration.

Popularity of Programs

Radio stations, advertising agencies, and special agencies conduct surveys to determine the popularity of programs and types of presentation. Tastes vary from time to time; however, there is slight change evident in audience response to program types. Thus, the program type has less to do with its popularity than has its presentation. In order of wide appeal, the panel or quiz shows come first, followed by comedy and drama. Then comes the sports broadcast, followed by music. The speech programs are next in the popularity ranking, then news, talks, religion, education, children's programs, special features, and finally women's programs.

The program builder should be familiar with all the programs that are being broadcast by various stations. He must evaluate their ideas and improve upon those that have been originated by others. He should have a complete knowledge of just about everything in the broadcasting station, particularly dramatics and music. He need not be the last word as a dramatic director but he should be surrounded by persons in that field who are capable.

Local Features

The alert program director will study the community in which his station is located and build programs to appeal to listeners. One Detroit station, recognizing the fact that that city has over 400,000 Polish listeners, has arranged programs in Polish for the listeners. Because of the large listening audience, this program is sponsored and the price that is charged the sponsor is more than that charged for the ordinary program in English. This station also presents programs in German, Czechoslovakian, Bavarian, and Italian. A foreign resident speaking these languages is put in charge of the program and sells time. The announcements are all made in the language; and the musical portion of the program consists of recordings, which are generally obtained from the native land, and live talent from the local foreign settlement. These programs are presented at hours when the small station would find it difficult to compete with the excellent chain programs that are offered by local stations. They are very popular and have a distinct and positive audience. Frequently competition between various language groups makes for better programs. Nearly 400 stations now accept foreign-language programs.

A few stations are recognizing the fact that a large proportion of laborers work all night in the cities; thus some stations are on the air for 24 hours a day. One station broadcasts programs that would appeal to the owners of beer gardens between twelve and two o'clock in the morning, presenting 10 minutes of dance music, followed by 10 minutes of music of a character that will force the listener to sit at a table where it is hoped he will drink beer. Such programs also find sponsors among the all-night barbecue stands that are equipped to deliver food. The early-morning programs from five-thirty on are excellent mediums to reach the invalid, the milkman, and the all-night worker. They largely consist of requested musical selections. Such programs furnish an excellent advertising medium, building up a listening audience for the station. This is one of the problems of the program director—the creating of an audience that will be a sales factor for daylight programs.

While the evening hours bring the finest programs from the networks, the local station relies upon the daylight programs for its greatest audience and income; consequently its daylight and evening rates are usually the same. In the evening the local manager must arrange special features, such as the foreign-language programs, local news broadcasts, and club programs, to attract the resident from the networks. Local merchants would be wise to recognize that competition is less during the daytime. A high proportion of existing radio stations are licensed to serve the particular needs of the areas in which they are located. Station managers are searching for good local-program material. The most important developments in broadcasting will probably occur in the improvement of local programs rather than in any change of national programs. The gauge for the successful program is threefold: (1) the popularity of programs which compete with the one being evaluated, (2) the attractiveness of the first two or three minutes of the program, (3) whether the whole content of the program, rather than some part, holds the interest to the end.

Special-day Programs

Various transcription services prepare a special-day program for the use of those who have subscribed to its transcription library. Special-day programs may be arranged by local stations. There are patriotic and religious holidays, sentimental holidays, as well as national holidays. Many excellent scripts have been written for Memorial Day, using the theme of the Unknown Soldier. A brief sketch of this type follows.

THE UNKNOWN SOLDIER

ANNOUNCER: The scene is Somewhere in Heaven on Armistice Day. As the scene opens, Red is looking down upon the earth. National airs can be heard played by a band and the atmosphere is created of a dignified, solemn, imposing ceremony at the dedication of the Tomb of the Unknown Soldier being conducted below on earth. The presidents, kings, emperors, and rulers of the countries of the world are in attendance to pay tribute to the Unknown Soldier. Red is gazing attentively at the ceremony.

QUINTON: What's going on, Red?

RED: Big doings down there—bands, speeches, and everything.

QUINTON: Boy, that's a wonderful sight! Never saw so many people in one spot. What's it all about?

RED: That's the Tomb of the Unknown Soldier and all the "head men" of the world are there to—what do you call those affairs?

QUINTON: Memorial Service.

RED: That's it. I've been watching and listening for half an hour—all the presidents, kings, princes, generals, admirals, the Pope, bishops, rabbis—they're all there, from all over the world.

QUINTON: What's the idea back of it all? I'm sorry I missed it.

RED: It's great—the finest notion that came out of the lousy war. It seems that a little country preacher thought it up—with all the hate, blood, guns, gases, subs, propaganda running wild, he donated to the world this simple, wonderful thought. You know there were thousands killed in the big scrap that were unidentified and their folks never heard from 'em. This preacher thought up the idea of picking one from the unknown bunch and burying him with great honors. You see, all the mothers of the missing thinks that's her boy—

QUINTON: And she's right—maybe it is her boy.

RED: (Cynical laugh)

QUINTON: Why the laugh—what's funny?

RED: That's me down there and all the world is around my tomb. (Laughs)

QUINTON: You lucky stiff, put it there. Glad and proud to meet you, kid. What's your name?

RED: Red.

QUINTON: Red—what?

RED: Just "Red."

QUINTON: Cut the kidding. What's your last name?

RED: Don't know—that's why I'm laughing. Never had any. On the square.

QUINTON: Never had a mother?

RED: Never knew who she was—or a dad either.

QUINTON: You don't mean to say you're a—

RED: Yes, isn't it funny, of all the thousands of guys unidentified they just happened to pick on me. The Unknown Soldier. I'm a real Unknown Soldier. When I tried to check up on myself I found out that I was left on a doorstep—raised in an orphan asylum—ran away—peddled papers—hung around the curbstones—worked in a factory—went to war and got knocked off in the Argonne.

QUINTON: What a break!

RED: Now you know why I laughed. But listen, kid! I know this is Heaven 'cause I got more mothers than any guy in the world!

Filling Time

The local station in a small community, where there is little talent, and the educational broadcaster have the problem of filling their time on the air at the least expense. Such stations average 84 hours a week on the air—336 quarter-hour programs, 52 weeks in a year. Their greatest blessings are the transcribed services which provide music and continuity. A station will use about 25 hours a week of transcriptions and additional recorded programs. Many popular selections are received free for use upon disc jockey programs as promotional advertising for the manufacturer. Victor, Columbia, Masque, Standard, and M.G.M. are but a few who provide "special purpose" current recordings.

These stations will subscribe to a news service—Associated Press, International News Service, United Press—and as a result will be able to present about 18 hours of news, market reports, sports, features, and commentaries.

Many excellent transcriptions are obtainable free from public-relations sources such as those of foreign nations—French, Dutch, and British. In addition the various departments of the United States government will provide public-service programs which highlight the Army, the Treasury Department, the U.S. Office of Education, the Navy, and the Veteran's Authority. The advertising on these programs is in the public interest and is carried by the station gratis.

There are a number of manufacturers who provide free institutional transcriptions with only indirect commercial material. The educational stations in the region will gladly supply transcriptions of their programs to gain greater coverage and to publicize their institutions. Other non-profit organizations also provide programs, such as the American Medical Society and Alcoholics Anonymous.

These three program sources—transcription service and recordings, news service, and public-service program transcriptions—should account for about one-half of the weekly program fare.

Mass or Selected Audience for Radio and TV

The commercial broadcaster gears his program day to appeal to a mass audience. Commercial radio and television are mass media in which broad appeal is inherent. The programming of these media must be such as to appeal to all kinds of people in all parts of the country, and in different age, income, and educational brackets—all, or nearly all, the different kinds of Americans there are. A mass medium must concern itself with the common denominators of mass interest. Not that every program broadcast will appeal to everyone, but the total program structure is intended to reach the widest possible audience. To do this the appeal can not be unduly special or excessive or selective. Yet, the listener and the viewer are not a mass. They are individuals, and in terms of the construction of any audience they are separate segments of the totality that is the listening and viewing public. It is the problem of management, and specifically of the program department, to choose a menu for the many different segments and to satisfy their average appetites for interests and needs. It does not cater to one listener or one viewer.

The true function of broadcasting relates quite specifically to the community it serves. It bears upon the needs, the differential needs, of that community. The function of the broadcaster is not to force his own opinions or attitudes upon his audience but to listen to the voices of his community which express the needs and problems of the individuals who are his listeners and viewers and to attempt to satisfy these voices.

Not all the listeners in the 46,600,000 radio homes nor all the millions of television viewers like the same things. With the networks and the big commercial stations vying for the mass audience, the independent locals and the educational stations have easy picking in the minority groups. These stations can and do present the finest music, the best experimental programs, and local events.

The independent station will go out after a share of a large potential audience or seek to attract the whole of a smaller group which it can more or less monopolize. Specification in a particular field, such as classical music or sports, always poses difficult problems. More often than not, there are as many people that do not like these programs as there are that will tune them in. If, for example, an FM station expects to counter AM and television with good music, it must first make certain that a potential audience for such music is large enough to become a market which will support the station. By the same token, if a TV station expects to compete with the network outlets by stressing sports programs, it must make certain that there is a sufficient audience in the market, as well as sufficient events to make up a schedule.

The station which continues to specialize and hold an audience which is essentially its own will continue to attract sponsors. Unfortunately there is no magic formula for a specialized station. Success will depend upon individual initiative, imagination, and experience.

TELEVISION PROGRAMMING

Television has grown up as a younger brother of radio. A high percentage of television stations are owned by companies that have been operating radio stations. The three major national networks in television are also the big radio networks. Many performers, writers, directors, producers, and executives who achieved success in radio have moved into television.

The advertisers and advertising agencies have furthered the ties between radio and television. Because of this sibling relationship it is only natural that television programming should follow most of radio's underlying principles.

Television programs fill a large part of the day. Two of the major networks begin the TV day at 7 A.M., for both the Eastern and Central time zones. Most stations stay on the air until midnight, or after. The early-morning shows are geared to the family as they prepare to leave for work or school, or to farmers. The late morning and early afternoon hours are largely aimed at the busy homemaker. Late afternoon ushers in the children's programs. The dinner-hour shows are news, sports, or light musical programs. The 7 to 10 P.M. evening hours are the prime Class "A" time, and it is here we find the high-budget entertainment programs. Audience appeals and sponsor use of such appeals correspond very closely to radio. More often than not the breadth of the appeal is the all-important factor. The rating is the thing. Perhaps it is even more true in television than in radio because of the greatly increased cost, and the advertiser wants his message to reach enough people to justify this cost. Programs designed for special audiences are rare.

The obvious conclusion is that in regard to programming television operates according to the same principles, the same working philosophy, as radio. The differences between radio and television programming arise because of the addition of the visual element in television, and not because of different purposes or objectives.

The Elements of a TV Program

The television program, like its counterpart in radio, is cast into a framework known in the industry as a "format." The format provides for some kind of opening (usually involving an effort to attract attention, commercial identification, and credit), the body of the program, closing credits, some type of pad that can be shortened or lengthened as time demands, and a close. The body of the program, which is usually interrupted at least once for a commercial, contains the main elements of the program. These are usually identifiable as quite separate segments, most of them rather short, and strung together with some kind of continuity. Variety and tempo are determined by the length of these program segments and the manner in which they are strung together. Even in the more formal program, such as a drama, scenes tend to be short, and an effort is made to keep the story moving.

Try analyzing a variety show or a comedy show. Notice how many program elements there are, in what order they are used, how long they last, and how they are strung together. If you watch programs critically you will soon find a tremendous similarity in the structural aspects of different television programs. Then, too, take a stop watch and time the change of scenes in a TV program or a film. Remember, photographically, it is a change of scene every time there is a cut to another camera, a dissolve, or a fade. If you have never done this you will be amazed at the fabulous number of changes that occur in the moving panorama that passes before your eyes. This is all a part of the conscious effort to keep the audience interested.

Television uses the speech and music elements of radio and adds to them the endless variety of visual impressions that can be achieved. It is contrary to F.C.C. regulations to use a television channel for broadcasting of audio only. However, it is perfectly legitimate, and perhaps practical, to broadcast a program that has no audio, or very little. The use of pictures, motion, pantomime, gestures, demonstration, and the hundreds of other visual patterns, greatly enhance the potential of television programming. While the underlying program structure is the same for radio and television, the variety and ultimate interest is greater in television. In the field of sports, for example, listening to someone describe an athletic contest is not as effective as watching it on a television screen. In some sports, like boxing, the sport is better on television than it is for most of the fans in the arena. On television, everyone has a ringside seat. Television's superiority is clear in any program area where sight adds to the understanding or appreciation of what is going on. On the other hand, what about programs like news and music? Television hasn't solved the problem of effective news reporting. The ever-popular disc jockey program is usually dull fare on TV. So, it cannot be said that TV is better for all types of programming.

The visual aspects of television also introduce some problems that must be considered in connection with programming. Of greatest importance is the added complexity of producing programs and its companion problem, cost. The program planner is never free, in television, to let his imagination run completely wild. The hard facts of production will certainly slow him down to a realistic pace. While a small studio crew can put on a fairly complicated radio show, a similar show on TV will require five, six, or even ten times as many people. Cost goes up proportionately. It is common for major network shows to have a weekly production budget of between \$30,000 and \$50,000. Some single-shot TV programs cost the sponsor a half million dollars. At these prices one can readily see that TV programming is a compromise between creative ideas and the size of the purse on which you have to draw.

Summary of TV Programs[1]

It is well-nigh impossible to indicate relative percentages of program types without being guilty of generalizations which needn't apply to all stations. It happens that there is excellent data available for the seven stations in New York City. This data was gathered over a four-year period, and is quite generally typical because it contains all of the network programming. It can safely be assumed that other stations throughout the country will not vary significantly from this pattern. The four-year study also indicates that programming trends have begun to stabilize to a great extent.

In 1954, the programming was divided by percentages of total program time into the following major categories:

Drama	46.2
Information	11.3
Variety	11.0
Music	6.7
News	6.1
Quizzes, contests, etc	5.0
Orientation	4.9
Personality	4.8
All other entertainment	4.0
	100%

The summary shows that 77.7 per cent of the total time was devoted to pure entertainment. Informational programs of all types, including news, accounted for 17.4 per cent, and the orientation type of program supplied the remaining 4.9 per cent. "Orientation programs," as used here, means areas such as family or personal relationships, religion, public affairs, discussions, debates.

[1] Most of the statistical data in this section is taken from the television monitoring studies done by the National Association of Educational Broadcasters, with financial aid from the Fund for Adult Education, an independent agency established by the Ford Foundation. There are seven such studies available from N.A.E.B., 14 Gregory Hall, University of Illinois, Urbana, Illinois. Specifically, I have taken data from studies number 6 and 7, *Three Years of New York Television* and *Four Years of New York Television.*

It will be noticed at once that sports are not specifically mentioned in this table. Actually, televised sports accounted for 3.4 percent of the total time. The four-year record shows a steady decline in the amount of time devoted to spectator sports. These studies were also made during the winter months, so we can safely assume that at other times of the year, and in other markets, sports would occupy a more prominent place.

One interesting thing to note is the heavy reliance on drama. These figures include, of course, both live and film programs. Drama has become to TV what music has always been to radio, the hard core around which the rest of the programming structure is built. In TV, music takes but 6.7 per cent of the available time. This is easy to understand when you try to figure out some way of adding visual appeal to popular music. Programs built around cooking, sewing, fashions, and other homemaking techniques, gardening, and handicrafts are responsible for the high percentage of informational programs. This type of show offers interesting and usually easy-to-achieve visual appeal. It will be noted that comedy is not listed as a separate category. TV comedy has found its way into more basic formats. For example, approximately one-fourth of the drama can be classified as comedy-drama. Comedy also appears in the larger framework of variety shows, in the quizzes and contests, and in the personality shows. So, while comedy is not shown separately it remains one of the most common, and certainly one of the most successful, program types.

The order of programs in any popularity poll varies from season to season. The basic tastes, however, remain about the same. It is possible that the level of popular taste is ever upward—mobile, but the rate is painfully slow. The amount of time given to different types of programs is one clue to popularity. To this can be added the fact that representative programs of certain basic types are almost always included in the "top ten." There will always be at least one quiz or similar kind of show, one or more situation comedy-dramas, one or more of the currently popular comedians in a sort of personality show, at least one variety show, and it appears that there will always be a mystery—a whodunnit—a crime show.

Official popularity standings are determined by commercial survey organizations. Stations and networks employ such concerns to keep them abreast of how their audience compares with that of the competition for every hour of the broadcast day. These ratings are combined into a national picture and lists of the top ten programs are published. It is not practical to include such a list in a book of this sort since it would be out of date before the book was off the presses. The current ratings can always be found in the trade papers *Broadcasting, Variety,* and *Television.*

The Program Year

In broadcasting, both radio and television, it has become standard practice to sell time and to book programs for periods of 13 weeks. This breaks the year into quarters, which have proved to be workable fractions from the business point of view. A sponsor can buy a program for 13 weeks, 26 weeks, 39 weeks, or for the full 52 weeks. The most common formula for the more or less permanent programs is to buy 39 weeks and take a 13-week "hiatus" in the summer. This accounts for the rash of fill-in programs through the summer months. Many advertisers feel that the listening and viewing public is too small during the summer to warrant the cost of high-budget shows. So, the summer is used for lighter, less expensive shows, and for trying out new program ideas or talent.

The summer hiatus is especially important in television because of the high costs. The optimum audience must be available to justify the large sums which the sponsor has to pay. When many thousands are off on vacations, on picnics, or out riding in the family car, it is not the ideal time for high-cost TV programs.

Another development in television programming which never became common in radio is the alternating sponsorship of top programs. A show will appear one week sponsored by a certain product, and come on the next week with a different sponsor. This is another effort on the part of advertisers to beat the high costs of TV programming. Participating sponsorship is also popular in TV. Here, a major program will have several sponsors, each getting equivalent time during the program. Perhaps on an hour-long program there will be three sponsors, each having bought 20 minutes of the show. Some programs are too costly and too complicated for weekly production. They will be broadcast once a month, or in some cases every two weeks. All of these exceptions to the old rule of the same show, the same sponsor, the same time every week grow out of television's complicated and costly production requirements. Irregular sponsorship is justified by the proven impact of TV advertising.

Live and Film Programs

A live program means that the show is actually being performed at the time it is broadcast. The terms "filmed" and "recorded" are frequently used interchangeably and indicate that the program has been prepared ahead of broadcast time. Some producers and performers believe that the spontaneity and sense of immediacy attendant on a live show are important and desirable qualities. They have a good point. On the other hand, a live show is always subject to flubs and other production mistakes. Also, there are some things which are possible on film and aren't practical for live productions. So, to make these things possible and to achieve a slickness of production, many shows have turned to film. This includes programs of all types except those that depend on immediacy or current information, such as news programs, or remotes of actual events.

In the early days of television most programs were done live. There were few films available, and producers and performers were experimenting with the new medium. Today, there are many companies making films for television, and filming programs of types not normally made as films, such as quiz programs, variety, etc.

In 1954, on the seven New York City stations, 44.9 per cent of all programs were on film. Of those programs classified as entertainment, an even higher percentage prevailed, 52.4 per cent. The total percentage was reduced by those programs that could not, by their very nature, be filmed. The four-year record in New York City showed a decided trend toward increased percentage of film programs up to 1954. It is possible that the ratio has now more or less stabilized. The values of filming programs, as discussed above, are further enhanced by the residual uses. There is always the possibility that a series of shows can be syndicated and sold locally after the network run. Or they might be reused at a later date. On some programs, the best shows from the winter season are used again during the summer months. In this way the added cost of film is turned to advantage, and the sponsor saves the production costs during the summer months.

Whether there is an increase in film programs in the future will depend largely on the types of program that appear on future schedules, and such technical advances as are made. If magnetic recording of television becomes a reality in the near future, this will be widely used for the pre-production of complicated shows. It might be pointed out that this is a very real possibility.

CHAPTER FIVE

RADIO AND TELEVISION ANNOUNCING

RADIO ANNOUNCING

Radio announcing, as a profession, has come of age. The day of the transient, station-to-station, journeyman announcer is past. Though all qualifications are not firmly established as yet, this is largely due to the fact that radio is still in a stage of transition. Television has added new requirements to the general confusion; and announcing, as a profession, needs unbiased analysis.

Announcers themselves have come to realize that training and experience must be an integral part of their equipment; that a good voice and a pleasing personality are not enough, as they might have been even five years ago. Many station managers still consider announcers as of little consequence, limiting initiative and authority to the minimum. This attitude may have been justified in the past, but today announcers must be considered as belonging to a profession which is fast gaining both dignity and respect, capable of attracting men and women of education and ambition. The more progressive stations have trained their announcers to shoulder responsibility and assist in planning programs. They have encouraged specialization in fields where the announcer seems to have particular aptitude. It is true that many of the top-notch announcers of today began with very little formal training and developed with the growth of radio, but they, more than any others, realize the potentialities of the profession and the need for adequate training.

As one radio executive has said, "an announcer should be such a friendly voice in the house that the listener is tempted to answer him back." Like most things which sound easy, however, the mere fact that an announcer can do this requires a background of intensive training and specialized education, which must become so much a part of him that he

66

and the listener both are unconscious of it. The radio announcer must also bear in mind that he is the station's representative while on the air. The listener judges the caliber and character of the station by its announcing staff. Therefore, voice and speech training are a *must* for success in announcing. The training must extend beyond the limits of formal education. No one should consider radio announcing as a profession unless he has a healthy curiosity and interest in speech and in people. He must be ready and willing to practice, drill, and study every day for the rest of his life. Dramatic training is helpful, for the announcer must sound convincing at all times and this occasionally requires acting ability. Many good announcers have been either actors or singers.

Here is a note of warning to the careless radio announcer who may tend to allow his lack of interest in or his disagreement with his announcements to reflect itself in his voice. An exercise in mental hygiene seems to be indicated for one who would be successful. As Milton Cross put it, "An announcer's voice must be healthy, well dressed, and cheerful." A continued conscious effort must be made toward that end. Many American colleges and universities offer excellent courses in speech training which provide drill in pronunciation needed to free the announcer from the handicap of regional dialect and local peculiarities. Here, he can study voice improvement, public speaking, and oral interpretation.

Training

There is no better training for radio speaking than the reading aloud of all types of material. Stumbling over an announcement is an unforgivable sin on the part of the announcer. There may be brief pauses—the slight hesitancy used by speakers to emphasize the choice of a carefully selected word. Reading is a tremendous handicap to spontaneity, and the difficulty is emphasized in the announcer's case, for when a man is giving various items daily, in many cases repeating what he has read previously, the opportunity to wander mentally is all the more attractive. To avoid the trap of this too easy job of reading words, one must concentrate upon the mood and the meaning of the words. Proper pause, stress, and intonation can be obtained only in this way. When the announcer or speaker has completed his radio address, he should be able to give a clear résumé of what he has just said.

William Shakespeare, although unacquainted with radio, once delivered some excellent advice to announcers when he said, "Speak the speech, I pray you, as I pronounce it to you, trippingly, on the tongue; for if you mouth it, as many of you players do, I had as lief the town crier spake my lines." To be acceptable to the radio listener, the announcer must avoid all forms of affectation such as gushing, evangelical exhortations, pleading sweetness, aggressive overemphasis, spiritual ecstasy, and the precise pronunciation that results in an obvious division of a word into its syllables. Today, sponsors prefer the chatty, chummy type of announcing.

If you want to be an announcer, Pat Kelly recommends a college liberal arts course, an English major, a course in speech, and as much acting as you can work in. The announcer needs training in mike technique, which a small station can provide, though not so well as many colleges and universities do. More important than either schooling or dramatics for the beginner is a good education with an all-around knowledge of music, sports, current events, and books. Along with this he should have the ability to learn the actual mechanics of radio announcing. Radio announcing is nothing more than an attempt to communicate information; to make something known. Although the information may reach millions, it is directed to the individual listener, and the communication is complete only when the listener hears, comprehends, is interested, and then acts upon what he hears. If the listener does not act upon the announcer's message the communication is still not complete, because in radio, as in almost all other speech activities, the purpose is the stimulation of action. The action may be merely that of remembering something, or it may be that of doing something, but unless the announcer's message is acted upon there is no real communication. If you fail to send in your bottle top or fail to "stay tuned to your friendly station" then the announcer has failed.

Skills

A partial list of skills, evolved from many discussions, although not entirely inclusive, consists of communication of ideas and emotion, as well as projection of the personality through naturalness, vitality, friendliness, adaptability, and pronunciation. Voice control is a skill which depends upon pitch, volume, timing, and quality to a large degree. Many other skills can be developed and added to these, but here, briefly, are those which any announcer needs, plus whatever education and experience he can obtain.

An announcer can achieve complete success, in selling his idea to his listener, if he rethinks his copy and makes it his own without mechanically employing the techniques of phrasing and emphasis. By knowing and understanding technique he can fortify his natural ability for the occasions when he is obliged to fall back upon them as aids when the continual reiteration of an announcement has robbed it of its freshness.

Phrasing is indicated by inflection, and an inflection is either upward or downward in pitch. In the English language such pitch comes at the end of each phrase, uniting the words in the phrase and indicating by the pitch movement whether the phrase is complete in itself or connected with what follows. A downward glide in the pitch usually expresses completion of the phrase; an upward glide, the opposite. Inflection can be varied to express any mood or emphasis, such as indecision, disbelief, a question, and courtesy. A circumflex inflection of the voice usually indicates insincerity or irony, or a state of mental confusion.

Emphasis can be achieved by variations in tone or volume. A phrase can be varied in this way to call attention to key words or can be increased in a crescendo, as in music, to gain the required feeling of mounting excitement and anticipation, as is sometimes used in variety shows. Emphasis can also be achieved by variation in timing. Time emphasis on a word or a phrase can be gained in the three following ways:

1. By the use of a pause after or before the word or phrase.
2. By prolongation of the sounds within the word or phrase.
3. By variation in rhythm.

Relaxation of the body may also contribute to the emphasis of speech. Within range of the microphone an announcer may move his arms or body, just as he would to a visible audience, and thereby gain more naturalness in his speech. Announcing and radio speaking, which is dealt with elsewhere in this book, have much in common; the rules for one apply also to the other. Genuine sincerity is, of course, one of the greatest attractions in any speaker, but it is especially to be desired in an announcer. The microphone is a sensitive instrument and records with utter fidelity the slightest variation in tone or meaning.

The pause, if well used, is one of the most effective devices an announcer can use, and it is often the most frequently ignored. Some announcers are still afraid of silence. They are convinced that the air must be constantly full of words. Sometimes this fear is conditioned by station managers who cling to the old methods and ideas of advertising. Newspapers learned long ago that white space has as much value to the advertiser as the printed word. The skilled and experienced announcer realizes that silence, if effectively used, is radio's "white space."

"Personality is reflected in the voice." We seldom think of personality except in positive terms, and the radio announcer is expected to have such a positive personality. That is, the listener enjoys hearing a voice which suggests naturalness, sincerity, believability, vitality, friendliness, and warmth as well as adaptability. The microphone picks up insincerity, disinterest, guile, and irritability very clearly. The beginning announcer may be nagged by qualms of mike fright and will realize all at once that he is addressing a mechanical instrument rather than an audience. He must speak with his mind on time and on the second hand of the clock ticking off each breath. He must say words that are not his own in a voice which is supposed to sound natural. Under these circumstances this is difficult to do, but the words and thoughts must be mastered until they *are* his own. He must imagine that he is speaking to just one listener and direct his message to that one person, sell his thought to that person. He will help himself most by following the advice which actors and performers give themselves:

1. Everyone has had a similar experience and lived through it.
2. Don't think how you feel. Think of what you are about to say.
3. Assume a vital, positive, assured manner and you will be more apt to be just that.
4. Know what you are going to say so thoroughly that you are saying it before you have a chance to worry about it.
5. Breathe as deeply and naturally as possible.

The would-be announcer should listen carefully to the station with which he hopes to affiliate himself. He should try to emulate the better announcers of that station but never to imitate them. The beginning announcer may be a "nobody," but he is better as a nobody than as an imitation of someone else. To be natural, to be himself, the announcer must react normally to each announcing situation. This does not mean that he must be colorless. It is as natural to be gay, enthusiastic, folksy, or chatty, as it is to be dull, bored, or aloof. Vitality is a personality trait most required of announcers, but even this can be overdone. Everyone who listens to radio is aware of this; in fact, many listeners would be happier if some announcers were not quite so vigorous and full of bounce.

The announcer should have a personality so varied that he can adapt himself and his announcing style to the constantly changing demands of the listener and the program. Listening audiences change from hour to hour, program styles often change every 15 minutes. The announcer must be ready to change with them without losing any of his individual integrity.

In the case of the radio announcer, the same individual is compelled constantly to change his style from one form to another, so that he is confronted with the difficult task of attempting to handle all types of public speaking equally well. Very few announcers specialize in one type of work. The average announcer must be prepared in the same day to give the dramatic ballyhoo of a spectacular program, to read the 3-minute commercial advertisement for a so-called health salt, to read the announcements for a program of classical music, and to introduce a professor or a minister. All these variations and many more come as grist to his mill.

The announcer should be aware that styles in pronunciation change just as clothing styles do. He should keep his standards high but flexible, for what was correct yesterday may not be acceptable today or preferred tomorrow. The International Phonetic Alphabet, sometimes called the "IPA," transcribes all sounds of spoken language into symbols, each representing only one sound. At first glance, it looks like an entirely new alphabet and some announcers shy away from it because it looks difficult. It is simple and is being utilized more and more in radio, and is used in nearly all college foreign-language courses and in many speech courses in vowel and consonant drill.

An announcer must be more conscious of time than of any other element in broadcasting. Although he must continually think of his listener and his message, he must always be aware of the clock and the constant sweep of the second hand. He must know how and when to take up the slack in a program when time is running short and how to stretch it out by prolonging phrases and other variations of speech. At first this is difficult to do unless one is born with a perfect sense of timing, as sometimes happens. Generally, however, it is knowledge which must be gained by constant observation and practice. It is one of the most essential skills an announcer can have.

The announcer's voice must be natural, a universal voice—one not tied to any locality or sectional dialect; he must have ability to be formal without being stiff, to be informal without gushing; he must be versatile in his ability to handle names, musical terms, and foreign words.

The National Broadcasting Company, in the pamphlet on *The Selection and Training of Radio Announcers*, states:

An announcer in the N.B.C. is expected to average well in the following: a good voice, clear enunciation, and pronunciation free of dialect or local peculiarities; ability to read well; sufficient knowledge of foreign languages for the correct pronunciation of names, places, titles, etc.; some knowledge of musical history, composition, and composers; ability to read and interpret poetry; facility in extempore speech; selling ability in the reading of commercial continuity; ability to master the technical details in operating switchboard; a college education.

The qualities that make the best announcers are personality, charm, naturalness, sincerity, conviction, enthusiasm, spontaneity, accuracy, culture, and salesmanship, to which add a dash of voice with an excellent vocabulary, and you will have an ideal radio announcer.

The commercial announcer must follow the principles that are laid down for radio speaking in general. However, he must also develop some special characteristics that are different from those used by the person giving a radio address.

Simply because all recognized announcers have good voices, it has been assumed that this is the most important requirement for the announcer. The ability, natural or acquired, to control the voice apparatus with which he is endowed is more essential than natural tone quality. Often the ability to control his voice earns for an announcer with meager volume and vocal equipment the reputation of having a good voice.

Physical relaxation of the vocal cords and of the muscles of the neck and throat is the foundation upon which all voice control is based. Without such relaxation, the tenseness of the throat muscles and vocal cords will limit the range of the voice and cause a readily detectable rasping quality; a breathy, harsh effect is imparted to the voice, and all opportunity for effective intonation is gone. Apart from the obvious restrictions of tenseness of the mechanism upon the voice, the listener is aware of the uneasiness, the strain, on the part of the announcer, and this destroys his confidence in what he hears. Tenseness is seldom obvious in ordinary conversation; therefore, it is obviously produced by a mild form of "mike fright." Even experienced announcers feel some excitement when they are addressing the mike, but they do not allow their feeling to tighten their throat muscles or to influence their speech. The best method of keeping mental strain at a minimum is to concentrate upon the material at hand, the script, the message to be given, the service that you feel you are giving to your listeners.

The position at the microphone is important. The best "punch" announcers talk up to the mike. Such announcers hold their copy above and beyond the mike and talk up with considerable verve. If the announcer talks down, his throat muscles are inclined to cramp and tighten. The man who is of average height seems to be more acceptable than one who is either very short or extremely tall. (I have never been able to do anything in my classes either to lengthen or to shrink an announcer.)

The students who have successfully placed themselves as commercial announcers are those who have practiced tirelessly in reading commercial announcements over the public-address system. It takes a lot of practice to gain naturalness and fluency. The average radio speaker has a very conversational style; the commercial announcer puts more punch into his delivery and, as a result, requires more voice volume and reserve breath.

The commercial announcer's sense of phraseology and immediate recognition of important words is essential. He must read his copy and determine what his punch words and phrases are to be. He must vary his tempo and his volume accordingly. As a general rule, tempo is slightly decreased for a punch line and slightly increased for supplementary material. Of course, in such change of tempo, there must never be a loss of clarity in enunciation. If a phrase is speeded up, the words that are in that phrase must still be clear and distinct. When an announcement is to be given rapidly, and most commercial announcements are given with considerable speed, success depends not only in skimming lightly over unimportant words, but in knowing what words require stress to make the advertising message vivid and clear. In actual practice, many simple words are skimmed over by a commercial announcer. In the following simple spot announcement, the italicized words are those which can be effectively run together.

Clapp's Strained Baby Foods *are made from* tender, select vegetables, *rushed fresh from factory garden* to spotless, sunlit kitchens where *every step in their preparation* is carefully supervised by *hospital-trained* dieticians.

The sponsor or his advertising agency infrequently gives instructions to the announcer about emphasis and style of delivery, depending upon his individual interpretation. Here, however, is one announcement with instructions that appeared in *The New Yorker:*

ANNOUNCER: CIGARETTE STAIN ON YOUR FINGERS IS NOT NICE! PELL MELL Famous Cigarettes are smoked wherever particular people congregate—because independent research proves that with PELL MELL there is noticeably less finger stain, or no finger stain at all. (*Pause*) Try PELL MELL CRITICALLY!

Note to announcer:

The first sentence of the above commercial should be read with great emphasis, particularly on the words "not nice."

In our previous instructions this was expressed by suggesting that "not nice" be said with a snarl. The *emphasis* gained by this instruction should be retained, but the tone of disgust should be dropped.

Keep the emphasis—but forget the snarl.

Effectively linking words together to bring out the meaning to best advantage is the secret of many an announcer's success. It is the keystone to his most important task—driving the sponsor's message home to the listeners—and often is the hardest feat to master.

The best means of mastering correct articulation for the punch announcement is simply to practice reading copy into a microphone for an unseen auditor, reading and rereading those passages which do not come through clearly until the articulation is satisfactory. Often it will be found that a single, short word is the source of difficulty, and that this one word will have to be separated from the rest of the phrase by a very short pause. Often, too, the trouble will be not that the words in themselves are not clear, but that a definite pause is needed between phrases to allow a rush of facts to sink home in the listener's mind before continuing.

The importance of a winning radio personality to a commercial announcer can hardly be overemphasized. His responsibility as the personal representative of his sponsor requires that his speech introduce him as an individual rather than as a puppet. This individual must be affable. He must be attractive in one respect or another. He must project the picture of a person who would hold one's attention if he were talking in one's living room. Most important of all, he must be *different, individualized.* He must call to mind a definite image, not simply the idea of a man talking.

Proper breath control is more important to the commercial announcer than to the average radio speaker, because of the frequency in his scripts of punch lines which require more voice volume than ordinary conversation. He must be constantly prepared to deliver full volume when the script demands it. He should always be sure of a reserve supply of lung power to fall back on.

The application of this principle of suiting the style of delivery to the type of listening audience and the type of product explains alike the staccato, vigorous style of the sports announcer who "plugs" a product during a sports résumé at suppertime; the easygoing banter interspersed with the variety show; the weaving of plugs into the nonsensical plots of a comedy program; and the dignified statement of sponsorship which opens and closes the United States Steel program.

Perhaps the newest and most interesting innovation in style in commercial announcing is the technique used on one of the "soap operas" —a technique which already shows signs of spreading. It is one of glorified informality, in which the announcer virtually twiddles his thumb in the listener's ear to the following words: "Well, ladies, you admit there's a definite problem connected with washing hosiery and delicate fabrics, don't you? Un-huh, I thought so. Well, you know, I've just got an idea you've never thought about using . . . " How far this new naïveté in commercial speech will go, and how successful the Little Boy Blue style of commercial announcing will prove, it is impossible to tell. However, it will be interesting to watch its progress.

TELEVISION ANNOUNCING

Announcers are used in television in the same ways as in radio. An announcer opens and closes the show, frequently connects segments of the program, and does the commercials. It can be seen almost at a glance that the announcer is no less important in television than in radio. All television has done is to make the announcer's job more difficult.

Many of the qualities of good radio announcing apply to television. A good voice, clear speech, naturalness, intelligent and effective reading are still important. The dependence of programs and stations on good announcing has not changed. The addition of the visual elements has divided television announcing into two types, one more difficult than the other.

Off-camera Announcing

There are many occasions in television where an announcer is used, but need not be seen. Such instances include some commercials, station breaks, promotional spots, narration, openings and closings. This job is quite similar to radio. The announcer is usually located in an announce booth somewhere near the main TV studio. He can sit comfortably at a desk or table with the microphone in front of him. He can read the copy. He need not be at all concerned about his appearance.

In some cases, off-camera announcements are but loosely tied to the picture on the screen. At other times the audio is very intimately tied to the picture. In this case the announcer must read with the picture. In the announce booth a monitor (TV screen) will be available for this purpose. Sometimes film is narrated live, or a commercial will consist of audio copy and a series of slides. In this kind of situation the announcer must fit his reading to the ever-changing video pattern. Thus, the major difference between radio announcing and off-camera TV announcing is the necessity for coordinating the delivery with pictures. An additional minor difference is that cues are almost never received visually from the control room. More often than not the control room cannot be seen from the announce booth. The announcer is cued through a headset, by a light, or directly from the picture itself. In most other respects, off-camera announcing is just like radio announcing.

On-camera Announcing

When the announcer has to appear on camera a whole host of new problems arise. On-camera announcing is far and away the most challenging task for an announcer. Let's consider the problems one by one.

When he is on camera, the announcer can't read his copy. At least he can't read it while holding sheets of paper in his hand in the usual fashion. One solution to this problem is to memorize the copy. Frequently, this is the best answer. If the material isn't too long, if the announcer has a quick and accurate memory, and if exact word-for-word reproduction is desired, memorization works well. However, if the copy is long, or if rehearsal time is short, or if the announcer's memory is not of the best, memorization is a poor answer. One way of getting around memorizing is the "Tele-Prompter." This is a patented device that attaches to the camera and unrolls the copy, which has been typed in very large letters. This system requires complete coordination on the part of the person controlling the speed of the roll so that he stays with the announcer. It also requires skill and practice by the announcer so he will give the impression that he is looking into the lens, when actually he isn't, and that he is talking to us rather than reading. The Tele-Prompter is not for the inexperienced.

Another partial answer to the memory problem is the "idiot board." Here the copy, or part of it, is written or printed on large cards, a blackboard, or other large flat surface. Of course, its function is quite similar to the Tele-Prompter, but not all stations have a Tele-Prompter. The location of the idiot board is important, for announcing is usually delivered directly to the audience, and this is impossible if the board is any distance from the camera lens.

On many shows where time is elastic, and where word-for-word detail is not mandatory, the best answer is announcing from learned notes. Here the main points and facts are memorized by the announcer but he speaks the message in his own words. A Tele-Prompter or an idiot board can be used for notes rather than full copy. If an announcer has a facility for extemporaneous speaking, and he should if he is a good announcer, it is possible in this last system to achieve a naturalness and conversational quality that is well-nigh impossible in any other way.

The minute the announcer steps in front of a camera his appearance becomes of the utmost importance. His face, how he combs his hair, the clothes he wears and how he wears them, his smile, the evenness of his teeth—all of these things combine to give the viewer an impression about the announcer. Moreover, his physical behavior adds to this impression; how he stands, how he moves, what he does with his hands, etc. The announcer is no longer a disembodied voice. He is a real person standing where everyone can see as well as hear him. Now the announcer must become an actor, too.

The television industry is not concerned with whether an announcer is the handsome, glamorous type. Rather, producers are interested in the same qualities that radio looked for in the voice. A pleasant, natural person both physically and vocally is the desired announcer. The voice and the body must indicate a certain degree of harmony. It would be ridiculous for a scrawny little man to appear and then to speak in a rich, full bass voice. In the truest sense of the word it is personality, and not beauty, that is at a premium. Of course, the television announcer must also be able to sell, to read well, and to perform all the many jobs that have come to be expected of him.

The television announcer must always appear completely at ease and avoid mannerisms which give the impression of self-consciousness. He must walk well, stand well, sit well, know what to do with his hands, and always look as though he were comfortable. This clearly indicates that students looking forward to a career of television announcing need to perform as much as possible before audiences—acting in legitimate plays, speaking to groups, and getting live TV experience. Ease and composure before audiences come only with long experience in such situations.

The on-camera announcer must also be able to talk to a camera lens with the same directness and sincerity that he would use in talking to a person. Remember that television is like radio in that your audience is really a large number of individuals or very small family groups. You aren't speaking to a large group, but many tiny groups. So, talk to the lens as though it were a single person. The announcer talks to the camera which is on the air, and this is indicated to him by red tally lights on the front of the camera. As the director changes from one camera to another the announcer must be able to shift smoothly to the new camera. If the announcer fails to notice the tally lights go out on one camera and come on on another, a very awkward picture can result. Another awkward situation occurs if the announcer fails to notice his cue to start talking. In this case his picture can be seen for several seconds before he starts to speak. Frequently the announcer is seen, obviously waiting for a cue. His whole expression changes as he gets the cue, and he starts to talk. Don't let this happen to you!

Placement of the microphone is seldom of concern to the on-camera announcer. Either the microphone will be worn by the announcer or it will be on a boom. In neither case does the announcer have much to do with its location. He will trust the engineer who puts the mike around his neck or on his lapel, or the boom operator who positions the mike above his head. Naturally, he avoids looking around to see if the mike is there, for this would appear most peculiar to the viewer.

In black-and-white television an appearance requires some attention to the clothing worn. Very dark or very light suits or dresses are to be avoided. Medium shades work much better. Pastel-colored shirts and blouses are preferred to white. Remember that the television system is limited in the tones of grey that can be reproduced. Enough contrast to indicate a different color between garments is desired, but too much contrast only causes trouble. Black and white together should always be avoided unless special arrangements are made with the engineers. In color television it is necessary to check in detail, ahead of time, the colors and fabrics that will be worn. Not only are certain colors desired and others not, but the total color scheme among all of the talent must be balanced and harmonious.

Success in television announcing depends on the same ingredients as success in other performance-type fields. One must start with certain physical and vocal characteristics, with a talent for this kind of work, and then develop these through years of study, practice, and experience.

CHAPTER SIX

RADIO AND TELEVISION SPEAKING

RADIO SPEAKING

In discussing the problem of how to be effective via the microphone, my task really is to adapt modern principles of effective speech to their use in the particular case of radio. A study of speech principles will reveal the little-realized fact that, aside from a few allowances due to the mechanical limitations of a microphone, the best radio speaker is the one who follows most closely the dictates of a competent textbook on public speaking. The added difficulty that lack of a visible audience presents in broadcasting only increases the necessity of observing speech rules. The often-remarked fact that many good announcers know nothing of platform speaking, while many good platform speakers are a failure on the air, is not a refutation of my statement. Reference to a speech textbook would confirm the technique unconsciously used by these announcers, while an analysis of the so-called good platform speaker would show that his success grew more from showmanship and dramatics than from effective speech. A textbook on speech usually is divided into chapters devoted to advice concerning each type in turn: the argumentative speech, the humorous talk, or the expository discussion. Obviously, all these possible types of talks have their turn on the air.

An added complexity in the study of radio speech is the increasing attempt of radio-program planners to get away from straight speaking, through the use of other interest-catching devices. The interview, composed of questions and answers, is being employed to hold the listener's attention. Round-table discussions by a small group of authorities are used to gain informality and, at the same time, to make the speakers feel more at ease. Debates and dramatic skits are also heard over the air.

All are interesting variations and require training different from that given to the orator.

The absence of a visual audience and the inability to aid his delivery by gestures is a serious handicap to the speaker. Allow me to make clear just what the lack of a visible audience means to the speaker. First of all he notes the absence of circular audience-speaker responses. In any speech textbook one will find a discussion of the stimulation that an audience gives to the man addressing it. Public speaking is usually a type of circular social behavior, in terms of social psychology. The speaker first stimulates his audience, but we sometimes overlook the fact that the audience in turn stimulates the speaker. This circular process goes on throughout the entire speech, playing an important part in its success. Anyone who has done much public speaking will realize the subtle but potent influences the audience has upon the speaker. The best speaker is inclined to be the one most sensitive and responsive to these influences, one who has the "feel" of the audience and who adapts himself to it both in his manner and in the content of his material while talking. It is needless to point out that the radio has entirely broken the chain of this circular process for the speaker. Radio performers drafted from the stage and platform are the first to feel the handicap of this situation.

Another important psychological factor in broadcast speech as differentiated from platform speech lies in the distribution of a radio audience, for an audience divided into a series of small family groups deprives a speaker of all the advantages to be gained from interstimulation, so commonly noticed in crowd psychology. Those infectious waves of emotion that sway a large mass of people, seated elbow to elbow, are lost in radio.

Furthermore, radio listeners are entirely free of those social inhibitions, compulsions, and conventions which dull speakers often rely upon to keep a visible audience in their seats. People who would be embarrassed to walk out of an auditorium while some would-be spellbinder is speaking do not hesitate to shut off the radio speaker. These factors force the radio speaker to be more painstaking in the preparation and in the presentation of his talk, if he expects to hold his audience.

The radio speaker has only one set of stimuli to work with instead of two. He can use only the audible speech symbols and he has no appeal for the eye. To quote from the *Little Book of Broadcasting* put out by the National Broadcasting Company, "Few of us realize, until put to the task, the extent to which the eye and the ear, when working together, are influenced by the impressions that come through the eye. We early found by experimentation that, when the sense of hearing alone is involved, we have a very different and a much more difficult problem on our hands." The problem that must be met here is not merely that of more strenuous effort at good speech, but it also involves more careful attention in the writing of the speech.

Added to this complete dependence upon one set of stimuli is the fact that this concentration seems to help the auditor more easily to detect the mental attitude of a speaker. Harvard psychologists recently announced that insincerity seems to be detected more easily over the air than from the lecture platform.

As a last preliminary consideration of the subject, remember that practically all programs of every kind are prepared in advance to be read. Those which are extemporaneous are rare exceptions when compared to the general mass. This rule is due to several factors: (1) the necessity of split-second timing makes it imperative that a speaker be chained down to a definite timed manuscript; (2) lack of a visible audience makes extemporaneous speaking a difficult task for anyone, even if it were allowed; (3) self-imposed rigid standards as to the nature of material allowed on the air requires the station to ask for a manuscript in advance of its broadcast. The necessity for reading imposes a preliminary hurdle which must be jumped in attempting good public speaking on the air.

Style of Delivery

The cardinal principle of good speech is the use of a direct conversational tone. The whole emphasis is upon a sincere direct contact with the members of an audience, which will achieve the effect of face-to-face conversation. A moment's thought will reveal that this is exactly the effect the radio speaker desires to achieve. Many delivering their first speech on the air seem to forget the distribution of their unseen audience and to remember only its size. While they are usually impressed with the fact that their potential audience runs into the millions, they fail to realize that this large number is divided into smaller groups of usually not over three or four individuals. A radio speaker must consider the atmosphere in which his voice is to be heard. He must visualize a small family group, distributed about the living room, engaged in domestic tasks or pleasures. People thus situated resent an oratorical or strident tone of voice in a guest, seen or unseen. They want the radio voice to talk to them, not shout at them. The speaker must fill the role of a guest, not that of an intruder.

Proceeding on this understanding, we have only to ask ourselves: What are the most effective means of speech in an ordinary conversation? What is the winning and attractive tone to use? The situation calls for an intimate and informal tone; insincere gushing is to be avoided as in everyday conversation. The speaker must be warm, sympathetic, and sincere, eliminating any trace of ostentation. There is no need to raise the voice—that instinctive lack of confidence in the microphone's sensitivity is entirely unjustified. A quiet, easy voice is the best.

Many speakers put too much stress on the need of adopting a personal style when broadcasting. A few of them go to the opposite extreme, which is also unacceptable; it is equally wrong to change to a colorless discourse, in which the voice loses power to express the variety of thought and feeling needed to give life to an address. A good speaker, well qualified to speak on a subject, should maintain a tone in keeping with his topic even though it is not personal or conversational. The effort to carry on an imaginary conversation may result in the loss of forcefulness somewhere between the microphone and the listener. Words have eloquence and power, but, if the speaker neglects to consider the cardinal principle that he cannot be seen and relies upon the animation of his facial expression and gestures and indeed of his whole body to hold the attention of the listener, he has gone too far in his picturing of the radio audience in order to obtain a friendly, personal intimate connection. Possibly it is better for the radio conversationalist to visualize the imaginary listener who is sitting opposite him during his radio address as being blind. Thus, in order to convey his thoughts and the emotions which he feels, he must express everything in his voice by variations in volume, in pitch, in intensity, by pauses, and by holding certain words.

Of course, to create the mood of a face-to-face conversation successfully requires the right mental attitude. The speaker must have a sincere interest in the material he is delivering and in the people who are listening to him. This must be especially remembered by the radio announcer, for the necessity of continually reading statements that he does not believe makes it easy for him to allow a tone of insincerity or boredom, the hint of a sneer, or an indication of a supercilious attitude to creep into his voice.

The necessity of reading from a manuscript adds greatly to this difficulty of maintaining a sincere conversational tone. Reading is both the easiest and the hardest manner of presenting a speech. It is the easiest because all one has to do is to read the words without any effort at choosing them except with the eye. But for that very reason it is difficult to read them in an interest-compelling manner. It is so easy getting the words that most people merely find them with their eyes, say them with their mouths, and permit their minds to wander away from the subject.

There is no better training for radio speaking than the reading aloud of all types of material. A person who is going on the air should sit down with a friend and tell that friend what he intends to say and then read a part of his talk. The listener can tell him just how his conversation differs from his reading style and tone. It would be a better test if the friend would close his eyes or turn from the speaker while listening. Of course, the faults in diction, pronunciation, and construction which are frequent in conversation must be avoided in good radio talking. Unfortunately the radio address must be read, but the speaker should be so familiar with the material that he merely uses the manuscript as an outline. Talk from the paper, follow what is written, but do not worry about the exact phraseology of the written words.

It has been said that the system of college teaching by lectures "is a process whereby the notes of the professor become the notes of the students without having gone through the minds of either." This applies to most beginners in oral reading. The written symbols become speech sounds in a mechanical manner which in no way involves the understanding of the reader, with the result that they are produced in a steady patter totally devoid of expression.

Psychological experiment has shown that the muscles of the body respond in perfect accord with speech efforts. If one were to record in waves, on a strip of paper, the voice of a speaker and also the subconscious movements of any part of his body, for instance the arm, one would find that these two curves agree. A close correlation exists between body movements and thought processes. When we watch a prize fight, we frequently become aware of the fact that we are duplicating the motions of the fighters, clenching our fists and tensing our muscles. Thus it is that, when we speak extemporaneously, our utterances are controlled by our thought processes and the correct grouping and stress are automatically achieved. While one is reading, one's speech organs are to a great degree controlled by the mechanical movements of the eye in following along the printed line. This uniformity of movement is reflected in one's delivery, and there is but one way to overcome this. That is to think what one is reading. By so doing, the influence of thought processes in controlling the speech organs can be made to overrule the mechanical influence of eye motion. A little practice will convince the most skeptical that thinking can easily solve most of the problems of oral reading. The grouping of words into thought units, the placing of emphasis, and correct pauses are easily achieved in this manner, and the rewards are well worth the time spent.

Simple Anglo-Saxon words are the best—the ones in every person's daily vocabulary. Some words are difficult to understand over the telephone or the radio. Excessive use of sibilants, the recurrence of words ending in the same sound, alliteration, and "tongue twisters" should be avoided. Where there is difficulty in enunciation, chop off a word and use it as a springboard to leap into the next word. Dwell longer on the vowels of important words than on those of relatively unimportant words; for example, usually you should give more time to nouns, adjectives, verbs, and adverbs than to other kinds of words, especially the articles and expletives.

Inflections of the voice are vital to the good radio speaker for they give what he has to say color, life, and emphasis. Do not allow your delivery to have a seasick wave of equal highs and lows. The rising inflection is far more effective than the falling inflection, except for humorous effect, because it suggests "I am going on."

If the use of quiet gestures will help your delivery, by all means use them. Point your finger at an imaginary listener. Shake your fist. A smile is heard over the radio because it changes the quality of your voice. A person a thousand miles away will "hear" you lift your eyebrows. Do not neglect these aids to speech. Make no gesture or movement, however, which might cause extraneous sound. Do not shake the hand that holds the manuscript paper. Do not rub an unshaven chin. Do not smack your lips or snap your fingers. Do not sigh or pound the desk, for these sounds will not be understood by the distant listener. Here is the lament of a radio announcer:

> I introduced the Duchess of Dundee
> Over the facilities of WABC.
> Her organs internal
> Made noises infernal
> And everyone thought it was me.

The most important thing for the radio speaker is that he should have a pleasing personality and be able to project this personality through the air to his audience. He should carry his eye picture of a scene through his mind and into his speech. He must never forget his listener in his own enthusiasm but should project this enthusiasm into the air. He must find interest or thrill in the scene that he is describing and give the same feeling to his audience. He must have a purpose in his speech or his description and know exactly what he intends to convey to his listening public.

Breathing

Groups of words count more in a radio talk than individual words. The listener picks up phrases and clauses that constitute thoughts. The wise radio speaker does not rely on ordinary punctuation, but goes through his manuscript and marks off groups of words which, put together, bring out his thought. These groups should vary in length to avoid monotony but none should be too long for natural breathing. Correct breathing is natural breathing in the sense that it is free from physical restraint and conscious self-control. While the orator can take a deep breath through his open mouth, such an intake is clearly heard over the radio. Consequently the radio speaker must inhale more quietly and deliberately through the nostrils or above the tongue. The radio speaker should never permit himself to exhaust his breath entirely but should breathe quietly and naturally. Frequently speakers are hampered with tight-fitting collars or belts, which should be loosened to allow greater freedom in breathing. Do not breathe directly into the microphone, for you will sound like a windstorm if you do. Stand erect with squared shoulders, with your head up so that your throat will not be cramped, and with feet flat on the floor.

Position before the Microphone

It is unwise to give definite rules on how far from a microphone a person should speak. The rule would have to be changed for different types of microphones, for different voice qualities, for the acoustics of different studios, and, if more than one speaker is on the program, with the placing of the speakers. However, if you are alone on the program and have learned to control your volume, 18 inches is about the right distance to be away from the ribbon type of microphone or the other modern types. Talk to a person who is presumably about 4 feet away. If you are to be confidential or sentimental in your style, you may talk very low and close to the microphone. This is the principle of crooning which is used by some singers and frequently by announcers. The majority of microphones are directional, and the speaker must talk either at an angle to or directly into the mouthpiece. In every case, have a test before going on the air to determine where you should be placed in relation to the microphone. Also have the microphone placed at the right level so that you may comfortably talk directly to it. Physical comfort is essential. When you have an immediate as well as an invisible audience, use more than the conversational volume but stand a little farther from the microphone than for ordinary announcements, in order that the proper volume will enter the instrument.

Moving about the studio before the program goes on the air is certainly better than sitting rigidly with eyes glued to the "On the Air" sign. Place yourself in a comfortable position before the microphone. Some people prefer to sit, feeling that they will be more conversational in such a position; but the diaphragm of the seated speaker is cramped and, consequently, those who are giving longer radio addresses prefer to stand. Do not lean upon the pulpit while giving a long talk because you will have to straighten up in order to rest your muscles and when you straighten up you unconsciously recede from the microphone, so that the listener has the impression you are leaving. Maintain the same distance from the microphone all the time that you are talking and do not throw your voice from side to side away from the microphone as you would upon the platform. Do not rock back and forth while talking because when you come forward your voice will become very strong and as you sway backward it will become faint.

If it is necessary to cough or to sneeze, turn as far from the microphone as possible. While the platform speaker may pause and take a drink during the delivery of his address, the radio speaker would broadcast the sound of swallowing the water if he did the same thing. Do not play with a lead pencil, rolling it between the hands. The rattle of paper before the microphone sounds like sheet-iron thunder. If you are to use a manuscript or an outline, be careful not to rattle it. Do not allow the paper to touch the microphone and by no means bump into or handle the microphone or its standard in any way.

Pitch and Volume

In radio the matter of volume is of utmost importance. If one speaks too loudly, the control operator must reduce the volume by mechanical means, thus interfering, to some degree, with its transmission in perfect naturalness. If one speaks with insufficient force, the control engineer must amplify the volume mechanically, again producing an effect that is not entirely natural. It is important also not to use too great a variety of emphasis, producing sudden peaks in the energy delivered to the microphone. The volume resulting from the overemphasis of a word or syllable may be too great for the apparatus to carry adequately. The control engineer, taken unawares, is unable to neutralize the effect mechanically and what is called a "blast" results. This is an overloading of the sensitive apparatus and a discordant rattle in the transmission and reception results.

The microphone magnifies the qualities of the voice. If the microphone and loud-speaker are properly adjusted, free tone has its resonance enlarged. The good voice then comes over with all its qualities enhanced. A speaker with such a voice may stand close to the microphone and talk intimately into it. A speaker with a voice of less pure quality gets a better effect by standing at right angles to the microphone. The volume of voice that the speaker may use varies with the distance from the microphone. As the volume of the voice is varied, the speaker should move back and forth from the microphone. The rasp of the metallic voice and the twang of the nasal are always magnified; when the current of transmission is too great, they come over with ear-splitting harshness. Excitement and nervousness are obvious and cannot be minimized.

The student of speech, the minister, the actor, and the stump speaker have all been trained to throw their voices to a far-reaching audience, but when they come before a microphone they must learn to retain all the vibrant qualities of the strong voice, yet maintain a level of volume that will not force the control operator to impair their tone qualities by mechanical means. There are many points in common in the correct techniques of addressing a visible audience and in speaking over the radio but the factors of pitch and volume are decided differences. The pitch of the voice of the public speaker is inclined to be raised a tone or two. If you were in a great hall speaking very loudly, the volume would be considerably greater, and the pitch would be perhaps three or four tones above the conversational level. The radio speaker, on the other hand, must keep his pitch down to his conversational level.

A good radio voice must have proper placement, range, flexibility, good control, and proper pitch. The pitch best suited to radio, owing to the fact that the microphone favors certain vibration frequencies, is baritone for men and contralto for women. The dangers, encouraged by reading, that the voice will fall into measured and rhythmical patterns with set inflections at regular intervals must be avoided. Voice variety of the proper sort is as important as the voice itself.

Speed of Delivery

Speakers vary greatly in the speed of talking. Some speak much faster than others, and the sponsors of programs may receive complaints about the difficulty of following them. A commercial station generally sells a 1-minute announcement and limits the topic to 100 words. A speedy delivery tends to reduce sincerity. News commentators frequently get as high as 225 words a minute. However, the best speed to maintain for the longer radio talk is about 140 words a minute. Franklin D. Roosevelt spoke between 110 and 135 words a minute. The one variable factor that sometimes upsets all the advanced estimates of length is the emotional tension. This factor frequently affects the speaker's natural tempo. The radio address should never be given too fast, because it is hard for one who is listening and unable to see the speaker's lips to follow the talk. Speedy delivery also results in slurring, in the dropping of finals, and in the speaker's getting ahead of himself in his manuscript, with the result that he stutters or loses his place. On the other hand, too slow a delivery may make an audience restive. Suit the rate of utterance to the weightiness and importance of the material—not only to a passage as a whole, but to particular paragraphs, sentences, and phrases within the passage. The result will be not only a pleasing and *logical* (not mechanical) rate variation, but also that justly applauded quality of vocal composure.

One should rehearse at home to determine the preferred rate of delivery for each manuscript. The split-second requirements of the radio require that the speaker time his copy before going onto the air and maintain the speed of the rehearsal in actual delivery. The actual time of a 15-minute program is 14 minutes and 30 seconds, the remaining 30 seconds being used for technical shifts from program to program. The announcer's introduction and conclusion generally require 1 minute, reducing the actual speaking time to 13½ minutes for a 15-minute program.

The Manuscript

The manuscript should be double spaced in order to allow for easy reading. It should be clean so that it will be easy to follow. It is best to have it typewritten. Be sure that the pages are arranged correctly so that you will not have to search for the correct page when you are before the microphone. Do not clip the sheets together. Use a type of paper that does not easily rattle. Onionskin paper is perhaps the worst. Typewriter bond paper is decidedly noisy. The pulp copy paper used in newspaper offices is probably the best. When you have completed reading a page, let it flutter to the floor. Do not attempt to slide it to the bottom of the pile, for this will be heard.

TELEVISION SPEAKING

Delivering a speech over television is not like speaking from a platform before a live audience, nor is it quite like giving a speech over radio. There are similarities to both live speechmaking and radio speaking. But, there are also major differences.

Let us examine some of the elements of the television speech situation. The speaker has the advantage of the microphone and electrical amplification of his voice. There is the impersonal character of the microphone and the camera, and rarely is there a live audience to provide feedback, or audience reaction. As in radio, the audience is many small groups or perhaps even individuals. Most of all, because of the ability of the camera to obtain close-ups, a degree of intimacy is possible far beyond that obtained in any other way. In television, the speaker has the opportunity to talk to his audience as intimately as he would if two or three people were sitting across a desk from him. This intimate nature can be a powerful speech weapon in the hands of an expert.

In preparing the speech for television the speaker has to decide what method of delivery he will use. He can read the speech from a manuscript, he can read it from a Tele-Prompter or idiot board, he can memorize the speech, or he can speak extemporaneously from previously learned notes or an outline. Of these methods the memorized speech is by all odds the poorest choice. The memory can fail frequently for most people, and it usually happens at just the critical moment. Then, too, it requires a skilled actor to recite memorized speeches with meaning and feeling. Reading the speech from manuscript is entirely acceptable for speeches given at important events which are being televised. This is not a television speech in the strictest sense of the word. Rather, television is eavesdropping on the event at which a speech is given. There are occasions when word-for-word accuracy is essential. This is true when the President of the United States delivers an important policy address. In such cases the speech must be read. Whether it is read from manuscript, or from a Tele-Prompter, depends on the personal preference of the speaker and his facility at speechmaking. Generally it would be better to read from a Tele-Prompter, since this method permits much more vital eye contact with the audience. The most effective method of speaking on television, in the majority of instances, is to speak extemporaneously from a prepared outline. Whether the notes are learned or whether they are available on Tele-Prompter or idiot board is not important. The important thing is that this style permits sincerity, direct contact, naturalness, and genuine conversational communication. Sincerity, simplicity, and intimacy are among the most significant characteristics of television, and these are best achieved by a speaker who speaks extemporaneously.

The Delivery

In television speaking the voice is not the speaker's only ammunition. The body, the face, the gesture, what you do and how you look are almost as important as what the audience hears. Remember, when you look into the lens of a TV camera you should see one, or two, or three people very close, and looking back at you. They see you from a close position and with an intimacy that has never been known before. It will be impossible for you to kid them or trick them. You had better have something to say and say it directly, sincerely, and conversationally.

To anyone who has watched Bishop Fulton J. Sheen deliver a television talk there can be no doubt about the impact of a good speech on television. It must be granted that Bishop Sheen is a brilliant speaker. So, what does television add? Where else can you look, from close up, into those snapping eyes, and watch at firsthand the set of the firm jaw as he makes his major points? In an auditorium, a speech by Bishop Sheen is stimulating. On television, where everyone sits across the podium from him, the speech is electrifying.

It must also be pointed out here that Bishop Sheen does not read his speeches. I don't know for certain, but it seems safe to wager that he doesn't memorize them either. He *talks* to the audience. Lest someone misunderstand, an extemporaneous speech is not an unprepared speech. Just as much thought and effort can go into preparing such a speech as into writing a manuscript. "Extemporaneous" applies to the manner of delivery. Never assume that you can make a successful television speech, or any other kind for that matter, without preparation. It is the well-planned and rehearsed casualness that is effective, not the aimless wanderings of the unprepared mind.

Microphone Placement

If the television speech is given from a lectern, or in some other situation where the microphone position is fixed, the speaker observes the same procedures as outlined for the radio talk. More often, in television, the microphone position is not fixed. Perhaps the situation, or the speaker's preference, suggests that movement and more fluid action would be desirable. In such cases, the microphone will be on a boom, and the boom operator will see to it that the microphone is kept in the proper position to pick up the speaker's voice. It is well to remember that a microphone is still used, and therefore the speaker doesn't have to project as much volume as he would if he were addressing a crowded auditorium.

Appearance

The television speaker should be just as concerned with his dress, his manner, and his naturalness as is the television announcer. Some of the considerations in this regard are covered in the section on television announcing. If the speaker provides any visual distraction, for whatever reason, he is lessening the attention that the audience will pay to his speech.

Make-up is rarely needed for television. Sometimes a man with a very heavy, dark beard will need a little powder or pancake base to avoid looking as if he hasn't shaved. Occasionally, someone with sunken eyes will look better if the caverns are lightened a little. For the most part a speaker should not consider himself an actor, and should realize that if he looks natural he is putting up his best possible appearance. Most of the time a TV speaker needs adequate lighting rather than make-up. Women can wear ordinary street make-up. A woman's main concern should be to avoid hats, veils, and other female accoutrements that might provide distractions.

Dress and make-up are more critical for color television. If the speech is to be given on color TV the speaker had better check with the station in advance and follow the advice given him.

What to do with one's body, feet, and hands is frequently a problem for television speakers. The first rule to keep in mind is to fit your behavior to the nature of the occasion. If the situation calls for dignity, that means one kind of behavior. If the situation is informal and friendly, it means something entirely different. In any case, try to appear natural and relaxed. Because of the inherent intimacy of the television medium, stiffness and exaggeration are painfully obvious.

Stand or sit naturally and comfortably, but never relaxing to the point of sloppiness. It is well to remember that you are a guest in the home of each viewer. Avoid petty, meaningless, nervous movements—they are exceedingly wearing to an audience. If it is necessary to move about the set, do so with ease and as naturally as you can.

Gestures become an important part of a television speech. If you are ever in doubt about the use of a gesture, cut it out. Make every movement count. If the gesture adds nothing definite, it will only annoy the viewer. Gestures need to be smaller and more deliberate than those used for platform speaking. Never forget that television is *intimate!* A little movement goes a long way. Swift, darting movements are less meaningful than more deliberate ones and frequently are impossible for the cameraman to follow.

Facial expression is more useful than in platform speaking. The close-up TV camera will catch even the slightest variation in facial expression. Properly used, such expression can add to the effectiveness of a speech. Exaggerated or insincere expression is only magnified and made worse. Possibly the most effective expressions come without any effort on the part of the speaker. If a speaker is at all animated, it is probable that his face will also be animated. There is nothing quite so painful as the TV performer who can be described as "a great stone face."

If visual aids are to be used, check with the director as to their location, how they will be used, where you will be in relation to them, and how you will point to them, hold them, or whatever. Movements in relation to visuals must be slow, deliberate, and in accordance with the plan previously arranged. If this kind of routine isn't followed the director will be unable to get close shots of the visuals on the air.

When preparing for a television speech, consider your physical behavior in the light of the following guides:

1. Television is a highly intimate, close-up medium.
2. When in doubt, do less rather than more moving, gesturing, facial expression, etc. Economy of visual impressions is important. Make every one count.
3. TV demands ease and naturalness. Don't try to act!
4. Be as relaxed and informal as the dignity of the occasion allows, but never be sloppy or allow any feelng of disrespect to show in your attitude or look.

CHAPTER SEVEN

PRONUNCIATION

The standard of pronunciation, enunciation, and articulation required of announcers, news commentators, and masters of ceremony of radio and television programs does not tolerate inaccurate, careless, or slovenly diction. Good speech must be clear, precise, and correct and must be devoid of provincial and even colloquial pronunciation. The student who aspires to a career in radio or television cannot begin too early to mend his pronunciation.

The first requirement in improving one's pronunciation is an ability to hear the slight variations in enunciation which distinguish the correct from the incorrect pronunciation. The ear must be trained to detect the difference between the correct pronunciation of "catch," which rhymes with "patch," and the incorrect pronunciation, which rhymes with "fetch."

The second requirement is an ability to make the same distinction in one's own speech. The organs of speech must be trained to enunciate the difference between the correct pronunciation of "any," which rhymes with "penny," and the incorrect pronunciation, which rhymes with "skinny."

Last, the student must acquire the habit of using discriminatingly correct pronunciation in his everyday conversation.

Drill

In a drill to acquire the correct pronunciation of frequently used words whose pronunciations often disclose a careless and inelegant diction, use the word concerned in an expression or sentence which includes its correct rhyme word and repeat the expression or sentence over and over again until the correct pronunciation becomes automatic. The following sentences are illustrative:

1. He did not *seek* to join the *clique*.
   (*Clique* rhymes with *seek*, not sick.)
2. Don't *rebuke* the *Duke*.
   (*Duke* rhymes with *rebuke*, not spook.)
3. The car *looks de luxe*.
   (*De luxe* rhymes with *looks*, not spooks.)
4. He *bade* the *bad* boy go.
   (*Bade* rhymes with *mad*, not made.)

Word	Correct Rhyme Word	Incorrect Rhyme Word	Word	Correct Rhyme Word	Incorrect Rhyme Word
*across**	toss	tossed	*err*	burr	air
again	pen	pin	*feat*	feet	fate
am	jam	gem	*fete*	fate	feet
and	sand	send	*fish*	dish	mesh
any	penny	skinny	*flew*	moo	mew
asked†	masked	past	*flute*	boot	cute
assume	fume	doom	*for*	or	fur
aye (yes)	pie	pay	*friend‡*	bend	hen
bade	mad	made	*from*	Tom	sum
because	pause	buzz	*gap*	tap	tape
been	din	den	*gape*	tape	tap
begin	tin	ten	*get*	bet	bit
beyond	fond	fund	*ghoul*	pool	pole
blew	moo	mew	*goal*	pole	pool
blue	moo	mew	*grew*	moo	mew
brick	slick	neck	*gross*	dose	toss
bruise	booze	fuse	*guess*	less	kiss
bury	berry	hurry	*gum*	glum	gloom
can	pan	pin	*grin*	pin	pen
catch	patch	fetch	*hoax§*	jokes	tax
cent	dent	dint	*hundred*	Mildred	thundered
chew	moo	mew	*if*	cliff	cleff
choose	booze	fuse	*ink*	sink	"enk"
clique	seek	sick	*inquiry*	wiry	bleary
clue	moo	mew	*instead*	bed	bid
college	edge	itch	*jowl*	howl	hole
corps	store	corpse	*juice*	goose	abuse
creek	week	wick	*June*	spoon	hewn
cruise	booze	abuse	*just*	must	mist
crux	trucks	spooks	*last‖*	past	lass
de luxe	looks	spooks	*loot*	boot	cute
dew	mew	moo	*lure*	pure	your
did	lid	led	*lute*	cute	boot
do	moo	mew	*many*	penny	skinny
doughty	gouty	throaty	*maybe*	baby	webby
dour	tour	sour	*men*	ten	tin
drew	moo	mew	*merely*	dearly	barely
droll	dole	doll	*mess*	less	kiss
drought	out	mouth	*mien*	mean	main
drouth	mouth	out	*milk*	silk	elk
due	mew	moo	*miss*	kiss	less
duke	rebuke	spook	*mix*	sticks	necks
dune	hewn	soon	*most‖*	ghost	dose
duty	beauty	booty	*nap*	tap	tape
egg	peg	vague	*nape*	tape	tap

* Don't add a *t*.
† Don't drop the *k*.
‡ Don't drop the *d*.
§ Only one syllable.
‖ Don't drop the *t*.

Word	Correct Rhyme Word	Incorrect Rhyme Word	Word	Correct Rhyme Word	Incorrect Rhyme Word
new	mew	moo	*suit*	cute	boot
next‖	vexed	necks	*suite*	sweet	boot
nude	feud	food	*swell*	bell	bill
our	sour	are	*tell*	bell	bill
pen	ten	tin	*them*	hem	hum
plague	vague	beg	*thick*	slick	deck
poor	tour	sore	*think*	pink	"thenk"
pour	sore	poor	*this*	kiss	less
pretty	witty	Betty	*to*	moo	mew
program	telegram	glum	*too*	moo	mew
queerly	dearly	barely	*toot*	boot	cute
rather	lather	other	*true*	moo	mew
rid	bid	bed	*tune*	hewn	soon
rinse	prince	sense	*two*	moo	mew
room	whom	fume	*was*	rahs	buzz
root	boot	foot	*wash*	josh	harsh
rout	bout	boot	*went*	dent	dint
route	boot	bout	*what*	dot	rut
rude	food	feud	*when*	pen	pin
rule	fool	mule	*where*	bear	whirr
sent	dent	dint	*which*	itch	etch
set	let	lit	*whole*	pole	hull
shoe	moo	mew	*will*	mill	wool
sure	your	fur	*win*	pin	pen
since	prince	fence	*wish*	fish	bush
sink	pink	"senk"	*very*	berry	hurry
sit	lit	let	*worst*‖	first	nurse
slew	moo	mew	*yes*	less	kiss
soot	foot	boot	*you*	moo	mew
stew	mew	moo	*your*	tour	per
such	dutch	fetch	*youth*	tooth	smooth

Additional Words

1. *Bogey* (bogeyman) rhymes with *fogy* (an old fogy).
2. *Chic* (smart) is pronounced *sheik* (Arab) not *cheek* or *chick*.
3. *Chute* (laundry) is pronounced *shoot*.
4. *Elm* is pronounced as one syllable to rhyme with *helm*.
5. *February* is pronounced *Feb'-roo-ary* not *Feb'-u-ary*.
6. *Film* is pronounced as one syllable, not *fill-um*.
7. *Folk* drops the *l* to rhyme with *joke*.
8. *Golf* has the *o* in *odd* and the *l* is pronounced; it is not *gulf* or *goff*.
9. *Height* drops the *g* and *h* to rhyme with *bite*.
10. *Honk* (a horn) has the *o* in *odd*, not the *u* in *hunk*.
11. *Hoof* rhymes with *proof* and does not have the *oo* in *foot*.
12. *Kowtow* (to toady to) drops the *w* in the first syllable to rhyme with *go*, not *cow*.
13. *Length* rhymes with *strength*, with the *g* pronounced.
14. *Logy* (dull, heavy, tired) rhymes with *fogy* (an old fogy).

15. *Often* is pronounced *Off-en* without the *t.*
16. *Poem* is pronounced *Po'-em*, not pome to rhyme with *home.*
17. *Quote* is pronounced *kwote*, not coat, with the *w* sounded.
18. *Roof* rhymes with *proof* and does not have the "oo" in foot.
19. *Sophomore* is pronounced *Soph'-o-more*, not Soph'-more.
20. *Stodgy* (slow, dull) rhymes its first syllable with *Dodge* (automobile).
21. *Strength* rhymes with *length* with the *g* pronounced.
22. *Student* rhymes its first syllable with *mew* and its last with *tent.*
23. *Sword* drops the *w* and is pronounced *sord*, to rhyme with *ford.*
24. *Tuesday* rhymes its first syllable with *fuse.*
25. *Wednesday* rhymes its first syllable with *lens.*
26. *Who* drops the *w* to rhyme with *do.*
27. *Whom* drops the *w* to rhyme with *boom.*
28. *Whoop* drops the *w* and is pronounced *hoop* to rhyme with *stoop.*
29. *Whose* drops the *w* to rhyme with *snooze.*
30. *Yolk* (egg) drops the *l* to rhyme with *joke*, not *elk.*

The rhyming exercise is satisfactory for monosyllables, but cooperation by two students is more efficient and more enjoyable for practicing the correct pronunciation of more difficult words. Using a story such as is told in *You Don't Say! Or Do You?*,[1] one student can read the following one-page chapter while his critic, facing him, can check on the correct pronunciation, which is given on the reverse side of the page.

"Coming to the musicale tonight, Jim?" asked Peary, as they strolled along the deck with Professor Bayard.

"Will they have any calliope or xylophone numbers?" grinned Jim. "I like plenty of action."

"It's not very probable," smiled the professor, "but if you want life and movement, the *Anvil Chorus*, from *Il Trovatore*, and the stirring *Soldiers' Chorus* from Gounod's *Faust*, should appeal to you."

Scanning the program, he continued, "A string quartet offers Tschaikowsky's *Andante Cantabile*, and the Chopin *Berceuse*. For the violin, we have Dvorák's *Humoresque* and the *Meditation* from *Thaïs;* and the cello offering is the *Song to the Evening Star*, from *Tannhäuser.*

"If you like tenor solos, you'll enjoy *Rudolph's Narrative*, with its glorious love motif, from Puccini's *La Bohème*. The soprano number is one of the most beautiful melodies in opera—*Knowest Thou the Land*, from *Mignon*. I was fortunate enough to hear it sung by Geraldine Farrar. There are excerpts, too, from the opera twins, *Pagliacci* and *Cavalleria Rusticana.*"

"Didn't they include the *Sextette* from *Lucia?*" asked Jim, adding, with a grin, "I guess I know my opera."

"After an hour of classical music," Peary said, laughingly, "you'll probably be so homesick you'll want Verdi's duet, *Home to Our Mountains.*"

[1] E. F. Tilden, Melrose, Mass.

(Accent the syllable printed in italics. When two pronunciations are allowable, they are given in order of preference.)

musicale	mew zih *cahl*	not *mew* zih cal
calliope	ca *lie* o pee	not *cal le* ope
zylophone	*zi* lo fone	not *zill* o fone
Il Trovatore	Eel Troh va *toh* reh	not Il *tro* va tore
Gounod	Goo *no*	not *Goo* no
Faust	Fowst	not Fawst
Tschaikowsky	Chi *kof* skee	not Chay *kow* ske
cantabile	cahn *tah* be lay	not can *tab* ih le
Chopin	Sho *pan*	not *Sho* pan
Berceuse	Ber *serz*	not Ber *soose*
Dvořák	*Dvor* zhahk	not De *vor* ak
Thaïs	Tah *ees*	not *Tha* is
Tannhäuser	*Tahn* hoy zer	not *Tan* haus er
cello	*chel* o	not *cell* o
motif	mo *teef*	not *mo* tif
Puccini	Poot *chee* nee	not Poo *se* ne
La Bohème	La Boh *em*	not La Bo *heem*
Mignon	Meen *yon*	not *Min* yon
Farrar	*Far* rar	not Far *rar*
Pagliacci	Pahl *yat* chee	not Pal e *ah* che
Cavalleria	Cah vahl-lay *ree* a	not Cav al *le* re a
Rusticana	Roos tih *cah* na	not Rus tih *can* a
Sextette	Sex *tet*	not *Sex* tet
Lucia	Loo *chee* a	not *Loo* sha
Verdi	*Vair* dee	not *Ver* de

Any person broadcasting over a medium that penetrates to the four corners of the continent, however, cannot satisfy all his listeners in his use of the king's English. In this country there is no fixed standard of pronunciation that is nationally recognized. If large bodies of educated people are using a certain pronunciation of a word, that form is good American usage and has a chance of becoming accepted in our national speech. Correct pronunciation is like correct behavior, depending upon the custom of the educated and conforming to public taste. If this doctrine seems to open the door to degraded pronunciations, it must be remembered that the so-called correct pronunciations have been accepted upon the same basis. The dictionaries record the usage of large bodies of intelligent and cultured users of speech. A degraded pronunciation of the past decade may be the accepted form today. Dictionaries go out of date as rapidly as the public accepts new standards. Possibly the only criterion to which pronunciation should conform is set up by Whitman. "The subtle charm of beautiful pronunciation is not in dictionaries; it is in perfect flexible vocal organs and in a developed harmonious soul."

A speaker should ask himself, "How shall I pronounce the word?" and "How good are the reasons for pronouncing it some other way?" In answering the first question, the speaker will consider two elements: the placing of the accent and the sound of the letters, which may be affected by their relations with other letters. Both the accent and the sound element are of equal importance if the pronunciation is to be understood by, and be pleasing to, the listener. Here the speaker will find his first difficulty because, if rules are obeyed, the word may prove to be an exception to the rule. Such rules found in dictionaries and handbooks are confusing. It is better to study the pronunciations as given by the phonetic key in the dictionary and then to follow the crowd. A good dictionary will tell us what the majority say, what the correct fashion is —except, of course, that the dictionary is always at least some years behind time. Pronunciation also varies from district to district, from class to class, from individual to individual, in proportion to the local, or social, differences that separate them. Announcers must remember that the intelligent listener's ear is always right. Yet the pronunciation must never be wholly wrong; it must be justified by authorities or by the usage of the majority of the listeners who are to be pleased.

Notice that the best announcers will not add letters to the word that are not in it—"idea" is not "idear"; they will pronounce the word as it is spelled—"nothing" is not "nothin"; and they will not slur words into one another—"don't you" must not be broadcast as "donchew." Possibly these are not so much faults in pronunciation as laziness in the use of lips, jaw, and tongue for articulation. Although on the stage "been" is like "seen," the American *Standard* and Webster's *New International* decree "bin." "Either" and "neither" give up that long ī under popular pressure in favor of long ē and are "ēther" and "nēther"; the public likes to hear words its way. While the announcer is advised to use the dictionary pronunciation that most closely conforms to immediate public usage, he must not compromise to the extent of deliberate mispronunciation. Probably a neutral pronunciation is best, for, while "cement" may be pronounced "sĕm' ent" (as some authorities incline to prefer), such pronunciation will be considered by the average listener as evidence of ignorance or affectation.

When the radio writer finds that he has included in his script a word whose pronunciation is difficult or doubtful, he should refer to a thesaurus for a satisfactory synonym, because the announcer is rigidly bound by the script.

Classical Music

Titles of musical compositions and names of composers should be pronounced with the correct foreign intonations. The larger network stations require of their announcers a knowledge of foreign languages. The announcers in smaller stations frequently have to rely upon the pronunciations given by the directors of their orchestras, who, it is presumed, have a musical education or foreign training. The World Broadcasting Company sends out with its transcribed programs a pronunciation sheet to be followed by the local announcer. Those who listen to classical and operatic music are critical of the announcements and are familiar with the names and titles; hence, the foreign pronunciations will not be foreign to their ears. Regardless of the research done by the announcer and the care with which he pronounces the foreign names, he will be criticized by his listeners.

Foreign Names in the News

Probably the news commentator faces more foreign names than does the announcer of operas. The news commentator is speaking to a more general audience, however, and it is permissible for him to Anglicize the names of places mentioned. Few listeners would recognize the names of cities in Europe if they were given their correct foreign pronunciation— in fact, the foreign spelling in many instances is different from that with which we are familiar. The announcer should be permitted to exercise his judgment as to whether his audience will better understand "Venice" or "Venezia," "Florence" or "Firenze." In most cases all will agree that the names should be spoken as they are spelled and pronounced by the majority of radio listeners.

Foreigners in the day's news, on the other hand, are best introduced in their native pronunciation. It is only courteous to pronounce a man's name so that he will understand it himself. "Pierre" should not become "Peer" when he is introduced to the radio audience. We are all inclined to be rather fond of our names, and incorrect pronunciation of them is decidedly distasteful.

Another problem that confronts the announcers is the matter of place names. It is not enough that these men know the correct foreign pronunciations of these names and phrases; they must know the Anglicized version of them.

Regional Dialects

It would be well to preface any discussion of regional accents in announcing with the following excerpt from N. Denison's article, "Why Isn't Radio Better?":[1]

Whatever its duties and obligations to the public may be, broadcasting in America is a profit-making enterprise whose first necessity is to pay its way. The broadcasting industry has a definite commodity to sell. The most elementary law of merchandising requires that the seller remain on good terms with the customer.

The announcer is the salesman on the program. Thus he has to be very careful not to create a feeling of antagonism. An easy way of doing this would be for an announcer in a Jasper, Alabama, station to use an irritating New England accent or even a pronounced Midwestern twang. As far as some people are concerned, there is still a civil war on.

Emancipation of language is a throwing off of belittling localisms and a finding of a common denominator. There is a very considerable difference of opinion among speech experts as to the desirability of an absolute standard of so-called speech. Many of the foremost authorities feel that it is far better and far more practical to strive for a standard of accepted speech which will admit of slight differences but agree in essentials and be easily understood throughout the English-speaking world.[2]

Avoid local terminology that would be lost upon distant listeners. That the top-line radio announcers do speak a common language greatly impresses Kenneth McKean.

Despite the fact that their homelands may be hundreds or thousands of miles apart, the radio announcers have no local speech. . . . The pronounced localist cannot get a job as radio announcer nowadays. It is speech which is a little of everything, a speech which is perhaps a little different from that of any one locality but which is strange to none. It is *the* American speech, and there won't be any other henceforth until the broadcasting systems decide to change it. You will find that the most highly cultured people of America, England, and the Continent speak very much the same, but that the speech of less cultured people is characterized by provincialism in pronunciation and rhythm. American speech is already the most geographically homogeneous in the world. Nowhere else in the world can the same speech be understood by all, over so

[1] *Harper's Magazine*, August, 1934.
[2] F. Purell, "Radio and the Language," *Commonwealth*, Apr. 10, 1929.

large an area, as in this country. Our dialects are nowhere found in the extreme variations characteristic of other tongues. So the radio here is in a comparatively fortunate situation. While the mere demand for uniformity for its own sake should not be pushed, there seems to be no justification for catering to what sectional idiosyncrasies of speech do exist in this country. Strictly local stations are inclined to cater to the dialect of their regions. Well-educated men may be chosen as announcers but, as they have been educated in the district they serve, they speak its language. The audience must be sold and the best way to appease the radio customers is by naturalness in dialect. This is to be found in the form of educated speech as applied to the dialect of the region.

Time was when the pronunciation of New England was thought to be far superior to that of the rest of the country. This superstition, however, is virtually dead. The persons who use the New England pronunciation are relatively so few in number that they may almost be said to speak a special dialect. The aristocratic period has passed; we are now on a thoroughly democratic basis. Hoosier and Wolverine, Badger and Sucker may hold up their heads when they use their native vowels, and the Southerners, who have always been justly proud of their beautiful speech, need no longer take the trouble to defend it. Districts still guard their local tendencies to dialect, and listeners may resent any effort made by announcers to force them to standard usage.

The individual claims many birthrights, not the least of which is his right to speak his language as, subject to the good will of his friends, it pleases him to do; perhaps next in importance must be ranked his right to think whatever he pleases of any style of speech that is different from his own. Radio is bound to have some effect on the national speech. This does not mean that the effect will be a standardization of speech in the dialect pattern of one particular group, such as the stage. It means a colligation of all the finest points of the speech of all regions. This would seem inevitable. Speech is a matter of imitation; we speak as we hear it spoken. It is only natural that we should gradually and perhaps unconsciously evolve a speech containing some qualities of all the dialects heard over the radio.

MUSIC PRONUNCIATION GUIDES

BAKER, DR. T.: *A Pronouncing Pocket Manual of Musical Terms*, G. Schirmer, Inc., New York.

BARNHART, L. D.: A recorded "Pronunciation Guide to Names, Titles, and Terminology in Classical Music." 1711 Hinman Ave., Evanston, Illinois. L.P.—Microgroove.

ELSON, L. C.: *Elson's Music Dictionary,* Oliver Ditson Company, New York. Pronouncing aids.

FARJEON, HARRY: *Musical Words Explained,* Oxford University Press, London, 1933.

HUBBARD, W. L.: *American History and Encyclopedia of Music,* Irving Squire, Toledo, Ohio, 1908.

THOMPSON, OSCAR: *The International Cyclopedia of Music and Musicians.* Dodd, Mead & Company, Inc., New York, 1949.

CHAPTER EIGHT

ARTICULATION, INTONATION, RHYTHM

Articulation

Closely related to the subject of pronunciation is that of correct articulation. The prospective radio or television announcer does well to practice speech before a mirror, or to watch the lip, jaw, and tongue action of the experienced announcer or singer, and then obey the rules for a pure and distinct speech. If an individual has a definite speech defect, my advice to him is to prepare himself to go into the sales or writing staff of a station rather than to attempt to prepare for announcing or dramatic work. In many instances, however, the individual with a slight fault can by conscientious work not only overcome that fault, but build himself into a better speaker than one who is not forced to work for perfection.

The criticism frequently given in auditions is that a voice is thin and nasal, that it has no depth. Such speakers are not originating their speech at the diaphragm. A listener can almost "see" the generation of the speech as he listens to the loud-speaker. The flexible lips, jaw, and tongue are to be used to form the sound, but it must float up from the diaphragm.

When the sound arrives at the mouth, the speaker should use his articulating organs; otherwise the criticism will be that he is lip lazy, that he has a tight jaw, or that his articulation is blurred. If the throat feels tight, open the mouth as wide as possible without stretching and attempt to yawn. There is no better throat relaxation.

Lack of clarity through a guttural or mixed quality of speech is sometimes caused through overtenseness of the jaw muscles. Since every normal individual uses a clear strident tone when he is excited and shouting, evidently the essential element is mental. Create a mental

104

picture of an exciting automobile wreck or of a football game. Get the vivid picture well in your mind. Then describe the incident as vividly as possible. Do not allow your excitement to decrease. Make it a short description at first and increase its length with repetition. If you feel that your excitement is decreasing, stop and start over.

Certain of the vowels, such as those in "way," "cat," "it," and "my," are formed at the front of the mouth. The same vowels in other words and additional sounds are created at the middle of the tongue, for example, "above," "but," and "bird." The location of the formation of the letters can best be determined by "feeling" the sounds in the mouth. Pucker the lips for sounds that come from the back of the mouth like those in "go," "put," "rule," "hole," etc. Don't be afraid to make faces unless you are on television, when you are speaking before the microphone. Certain sounds require jaw action, such as those in "father." There is a tendency on the part of the neophyte before the mike to tighten his jaws, with the result that there is no richness in his articulation. Before going on the air loosen up your face. Waggle the jaw up and down repeatedly; do not try to control its movements more than is strictly necessary to insure motion.

The microphone gives the speaker greater opportunity to speak clearly, for it saves him from straining his voice into a twanging nasality or from effort in the throat. Stage actors and public speakers are apt to strain and at the same time reduce the volume of their speech by the use of the tongue, with the result that resonance is interfered with. On the other hand, the person who first addresses the microphone and is impressed by the necessity of modulating his volume will often be affected by constraint and tenseness, which cause jaw tightness. The best articulation results from freedom from all inhibitions and coordination of all vocal controls; throat, nose, jaw, lips, tongue, and breath. The correct use of these speech factors is best studied in a course in linguistics.

A low, well-rounded voice is one of the prime requisites of pleasing speech; hence pitch and quality have an integral relationship. A high-pitched voice is thought typical of a scolding woman; in a man it is considered effeminate. High pitch itself is not nearly so undesirable as the quality that goes with it. The public does not object to high pitch as such. It does object to the harshness of tone of a high voice and to the amplification of this harshness that present broadcasting and receiving facilities seem to produce. When we speak slowly we usually have a lower pitch than when speaking fast and we are better understood. The overtones may be removed and the quality considerably improved by humming during practice.

I am very much in favor of social intercourse for radio announcers and speakers. Each must develop a personality and the ability to project this personality through the air. Those who are successful at this will find that they no longer merely read their copy. Be somebody; make yourself a personality. Your voice reveals the personality you are. The best radio announcers seem to be men who have seen something of life and show it in their speech.

Sincerity is vital to the announcer as well as to the speaker. Compose a speech of about 2 minutes on the subject in which you are most interested. If possible, make it a speech advocating a course of action. Try to persuade someone to do something in which you have a tremendous interest. It is best, at first, to have someone actually to talk to. Plead violently. When you have succeeded in this, transfer the same feeling to less and less interesting subjects. Bodily alertness is equally important. Before beginning to speak always breathe deeply, and use your body to develop a sincere delivery. Mental alertness is the final step in this road to vitality. A few minutes of stimulating reading, before speaking, is good practice for gaining vitality, as is also an argument, mental or oral. If mind and body are thoroughly alert and eager, if the speaker can feel a burning sincerity (at least for the moment), and if he feels that he is talking to someone directly, there is every reason to suppose that his voice will be vital.

It is apparently no accident that so many singers have found permanent employment as announcers. Singing by its very nature helps to vary the pitch of the voice. Sing two or three songs a day, any tune at all so long as it takes you a little bit higher or a little bit lower than you go in ordinary speech. Then try to speak the words of the song while remembering the tune.

Your breath intake is very noticeable through the microphone, but it will be less so if you are calm. Take a few deep breaths before you start your radio speech. The radio speaker must know how to breathe and how to control that breath. The breath stream must directly and clearly contact the resonators of the mouth and at the same time form indirect, but true, contact with the resonators in the nose and in the face frame, Any tension or stiffness of the neck and head, any rigidity of the upper chest and shoulders, has a tendency to produce harshness, thinness, and rigidity of tone. Therefore breathing must be free and relaxed. At all times the speaker must strive for freedom of the head, neck, and upper chest. Any exercises designed for relaxing these parts will serve the speaker in good stead, for once he is relaxed he can begin the business of control—the business of learning to talk *on* the breath, rather than with the breath. Learn to space your speech and do not attempt to say too much on one inhalation. Breathe freely, breathe normally, and breathe frequently; do not exhaust your breath.

In certain words the articulation must be snapped out, while in others the sound is prolonged. It takes longer to utter "see" than to chop off "sit." Practice the long vowels and consonants. Wriggling the nose will help in the pronunciation of "news," which is apt to be pronounced "noose." However, when you are before the camera do not pucker your lips, waggle the jaw, or wriggle your nose. Get the feeling of these actions in rehearsal and carry that sensation to the television microphone. The yodler uses the correct method for pronouncing the diphthongs that require two shapes of the mouth. "Way" is pronounced "wā-i"; "my" is clearly heard when it is emphasized to "ma-i."

In speech, as in many other social conventions, it is easier to explain what disqualifies than what qualifies. It is easier to choose a speaker by observing his bad spots than by noting his good ones. It is surprising what an effect a small detail can produce upon the whole. Has he poor voice quality? Is he too nasal? Is he monotonous (not giving a sufficient variety of voice pitches)? Is he drawling (not giving a sufficient variety of sounds)? Is he slipshod (underarticulating *t*'s and *d*'s)? Is he pedantic (overarticulating sounds)? Is he clerical (using certain unusual details of intonation)? Does he speak from high up in the head, from back in the throat, or from the nose? The acceptable speaker launches his volume from the diaphragm and forms his sounds in a flexible mouth. Each vowel requires a distinct shape of the mouth. Tongue, lips, and jaws are all used. He is advised to practice vowels and consonants with spoken words and in song to improve the articulation. "Nasal," "thin," "shrill," "metallic," "twanging," "throaty," "muffled," "growling," "furry," "breathy," "full," "rich," "free," "resonant," "unobstructed," and "clear" are adjectives used to describe various voices.

Rhythm and Intonation

There is rhythm in all well-constructed speech. The easiest way to be unintelligible in a language is to speak it in wrong rhythm. Rhythm, and rhythm alone, is often the determining factor in intelligibility. What the

English call the "American drawl" and what Americans call the "British clipping of syllables" are in reality differences of rhythm.

Speech is an affair of rhythm and intonation, and these all have to do with sound. Our speech has a clear-cut system of long vowel sounds and short ones, and a very decided feature which we call the "accent," without knowing precisely what accent consists of. English speech is pre-eminently a speech of strong rhythm, long and short sounds, long and short pauses between sounds, clear-cut vowels, and obscure vowels. Just as there is a peculiar English rhythm, so there is, although we are not generally aware of it, a purely English speech melody. We are so used to it that we are usually oblivious of its existence and generally ignorant of its nature. But it is there, and we are wide awake indeed when we are suddenly presented with a speech melody that is unfamiliar. We sense it at once; there is probably no aspect of this speech business to which we are so sensitive as we are to this intonation factor. What we call "expression" in reading is really the finesse of putting intonations, accents, and rhythms onto the bare words so as to make them resemble speech.

Rhythm requires thought, and, if the speaker thinks about what he is saying, his rhythm will be smooth. If he is reading, that material must have been written with thought units varying in style and length. Do not break thought units. Seek the most effective groupings of words by means of gestures or tapping.

Criticism and Analysis

The importance of a competent teacher to check on results and quality cannot be overestimated. No person is competent to correct his own vocal faults. Even great singers take lessons occasionally. The student should be encouraged to work by himself but this should never be allowed to take the place of competent guidance.

The only way in which the radio speaker can get a convincing criticism of his voice is for him to have an experienced teacher of speech analyze a recording of his speech. The disc record permits him to make a short cutting, listen to it, pick out the faults, and attempt to correct them in the next short cutting. A student is inclined to be skeptical of criticisms by teachers of faults which are not obvious to him, but the recorded talk will accurately deliver to his ear matters of articulation, enunciation, pronunciation, and rhythm. The tone quality may not be perfect but variation in tone will also be obvious. Such recordings may be taken home and used for constant analysis.

Students of speech have found the magnetic-tape recorder helpful, inspiring, and enjoyable. With such a device the student delivers to the microphone a 1-minute announcement or speech which is preserved as local variations in the magnetization of a steel tape. By turning a switch the recorded speech is immediately played back. At any word the voice may be silenced for analysis and then the speech resumed as many times as desired. Turning another switch erases the recording and prepares the tape for a new recording. This method is admirably suited to practice techniques, but the recording is not kept to evidence improvement.

A combination of recording equipment and motion pictures is used in many speech classes to show to the student the use of lips, jaw, and facial expression in perfecting enunciation and intonation. There is always a problem in timing, but the results, even if imperfect, are worth the experimental efforts of the teacher and student.

CHAPTER NINE

NEWS PROGRAMS

NEWS BY RADIO

Program types

There are many types of news broadcasts, each one presented in a different manner and prepared in a different style. Probably the most elementary type of news broadcast is the one presenting news carried by the wire of the Associated Press, the United Press, or the International News Service. These various American news services were originally organized to service newspapers, and the items that came over the teletype were written in newspaper style rather than radio style. Consequently, radio reporters found it necessary to "process" such items, making them hearable rather than readable. Now, however, both the Associated Press and the United Press offer prepared radio news services designed for oral delivery. Programs made up from these sources stress facts and, at regular intervals, comments of an analytical character.

Other sources for news include items adapted from newspapers. This is a legal procedure, since stories have no property rights after publication unless they are copyrighted; however, to be doubly sure, change the wording. While a newspaper item is not ordinarily copyrighted, the newspaper may sue the radio or television station under the laws relating to unfair competition. A commercial station may not appropriate the results of the efforts of a competitor, whether that competitor is another station or a newspaper. A commercial station may not read from a newspaper copy which might interfere with the sale of the paper without first securing the consent of the publisher. The larger broadcasting stations maintain their own bureaus in Washington and other national capitals, which are used as the basis for the manuscript prepared by the local commentator. In many instances the commentator will endeavor to bring in a personal touch by commenting upon his own experiences in the country concerned in the news, or his acquaintance with and observation of individuals. In many progressive stations there are facilities for gathering local news.

Then there are the news commentators, who take the news of the day, relate it to happenings of the past, and to those of the probable future, and analyze its significance. These broadcasts are given in a less formal manner by the speaker, who puts a great deal of his personality into such presentation. The news that is presented by the commentator may be colored by his own attitude or by the policy of either his station or his sponsor, if he is sponsored. Because listeners were tuning in a program, newscasters formerly were inclined to save their most important item for second place. An item of national or international aspect is considered most important. In recent years, however, a different practice has developed. The commentator begins with the major headlines of his broadcast. The announcer then reads the commercial, followed by the newsman with the complete detailed stories. This system is tailor-made for the listener. Before the commercial he is advised as to the exact content of the broadcast. Thus fully informed, he can change programs if the prospectus fails to interest him. The result is that the headlines must be selected to hold the listener's attention for the expanded news reports and comments. The conversational news of the commentator is not so immediate as that presented in press news reports. Some commentators speak extemporaneously from notes, cleverly changing their pace and pitch to conform to the content of the items and to make a change of subject. As the radio listener has been taught to visualize what he hears from his receiving set, it is difficult for him to jump from a New York item to Paris and then back to Washington. The news commentator writes his material so that the listener can visualize the scene, feeling that he is an eyewitness.

During the course of his program the newscaster includes some human-interest stories. It is good practice occasionally to insert short, bright, and fast-moving items between long news features; however, no monotonous pattern should be created. As the editor of the invisible newspaper, the commentator must have a sense of what will appeal to the greatest number of his listeners. The commentator must not allow his items to cause alarm or anxiety for the safety of friends or relatives of the listeners.

Some newscasters introduce the commercial announcers with a sentence which is a commercial plug in itself. The National Association of

Radio and Television Standards of Practice [Revised 1955] suggests a total of 1:15 minutes of commercial copy in a 5-minute program, and three minutes in a 15-minute program. The announcer now delivers the commercial announcements near the beginning and end of the broadcast only. In this way the newsman is freed of commercialism.

Also, there are the programs that deal with topics and personalities of current interest, given by "columnists" who are not so much concerned with the news of the moment as with anecdotes, inventions, or gossip. Some of them are merely answering inquiries that have been mailed to the commentator.

Trying to tell a news story in dramatic terms takes practice, but a finished product makes an absorbing program. As in any form of drama, the suspense factor is important; important scenes should end with plenty of punch to sustain interest.

One common device is used to achieve the realistic effect of a narrator's voice backed by less important incidental conversation. When, as a writer, you want to bring this main voice into prominence (the narrator perhaps), write in parallel columns, with the narrator's speech on the left, and background words on the right. Keep in mind that news drama must have conflict and suspense, make the conflict clear at the outset, and complete the picture with well-identified characters. Remember that natural, easy conversation will make your characters become flesh-and-blood people in a real-life drama.

During the Second World War, news broadcasts dominated the radio day. Because of their popularity, every conceivable type of news broadcast is being tried out in peacetime. News programs devoted to local, church, society, health, and education items are tried out. The microphone is taken into the marriage license bureau, the traffic court, police department, to the railroad station to broadcast the departure of a famous train filled with famous travelers. There are garden, labor, sports, civic, and campus news programs. There are news programs especially designed for children or for women, programs which contain only human-interest stories, and those which are titled the "Sunny Side of the Street," the backwoods philosopher type. The person who can think up a new and popular news program is assured a place in the air.

The great problems of the news broadcaster is that his program is a daily feature. Newscasts run from 12 to 18 per day in 5- or 15-minute programs. Most stations broadcast four major daily newscasts; the morning eight o'clock news informs the office worker before he leaves, the noon-hour news sums up morning events. The six o'clock news is designed to jibe with the dinner hour, and the late, eleven o'clock, is a résumé of the day's happenings. Finding material to fill all this time is a real problem; new methods of presentation constitute an even greater challenge. Most news commentators are former newspaper men who have developed a sense of news values.

Selection of Material

The elements that enter into the selection of what is called in the newspaper "front-page news" are the same for the radio commentator as they are for the newspaper editor. Briefly, these may be considered as the significance of the item and, in the case of feature stories, the *conflict* between man and other men, or with animals, things, ideas, or the elements. There must be some sort of conflict. The second element is the fact that people are always interested in placing themselves in the role of the character who is making news. Consequently, an item about an individual or in which an individual plays a part in the conflict is better. The news should be of interest to a widely separated audience.

The "here and now" quality of radio news is an important requisite. If an event "just happened" radio alone can report it immediately. Television can literally be "on the spot" to give the story in some cases. Equipment has been brought to the scene of a fire or riot in time for the action to be televised to the video audience. That's what the radio audience wants—immediate news. Thus the radio and the newspaper have clearly defined respective news functions. In one sense, they do not compete but complement each other. Radio quickly sketches the picture, the newspaper can use sufficient space to fill in the background with all additional details.

Action is important in radio news. The listener interest in a conflict of any kind has already been mentioned and conflict means action. The four main news categories are local, state, national, and international. Radio's job is to bring to its audience up-to-the-minute major developments on all four levels. These divisions became customary in wartime and remained as a legacy for a well-balanced newscast. The particular interests of a listening area should be considered. In a highly industrialized area, news of a special manufacturing process or labor problems would have appeal. In local stories, "follow-through" is a must. The community is alerted when a child is bitten by a rabid dog. Listeners will also want to know what medical treatment was given, how successful it was, and whether complete recovery was achieved. Thus, follow-through is obligatory in many cases under libel laws in court cases.

That brings us to human-interest stories, important for their universal appeal. If such a story involves an amusing twist it is even better. Local incidents are particularly good. Many stations and sponsors require that their broadcasts combine information with entertainment, and consequently humorous and human-interest stories are interspersed between the more significant items or are used in the conclusion of the broadcast.

The United Press warns its radio affiliates to avoid "gruesome" stories; court trials with unpleasant angles, particularly of sex; birth control, unless handled with care; divorces, except those of famous personalities, and with these the sex angle should be avoided; crime, only outstanding cases, and then minimized; capital punishment, except that which has resulted from trials that have been in the public eye. This does not mean that all unpleasant cases or unpleasant items are discarded. It does mean that as far as possible the radio reporter attempts to avoid being an alarmist. This undoubtedly is the result of the radio's whole-family audience. Furthermore, in the selection of news the radio editor must take into consideration that he may be held for libel, blasphemy, immoral publication, contempt of court, or sedition, and select items to avoid any such charges. The time of day when the news is to be broadcast influences the selection of items: cancer, reptiles, false teeth are not topics for a mealtime broadcast.

Accuracy is essential in the report of the newscaster. An inaccurate news item cannot be killed on radio as it can be in a newspaper, and a correction sometimes does more harm than the original statement. If the news is based upon some previous report, it must be tied up with what has gone before. The newscaster cannot assume that the listener has heard the previous news report and consequently must summarize very briefly.

Radio is a means of communication ideally suited to the pace of modern life. It reduces news to its simplest terms and gets it across in a small capsule of time. A complex situation of world-wide importance will be dealt with very fully by a newspaper. But many individuals may have neither the time nor inclination to study such an analysis with sufficient care to gain a clear understanding of the related events. The radio news version should make it relatively easy for the listener to grasp the significance of such events. As the United States assumes a role of increasing prominence in world affairs, it is essential that the nation be well and accurately informed. From knowledge comes understanding, and this is the vital ingredient of the "one-world" concept. The radio writer can further this aim by making the message clean-cut and simple. Public attention and esteem is the result of such effort.

Diction

Like all other forms of continuity for broadcasting, news must be written for the listener. This requires that the reporter should always be concerned with how his material will sound. He will find if he reads from a newspaper that there are many words which are difficult to enunciate and sentences that are so complex that they would be lost in the ear of the audience. He must keep in mind that radio news is told by a storyteller and must be written in the form of an oral story. At the outset the radio news reporter tries to get friendly with his listeners; consequently the "yellow" or "shocker" story should not be used as an opening. The news program is considered by all stations to be educational and informative, but even the educational program must be entertaining to hold the listener's attention. In the preparation of news copy consider the listener's interest angle and attitude, not your own.

As in other forms of radio writing, the selection of just the right word is all-important; because of the time limitation every word must have real value from an informative or picture-producing standpoint. Too many adjectives are inadvisable, although simple adjectives frequently make the scene more vivid. For instance, it is better to say, "It is a bitterly cold morning," than merely, "It is a cold morning." This is where good radio jibes with good showmanship. Words that catch and hold your listener's attention are essential. Radio news must compete for attention with countless diversions—conversation, reading, household duties and activities. Verbs are particularly helpful in portraying action and in creating a mental picture and should be chosen with that in mind. Words with double meanings should be avoided. The reader of copy can differentiate between two words that sound alike but are spelled differently and have a different meaning; however, this is not at all possible for the radio listener. If there is the slightest chance of a misunderstanding, change the word, because your audience is decidedly critical. Some words are hard to pronounce over the air, particularly those containing sibilant sounds like "reminiscences." If possible, a synonym should be found for all such cumbersome words. This means that many expressive and descriptive words are eliminated from the radio commentator's vocabulary. Form the habit of eliminating these tongue twisters by reading over your work to yourself. This will also help you to build a good vocabulary of oral words.

Don'ts

Some of the instructions given by news agencies to their correspondents are equally applicable to the writer of radio news copy. For instance, the following hints from the United Press Service may well be considered:

Send something—don't always "transmit" or "dispatch" it.
Call a person, or persons, or a meeting—don't always "summon" them.
Buy something—don't always "purchase" it.
Leave some place—don't always "depart."
Act—don't always "take action."
Will—not always "is going to."
Arrest or *Seize*—not "take into custody."
Show—don't always "display" or "exhibit."
Get—don't always "obtain."
Need—don't always "require."
See—don't always "witness."
Can—not always "is able to."
Help—not always "aid" or "assist."
Hurt—not always "injured."
Break—not always "fracture."
Build and *Building*—not always "construct" and "construction."
Meet—not always "confer," "convene," or "hold a conference."
Doctor—not always "physician."

Among journalists it has become customary never to draw attention to the fact that information is lacking. This very fact may be of interest to a radio audience—and may be one step in the follow-through process mentioned before. If there has been a local jail break, for instance, residents want to know if the prisoners are still at large or if any one district is even suspected as a possible hide-out. There is no reason to avoid a negative news lead of this kind.

An important requirement of radio news is repetition. The first sentence of a story may contain the essential facts, but perhaps key words have only attracted the listener from another simultaneous interest. Now that his undivided attention is yours, give him one or even two more chances to get the story straight by presenting the facts in varied forms.

Don't give the listener your opinion of an item before you present it; that is not reporting. News is "good," "bad," or "interesting" according to how you look at it, so get into the story immediately so the listener may pass judgment.

Avoid introducing a story by asking a question. Instead of writing, "Who will win the Big Ten Championship? that is the current question tonight"; say—"The question—Who will win the Big Ten Championship —is current tonight."

All regulations concerning offensive material, immorality, and sex should be observed, and anything that is offensive to any race, sex, or creed should be avoided. A word that has recently come into disrepute is "blood." In a recent broadcast of a prize fight, when one of the contestants was given a bloody nose, it was announced that his nose was red. Other words, like "bugs" and names of vermin, should be avoided. The newspaper reporter is very much inclined to use stock phrases; trite expressions should be avoided. An interesting story about this practice is "Calloway's Code" by O. Henry. Certain words are overworked; for instance, "rush" is too frequently used in place of "hurry" or just plain "go." Reporters and radio men consider that all kinds of motor cars are "high-powered." We are guilty of failing to differentiate between the verbs "can" and "may." There is some redundancy in news reports; for instance, only a grand jury can indict and it is unnecessary to state that a certain man was indicted by the grand jury. Transitional words and connectives in writing are placed in the body of a sentence; however, for radio they are generally placed at the beginning of a sentence. If they are placed in the middle of the sentence, the thought is broken for the ear.

The broadcaster is particularly interested in making his program sound like fresh news. He attempts to give the impression that the action of the story is immediate. Various devices are used to accomplish this purpose; fresh angles should be sought which will make the use of the present tense possible. The radio listener is accustomed to bulletins taken from the wire and expects that all news is of the moment. On the other hand, use the word "today" sparingly, particularly in the opening sentence, and do not repeat it in various items. Expressions such as "this morning," "this afternoon," and "during the day" may be used, or the same expression may be created by using the present tense. If the verb in the present tense denotes action, this also gives the item more timeliness. Of course, if the event is decidedly over, the past tense may be used.

The newspaper report, with a narrative news lead answering the six questions (what, why, where, when, how, who) is too complicated for the opening of a radio news report. Do not try to give too much information in the opening sentence. The best policy is to permit the listener to get the setting before proceeding to the important part of the story. If you pile too many details into the first sentence, the listener gets lost. Don't start off with an unfamiliar name. It is wise to give the source of the information quite near the start in the body of the report, rather than as a date line for the story as it appears in the newspapers.

Some stations attempt to make transitions between the sources of material. Either an announcer will come in and state "News from the nation's capital," "The state in review," "Now to foreign shores," or the commentator will in some like way transport the listener from locale to locale.

Many newspapers resort to extreme caution in presenting items by using some such phrase as, "It was learned." There is no point in this because it implies that the reporter is not sure of his facts. During the war years there were exceptions to this rule. News was censored by the warring nations and much of it was propaganda. Thus in many cases it was entirely necessary to comment on the source or authenticity of an item. Another style that is in bad repute is the use of the words "quote" and "unquote" in reporting an interview or speech. The radio writer should compose the material in such a way that these expressions can be avoided. It can be done by introducing the quotation with such words as "what he termed," "what he called," or "he said." The combination of the writing and of the delivery should make the listener understand that the announcer is really quoting. Using pauses just before the quotation and at the end of the quotation will to some extent take the place of quotation marks. If the quotation used is a long one, the source should be inserted again in a different form, sometimes in the middle of the sentence, sometimes introducing the sentence. Such phrases as "the visiting speaker continued" or "the lecturer added" may be used to make it clear that the views are quoted, and the listener is not hearing the opinions of the announcer. Make your source of information clear but use "quote" and "quotation" as little as possible. If it is absolutely necessary, weave them into your script as skillfully as you can. And a last reminder—don't use "unquote."

Make the various news items short. Not even the biggest news story is worth much more than 500 words. The radio listener likes variety and is disappointed if only a few items are given to him by the broadcaster. It is difficult to hold the attention of a listener on any single subject for a great length of time.

As a general rule short sentences are most desirable in the writing of copy; however, they can be overdone, resulting in jerky or choppy delivery. The writer should strive for smoothness and rhythm. The rhythm style enables the announcer to get a swing into his delivery. It is possible even to forget rules of grammar because some of radio's most expressive statements are descriptive phrases rather than complete sentences.

Be careful in using relative pronouns; there must be no doubt about their antecedents. For the late tuner-in it is better to repeat the person's name or the place. Clarity is important. Don't trust announcers to pronounce difficult words and phrases properly. News copy is not completed until a few minutes before it is put on the air, with the result that the speaker does not have the opportunity to study the copy and audition it. Make use of the apostrophe—use dashes freely; they are effective in radio writing for setting the pace and emphasis of the announcer. In handling figures do not write $25,000,000, but write it out in full in the copy, 25 million dollars, for then the announcer cannot go wrong. It is best not to use exact figures; put them in round numbers, even if you are guilty of a slight exaggeration. Do not bother with ages in broadcasts unless they really play some part in the story; in death stories older listeners, however, like to know at what age some other person dies. Full names of well-known people are not necessary; use their common identification. In the case of senators or representatives, name the state they represent. Don't put out stories about local accidents in which victims are unidentified. Of course a major catastrophe constitutes an exception to this rule. In processing a wire report for the air, do not deviate from the facts contained in the wire story.

The radio news services give stations 24-hour service. Five- and fifteen-minute summaries come through at specified intervals. These are designed to be used as complete programs for those time periods. Between summaries, numerous daily features are filed—sports, women's commentary programs, and farm news. Other items are individual stories, 1-minute roundups, and local and regional news.

Too much reliance must not be placed on this material however. When a station must broadcast the same news it should be rewritten to avoid monotony. Initiative and imagination are needed to pep up a stale story. Newswire stories may give you an important lead for a local angle. Check up on a government announcement and point out how it affects people in your community.

Before starting to edit and rewrite the news, take time to understand the item fully yourself. This is the time to check the story if it isn't clear. Phrase the story your own way but take care not to be misleading. Compare your version with the complete original story to be certain the meaning is not obscured or changed. If you have more than one source of information, pool all the facts and check differences of interpretation, then choose your rewrite facts from the total. Read your story out loud; what looks well on paper may have many concealed pitfalls for the announcer.

Style

Unless the newscaster is introduced by name, it is advisable for him to open his program with some sort of greeting—"Good evening," or some other such phrase. A person does not ordinarily walk into another's living room and immediately start to talk. While subtle humor which results from a clever choice of phraseology enlivens the program and brings lightness into it, the newscaster should never allow himself to be considered silly. Sarcasm and irony are also dangerous since they are frequently misunderstood. The news commentator is presenting facts, and he should sound as though he considered these facts worthy of the attention of his audience.

He should also sound familiar with the material because the public is getting its information from him. To the listener he is the first reader of the story. Words that are unfamiliar must be checked for accuracy of meaning and pronunciation. Foreign place names and unusual personal names warrant particular care. Write them out phonetically so there is no danger of forgetting where the emphasis falls when you meet them again on the air.

Frequent criticism is aimed at radio speakers for falling into one of two equally bad categories. In their desire to read with expression, some develop a "voice pattern," a singsong sort of delivery with meaningless rising and falling inflections. The other extreme is a monotone. It is most important to keep the voice flexible, and vary pitch, speed, and tone. But you will find that if you concentrate on the meaning behind the words, a natural correct pacing will result. Words are merely symbols of thoughts and ideas—try to forget that they are on a printed page and turn them into conversation. Find out what the script is about and then "tell" your listeners. Individual voice problems have to be worked out, and there are many techniques that may be learned to make your voice say just what you mean it to. The best advice to the would-be commentator is to develop a personal plan or credo that will conform to and establish his personality. Study the radio public and cater to it. The listener is always right.

There is no reason to broadcast sitting down if you would prefer to stand. Most telenewscasters are seated before a map or a picture screen. A comfortable position generally results in better delivery. By the same token, clearing your throat or coughing slightly is perfectly permissible if you turn from the mike. Certainly it is better than finding it difficult to use your voice properly because you have failed to do so. Some microphones have a "cut-off switch" to take care of this, and some announcers and commentators use the throat-cutting signal to the control room to get them off the air momentarily. All radio speakers "muff" or "flub" words at some time or another; most enjoy recounting their worst ones. If this happens, a quick correction may be possible but going back may result in a worse tangle than the first time. You can't take back the mistake so go on and let the listener forget it.

The newscaster should present his material in a clear manner without making any attempt to force his opinion upon the listener. It is wiser to lead the listener to the same point of view, and compliment him at the same time, by allowing him to reach his own decision. The "newscaster" is a real personality, and, consequently, he should project that personality. News commentators usually develop the personal style that creates for them friends and listeners and makes their programs distinctive.

To announce a transition from one news item to another, the speaker should pause briefly, change his voice slightly, or announce the transition. Frequently, it is good practice to present the news in the style that one person might use in telling it to someone he does not know very well. Crime stories are seldom broadcast unless the crime is one against the public. A crime of passion committed in the slums or underworld has little value as news to the radio listener. Certain stations have definite policies forbidding unnecessary injury to any person's feelings by the spreading of news. Stations are inclined to be unbiased in political attitudes, but news commentators frequently imply their personal bias. Sponsored programs, however, too frequently are influenced.

The speed with which most announcers speak is about 150 words a minute. However, delivery is very deceptive inasmuch as some announcers dash along and then waste seconds upon unimportant transitions. Frequently, those whose delivery sounds slow will put more words into a minute than the speaker with the machine-gun type of presentation. Placing emphasis upon every final syllable, giving it a slight accent whether it truly should have a final accent or not, will enable the deliberate speaker to cover ground. The average is about 2500 words on a 15-minute program. Too rapid delivery of news copy is unsatisfactory to the listener. While people hear at the average rate of 150 words a minute, they are accustomed to reading news at a little less than 100 words a minute. If the news delivery is too speedy, the listener has little left at the end of the report but a mixed impression that somebody did something somewhere. The listener does not have an opportunity to absorb rapidly delivered news.

Code of Self-regulation

The provision about news broadcasts included in the Code of Self-regulation of the National Association of Radio and Television Broadcasters reads:

News shall be presented with fairness and accuracy and the broadcasting station or network shall satisfy itself that the arrangements made for obtaining news insure this result. Since the number of broadcasting channels is limited, news broadcasts shall not be editorial. This means that news shall not be selected for the purpose of furthering or hindering either side of any controversial public issue nor shall it be colored by the opinions or desires of the station or network management, the editor or others engaged in its preparation or the person actually delivering it over the air, or, in the case of sponsored news broadcasts, the advertiser.

The fundamental purpose of news dissemination in a democracy is to enable people to know what is happening and to understand the meaning of events so that they may form their own conclusions and, therefore, nothing in the foregoing shall be understood as preventing news broadcasters from analyzing and elucidating news so long as such analysis and elucidation are free of bias.

News commentators as well as all other newscasters shall be governed by these provisions.

The policies and standards of the National Broadcasting Company regarding the broadcasting of news have been set as follows:

All standards of the company apply to news programs. Specifically, the following standards must be followed:

1. All news shall be reported from an unbiased, non-partisan viewpoint.

2. News shall be treated factually and analytically, never sensationally.

3. News announcements involving crime or sex shall be avoided unless of national importance.

4. News shall not be broadcast in such a manner as might unduly create alarm or panic. No flash stories about accidents or disasters shall be broadcast until adequate details are available.

5. No suicide shall be reported, except in the case of a nationally known figure.

6. No lotteries, gambling odds or similar information shall be broadcast which might tend to cause listeners to gamble on the outcome of an event.

7. No libelous or slanderous news is permitted.

8. The news announcer shall not deliberately distort the news by any inflection of the voice.

9. Fictional events shall not be presented in the form of authentic news announcements.

10. No legal or medical advice is allowed in news broadcasts except when it is an essential part of legitimate news from official sources.

NEWS ON TELEVISION

Since television is part of the broadcasting industry, many of the problems of news presentation are the same as they are in radio. This is particularly true in such matters as fairness, accuracy, timeliness, aural style, and interest. Thus, many of the basic principles discussed under radio news apply equally to television.

Program types

The sources of television news, at least the verbal portions of it, are the same as for radio. Most television stations have the A.P. or U.P. radio wire, and many supplement this with a straight news wire. I.N.S. also provides this type of service. The larger stations might add a state wire service, and some method of gathering the local news. Where the same company operates a radio and a television station it is common practice to share the newsroom and the news-gathering sources. The verbal parts of TV news present no new problems. Radio experience has provided television with considerable know-how in assembling and editing the news information.

Visual Aids

The real problem in television news arises when some effort is made to supply visual elements. What is gained when we can see the newscaster seated at a desk reading the news? Or to put it another way, and very possibly more accurately, isn't there danger that such a presentation of the news will be distracting? What, then, can be done visually during a news program?

The most obvious answer, film, is only a partial answer. Many difficulties are encountered in the use of news film. Film of world and national news events must be purchased from the major news-film companies. How does film shot in Rome get to Ames, Iowa, in time to be used while the story is still news? Clearly this isn't easy to accomplish. Newsreel film does supply part of the answer for network news programs. They can get the film, process it quickly and have it on in a matter of hours. News film of widespread events is not very practical for local-station newscasts. Newsreel footage of local events can be incorporated into a news program with marked success. It is an expensive operation, but where the station can recover this cost it is a definite audience builder. Station WHAS in Louisville, Kentucky, has done a remarkable job with a local newsreel. This answers only a part of the problem of TV news, but does provide something interesting and worthwhile. The use of morgue film footage is fraught with dangers. In the first place, the job of collecting, cataloguing, and filing film footage for future use is too much of a job for the average local station. Then, too, incongruities occur so often between the pictures used and the current story being read that the result is apt to be more distracting than enlightening.

Film also tends to overemphasize certain kinds of news stories. Fires, floods, and other dramatic events which lend themselves well to filming get a disproportionate amount of attention. Many of the most important news stories do not involve physical action, so do not lend themselves to film coverage. A good newscast is organized according to the importance of the news and not by what makes the most dramatic pictures.

Still pictures offer another partial answer. In many ways the timeliness of stills is more valuable than the motion offered by outdated movies. The major wire services have made their wire-photo pictures available for TV use. Facsimile is also used to provide current news photos to TV stations. At least one wire service, I.N.S. includes with its facsimile pictures sound which can be tape recorded and used with the pictures. In this way, two or three shots of the President might appear on the screen while a brief highlight from an address is played on audio. The continuing growth in the use of newspaper pictures indicates that the public does like news photos. There is no reason why they shouldn't like them on television as well, if they are properly used, and if they are timely.

Yet another partial answer is the use of visuals such as maps, charts, graphs, etc. These are valuable additions when they apply, and when a definite contribution can be made by their use. There are many news stories for which no such visual is appropriate.

All of this adds up to a difficult task in news reporting on television. The only known answer is a combination of imagination, judgment, hard work, many man-hours, and enough money to provide the necessary resources. Despite the many difficulties, and even though there may be no advantages in television news over radio news, stations should not fail to provide this service on television. Whatever the merits of radio over television in this field, if people are watching television, and not listening to the radio, they will not get the news unless it is on TV. So, television owes it to the audience to provide this important service, whether or not it can add a lot in the way of visual interest.

News Background Programs

In the area of news background programs, television proves its worth. One need mention only the work of Edward R. Murrow and Eric Sevareid in this connection. It is here that film and visuals take on significance. It is, of course, an entirely different kind of thing from reporting the current news. In the background program there is time to prepare the elaborate visual elements.

Television can add a major dimension to the public's understanding of important news events. If some unfamiliar geographical area becomes important in the world news, a few TV programs can show what such a place is like, who lives there and what they are like, and why it is all important. A piece of documentary film on a slum area is worth many words in an effort to make the subject clear to an audience.

Here is one news job that television can sink its teeth into, and can develop into a powerful force for public enlightenment. Nor is this type of program limited to the networks. Every community and every state contain a wealth of information for background programs. The people and the information are there. All that is needed is an imaginative person on the station staff, and meaningful and interesting programs can be developed.

The TV Newscaster

In radio it is fairly common to find the newscast prepared by one person and read by someone else. Frequently, the man who reads the news is a capable announcer rather than a newsman. All too often, this same situation obtains in television. It is best if the man who presents the news on television is also a news specialist. The best delivery for TV involves more than the straight reading of copy. Eye contact with the camera is essential. It is helpful if parts of different stories can be embellished with pertinent references, and ad-lib details. This helps to create a slightly informal atmosphere. If such a technique is to be used, it is essential that the announcer be a qualified newsman, who follows the news closely, and whose remarks will be accurate. The impression to be made is that the person is an expert and an authority on the news.

The good TV newscaster, then, is a person who knows the news. He is able to do more than read wire copy. He can present the news with authority. He is able to use visuals smoothly and to blend all of the elements available into a meaningful summary of what is going on. He must avoid mannerisms that will distract from the information he is presenting.

None of this should be understood as an excuse for corning up a newscast. A news program is not a variety show. The information is the important thing, and the manner of presentation should enhance that information in the greatest possible degree. Anything that interferes with clear understanding of the news should be avoided, no matter how visually tempting.

CHAPTER TEN

SPORTS PROGRAMS

SPORTS ON RADIO

There are various kinds of sports programs. There is the on-the-spot broadcast of an event, the descriptive account based upon telegraphic reports, the after-the-event résumé, the dramatized sports program, and the straight recapitulation of wire news; there are also combinations of these. The type of broadcast which attracts the largest number of listeners is a running description of a sports event which is taking place at the very moment that the news comes over the air. Examples are broadcasts of football, baseball, hockey, and basketball games, tennis and golf matches, boxing bouts, and boat races.

Of these, hockey is the most difficult to broadcast and rarely is done well. It is such an exceedingly fast affair that the man at the microphone is almost always behind the action. The other extreme is baseball. Taking advantage of the fact that he has all the time in the world between pitches, the commentator employs a slow delivery and uses a great amount of fill-in material. The baseball game is comparatively easy to broadcast because there are few line-up changes after the season starts. Fans are extremely critical if you err. Describing a basketball game requires a thorough knowledge of the game. The broadcaster must have a very fast speech rate and excellent eyesight. Aside from naming substitutions, the "spotter" does not help much. Obviously, the spotter is also useless in describing a boxing match. Knowledge of boxing is necessary for broadcasting, since big fights are televised widely and listeners can check up on any important radio error. A speedy delivery is also called for. Football is not difficult to broadcast because of the exceptional facilities in press boxes and the extensive pregame preparation. One man usually does color while the sports announcer does the play-by-play. A tennis match is difficult to broadcast, for the strokes are difficult to call and possess technical names. A combination of a thorough knowledge of the game and the ability to fill are essential qualities in the announcer. Golf reportage is also difficult. There is such a long time between strokes that a tremendous amount of ad-libbing is necessary. Furthermore, the voice has to be controlled so that it will not annoy the players.

The Sports Announcer

There has been an idea that the sports announcer should be an athlete who has participated in the sport he is describing. One of the outstanding professional football players of the day has expressed a desire for a college-trained football man to announce programs; on the other hand a famous coach says that it is dangerous for the sports announcer to have too much knowledge about the game because he is inclined to get ahead of the play, and, instead of talking to the average fan, give a more technical explanation which might be understandable only to the football player. Undoubtedly a good background knowledge of sports is essential; but the knowledge of how to dramatize the voice, to pick vivid, descriptive words quickly, to keep on giving information in the midst of excitement, and to inject the thrill of the game without hesitation into the microphone, is more essential than previous participation in the sport.

A would-be sports announcer would do well to learn all that he can of the different sports that are broadcast. The rules and requirements of the games must be thoroughly absorbed. He should study the phraseology that is distinctive of the game or sport, which he may use in his broadcasts if it is generally understood by sport fans and by the average listener. The sport pages of newspapers written by experts will form his textbook, for they will give him a diction that is picturesque and a style that is speedy. He should study the history of sport and of those who have participated and gained renown. He must know the signs or gestures used by the officials to signify penalties, etc. But most of all, he must never forget that he is not watching a game for his own amusement, but is reporting it to listeners who are hanging on his word description.

When the announcer has received his assignment, he should go to the scene of the contest well in advance of the event. There he will pick up all the gossip about the game that he can. He will absorb local color, stories about the participants, and the history of the competition. He should find out what selections the band will play in between halves, so that the network will not be caught with an uncleared tune, and he should otherwise anticipate any difficulties that might arise before or after the program. If he is to broadcast a football game, he will get acquainted with the players, watch their practice, learn their formations, discover what plays are used under given circumstances. The sports announcer is generally trusted by the coaches and is provided with the records that have been brought in by scouts who have watched the opposing team in action. If possible, the announcer will attempt to get the coach to tell him of any radical departures from the normal style of play, so that he will not be unprepared. Bill Stern arrives nearly a week before the game and has even practiced with the teams. All this preparation gives him confidence.

The announcer is supplied by the college publicity departments with material concerning each player, his age, weight, experience, class in college, where he played in preparatory school, home town, and position on the team. From this advance information he prepares his opening account to be used before the game, the filler material to be used between halves, and short fragments to be used when time out is taken. This is all the material that is written in advance of the program. When the whistle blows for the kickoff, the announcer is on his own. His tongue and mind must be as quick and as true as his eyes. Some colleges supply a tabulation of the game to the announcer immediately after the final whistle which he can use for his summary; other announcers have a man with them who tabulates the game as it progresses. This tabulator usually is capable of announcing his findings and in this way relieves the announcer.

When the day of the game arrives, the announcer, who alone is responsible for the broadcast, tests his mikes and his lines, instructs his technician, sees to it that he can observe the play upon all parts of the gridiron from his booth, selects locations for additional mikes to pick up the bands and crowd noises. He generally is provided with two spotters who can identify players on both teams by their walk or mannerisms, as well as one to watch the officials. These assistants can immediately give the announcer the names of the player carrying the ball and of the one who makes the tackle, as well as the names of other players who have taken important parts in the play. The third spotter will have a series of cards upon which are printed the penalties and rules. These cards are handed to the announcer for his use when occasion demands.

As the broadcaster takes his seat to begin work, he makes a mental

calculation as to the dramatic possibilities of the pregame description.
He decides on how much time he will be able to devote to the various
subjects. He roughly allots a certain amount of time to the weather, the
spectators, distinguished guests, and perhaps music, cheering sections,
and the like. He calculates a certain length of time for announcement
of the personnel and sets aside the last 2 or 3 minutes for the commercial, the anticipated high light of the contest, and the opening play. It

Fig. 26. Sportscaster's spotter board. (*University of Michigan.*)

is customary to start a sports broadcast several minutes before a contest
is scheduled to begin. This permits the observer to set the scene.

Every sports man who is announcing football games makes a spotter
board (Fig. 26) which he uses to check on the players. This device has
two boards which are hinged together to form a folder, but the hinge
pins may be removed so that the two sides can become separate boards.
On the back of each section are hinged raisers at each end which tilt
the board when it is placed upon the shelf. These two sections are on
each side of the microphone during the game, placed as the two teams
are on the field. The board for each team is set up in its offensive formation. For instance, if Michigan is using a "T" formation its player cards

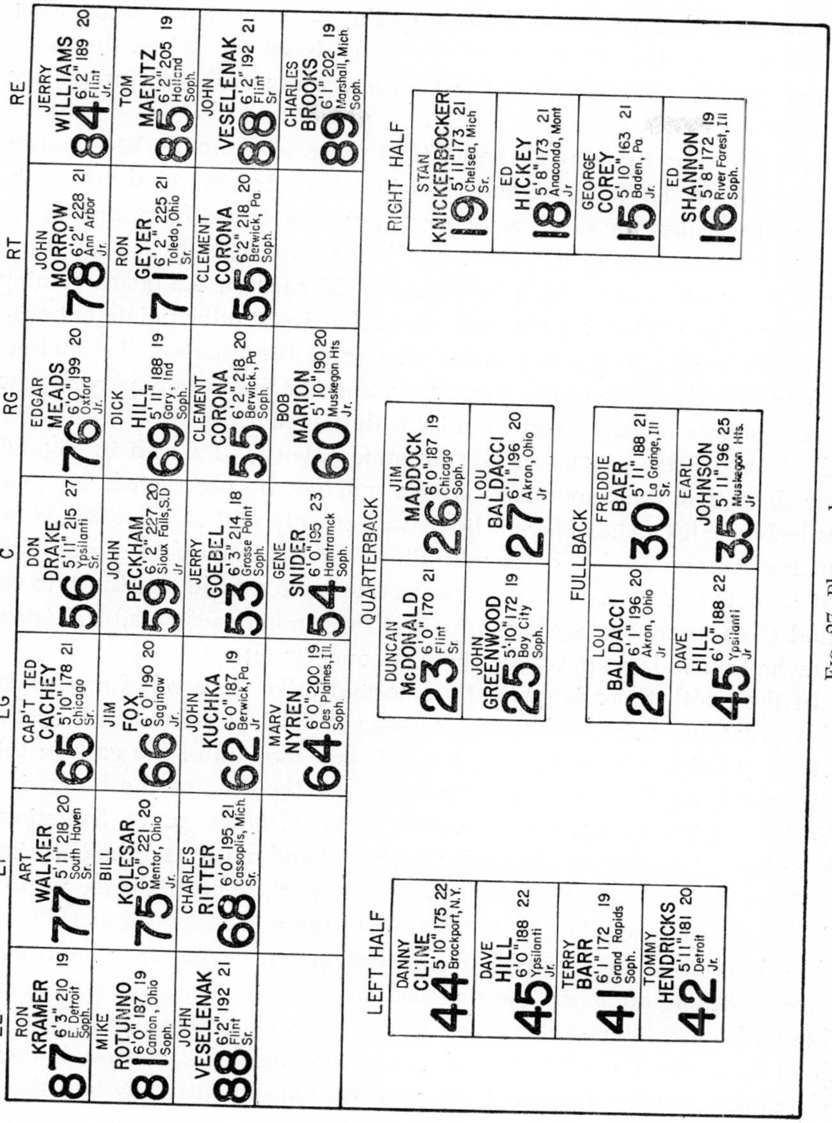

LE
- RON KRAMER 87 — 6'3" 210, E. Detroit, Soph., 19
- MIKE ROTUNNO 81 — 6'0" 187, Canton, Ohio, Soph., 19
- JOHN VESELENAK 88 — 6'2" 192, Flint, Sr., 21

LT
- ART WALKER 77 — 5'11" 218, South Haven, Sr., 20
- BILL KOLESAR 75 — 6'0" 221, Mentor, Ohio, Jr., 20
- CHARLES RITTER 68 — 6'0" 195, Cassopolis, Mich., Sr., 21

LG
- CAP'T TED CACHEY 65 — 5'10" 178, Chicago, Sr., 21
- JIM FOX 66 — 6'0" 190, Saginaw, Jr., 20
- JOHN KUCHKA 62 — 6'0" 187, Berwick, Pa, Jr., 19
- MARV NYREN 64 — 6'0" 200, Des Plaines, Ill., Soph., 19

C
- DON DRAKE 56 — 5'11" 215, Ypsilanti, Sr., 27
- JOHN PECKHAM 59 — 6'2" 227, Sioux Falls, S.D, Jr., 20
- JERRY GOEBEL 53 — 6'3" 214, Grosse Point, Soph., 18
- GENE SNIDER 54 — 6'0" 195, Hamtramck, Soph., 23

RG
- EDGAR MEADS 76 — 6'0" 99, Oxford, Jr., 20
- DICK HILL 69 — 5'11" 188, Gary, Ind, Soph., 19
- CLEMENT CORONA 55 — 6'2" 218, Berwick, Pa, Soph., 20
- BOB MARION 60 — 5'10" 190, Muskegon Hts, Jr., 20

RT
- JOHN MORROW 78 — 6'2" 228, Ann Arbor, Jr., 21
- RON GEYER 71 — 6'2" 225, Toledo, Ohio, Sr., 21
- CLEMENT CORONA 55

RE
- JERRY WILLIAMS 84 — 6'2" 189, Flint, Jr., 20
- TOM MAENTZ 85 — 6'2" 205, Holland, Soph., 19
- JOHN VESELENAK 88 — 6'2" 192, Flint, Sr., 21
- CHARLES BROOKS 89 — 6'1" 202, Marshall, Mich, Soph., 19

LEFT HALF
- DANNY CLINE 44 — 5'10" 175, Brockport, N.Y., 22
- DAVE HILL 45 — 6'0" 188, Ypsilanti, Jr., 22
- TERRY BARR 41 — 6'1" 172, Grand Rapids, Soph., 19
- TOMMY HENDRICKS 42 — 5'11" 181, Detroit, Jr., 20

QUARTERBACK
- DUNCAN McDONALD 23 — 6'0" 170, Flint, Sr., 21
- JOHN GREENWOOD 25 — 5'10" 172, Bay City, Soph., 19
- JIM MADDOCK 26 — 6'0" 187, Chicago, Soph., 19
- LOU BALDACCI 27 — 6'1" 196, Akron, Ohio, Jr., 20

FULLBACK
- LOU BALDACCI 27 — 6'1" 196, Akron, Ohio, Jr.
- DAVE HILL 45 — 6'0" 188, Ypsilanti, Jr., 22
- FREDDIE BAER 30 — 5'11" 188, La Grange, Ill, 21
- EARL JOHNSON 35 — 5'11" 196, Muskegon Hts., 25

RIGHT HALF
- STAN KNICKERBOCKER 9 — 5'11" 173, Chelsea, Mich, Sr., 21
- ED HICKEY 18 — 5'8" 173, Anaconda, Mont, Jr., 21
- GEORGE COREY 15 — 5'10" 163, Baden, Pa, 21
- ED SHANNON 16 — 5'8" 172, River Forest, Ill, Soph., 19

FIG. 27. Players chart.

are arranged that way, and if the opposing team uses the single wing, that is the way the other side of the board is set up. When the teams change positions on the field, the boards are reversed and turned end for end.

Each card has the player's name (last name in capitals), his number, height, weight, home town, and class in school. In case of substitution, the spotter makes the necessary change upon the board from a complete roster of players arranged numerically. The spotter usually has a pointer, a pencil, or stick with which he points to the card on the board naming the man who is carrying the ball; the defensive spotter points out who made the tackle. When the teams change at the quarters the spotters shift to the other side of the announcer. Spotters are usually players who are on the injured list or very familiar with the team.

In front of the announcer is a low microphone, as shown in Fig. 36, placed so that the announcer's vision will not be obstructed. He generally has a list of all players listed numerically and of the officials for quick reference. He has cards with filler material to be used during time out or between periods. Many announcers have a little egg timer to remind them to announce the score every three minutes if possible. Listeners who tune in late appreciate these announcements.

In the booth there is generally a second mike for a relief announcer who gives the color and game statistics (which are furnished by the college publicity department at the half and the end of the game); this announcer usually does the commercial. At the rear of the booth is a Western Union operator who receives scores of other games. Sometimes there is a third mike on the field to pick up band music and the cheering.

The whistle blows as the announcer has worked his audience up to a climax of suspense. He adopts the present tense in his account. He must place himself in the position of one viewing the game and describe it to his unseeing audience. He must assume that in his audience there are those who are interested in the technical details of the play as well as those to whom the dramatics of the contest hold the greatest interest. The announcer at a football game concerns himself with only four things —who is carrying the ball, what sort of play it was, who made the tackle, and how far the ball was advanced. These four things must be answered. Other descriptive material may be included, but if these four questions are answered the listener can always locate the ball upon his imaginary field. The description should reach the ear of the listener as if the play were in progress as it is described. The play may be completed but still

FIRST DOWNS:	MICHIGAN STATISTICS
1 2 3 4 5 6 7 8 9 10 11 12 13 14 15 16 17 18 19 20 21 22 23 24 25 26 27 28 29	

RUSHING:	YARDAGE GAINED	PASSING:

Cumulative tally of yardage gained or lost play by play. The last figure always gives the total yardage gained or lost.

Same as under Rushing.

Circle passes as attempted, complete, incomplete, or intercepted.

PASSES: 1 2 3 4 5 6 7 8 9 10 11 12 13 14 15 16 17 18 19 20 21 22 23 24 25 26 27 28 29 30 31 32 33 34 35 36 37 38

COMPLETE: 1 2 3 4 5 6 7 8 9 10 11 12 13 14 15 16 17 18 19 20 21 22 23 24 25

INCOMPLETE: 1 2 3 4 5 6 7 8 9 10 11 12 13 14 15 16 17 18 19 20 21 22 23 24 25

INTERCEPTED: 1 2 3 4 5 6 7 8 9 10 11

FUMBLES	PENALTIES
Circle around recovered. Square around lost.	Accumulated penalty yardage.

	1	2	3	4	F	
MICHIGAN						
OPPONENT						

FIRST DOWNS:	STATISTICS [OPPONENT]
1 2 3 4 5 6 7 8 9 10 11 12 13 14 15 16 17 18 19 20 21 22 23 24 25 26 27 28 29	

RUSHING:	YARDAGE GAINED	PASSING:

PASSES: 1 2 3 4 5 6 7 8 9 10 11 12 13 14 15 16 17 18 19 20 21 22 23 24 25 26 27 28 29 30 31 32 33 34 35 36 37 38

COMPLETE: 1 2 3 4 5 6 7 8 9 10 11 12 13 14 15 16 17 18 19 20 21 22 23 24 25 26

INCOMPLETE: 1 2 3 4 5 6 7 8 9 10 11 12 13 14 15 16 17 18 19 20 21 22 23 24 25

INTERCEPTED: 1 2 3 4 5 6 7 8 9 10 11 12

FUMBLES	PENALTIES

FIG. 28. WUOM sportscasters are equipped with a mimeographed record sheet which enables them to keep track of the game as it progresses, and to report immediately upon statistics both for the home team (top) and the opponent (lower part of sheet).

the present tense is used to denote action. Instead of saying "Branoff tried to go around right end," he says "Branoff has the ball. He is going around right end." At times the announcer may use the progressive present tense; for instance, a tailback fades back: "Barr is falling back. He is going to pass." But when the man is tackled the tense is changed to the past.

While the announcer is familiar with the plays to be used between teams, he should never get ahead of the play and forecast any type of play because he cannot be absolutely certain just what is going to happen upon the field. His forecast of a pass or a kick, however, will convey to the listener the impression of the eyewitness, and, even if the play is changed, the same suspense is created for the listening rooter as for the fan in the stadium. It is essential that the sports announcer be sure of his facts before he impresses them upon the listener. He may know that a certain formation is used for an end run, and as a result he may start off on a description of the halfback dashing around end, only to find that the ball carrier has discovered an opening and is plunging through center.

Telling what is going to happen has its dangers. Something is likely to go wrong, plans may be changed, or the observer may be deceived. In such cases he must admit that he was wrong in his prediction. Announcers have been severely criticized for frequent inaccuracy in their statements of what is about to happen. But the dramatic value of letting the radio audience share the same speculations as are held by those in actual attendance probably more than makes up for the apparent error The commentator has introduced the element of suspense, and, in addition, the factor of surprise. It is contended that the play which follows is more thrilling to the radio listener by reason of the very fact that he had been misled in his expectations.

The announcer at times, however, will have opportunity for using the future tense. He may go to the point of predicting an action. The truth is that he is not guessing. He prophesies only when quite certain that such action will take place. For instance, he might say, "It looks as though Turley will walk Kaline to get at pitcher Gromek." From the standpoint of dramatic production the prediction possesses an unusual significance. It creates an element of suspense, one of the first essentials of showmanship. It gives the radio listener a feeling of being on the "inside," an intensified interest in what is to follow immediately thereafter. It arouses his curiosity as to the outcome of the predicted play. This practice of preparing the listener for something about to take place, or something which appears likely to take place, is an accurate reflection of what is going on in the minds of the rest of the spectators.

It has been said that sports announcers should be entirely neutral, showing no bias for either team. The danger of this requirement is that it makes the broadcast neutral, with no life, no interest. It is wiser for the announcer to be decidedly biased for both teams. Always give credit where credit is due but never condemn. If a runner is on his way to the goal line and the safety man is easily side-stepped, emphasize the skill used by the runner rather than the failure of the tackler. Every boy on the team has friends or parents whose feelings would be hurt if his poor playing were broadcast. Furthermore, injuries should not be emphasized since this would worry parents and relatives who are listening.

The sports announcer should remember that his listeners are those who wish they might be in the stadium. They want to watch the game, enjoy the crowd, see the color of the event. No one keeps his eyes on the players steadily for 60 minutes. The fan is amused by the antics of cheerleaders, by the activity of the officials; but these interests, while important, are subordinated to the progress of the game. Weather is important only as it affects the play. Distant landscape must not be described with the ball on the 1-yard line.

Announcers believe that their voices must not reflect undue excitement or put in thrills when there are no thrills. The delivery is important but the announcer must remember not to be unfair to his audience—not to be calm and dispassionate in an exciting climax, or to shout about a 1-yard gain in the center of the field.

In the excitement of a play a listener may lose track of the advance of the ball; hence it is frequently good practice when time permits to repeat the essential details of the play. A résumé of the play may be given between halves.

In sports broadcasting, the observer usually works very close to the microphone, his mouth within 4 or 5 inches of the instrument and a little above it. This position enables him to see over the microphone and to shield the instrument with his head and body from the noise of the crowds. As his voice increases in volume, he turns his head, or backs away from the microphone. At a distance, or with his face turned aside, he may be able to put on all the lung power he possesses without danger of ruining the effect. What comes out of the loud-speaker in this case is the sound of a man actually shouting.

A second factor in the creation of an atmosphere of intense action is changing the pitch of the voice. It is quite a natural thing that the announcer should raise the pitch of his voice as well as the volume to express excitement. The listener associates these changes in tone with the cause for them. When he hears a high-pitched voice, he immediately senses excitement. The atmosphere of stress can be supplemented in the use of staccato sentences. Long sentences indicate unhurried preparation and mature consideration; short sentences denote motion and speed, giving the impression that the speaker must hurry to keep pace with the proceedings.

It is desirable to sum up at frequent intervals just what has happened up to that time. This may be done by stating the score, or it may be enlarged to a detailed description. In most sports—baseball, football, boxing, and tennis—there are interludes in which changes are being made in line-ups or in positions on the playing space, time outs, or rest periods. There is opportunity for summing up the situation at such times.

The broadcasting of baseball games appears to the neophyte sports-caster as a job a great deal easier than broadcasting the faster sports of football, basketball, and hockey. But, oddly enough, baseball is some-times one of the most difficult sports to present to the radio listener. And one of the reasons for the difficulty lies in the fact that time is not pressing, whereas, in the faster-moving sports, the announcer has to be with the play every second, literally "spitting out" words as fast as he can articulate them. However, a good baseball announcer is really a "narrator." He makes his delivery slower and creates word pictures for the fan sitting by the radio. Let's take an example: Tippery of Michigan is at bat; there's a man on third base and one out; Tippery hits a long fly ball to left field. It's not enough for the announcer to say, "Tippery hits a long fly ball to left field . . . and . . . it's caught! Here comes Eaddy home with another Michigan run." As you can see, the listener has to fill in a lot of blanks. Now let's take the same situation with the announcer using the "narration" style of delivery. "Tippery swings . . . and there goes a long fly ball out to left field . . . the left fielder is mov-ing back . . . he flips down his sun glasses . . . Eaddy is tagged up at third . . . he'll try to score after the catch . . . there's the put-out in left field . . . and here comes Eaddy racing for home ahead of the throw for another Michigan run." You can see in this instance how a "word picture" is created for the listener, and he can visualize the par-ticular play almost as if he were seeing it with his own eyes. Further-more, the announcer should give frequent recaps of scoring, naming each team and its score at every opportunity.

TELEVISED SPORTS

The coverage of sports events on television typifies the whole field of remote telecasts. The radio remote has become a simple task. Tele-phone lines are nearly always available to feed the program back to the station. A remote amplifier and a microphone constitute the basic equipment. In television, none of this is true. Telephone lines will handle the audio but will not take care of the video signal. A whole truckload of equipment must be transported to the remote site. A very sizable crew must be on hand hours, and sometimes days, before the broadcast goes on. Television remotes are complicated and expensive.

Among the popular sports boxing, wrestling, football, basketball, baseball, hockey, golf, tennis, swimming, racing, and bowling have all been televised successfully. The impetus given professional wrestling by television is well known. Boxing, too, has hit its golden age, at least monetarily if not quality-wise, since it went on television. Some might argue whether wrestling and boxing are still sports, but, in any event, they do belong in our discussion of televised sports. The potential effect of television on football was clearly illustrated by the rigid N.C.A.A. policy of strictly controlled telecasts of college football. Certainly, next to actual attendance, a sport on television is the most rewarding experience. In some sports, like boxing, where the action is concentrated in a small area, the TV fans have a better view than the great majority of those actually attending. There are some Sunday morning quarterbacks who think they see more football on TV than they do a quarter of a mile up in a large stadium. Despite the appeal of a big sporting event on TV, to many there is no substitute for attendance at the event itself, with all of the atmosphere and color of the excited crowd. The ball parks, gymnasiums, and the stadia are in no danger of replacement by the TV camera.

Preparing for the Television Remote

The first requirement for televising a sporting event is to have a director who knows the sport to be covered. The camera positions, and other details of the coverage, must be planned to present the sport accurately and as realistically as possible. Assuming, then, that the person doing the planning has a working knowledge of the sport to be covered, he is ready to go to the site to survey the situation. If he has been in television for more than a day or two he will take a competent engineer with him. If his station does remotes often he will probably have a complete check list to make certain that nothing is overlooked. There are many things to be checked: camera positions, location of the mobile unit, adequate source of electrical power, location of the announcer, how cables can be run to the cameras, audio lines, lenses that will be needed, amount of available light and the direction of light if the event is outdoors, and—frequently the worst problem of all—where to put the microwave gear. Once it is decided that the event can be adequately covered, there remains the problem of getting the video signal back to

FIG. 29. Placement of cameras on second deck at Comiskey Park (Chicago) for WGN–TV telecasts of White Sox baseball games. Note use of external sight on foreground camera, and use of zoomar on the rear camera.

the station. The easiest answer, for the station, is to hire A.T. & T. to provide the video feed. Many stations, however, have found it more economical to use their own microwave equipment. In either case, the microwave transmitter dish must be located where it will have a line-of-sight shot to the station or transmitter. Then a coaxial video cable must be run from the truck to this transmitter.

The final arrangements for a remote pickup are always a compromise between what the station would like to have and what the operators of the event decide is feasible. There are usually good reasons why a camera can be placed in one place and not another. It may interfere with the view of too many fans. There may not be any structure capable of holding the camera and the operator. TV stations never have a complete carte blanche to do as they please. They settle for the best setup that can be made under the existing circumstances.

In setting up the plan for a remote, the engineering department and the program department have to work hand in hand. The arrangement must be capable of working from the technical standpoint, and this is not always easy to achieve. At the same time, the cameras must be located in positions, and equipped with lenses, that will allow the event to be adequately covered. This implies that the director has a plan for the coverage in mind right from the outset.

This plan cannot remain the sole property of the director. Everyone on the crew must be thoroughly familiar with it. For an example, take a baseball game. There is a runner on first base. We watch the pitcher work on the batter and occasionally check the runner at first. The count works its way to two balls and two strikes. On the next pitch the batter hits a sharp grounder to the shortstop. He fields the ball, fires it to second, and the second baseman fires it to first base for a double play. The question is, how do you cover the action? Think first of all about how much time you have between the crack of the bat on the baseball and the throw to first ending the play. Clearly there isn't enough time for the director to make a decision and to relay this to the cameramen. The plan is prearranged, and everyone follows the plan automatically. The only other choice is to stay on an extremely wide shot for the entire game, and this is completely unacceptable. This same situation exists in all sports. TV coverage is not a catch-as-catch-can situation. A definite plan, taking into account all of the things that can happen, is the only method that will insure adequate coverage.

The Coverage

Every event, in every different location, presents special problems for the TV crew. It is, therefore, impossible to cover every possible collection of circumstances. Furthermore, space in a book of this type doesn't

Fig. 30. WGN–TV (Chicago) baseball remote. Note side-by-side camera positions in booth with the announcer.

permit detailed coverage of all aspects of TV production. For a more comprehensive discussion of television remotes the reader is urged to examine the chapter on this subject in *Techniques of Television Production* by Rudy Bretz (McGraw-Hill). This outstanding book will supply many of the details that must be omitted from this handbook.

The first problem encountered in covering a sports event on television is the necessary dispersal of the crew. The cameramen are located at the

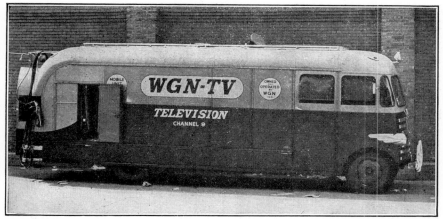

Fig. 31. WGN–TV, Chicago, mobile unit parked outside of Comiskey Park, home of the White Sox.

Fig. 32. Interior of WGN–TV remote mobile unit. In the foreground, technical director (switcher) position, and audio engineer position.

best possible positions for covering the event. The announcer is at another location where he can view all of the proceedings. The mobile unit, which serves as the control room on a remote, is located at another point, usually just outside the stadium or gym. The director works from inside the truck, and his only view is through the camera monitors. The microwave gear is at still another point. All of these widely-spread people must be coordinated into split-second production. A dependable intercom system becomes a necessity. The director must give his instructions clearly and without hesitation. The cameramen must be alert to what is happening and tell the director if something is going on which he should know about but can't see. A remote crew becomes a highly efficient team.

BOXING OR WRESTLING

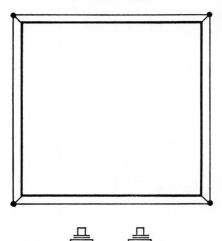

Fig. 33. Camera positions for covering boxing or wrestling bouts.

Some of the other basic problems can best be illustrated by brief discussions of the coverage of several popular sports.

Perhaps the easiest sports remotes are wrestling and boxing. Here the action is concentrated in the area of the ring. Usually, two cameras will do a very satisfactory job. They must have a clear shot of the ring area, which invariably means that they will need to be elevated so that spectators' heads will not get in the picture. The general plan would involve a medium long shot and a medium close-up. The director could then cut back and forth between these shots as the situation demanded. He is always protected because he has the medium long shot to cut to if the action gets more spread out and will not fit into the closer shot. In all sports the audience wants to see the things that are important. So, the moving of the contestants, footwork, etc., should be seen most of the time. Excessive use of close-ups will result in inadequate coverage because they won't show all of the important details. Secondary requirements would include shots of the corners for use between rounds, the referee, and the ring announcer.

It is clear that in boxing and wrestling, as it is in all TV remotes, care must be taken not to disorient the viewer. For instance, if we were to put a camera on sides of the ring opposite each other, and then were to cut from one to the other, what would the result be? Clearly the positions would be reversed. To the viewer we have suddenly turned the directions 180 degrees. This is extremely confusing and can only be condemned as poor planning. For ring sports, it is generally best to keep the two cameras fairly close to each other.

BASKETBALL

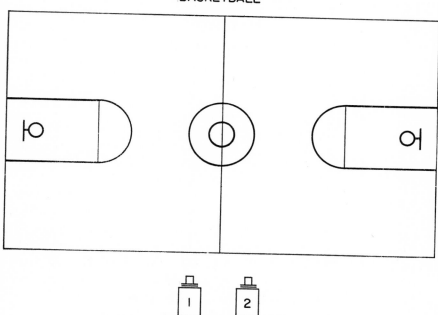

Fig. 34. Camera positions for covering basketball.

In basketball, a different problem is encountered. Here the action moves rapidly from one end of the court to the other. We must be able to see the offensive and defensive plays form as the action moves toward a basket. We should be able to follow the ball as it is passed from player to player. We should see the shots at the basket and whether or not they go through the hoop. This coverage should be intercut with closer shots of players dribbling, guarding, etc. Basketball can be handled quite well from a point near the center line and, if possible, some distance back from the sideline, and slightly elevated. Two cameras placed side by side will be able to cover all essential play. Again care must be taken to avoid excessively radical shifts in angle when cutting from camera to camera. The system outlined above will avoid this disorientation. Some stations use a third camera on the floor for occasional dramatic shots, but such a camera cannot add to the essential coverage of the game. Coverage of a basketball game is not complete unless one camera can get a clear shot of the scoreboard. The score changes rapidly in basketball, and toward the end of a period, or at the end of the game, time remaining is frequently of the essence. The director must be able to flash the scoreboard on whenever it is called for.

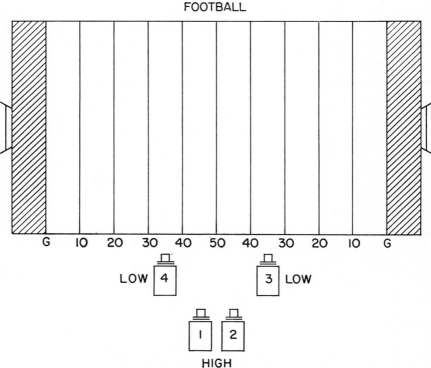

Fig. 35. Camera positions for covering football.

Football is fairly well concentrated except for long pass plays, punts, and kickoffs. Two cameras along the 50-yard line and elevated will provide excellent coverage. This is especially true if a vari-focal, or zoom, camera lens is available. Because of physical limitations these cameras are normally placed in or on top of the press box. This really makes for a sharper angle than would be desired, but serves very well if a lower angle is impossible. Some network crews use two additional cameras placed at the 35- or 40-yard lines and from a lower angle. This is nice if the equipment and crew are available, but two cameras will provide good coverage of a football game. Of course, the cameras must be on the same side of the field to avoid any change in direction when cutting. Actually, the basic coverage of the action can be handled on one camera with a zoom-type lens, if the camera operator is sufficiently skilled. By zooming in and out he can stay with the play almost all the way. The second camera is used primarily for cut-in shots, huddles, cheers, and perhaps the widespread formations such as the kickoff. In football, probably more than in other sports, the color, the crowd, the cheers, and similar game-related activities are extremely important. The director's plan should include as much of this spectacle as possible.

BASEBALL

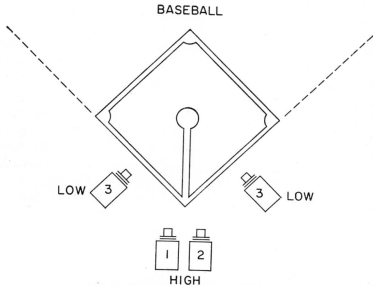

FIG. 36. Camera positions for covering baseball.

Baseball is, without question, the most difficult game to televise. The action is spread out over an enormous area. There are long periods of relative inactivity alternating with bursts of lightning-fast action. A high percentage of the game time involves only the pitcher, the catcher, the batter and the umpire. A heavy share of the remaining time involves the play at first base. Yet, anywhere in the infield or the outfield might be the location of the crucial play of the game. It is generally agreed that there needs to be one camera behind home plate that will get a good shot of the pitcher, catcher, batter, and umpire. Usually this camera is a little bit to one side or the other of the plate, but a straight line shot is good if a camera position can be found. Practice indicates that the second camera is placed beside the first. There is no agreement on a third camera. Some stations put one down the line toward first and try to get it on a lower angle than the first two. Some have a third camera at a ground level for dramatic shots of the batter, the pitcher, baserunner, etc. The location of a third camera can only be determined at a given ballpark. Each park has some peculiarities that make some positions impossible, and others entirely acceptable. The important thing in baseball is to get the two primary cameras situated, and then to make a precise and comprehensive plan to cover the game. This plan must be known by all of the crew, and they must be rehearsed in it to the point where they will automatically provide the necessary shots. Without this plan, coverage of baseball on television is impossible.

In all sports the director must remember that his job is to provide the audience with the essential information. The coverage of the game is the important thing. This is not the opportunity for creative and dramatic camera work. The viewer wants to see the game. The director's job is to analyze the important features of the particular game and then to provide the means for showing them. After a director has been at sports remotes for some time it is likely he will become bored by the same old routine over and over. The tendency to change and be creative in an effort to overcome this boredom must be resisted. The only reason to change is if something is thought of to make the coverage more complete. The viewer is not interested in the director's mental state, he only wants to see as much of the action as possible.

The TV Sports Announcer

The announcer for a TV sportscast is provided with a location similar to that afforded the radio announcer. He usually has a vantage point where he can see all of the action. He also is provided with a TV monitor so that he will always know what picture is being fed to the audience. The TV announcer must get accustomed to watching both the live action and the TV screen. Sometimes the director will call for the cameras to follow the announcer's lead, because he can see the whole field of action while the director sees only what is on his monitors. The announcer might say, "there's a right-hander warming up in the bull pen." On this cue the director will try to get a shot of the bull pen. At other times the announcer should follow the action on the screen and refer to it. He will make references to the screen such as, "that was so-and-so that you just saw make the key block," or "that man on the left of your picture is the head iinesman." The exact working relationship between an-

Fig. 37. Jack Brickhouse, WGN–TV sports announcer, in booth at Wrigley Field, with earphones, is in touch with remote crew in mobile truck and cameramen on intercom system. Brickhouse has announced more than 1000 televised major league games.

nouncer and cameras must be evolved for each crew. A few times working together will result in coordination between the two.

From a completely objective point of view, it would be supposed that the TV sports announcer would say considerably less than the radio announcer, because the audience can see most of the action, and there is little point in the announcer trying to describe what they can see. This isn't the case, however. Many TV announcers have come from radio, and certainly the majority of viewers are ex-radio listeners. The truth is that many TV sportscasters talk much more than is necessary, and for many people more than is desirable.

The TV announcer's job is to amplify and extend the video coverage. He can explain things that the audience may not know. He can keep the audience posted on the factual information accompanying the game, such as the score, the outs, the balls and strikes, the yardage, time remaining, etc. He can add information on the players, coaches, teams, and officials. He can explain the rulings of the officials. He can call attention to good or poor plays, or other things of interest. In short, he can add those things which the audience isn't apt to see, or might not understand, or can't find out from watching. There is little to be gained from the usual kind of coverage provided in baseball: "there's the stretch . . . and the pitch. It's low and outside for ball two." The viewer can see the pitcher wind up and throw the ball. Why shouldn't the TV announcer simply say "that pitch was low and outside for ball two," or just "low and outside for ball two." The TV announcer can also work in an easier style than can the radio announcer. The excitement is right there for the audience to see, it isn't necessary for the announcer to generate it. He should reflect the mood of the moment rather than create it.

Accuracy is exceedingly important to the TV announcer. He cannot be behind the action, and he can't afford many miscalls. His sins are there for all to see. Inaccuracies, excessive chatter, and artificial enthusiasm by the TV announcer can only detract from the visual coverage.

CHAPTER ELEVEN

UNWRITTEN TALK PROGRAMS

I have a feeling that impromptu and extempore speaking are neglected by the student of broadcasting, as well as by the teacher. One of the outstanding news commentators visited my classes and pointed out that there are many programs being presented which require the ability to speak spontaneously. Such programs as the round table, forum, interview, man-on-the-street, disc jockey, on-the-spot broadcasts, and some of the news-commentary programs require the broadcaster to be a fluent and spontaneous speaker. The art of announcing has become so standardized that at present one small bit of impromptu radio speech can be detected and frequently is a welcome relief if well done.

For these types of program a good vocabulary of descriptive words, particularly action verbs, adverbs, and nouns is essential. The impromptu speaker must have a good cultural background, for he is not forgiven for mistakes in grammar, pronunciation, or diction. The speaker in every instance is required to have excellent powers of observation, to be able to see ahead while he is talking about something that he has previously observed. In too many instances the broadcaster is inclined to "hem and haw" while he is groping for a word that he feels will convey the correct impression to the listener. In such unprepared programs there must be no dead air, although brief pauses undoubtedly will make the material sound more conversational. These pauses will be shorter than they would be if the speaker were conversing with a visible audience. Quickness in thought and expression are equally vital. Perhaps one of the best practices to use in the preparation for this type of broadcasting is talking to oneself, particularly describing things that are being seen.

Another requirement for such extempore and impromptu programs is an ability to time the material to be presented. The program will run for a definite period, and the broadcaster must time himself so that he will have rounded out his material, summarized if necessary, and come to a satisfactory conclusion at the second that he goes off the air. I place my students before the microphone with one of those 3-minute glasses made for the timing of boiling eggs and tell them they are to talk until the sand has dropped to the last grain into the lower chamber and no longer.

One of the faults evident in the impromptu speech of the novice is the repetition of certain phrases and words that pierce the ear of the listener. Some speakers, masters of ceremonies, man-on-the-street interviewers, are inclined to start their sentences with an ejaculation or connective, in most instances "Ah," because they have not definitely formulated ideas about what they intend to say. It is much wiser to be silent for an instant while the sentence, expression, or thought is developed. Possibly good experience in smooth delivery can be obtained by the practice of dictating to a stenographer.

If the program is a commercial one, the announcer is constantly aware of the fact that he must smoothly lead into the commercial announcement from his impromptu speech. Many masters of ceremonies have before them a page or two from a scrapbook in which they have pasted short stories or sayings which they hope will fit into their program.

Public Events; Special Features

Announcers are frequently sent out upon remote-control pickups when the station manager feels that public interest in the event is adequate (Fig. 38). From the skies the announcer will give a running account of a trip in an airplane or dirigible; from the depths of the sea his voice will come from a submarine. He describes vividly a flood from the banks of a raging river which furnishes sound effects, or from the shore of the sea he may bring all the thrill of a rescue from a burning ocean liner. Listeners can hear the crackle of flames and imagine the smell of smoke as the announcer carries his mike close to a burning building; they hear the bands and tramp of feet as a parade passes by a microphone in the reviewing stand. These announcers must have eyes that see what the public will be interested in, vocabularies that contain the most vivid and concise descriptive words, and tongues that wag conversationally and constantly. Such announcers experience all the excitement that comes to the newspaper reporter, they face danger, they must be alert to act in emergencies. It is their job to induce public characters to speak to the mike, to obtain the best placement for their equipment, and to satisfy the endless curiosity of the listener. These announcers work without manuscript, although they may have notes which will give them facts that are pertinent to their broadcast. They are the war correspondents of the radio and consequently must not only have all the qualities of a good announcer and of an excellent reporter, but must have a physique

FIG. 38. Remote amplifier Collins Type 12Z, used for remote pickups where there is no permanent installation. (*Collins Radio Company.*)

that will stand up under the strain and under the conditions in which they work.

Round Table

Since it is the aim of the radio program containing information to come into the home in the form of conversation, it is a good idea to project more than one person into the living room of the listener to discuss problems of the day. The radio listener cannot talk back but he finds that the radio discussion is more natural if there is a give and take of opinion by a group of radio speakers. This type of broadcast is the round-table discussion. Probably the outstanding example of the round table is that conducted by the University of Chicago.

The purpose in these spontaneous discussions is to permit the exchange of ideas, to attempt to arrive at some solution of a problem, and to avoid the formality of a lecture by using conversation. For some topics it is wiser to start the listener thinking, without arriving at a conclusion for him on such programs, by merely fading out the speakers, leaving the idea dangling before the listener. In order that this conversation may be natural, those who are participating in the round table do not prepare their parts in written form but merely outline the course of the discussion and the attitude that each participant will adopt during the period of the round table. In order to avoid any hesitation or divergence from the topic being discussed, the program must be discussed and an outline constructed with various parts assigned. The introduction may be written by the leader of the round table; and the outline showing the various subtopics, together with the individuals who will take up these subtopics, is in written form before the participants as they sit down at their round table. In order to observe the time limitation, it is advisable to show in this outline the time that is to be allotted to a discussion of each of the points. The leader also may have his summary written out, which is prepared after the rehearsal.

The conversational program may advantageously become a written program before it goes on the air. Participants go through the routine round-table procedure just as if they were to be on the air. However, instead of presenting their talk for air, it is taken down by a stenotypist. They are then given opportunity to look over the copy, change it to suit their best judgment, and go on the air with a script discussion program. By starting with this conversational basis, they are enabled to overcome some of the difficulties of a writing style which is quite often wooden and ineffective for broadcasting. This format is particularly appropriate for medical and scientific topics.

Usually three people will participate in a round-table discussion. Two of these will be experts holding different views or attacking the problem from different viewpoints. The third should be an intelligent layman desirous of information and questioning the opinions of the two experts. It is advisable to identify the various speakers at the very beginning of the discussion. Their questions and comments should also give their attitudes toward the topic. In order that their voices may be impressed upon the listener, they should be addressed by name for the first few minutes of the discussion. This requires a variety in the form of salutation in order that the discussion may sound conversational. The round table is designed to present clashes of opinion and to bring out different points of view, and yet it must arrive at some conclusion. It must not be merely talk but must be organized skillfully before the program starts. There cannot be too detailed discussion of any subtopic, and, while an individual may be assigned a subtopic in the outline, there is no reason for him to monopolize the discussion. It is incumbent upon the person to whom the subtopic has been assigned to see that there are no pauses while that topic is being discussed. In order to keep up the spontaneity of the conversation, the leader should know the attitude of the various participants and point to one or to the other when he desires an opinion concerning a point raised. In order to make for the greatest realism, the expression of personal opinion should not be hampered. In order that the listener may gain the impression that he is to listen to a conversation, the program may be faded in. This requires the speakers to be discussing some unimportant topic as their voices gradually become audible.

Some "do's and don'ts" for round-table panelists are:

1. Points made with enumeration—"1–2–3"—are far more listenable than three points made one after the other without such enumeration.

2. Everybody should participate. The program time should be balanced equally among the participants. Don't ever talk the ears off the other speakers, but on the other extreme don't be reticent!

3. Mention the names of fellow-participants whenever you speak, and have a uniform method of identification.

4. Address other participants directly, rather than throw an idea into thin air, or pick up another speaker's point without attributing it to him. Frequently a hesitant speaker may be drawn into the discussion in this way, or the conversation may be steered away from a speaker who is dominating the microphone. It is one of the surest ways of pinning a person down to an answer.

5. Normal conversation is the ideal pattern for a Round Table—normal conversation with normal interruptions, normal jokes and laughter, normal asides. Give your fellow-participants an opportunity to come in and break up your remarks. Not only do long speeches destroy the feeling of informality and spontaneity of the Round Table, but listeners do not have the benefit of a critical examination of each point in the argument.

6. Elbows on the table, please! For in that way the producer may be sure that each participant is the same distance from the microphone and, further, that he stays that distance throughout the broadcast! Don't tilt forward—or your voice will roar like Niagara! Don't lean back—or your voice will resemble a hoarse cry from the stadium bleachers!

7. Jot down facts, figures, and quotes on small cards for possible use on the air.

8. How the broadcast time should be apportioned will be decided before the broadcast. Once the time is apportioned—stick to it. Watch the studio clock and observe how much discussion time remains.

9. Emphasize your right to speak as an expert! Don't be modest! Speakers should document the authority of their colleagues; it is desirable for speakers to personalize their authority.

10. Personalization is always first-rate on the Round Table. You'll do more to hold the attention of listeners, authorize your remarks, and add life to the discussion by referring to specific things you, yourself, have seen or done, or to some piece of information you have obtained or have heard at firsthand.

11. Talk to the listener—as well as your fellow-participants. You know that he's listening. And he'll enjoy listening the more if you occasionally acknowledge his presence. Remember that you are speaking not to a large audience in an auditorium but to individual listeners in their homes. A direct candid conversational approach is best.

12. Identification of the topic is very necessary three or four times during the broadcast. Many listeners tune in after the opening announcement.

13. Human interest must be emphasized to make the problem one of personal importance to the listener; answer the questions of the public. Participants should try to answer the normal questions of the average listener.

14. Humorous stories and anecdotes often add a friendly tone to the discussion and succeed in making serious points too! And if what a fellow-participant says is funny, laugh. If it isn't, don't hesitate to say so—even that's funny. Whatever happens, be natural.

15. Controversy may heighten the listeners' interest in the discussion when it serves to emphasize fundamental arguments on both sides of a dispute. But controversy on minor points annoys rather than interests listeners. If you disagree with a statement, don't hesitate to say so, and state your reasons clearly. In building your case, don't be timid—speak out for your point of view. Too often participants are overpolite.

16. Avoid pauses by always being on your toes—you may have the "ball" tossed into your lap when you least expect it. Snapping in on the heels of another speaker adds to the pace and spontaneity of the discussion.

17. Don't all speak at once. When you wish to interrupt, be sure that the other speaker has completed the expression of his idea.

Each round-table group may adopt its own signals to be used to indicate the procedure of its discussion. A raised finger is a sign that the person desires to speak on the topic, and courtesy demands that he be given an opportunity. The leader may indicate that he desires an opinion from a member by pointing his finger at that person. The palm of a hand toward a speaker indicates that he should cut his discussion short. The announcer of the program should inform the group by means of some sign when the time is drawing short so that they can work to a conclusion. The conversation may, by its phraseology, indicate that one of the participants should come in and discuss a point. The great problem of this type of broadcast is the possibility of vague, aimless talk which serves only to confuse and bore listeners, and the solution of this problem is to have competent people who are sure of themselves and of their subject and who are willing to express forceful opinions.

It is well to develop certain personalities if the round table is to be a continuing program, to retain at least the leader for the entire series, and to bring back speakers frequently to the radio ears. The topics that may be discussed include problems of the day in politics, economics, literature, education, or religion.

Radio Interviews

The radio public is interested in interviews because of the human instinct to eavesdrop upon the thoughts of others. In fact, it is not essential that the interviewee be a celebrity, for the radio listener finds interesting the comments that are given by the man-in-the-street who is stopped by an inquiring reporter. The interviewer must have an idea of what the average listener would himself like to ask the individual. He must have natural curiosity and should visualize himself as the average listener.

Interviews are never rehearsed in advance of the broadcast. The interviewee is asked to suggest certain questions that he would be willing to discuss, but it makes for greater interest and spontaneity if the questioner does not know the inquiries in advance. The interrogator, however, must use good judgment and diplomacy in the selection. It is good practice to sit down with the person to be interviewed at a table upon which there is a microphone and talk with him in advance of the program in order to get him into the conversational mood and to ascertain his attitudes. This puts him at ease and eliminates the probability of "mike fright." When the broadcast starts, the interviewer will introduce the victim and ask questions, which will also tend to introduce him. It is not a bad plan to ask some rather light, frivolous questions that may start the program with a spurt of humor, for this puts the interviewee at ease and pleases the listener. It is essential that there be no pauses of any length; consequently the person who is doing the interviewing must be alert to discover leads in the answers he receives. Probably the first few minutes of the interview will be devoted to less serious discussion in order to brighten the subject and to encourage the interviewee to articulate comfortably. There is a tendency to allow the interview to become argumentative, but this should be avoided because it makes the interviewer express his ideas, which are not of importance. The interviewer must remember that he is not interviewing himself. His job is to ask stimulating questions, not to supply the answers; to bring out the interviewee's personality, not his own. Do not try to influence the speaker by leading questions. The man who is important enough to be interviewed has something interesting enough to appeal to the listener. Try to dig down and disclose the person off guard; by that it is meant that there should be revelation but not exposure. To be good at the radio interview, the announcer must have a rather general knowledge so that he may ask intelligent questions in the field of the speaker's interest. Most of the questions should be of such nature as to require more than "yes" or "no" answers. However, the interviewee should not be forced to give too lengthy a reply because the radio listener will be inclined to think that it is a prepared speech and not an interview. It is permissible for the announcer to raise his hand and interrupt the speaker if he gets started on an oration. If some definite topic is to be discussed, the questioner must strive to keep the speaker talking about the topic and lead him back to the subject if necessary. This type of broadcast must be natural and conversational. Mild laughter may be heard but it is inadvisable for the announcer to laugh too heartily at his own comments. Repetition in the style of questions should be avoided, such as starting questions with the word "Well" or using "I see" after each answer.

People who are well informed on special topics and who are close to their subjects are inclined to overlook the interest of the public. This form of broadcast gives an opportunity to the interviewer to bring out points of general interest which might be overlooked by the specialist himself. Long-winded generalization makes the interview a monologue; the skillful interviewer avoids this by deftly breaking in to demand particulars, concrete details, and answers to questions which will require decisive comments, or he may start the discussion on a new or more pertinent tack.

Other types of impromptu or extempore programs which are decidedly popular at the present time are the "Forum," and the "Town Meeting of the Air." Two factors contribute to the popularity of these programs: (1) the radio audience enjoys a dramatic verbal combat between personages or individuals; and (2) the majority of such programs are concerned with highly controversial topics. In many instances, the audience is permitted to inject questions; thus a cross section of the American public is introduced as interviewers.

Much of the success depends upon the ability of the chairman, who steers the discussion and must set the pace. He must be alert, well versed in the topic that is slated for discussion, witty, and diplomatic. Equally important are the participants, for if they do not enter into the spirit of the program their answers can be flat and uninteresting, regardless of their knowledge. Care should be taken that there is no overlapping of voices. Radio is a great teacher of manners, for it insists that no person shall start to talk until the other person has completed his speech. The only times that a chairman is permitted to interrupt the speaker are when he sees that the time limit is being reached, when the interviewee or speaker has ventured upon a topic which is dangerous, or when the participant shows evidence of giving a monologue.

Probably the most successful ad-lib programs are the panel and the quiz shows. These may be of either a serious or an amusing nature. The quiz shows generally have a panel of four: (1) an individual who is intent upon finding the correct answer, (2) a serious and determined straight man, (3) a comic who enlivens the program but seldom finds the answer, and (4) a well-known personality who slows down the pace of the quiz but is more intent upon light personal comments. There is also the moderator, who can control the panel members, maintain the fast-moving pace, and cope with any unexpected situation. Panel members do a great deal of preparatory research in the fields to be discussed upon the program, searching magazines, trade papers, and the news for topics that may arise. Panel members must listen carefully to avoid repetition and to find a possible lead for a humorous remark or a clue to the solution of the problem presented (many such clues come from the studio-audience reactions). The start of such a program must be entertaining and interesting; once the program is started the mood is easy to sustain.

The Television Talk Program

Many of the common, informal talk programs that were born in radio have been carried over into television. If anything, they are even more popular than they were on radio. This, very likely, is due to the fact that we can see the people, so they become more real. There is a widespread and genuine interest in people, and when they become real personalities this interest is intensified.

The nature of the informal talk program has not changed by being put on television. Most of the problems involved and the principles followed in radio are likewise applicable to television. To the radio technique must be added attention to the visual details: the appearance and dress of the participants, the ability to look natural as well as sound natural, the avoidance of annoying mannerisms, and the ability to move with grace and dignity.

Experience seems to indicate that the informal talk program is easier to do on television than on radio. Participants are usually arranged in a more lifelike situation. Less attention to the impersonal microphone is required. There is no necessity to avoid natural pauses. When you see people talking, the inevitable hesitations, pauses for thinking, and similar breaks seem natural and lifelike, rather than like gaping holes as they do in radio. Gestures, business, and facial expressions can be used to emphasize what is said. All of these things together tend to put people at ease sooner, and to result in a more genuine process of communication. Yet, the video medium is not all advantage. It is even more necessary in television than in radio that people listen to each other and answer each other. The most common fault in beginning interviewers is that they don't really listen to what the other person says. They are thinking about the next question, or something else only remotely connected with what is going on. Such a technique is bad on radio; on television it is murder! Talk between two or more people is a form of communication, and to communicate the participants must listen to the other people and respond to what they say. This requires some mental activity. If this genuine give and take of conversation isn't present on TV, it is as readily apparent as the loss of the picture on the receiver.

The same types of informal talk programs appear on television and radio. There are forums, quiz programs, interviews, and panel shows. Some of these programs are among the most popular on TV. Television has developed to a fine art one type of informal talk program that can only be classed with that venerable breed of drama known as the "tear jerker." Such programs use the unrehearsed talk formula to wring the hearts and tear ducts of the audience. Strange it may be, but people love it.

It is probably safe to say that the informal talk program will always be popular on television. When well planned, and with a workable format, it is popular, easy to do, and is the real luxury of TV production —a low-budget show. People can't very well read scripts on TV. Programs requiring memorization and a lot of rehearsal are extremely expensive. The informal talk program offers one solution to the problem of programs that sponsors with small budgets can afford. This emphasizes the point made at the opening of this chapter. Students planning a career in radio and television need all of the experience they can get at impromptu or extemporaneous speaking.

CHAPTER TWELVE

PREPARING THE BROADCAST ADDRESS

THE RADIO ADDRESS

Doctor, lawyer, merchant, chief (of police or fire department), preacher, teacher, politician—everyone, in brief, is likely to be called upon to speak to the radio audience today. Radio speaking is a one-way conversation with everyone (in the radio audience) as an individual. The radio conversationalist must not be a bore, he must have interesting material to discuss, he must present it in an attractive way, and his personality must be pleasantly projected to the distant listener. An examination of the best radio speakers shows that they have observed the interesting things in life and have developed what has been described by one writer as the "daily-theme eye." The majority have "done things," have lived lives teeming with interest or excitement, and consequently have become engaging conversationalists. They have discovered human interests and are wise in their judgment of proprieties and public appeal. A drab personality is wearying to the dial.

As the radio speaker has been introduced into the home by the announcer, it is unnecessary for him to open with any salutation; his task is to prove himself to be immediately an interesting, bright, and courteous guest. A pertinent anecdote that will lead quickly into the subject, which has been wisely chosen to interest the majority of average listeners, forms an excellent introduction. The speaker who uses homely expressions and introduces into his broadcast illustrations drawn from everyday life is much more likely to reach the intelligence of his listeners.

The "great speaker," the classroom lecturer, and the spellbinder politician have no place in the living room of the home. The radio talk must interweave information and human interest. Classroom methods are taboo on the air. Education must be adapted to radio, not radio to education. It is essential that the writer of a radio address forget textbooks, auditorium audiences, and congregations and think more in terms of human interest. Relate the subject to the listener, his life, his pocketbook, his everyday realities. The choice of a subject is of primary importance in order to compete with the entertainment on a neighboring kilocycle.

Make it easy for the listener to follow your trend of thought by carefully organizing the talk. Consider first the limited time on the air allotted to you and select a topic that can be adequately treated in that period. You will speak about 140 words a minute. How many minutes have you in the clear? Do not try to crowd too much into the ears and minds of your listeners. Do not depend upon your listener to fill in any gaps. Idea should follow idea with a naturalness that makes for clear understanding.

A good formula for the organization of the radio talk is as follows:

1. An interest-getting opening paragraph (a quip, wisecrack, or an anecdote; he may start with a reference to something that is certain to be in the foreground of the thinking of most of his listeners and work from that into the theme of his talk).
2. A summary of the points the talk is going to cover.
3. A swift, interesting development of the summary outline.
4. A final summary to clinch the points in the minds of the listeners.
5. A direction to the listeners interested in adopting the practice the talk has urged, telling them where to acquire further information.

The most difficult part of the radio address is the opening sentence. I have often read over radio lectures and picked out a sentence containing an important statement, a surprising fact, or a charming rhythm and transferred this sentence to the opening.

Although writing for the radio uses the same general forms and is governed by the same general rules of grammar and construction that govern writing for print, language—to be thoroughly successful when broadcast by radio—has certain specific requirements not necessarily met by the printed word. It is true that good stories, articles, and poetry written for print may prove to be good broadcasting material. Their success is not necessarily due to the fact that they read well from print, but to the fact that they happen also to fulfill the requirements of radio.

The first major problem of the writer for radio is the same as that of any writer—communication. Thus the first requirement is to make the ideas understandable to the audience. Whether the purpose is to instruct, to persuade, or to entertain, the writer must use language within the comprehension of his audience; he must explain new things in terms of old. But there is a fundamental difference between the relation of the radio writer to his audience and the relation of the writer of material for print to his readers. The words of the author who writes for print are a permanent record before the reader; the words of the radio writer fall on the ears of his listener and, unless they make an impression immediately, they are lost. Because he must make his entire impression on the audience through the sense of hearing, the radio writer must be more careful than any other to write in terms understandable to the audience and to make his sentences as clear as possible. A reader in doubt as to the meaning of a word usually can find the meaning in a dictionary without too much inconvenience. If he misses the point of a sentence, he can reread it as many times as are necessary. If he forgets a statement having some bearing on a later part of the paper, he can refer back to it as often as he wishes. The person listening to a speech cannot stop to look up unfamiliar words without danger of losing part of the speech. And if he does not understand every sentence as the speaker utters it, he immediately loses the continuity of the talk, and the purpose of the speech is defeated.

Vocabulary

Edgar Dale, in an article entitled "Vocabulary Level of Radio Addresses," reports the results of an investigation conducted with speeches that were presented over the Ohio School of the Air and The American School of the Air, especially for school children. The investigation involved a study of the words used by the speakers to determine how many of them the listening students did not know. After the speeches were finished, Mr. Dale selected the words that might possibly give some difficulty and asked the children to indicate which ones they could not define. In one instance he found that 12 per cent of the words were unknown to 29 per cent of the pupils. Many of the words unknown were the verbs and keywords of the sentences; among them were words like *aspire, attain, concentrate,* and *abstain.* Others which should have been easily recognized by the speakers themselves as outside the scope of grammar school pupils were *feasibility, ramifications, amenable,* and *forecasting.* Needless to say, much of a speech employing words of this type passed over the heads of the audience. Mr. Dale found, on the other hand, that the speaker who was voted by teachers as the most successful to broadcast in the Ohio School of the Air used in a speech of 1950 words only 10 words not known to 25 per cent of the children. It is interesting to note also that every one of these 10 words was a geographical term, the acquisition of which was in part the purpose of the speech. When asked how he went about writing his speech, the speaker accounted for his success by explaining that he took particular care in selecting words that would be within the scope of the listeners. Whenever he was in doubt as to the wisdom of using a particular word, he referred to Thorndike's *Teachers' Word Book,* which lists some 20,000 words and classifies them according to the ability of children of different ages to understand them.

This experiment, it is true, was carried on in a special field of radio broadcasting in which simplicity was absolutely necessary. However, the principle behind it is applicable to the general field of radio. For, although the audience may not be composed of children, the problem of the vocabulary level still remains. Indeed, there is the added problem of adjusting the vocabulary to a heterogeneous audience. There may be educated and uneducated people, old and young people, sophisticates from metropolitan districts and innocents from the backwoods in the audience; the writer of radio speeches must write for all of them. On special occasions, when a speech is directed toward a specific audience, the writer can have some definite idea of its educational and cultural background and adjust his vocabulary accordingly. But the majority of speeches are made under the assumption that anyone within range of a radio-receiving set can listen and understand; consequently the best answer to the question of vocabulary level for radio speeches is, aim them at the average radio listener. Thorndike places the average American intelligence at fourteen years. The radio writer will do well to use in his speeches for a general audience only those words familiar to the average high school pupil. Thorndike's book is probably the most reliable source for determining what words can be included in the list.

Fully as disconcerting to the audience as the use of unfamiliar words is the use of allusions to persons and events about which listeners have no knowledge. If the speaker is sure his audience is made up of college graduates, he can reasonably assume a knowledge of history and literature, but, if his speech is directed toward a general audience, he must explain most of the allusions he makes to things not immediately in the experience of the audience.

Sentences

The problem of making the radio speech understandable to the audience is not entirely a matter of vocabulary. The structure of sentences plays an even greater part in the clearness of the material presented. The meaning of a word may sometimes be guessed from the context in which it is found, but, if the thought is obscured by complicated and involved sentence structure, the audience will make no effort to solve the maze of words in order to find out what it is all about.

The first requirement of sentence structure is that there be absolute clarity. The best way to be sure of this clarity is to write in simple and compound sentences, and, when complex sentences are injected to avoid monotony, to make them free from all difficult clauses that might be ambiguous or obscure. It is easy for the writer who knows precisely what he means by the sentences he writes, and who can easily follow his own trend of thought, to forget how short the memory span of his listener is, and to go on attaching prefatory and attributive phrases to sentences which would have been precisely clear and effective standing alone but which are made difficult and pointless to the audience by the compilation. The material that is written into the added phrases can easily be put into other sentences, thus gaining much in the way of understandability and not losing heavily in emphasis.

A dangerous pitfall for the radio writer is the habit, of which he is sometimes quite unconscious, of adding idea after idea to sentences with the connecting word "which," trusting that the listener will trail along with him and make all the necessary connections. The solution is in breaking up the sentences into shorter ones, making complete simple sentences of the phrases.

Another practice equally as offensive to the radio listener, but nevertheless common among speakers, especially those whose subject is of a somewhat scientific nature, is the use of the relative pronouns "this" or "that" to refer to a whole complex idea which may have taken several sentences or even paragraphs to develop. The listener is unable to carry in his mind all the details of the idea and may have entirely forgotten the point to which the speaker wishes to refer. The relative pronoun calls up no answering response in his consciousness, and consequently he misses the point completely. If the writer would insert in a new sentence a short summarizing statement of the idea referred to by the pronoun, the familiar words would serve to stimulate the recollection, on the part of the listener, of the essentials of the idea, and he would make the correct connections, grasping the full significance of the sentence.

The use of other expressions to designate something that has gone before, such as "the above," "the former," and "the latter," is also out of place in the radio speech. Such expressions serve only to confuse the listener, for the chances are he cannot remember the statement or idea to which the speaker refers, if there has been any considerable amount of material presented in the interval.

The trouble with a great many writers is that they are afraid to write for the intellectual middle class because they think it may give the impression that they are not capable of writing for the learned. They throw into their writing big words just to give an impression of knowledge. Of course, there is the danger that, in attempting to keep the language on a level to fit the average of the American public, the writer will acquire the attitude of writing down to his audience, giving them the feeling that he knows they are intellectually inferior to him and that he is doing his best to explain things in words of one syllable. This result is just as undesirable as the confusion that is the result of too difficult language, for it produces an antagonism toward the speaker. To avoid an attitude of this kind in writing, the radio writer need only remember that there may be people in the audience who know just as much about his subject as he does, or a great deal more.

The person who reads the material over the microphone, whether he is the same one who wrote it or another, can do much toward the success or failure of the speech. A good reading may improve any material, just as poor reading may ruin the best. Likewise, the quality of the written material can influence tremendously the success of the reader. These possibilities must be considered seriously when the material is written.

The limitations of vocal expression must be recognized. All the sounds in the English language can be made singly without effort, but there are some sounds which, appearing in combination, are almost certain to cause the best of speakers to stumble. Many a man has tripped up on a phrase like "especially susceptible." No matter how carefully the speech is rehearsed before broadcasting, the tension before the microphone is likely to bring about an unforeseen difficulty in the pronunciation of some sound. Therefore, it is essential that the speeches be carefully checked for any possible tongue twisters before going on the air.

The diction should be vivid and colorful, presenting word pictures to the listeners. Most writers fail to search for verbs and adverbs to carry the burden of action description. There is a tendency to rely too much on adjectives. Sibilants, while not emphasized as they were by the carbon microphones, still do not broadcast well; when it is practicable to do so, other words with similar meanings should be used for words containing awkward sibilant repetition ("crime" in place of "lawlessness," "gratitude" in place of "thanks"). Slang and colloquialisms may be used, but they have a tendency to be local in character and may not be understood by the distant listener.

Modifying phrases should be placed so that no misunderstanding can exist as to what word or group of words they modify. Do not separate the subject and verb by long distances. If modifying clauses or phrases necessarily intervene, repeat the subject. Be very certain that the relation of relative pronouns is clear and correct. Conjunctions are inclined to drag sentences to great lengths; consequently they should be used sparingly.

Naturalness in speech will suggest the use of contractions. By all means use them. However, there are times when emphasis will require the avoidance of a contraction.

The style of the radio talk is conversational, with ideas so expressed that the listener not only may but must understand. Written style lacks the informality needed in radio. Every effort should be made in the written copy to make it sound like an extemporaneous talk when heard. The effective radio speaker writes and speaks in the first and second person, the active voice, and the indicative or imperative mood. So important is the use of the second person that one can almost judge the radio suitability of a manuscript by counting the number of times "you" appears on a page. If one does not find it used at least three or four times, the material may be suitable for print, but not often appropriate for the loud-speaker. An example that illustrates both the personal and the action-picture features needed in radio is the following opening from a printed article on "Spring Hiking":

This is the season when the lure of forest and field is felt by all. The fragrance of new-grown things is in the air. . . .

And here is the same, revised as it should be for radio:

When this season rolls around, you feel the lure to go out into field and forest. You want to fill your nostrils with the fragrance of new-grown things. . . .

Transitional words will serve to hold the plan of the address together for the listener. The speaker uses fillers, such as "now," for these expressions give spontaneity and conversational atmosphere. When the rules and regulations of grammar interfere with the transfer of an idea by words, such rules should be amended. Grammatical murder cannot be defended but, on the other hand, an occasional misdemeanor is inoffensively human.

Do not try to be funny, but allow a little humor to creep in, although never the slapstick, burlesque type. Humor should never be injected into a speech simply for the sake of being funny, unless, of course, the entertainer is listed as a comedian. Humor may be used in a radio speech to relieve the seriousness and heaviness of the speech and to create a pleasant feeling between speaker and audience. Avoid irony, which may not be understood by those who cannot see your expression. Sarcasm and bitterness are not pleasant to the listener. On the other hand, do not be a sweet Pollyanna.

The length of the address should be somewhat flexible with paragraphs toward the end that can be omitted or added as the time requires. Some speakers slow up under the emotional tension of the microphone; others accelerate. The talks should be rehearsed and timed. Speakers frequently place time notations in the margins of their manuscripts with which they attempt to conform.

The manuscript should be typed double space, on rough paper that will not rattle. Only one side of the paper should be used. The pages must be clearly numbered and arranged in order. They should be neither clipped together nor folded. Never continue a sentence from one page to another. While the speaker shifts his gaze from the bottom line of one page to the top line of the following page, there is bound to be a pause that will sound unnatural. Almost every broadcasting station requires a copy of the manuscript for its files.

It is wise for the radio speaker to furnish the announcer, well in advance, with brief introductory material to be used in presenting him to the radio audience and in defining his subject matter. This procedure assures the announcer of accurate and up-to-date information about the qualifications of the speaker to discuss the chosen topic and increases the attractiveness of the program.

THE TELEVISION ADDRESS

As was pointed out in Chap. VI, for most occasions the best kind of television address is one delivered extemporaneously. This style of speaking demands as much preparation as the writing-out of a complete manuscript. On the other hand, it offers the speaker a chance to be natural and to talk directly to his audience. Reading speeches from manuscript or from a Tele-Prompter is appropriate for certain occasions, but these should be thought of as exceptions rather than the rule.

In preparing the extemporaneous address the material is thought through and outlined in considerable detail. As in the radio address, or any other speech, the organization is important. It is necessary to attract attention and interest in the opening. The ideas must be presented clearly, logically, and in the proper order. There should be a concise summary and concluding section at the end of the talk. This kind of preparation and organizing is essential for any kind of speech. When it has been completed, the person who is going to speak from a manuscript begins to write. The speaker who is going to talk extemporaneously begins to rehearse and think through what he is going to say. In either case, the preparation needs to be thorough.

Television is a slave to the clock, just like radio. This might tend to discourage some people from attempting unwritten talks. It would be well to compare the precise timing possible with a manuscript against the more effective delivery possible with the extemporaneous technique. Not all stations will have a Tele-Prompter for the use of speakers. Even if they do, the use of this device requires considerable practice and skill. Lacking that skill, the speaker is apt to look like a complete incompetent. Reading from a printed manuscript is a high art that few are able to master. It is easier on radio because you never have to take your eyes from the page. Such a delivery on television would most certainly cause a high rate of channel switching. What could be duller than someone reading on TV with his head buried in a script? With the extemporaneous delivery the speaker is free to be completely natural. He can use his own words, gestures, and mannerisms. He can look into the lens of the camera, which is the eye of the audience. He can talk to the audience with directness.

It is possible with practice and rehearsal to give a nonwritten speech and make it fit quite closely into a time segment. This would indicate that practice in extemporaneous speaking is the long-range answer to the problem. There is no comparison between reading and talking on television. One is highly effective, the other is just short of hopeless. Is the precise time so important that it requires a tendency toward ineffectiveness? It hardly seems possible. It is true that a speaker will probably be cut off if he runs overtime. He must, therefore, be careful that this doesn't happen. On the other hand, if he is a few seconds short it is no great tragedy.

Visual Aids

It is very easy, and sometimes effective, to use visual aids in television talks. Such aids include maps, charts, graphs, slides, pictures, film, and three-dimensional models. This should not be interpreted as a plea to drag visual aids into a speech by the heels. There are many times when visuals are of no help. However, when a visual aid will help clarify a point, or give it greater emphasis, such a visual should be used.

Television stations are prepared to use these things and do use them daily in their regular programming. In preparing the television address the speaker should think carefully about any possible visual aids. They present no problem if a few simple rules are observed. Television pictures are always in a 3:4 aspect ratio, with the longer dimension being the horizontal. Visuals that are approximately of this shape are easily used. Visuals should be simple, with just the essential information shown boldly and clearly. Avoid excessive detail. Maps, charts, pictures, etc., which are to be used live on a studio camera, should have a generous border to allow the cameraman ample room to frame up on them. Colors should provide sufficient contrast so that the information will stand out clearly. Avoid black on white. The extremes of the black-white scale exceed television's capabilities, so almost-black on grey is better. All television stations are equipped to use 2- by 2-inch 35-millimeter slides. All stations are also equipped to show 16-millimeter motion-picture film, providing it is of acceptable quality and was shot at sound speed, 24 frames per second. Normally, there will be opportunity for the speaker to check details on the use of visual aids with the station over which he is to speak. It would be wise for the speaker to do this, and be certain that everything will work out as he hopes it will.

In planning the use of visual aids, it is important to remember that the director will be responsible for coordinating their use and getting them on the air at the right time. It is, therefore, necessary to devise some way of supplying the director with all of the information he will need to help you in using these aids.

CHAPTER THIRTEEN

BROADCASTING IN THE PUBLIC SERVICE

Local Community Service

The local or regional station has an opportunity, which is crowded out of the profitable life of the outlet station, of becoming a vital part of the community existence. While there is no immediate profit in assisting every worthwhile local project of the community, the good will and interest of the public are assets that will ultimately bring a return. Listeners and viewers are attracted to their local dial numbers by reports of local activities in churches and schools, in civic and health problems, in community-chest and Christmas drives. The wide-awake local station will participate in every project to build up its listening audience so as to attract advertisers. The local committees will plan and present sustaining programs for the Red Cross or fire prevention, for the local library or little theater, and all the friends of the actors or committees will be enthusiastic listeners. These programs serve both the listener directly and the organizations that indirectly serve the listener.

The broadcasting station, in applying for its license to operate, states that it will serve the public interest, convenience, and necessity. The entertainment features are usually combined with the sponsored programs, on which there are humor, music, and drama. In the category of programs that are of necessity to the listener are the farm-market reports and the stock- and bond-market quotations. Broadcasts of weather conditions and temperature predictions from the Weather Bureau are a necessity to certain businesses and individuals, particularly in times of extremes of temperature or of threatening storm conditions. Many local stations announce the time frequently during the day, and this service is of value to the housewife as well as to the laborer. A knowledge of what is happening in the world or the community is a necessity to some, a convenience to others. Local stations broadcast the news not less than three times a day and frequently augment news reports with spot news broadcasts, such as ball games, parades, and concerts. Shut-ins and those whose labors prevent their attending a parade or concert enjoy the description and the music. Outstanding choirs and school musical organizations of the city furnish programs of genuine service to the organization and entertainment to the listener. An inquiring reporter who visits the city officials and interviews them about their duties is instructive to the listener and stimulates civic interest. A microphone or a movie camera in the council chamber, the police court, or even in the chamber of commerce will give the citizen an insight into his local government. Distinguished guests and speakers would only be heard by a small minority of the citizens if it were not for the radio interview.

Such community programs also serve the organizations of the city, such as churches, schools, clubs, and lodges. Social and business meetings may be announced, and the radio may serve as a clearing house of information. A definite daily program will be helpful to listeners, although special bulletins may also be broadcast. The Better Business Bureau may give warning to the citizens of some house-to-house swindler who is obtaining money under false pretenses. Broadcasts from the police department and the traffic court have been very successful in reducing the number of accidents, and they are interesting; in some instances they have reduced graft and favoritism upon the part of judges. Committees that have charge of raising funds for the needy in Christmas drives, for the local Boy Scout troop, for the Red Cross, or for the Policemen's ball, which raises funds for pensions, will do well to enlist the services of the community-minded broadcasting station.

The most valuable program promotion for the local or regional station is an evidenced interest in serving the local community. This service to the local community builds up listener interest and appeals to local sponsors. The station that does not do this is missing one of the easiest ways to become a real factor and influence in the community. In some instances local Junior League women take over the distribution of free time by the station to local organizations, and in this way protect the station from having to refuse time or to allocate certain periods. Many local groups do not know what to do with radio time until a program is outlined for them. Schools, amateur musical clubs, women's clubs, parent-teacher organizations, need guidance of someone experienced in radio, which should be provided by the station. Local and regional stations offer many opportunities for both sustaining and sponsored programs in local interest. The only requirement is that whoever produces the show must do so under the supervision of those who are acquainted with radio showmanship. The contribution of time and facilities by the station must be enhanced by advice and leadership, also.

Programs may be arranged to inform the people of the community and the surrounding territory concerning the industries, business houses, banks, and outstanding public citizens of the city. A New York station broadcast the annual meeting of the stockholders of a corporation. While the station should assume no political influence it may present, by unbiased announcements to the local voters, different candidates for public office in election years. Local history and folklore may be presented in dramatic form. In the spring, summer, and autumn the beauties of neighboring drives may be pictured to the local automobilist. The search for missing persons, stray pets, and lost articles may be conducted by radio and television. Local religious congregations, especially the invalids who are unable to attend church, appreciate the broadcasting of services. The studio may arrange a series of religious discussions by various religious leaders, avoiding denominational controversies. Cooperation with the local chamber of commerce in promoting local celebrations and "bargain days" will advertise the city, obtain commercial announcements for the station, and increase public interest in all the programs of the station.

Medical and Health Programs

Medicine is as old a subject as radio and television are new; it is therefore significant that the two should combine mutual advantages, at times, for the benefit and relief of modern society.

Many firms, using radio and TV to advertise their products, carry on a campaign by stressing the appeal of the audience's health as a keynote. Naturally, these are often farfetched, making it difficult for the hearer to distinguish between the crystal gazer and the reliable physician. Hence, it is entirely justifiable for the medical profession to maintain a comprehensive popular health program to offset the broadcasting of unreliable information. Such a program must necessarily reach the greatest possible number of people. The programs must vary and should be presented so as to give the maximum benefit for the health of the individuals. Similarly, the frequency with which health talks may be given probably will vary in different communities, but once a week seems to be the common practice and is probably sufficient. Epidemics may also be combated by radio and television.

The purposes of medical and public-health programs are to attract the attention of those who are not already interested in health and hygiene and who are in need of information, to disseminate up-to-the-minute information by authorities, and to inspire listeners to health examinations and personal care and hygiene. It is important that the individual who wishes to present a worthwhile public-health program acquaint himself with what is being done in public-health education in other media.

The subject matter of health broadcasts should embrace all phases of health, written in language which the laity understands and which is not unpleasant to the hearer. Most talks in this type of broadcasting should be fairly short, so as to hold the attention of the audience. The speaker must answer in his talk any questions that may arise in the mind of the listener. While the doctor is delivering such a medical talk, he must take into consideration the fact that he might be developing a group of neurasthenics, or people who feel that they have the disease symptoms that are being discussed. Careful attention is necessary to avoid such a condition.

The program director must also consider the hour at which the listener is to hear the medical talk and should not offer talks on cancer or stomach disorders during the meal hour or alarming prophecies at bedtime. The radio-TV program committee must refuse all talks dealing with controversial medical or health topics. In all medical broadcasts the ethics of presentation must be watched carefully. Hence, programs must be sponsored by local or state medical societies and not by individual physicians. In some quarters the speaker remains unidentified; however, stations object to unnamed speakers because they recognize the fact that listeners, as a rule, desire to know the identity of the person to whom they are listening. Big names do not always help the program. Chances are that the lesser ones have more time to work upon the program, are more willing to take suggestions, and are apt to turn out a better script. Editing of talks by committees to eliminate uncontrolled expression of individual opinion is held to be desirable. The health program secures best results when supplemented by press releases and some amount of newspaper advertising, which can best be obtained by local medical groups.

The most popular method from the listener's viewpoint is the dramatic playlet. If the dramatic sketch is carefully constructed from the standpoint of both play writing and the scientific facts presented, it will hold more listeners and will reach them more effectively than either the monologue or the interview. These dramas, based upon facts supplied by the physician or group, should be written by a playwright and acted by a professional group. The characters must represent the average listener, and the subjects must be those health problems common in everyday experience. The general tone may be light, but the serious educational purpose must ever be present.

There have been good instances of dramatic programs using medical themes on both radio and television. For example, "Medicine in the News" on radio, and "The Medic" and "The March of Medicine" on television. Some programs of this type have been resounding commercial and audience successes. There is little doubt that the impact of such programs can be powerful, or that major concepts about medicine and health can be gotten across to the audience. However, despite their appeal and effectiveness, programs of this kind need to exercise caution. It is always a temptation to give too much weight to the dramatic elements. When this happens, the program can leave wrong or improperly emphasized notions. It is also possible to give too much weight to rare or medically unimportant diseases, accidents, and other health problems. This can only result in confusing—or, what is worse, unduly alarming—the audience.

Probably the easiest kind of radio program from the standpoint of the doctor and the station director is the straight talk or monologue, in which facts are presented in a conversational manner. Needless to say, such a talk must not be a dissertation such as one hears in a medical-society meeting. It should be popular in form and manner of presentation, but not sensational, and it should maintain an air of dignity suitable to its professional character and educational motive. This does not mean that it has to be dull. It can be sprightly in tone and need not be devoid of humor. It should deal with topics of public interest and should be timely with respect to season and local conditions. In many instances it is difficult to find a voice which will fit the listener's visualization of the doctor at the bedside.

Combining the simple directness of the straight talk with the dramatic quality of informal conversation is the interview type of program. A patient may interview the doctor in his office; two doctors may discuss a local health problem and how to combat an epidemic; or the doctor may, at the bedside of a patient, answer the questions of his interns. This type of broadcast has more interest and voice appeal than the monologue program. The doctor, however, must avoid allowing his answers to become lectures. A rather fast-moving exchange of pertinent questions and informative answers, given in an unstilted conversational style, is best. Use illustrations with human interest. The radio audience does not want to hear case histories; as such they mean nothing. It's what the doctors and scientists have been able to glean from the observation of these patients that the listeners want to hear.

The fourth method of presenting medical subjects over the radio is largely used by quacks and medical fakers; consequently it is inadvisable for the reputable doctor to adopt it. This consists of the question-and-answer type of broadcast. Questions relating to medical subjects cannot be answered by mail or radio except in very general terms, with instructions to the writer to consult his local physician. In every type of medical broadcast this advice should be given. A public-health program is not to take the place of the advice of the family doctor. If the question-and-answer method is used, it is advisable for the medical speaker to phrase both the question and the answer. Such a method allows the speaker to cover more ground and makes his monologue more human.

These program types, the straight talk, the interview, and the panel, which developed in radio, can frequently be used to even greater advantage in television. Medicine and health are fields that abound in visual material. There are all kinds of models, charts, pictures, slides, X-ray photographs, and instruments. These can be used to accent and make more interesting the material to be covered.

Another TV format that is appropriate to this field is the demonstration. Fascinating programs can be broadcast dealing with first aid, lifesaving, nutrition, infant care, and similar fields. There have also been actual operations broadcast for public viewing. While the value of this for doctors and technicians is unquestioned, there is some doubt as to the precise effect on the lay public.

One of the most powerful television programs I have ever seen was done by station WOI-TV, operated by Iowa State College in Ames, Iowa. A motion-picture photographer had gone to one of the large hospitals in New York City that specializes in the training and rehabilitation of the physically handicapped. Naturally enough, the photographer concentrated on a few individuals undergoing treatment and, in particular, on a girl about seven years old. The footage obtained was edited and then formed the basic unit of the program. The show opened on a narrator in the studio, standing in front of a large picture of the small girl featured in the film footage. He told about the problems of rehabilitating the physically handicapped. He pointed out that the State of Iowa had no such facility. Then, via the film, we visited the New York hospital. After several minutes of heart-tugging scenes showing the young girl learning to walk and learning to do things for herself even though she had been born without arms, we were entirely convinced that specialists in this field could work near-miracles. We were then returned to Iowa for an interview with a young mother. This woman, the mother of two children, had been stricken with polio and was confined to a wheelchair for the rest of her life. Local help was not available. But there was a brighter side. Fortunately she was able to go to the hospital in New York which we had just visited. There she learned to operate her chair and to do many other things. As a result, a few changes in her house enabled her to do all her housework, take care of her children, cook for the family, and do all the many things that a homemaker does. Film clips showed her washing dishes, cooking, and ironing.

After seeing this program no member of the audience could possibly deny that the State of Iowa should have such a hospital and a staff of experts in the field of rehabilitation of the physically handicapped. That, of course, was the precise purpose of the show.

Generally speaking, the medical performer has a topic of interest for every listener inasmuch as all are concerned with their own physical ailments. However, this existing interest must be held by a program that is distinctive, attractive, and authentic. As pointed out by Dr. W. W. Bauer, "Ether, when used for the transmission of health education, is not intended as an anesthetic. Nevertheless, if not tuned out first, certain health talks have precisely that effect."

Serving the Farmer

Among the more important public services is that rendered to the farmer. Programs addressed to the agriculturalist are broadcast over the networks from the Department of Agriculture in Washington and from local or regional stations using material supplied by the government. Agricultural colleges present programs over their own stations, and newspaper-owned stations often have farm editors who arrange programs taking the form of "farm shows," upon which old-time songs and music are mingled with weather and market reports. County farm agents are frequent performers, broadcasting agricultural bulletins, feed quotations, and livestock reports.

The radio program addressed to the farmer should not contain too many facts, and these facts must be presented in an interesting manner to catch the attention of a busy listener. Points must be explained in simple and direct language and must conform to the other fundamental requirements previously set forth for writing the radio address. The speaker should avoid percentages and statistics. He should speak in round numbers and use concrete illustrations. Figures of speech and similes should be picturesque. The solid facts presented should be enlivened by humor, anecdotes, or music. As in all broadcasting, the speaker should converse and chat with his listeners, using the personal pronouns "I," "we," and "you." The personality of the speaker must stand forth in the home where the receiving set is located; only the engaging personality holds attention. The speaker, while preparing his copy, should put himself in the place of his listener, formulating the questions that the listener might ask. In outlining the talk he should attempt to find some common point of farm interest as an introduction. Choosing a limited number of facts relating to the subject to be discussed, he should develop these thoroughly, using personal experiences, quotations from authorities, and some entertainment material. In conclusion it is well to announce any free publications that are available on the subject.

The farm-program manuscript should be carefully edited with the potential audience in mind. The editor must see that the topic and development are interesting and informative, that points are clearly made and emphasized, that it is not wordy, that it is human and friendly, and that the listener is left with some definite project and increased knowledge. Probably the old formula of first telling what you are going to tell, then telling it, and then telling what you have told is the best outline to follow.

Television, too, has found the farm audience deserving of special programs. Many of the same things that are done on radio are also found on television. The real and new contribution that television has made to farm programming is the demonstration-type program. Farmers can be shown the techniques of equipment maintenance, care of livestock, soil-conservation measures, milk-handling procedures, and all the many complicated processes that are a part of modern farming. The United States

Department of Agriculture and the colleges of agriculture have carried on far-flung extension programs for many years. The contribution of these programs to the efficiency of American farming is enormous. The extension workers are now finding television a valuable tool in further expansion of this informational job.

Religious Broadcasts

A recent survey disclosed that an average of 1 hour daily is devoted to religious programs by the average American radio station. The average was 22¼-hour periods weekly, with the peak load between ten and twelve o'clock on Sundays. Nearly all denominations are sending forth sermons, services, and hymns to bring to the shut-ins as well as to the unchurched the message of the gospel. Religious programs include services, sermons, secular talks, music, charity appeals, inspirational addresses, prayers, Bible reading, religious news, and announcements. However, I am concerned in this handbook only with the preparation and delivery of the religious sermon or talk. The secular speaker who talks on a religious subject should conform to the various requirements set forth for radio speaking in general and for preparing the radio address.

In the first place, the announcements of radio sermons have been too long, indeed in many instances have overshadowed the prayers. Such announcements should be brief and in good taste. Full information concerning the speaker and service may follow the talk but should not precede it.

There are two types of religious programs: those conducted from the pulpit for a church congregation and picked up by the microphone and those prepared primarily for the radio congregation. In the former the radio audience is secondary and the minister prepares to talk for his visual audience, with a possible reference to his unseen congregation.

For a specially prepared radio sermon, the preacher may write his sermon for the pulpit in the language of the clergy and then rewrite it for the radio listener. The phraseology of the church will be toned down to the language of the armchair listener. Figures of speech, colloquialisms, and metaphors will enliven the sermon of the ecclesiastic showman. The speaker cannot be too intellectual, but must deal with things vital to the life of the average listener in a human and direct manner. The oratorical, ministerial style used in the pulpit will not have the appeal that is found in a spiritually conversational style. The airway sermon is not of the ritualistic type but is nondenominational and non-sectarian, condemning no faith.

The radio can be of great value to the churches if religious broadcasts are kept on a high level. A well-known radio preacher has outlined his "Ten Radio Commandments" for the effective broadcasting of religious programs:

1. Speak in a conversational tone.
2. Take your sermons not from the Bible, but from life.
3. Leave out the word "I."
4. Neglect the needless.
5. No bunk.
6. No sob stuff.
7. Make the web of your sermon optimistic, cheerful.
8. Check and recheck your script before delivering . . . for absolute factual accuracy.
9. Keep the word "not" out of your sermon script.
10. Use no introduction. Plunge right into the middle of the sermon.

The radio preacher will use all the appeal of his personality. He will use the rising and falling inflection and observe the value of the pause. His enunciation must be sharp, clear, and decisive. He will be emphatic, soothing, or inviting through his flow of words, but at all times he must remember that he is speaking in a private home to an individual listener.

The straight religious program is also found on television, and usually combines some music with a sermon. For TV, the minister should develop the direct, intimate, informal technique discussed under the sections on speaking and announcing for television. From time to time, actual services are telecast from churches, especially on such occasions as Christmas and Easter. Some of the national organizations have produced stirring religious dramas for network presentation.

As in radio, it is necessary to blend the need for keeping the dignity of the service with enough informality and humanness to keep the audience with the program. In his own home, the viewer does not have the stimulation of the church atmosphere, the stained-glass windows, etc., to put him in the frame of mind for worship. The program must do this for him.

For the networks, the responsibility of selecting those who spread the gospel through the air has been placed under the control of such bodies as the Federal Council of Churches in America, the National Council of Catholic Men, and the United Jewish Laymen's Committee. Local stations usually work through similar local groups. This method provides for an equal distribution of time and attention on a basis acceptable to the religious organizations, and it relieves the stations and networks of a touchy responsibility. Programs arranged by such organizations are usually sustaining programs constituting a part of the public service of the station.

Politics and Government

The first notable use of radio in the political field was the broadcasting of the Republican and Democratic national conventions in 1924. Today, both political parties arrange their conventions with the radio and television audiences as much in mind as the delegates in attendance. The keynote speech and the nominations are staged in the evening, during the best listening and viewing hours, in order that the vast network audience may hear and see the proceedings of the convention. Radio and television pervade the whole field of government and politics.

During the 1930s the increasing use of radio in national politics drastically changed campaigns and campaign orators. No longer was the spellbinder able to sway voters as he had from the political rally platform. The flowery political speaker of the past has his career ended by radio. Politicians found it necessary to adapt their personalities and speeches to the microphone. The form of political campaigns changed. Much of the party budget went into radio. Via the networks, the national candidates could reach millions of people through one broadcast. This made it essential for the candidate, and the party, to prepare the speech with extreme care. This was something different from haranguing a few hundred or a few thousand people in a town square, or at a fairground. There was a marked trend toward more factual, more sincere, more rational campaign speeches.

Television has furthered this process. Today, a very high percentage of national campaign budgets goes into television. The candidate must learn to make a good appearance before the TV camera. He must be able to look and sound sincere, intelligent, and honest. He must realize that the impact of repeated appearances on national television networks is enormous. The entire voting public is now able to form very real impressions about the character and personality of the candidates. It is almost impossible to hide any secrets from the probing eye of the camera and the intent ear of the microphone. The time factor of radio and television has also helped political campaigning. Speeches must fit into a specific time segment. This prevents the candidate from becoming overly long-winded, and it also requires him to organize his material better to insure getting it all in. It can be said without argument that radio and television now form the core around which national political campaigns are built. Broadcasting carries the bulk of the load, and whistle-stop oratory is secondary.

The Communications Act has some provisions which are highly important to political campaigns. This whole subject will be treated in more detail in a later chapter, but it is appropriate now to mention some of the things that relate directly to political campaigns and their use of broadcasting facilities. Stations are not required to provide time for the broadcasting of political speeches by candidates. However, if they do provide time for this purpose, there are two vital requirements that must be met. Equal time must be available to all candidates for the office on exactly the same basis. That is, if the Republican candidate for President obtains a half hour of time during evening hours for X dollars, then the Democratic candidate is entitled to similar time for the same amount of money. Stations are not required to give time to candidates "for free." However, if they do donate time to one, they must also donate time to all. Generally, the tradition has grown up that campaign time on radio and television is sold on the same basis that is used in selling time to advertisers. The second major requirement established by the Communications Act is that a station has no right of censorship over speeches made by political candidates.

These rules apply only to broadcasts by political candidates. Officially, a candidate is a person running for a specific office after having received the nomination of his party. The F.C.C., however, has tended to apply these same rules to political broadcasting in general. In this way, the spirit of fairness intended by the Communications Act is spread to all political broadcasting rather than being limited to actual speeches made by candidates.

In addition to the profound effects made on political campaigns by radio and television broadcasting, we need to consider in further detail the effects on political conventions. As mentioned earlier, radio began covering the conventions in 1924. Television has broadcast the 1948, 1952, and 1956 national conventions. The bulk of the voting population now knows what goes on at these conventions and how the delegates behave. Thanks to the TV cameras and the radio microphones they have even attended the meetings in the traditional "smoke-filled rooms" where the real decisions are made. This has resulted in a much better-informed electorate and furthers the democratic process. Politicians know these things, and conventions are staged and run with full knowledge that the entire nation is attending.

President Franklin D. Roosevelt started a very important governmental use of radio and television. He took the nation's problems directly to the people in his radio "fireside chats." They were enormously successful and have since been continued on both radio and TV. It has become almost routine for the President, the Secretary of State, and other important government officials to make periodic reports to the nation over the combined resources of the national networks. Again, it is easy to see how this keeps the public informed about their government and its operation.

Radio and television coverage of legislative bodies, the United Nations sessions, committee hearings, etc., have added to the informing job that the broadcasting industry has undertaken in the political and governmental fields. The famous televised hearings of the Kefauver senate committee on crime and the even more renowned debates between Senator McCarthy and the Army are dramatic examples of how broadcast proceedings can alert the public. It is possible that these two events drew larger audiences than any continuing events ever covered.

It is no doubt true that broadcasting has up-graded political campaigning and the management of political conventions. Radio and TV have made it possible for almost everyone to keep informed about our government and the performance of its officials and agencies. Thus, in the areas of politics and government, broadcasting's influence has been all to the good. However, this great success should cause us to give serious consideration to the inherent dangers in political broadcasting. As we have seen, radio and television are powerful political tools. What happens when they are improperly used? We can look at the excellent examples in Fascist Italy, Nazi Germany, and Communist Russia. The inherent power of the broadcast media doesn't necessarily mean that this power will be used for worthy ends. It is up to us, as a democratic people, to see that a free, fair, and honest use is made of this great facility. It is not alarmism to say that the very survival of our democratic society depends upon our ability to do just that. Everyone in the field of broadcasting needs to realize that the political use of these media is a serious trust, and prejudice, bias, and irresponsibility cannot govern this use.

Law-enforcement Programs

An interesting variation of the usual type of crime program is the interview with the chief of police of a city of smaller than metropolitan size. Such a program might be broadcast for a 15-minute period during the morning hours and for a like period during the evening in order to reach different audiences. A veteran police reporter or a skilled interviewer would discuss with the chief of police the daily events in the activities of the local police department. Such an interview could take place in the office of the chief of police, where the sounds that are associated with the police department might be heard by the listener. If the local department has a short-wave station, the log of this short-wave station might be used as an outline for the interview. The chief should give the facts of various matters that have been brought to his attention during the period immediately preceding the interview. Evidences of crime, reports of lost and stolen articles, descriptions of missing persons, information concerning rackets that are being perpetrated upon the citizens, and other happenings of local interest are but a few of the topics that would interest and inform the public. These facts and the evidence should be interpreted by the chief of police in statements that are drawn out by the interviewer. Such a program would be a strong force in the maintenance of law and order in a community; because actual facts, true names, and places would be given in a broadcast with the same impartiality that they are given in the newspapers, the program would create a wide public interest. Stolen cars might be recovered if the general public were thus made aware of the theft. Rackets being conducted by solicitors and others could be stopped and the racketeers apprehended if advance notice were thus sent into the homes of the city. Lost bicycles and other articles might be recovered as a result of such broadcasts. Frequently, important witnesses of a crime or of an accident would report their evidence to the police department if they were appealed to through the local station. The police and sheriffs of surrounding cities and villages should be informed of the hours for these programs and should be invited to send their bulletins to be used upon this local program.

The types of program which I have described are but a few of those that are broadcast in the public service. An excellent series of programs has been presented to inform the taxpayers of one state about their schools. Many stations have carried series of programs informing the public concerning the industries, natural resources, educational facilities, and recreational opportunities of the state in which the station is located. Town-hall programs and forums have been built upon the idea of the old town hall and broadcast both nationally and locally. The community-minded station must originate new ideas and assume leadership in conceiving methods, writing continuity, training the broadcasters, and presenting the finished programs. Its reward will be a large and loyal audience that will attract commercial accounts.

Generally speaking, the broadcasting industry can be proud of its record in the field of public-service programming. Not that improvements couldn't be found, but year in and year out the industry has contributed generously of its time and talents to keep the country informed, and to assist in worthwhile campaigns. Several research studies have shown that people tend to think of radio as more free from bias in the handling of news and political matters than the other media of newspaper and magazine. There is every reason to believe that radio and television will continue this outstanding work.

CHAPTER FOURTEEN

MUSIC PROGRAMS

Radio Singing

Richness, smoothness, flexibility, expression, mellowness—these are some of the adjectives that may be applied to a good radio voice. The same adjectives may apply to an operatic voice, for today any voice that is good for opera or concert stage is suitable for broadcasting. It is only necessary that the singer be in a correct position before the AM or FM microphone, and that the technicians test his particular type of delivery.

In the case of an exceptionally powerful voice, it may be necessary to place the singer a little farther from the microphone or a little to one side. If the voice is capable of great range, and that range is to be utilized, then the singer's position should be such as to allow him complete freedom of action to turn away from or toward the microphone. It is true that the increased sensitivity of modern microphones has greatly reduced the necessity for this movement on the part of the singer. However, this increased sensitivity works against the singer as well as for him, because it registers more readily faults in quality, tone, pitch, or timbre. Hence the necessity for "smooth" voices.

The control of the voice is of greatest importance in radio. Operatic stars whose looks or acting ability help to detract from their pitch deviations are a disappointment to radio listeners when they are heard to "flat" notes in a simple song such as "Carry Me Back to Old Virginny." Control means maintaining the correct pitch and the acquisition and retention of a good tone, quality, and general technique. Expression is the attribute of a good radio performer. It is in the expression given to words and tones that real artistry lies. For instance, it is possible to say "I love you" by bellowing it out like a bull. But it is also possible to say "I love you" by drawing it out, sweetening it, and mellowing it. The difference is obvious; in that difference lies the *expression*—and often the greatness of a performer. Ezio Pinza is admired both for his expression and his dramatic quality. Expression, important as it is to any singer, is most important to the radio singer, because he must accomplish through expression and fine shading what the concert or operatic singer achieves through singing and partly through action. While voice quality is essential and of primary importance, it is personality that singles the vocalist from the crowd and stamps the voice with individuality. This applies not only to the "voice" personality but to those little accidents of voice and gesture and mannerism.

Microphone Position: Amplitude Modulation

The method of attaining the correct location or position before the microphone depends on several things: the type of accompaniment, the power and flexibility of the voice, the type of song, and the acoustics of the studio. These in turn are dependent on the type of mike in use. The rule most generally followed is to have the singer center up on the microphone and stand about 20 to 30 inches away from it. There is too great a tendency upon the part of the singer to hug the mike. (Leave that to Perry Como.) One foot should be placed in advance of the other —as on the stage—to assure balance and poise. When gradations in volume are necessary, the singer may bend toward or away from the microphone. A soft note is picked up better close to the microphone. Sometimes the singer, when hitting a shrill note or when vocal strength is necessary, will be told to turn his head away from the microphone. (This has the same effect as stepping back but is not considered to be so satisfactory.) Above all, the singer must observe the fundamental rule of being at ease. His position should not be cramped or unnatural. This is the procedure followed when singing with a piano accompaniment.

If the accompaniment is orchestral, the placing of the singer must be tried out. The singer must not be drowned out or interfere with the reception of any of the instruments. Often it is considered more satisfactory to place the singer at a separate microphone.

Microphone Position: Frequency Modulation

The same principles that are set forth in the chapter on announcing for the location of the announcer or speaker in relation to the FM microphone apply to the radio singer. The singer just sings in the studio, oblivious of the microphone, using any volume desired. While the singer is rehearsing, the music director should have the technicians move the microphone to various locations in the studio—above the singer—to one side—in a corner—to try out the pickup until the reproduction is satisfactory. The studio, it is to be presumed, is soundproof and acoustically constructed so that extraneous sound will not pick up when the engineer opens the gain. With such a setup in such a studio, the full range of the soloist's voice will be reproduced for the listeners, which is not possible when the singer sings into a mike and is conscious of the microphone.

There are, obviously, conditions which require multiple miking. Where vocalists are used, a special microphone is needed to provide the proper balance for the radio listener between the musicians and the vocalist or vocalists. The vocalist should be no closer than 3 feet to the microphone when a high-fidelity microphone is used, depending upon the volume range. In a solo with piano accompaniment, the mike is about 6 to 8 feet from the soloist, while well spaced from the piano. In the previous AM practice, the mike is within arm's reach of the singer and directly at the side of the piano, but no listener would enjoy the program if he stood where the mike is located.

The quality of a program is always conditioned by the equipment used. Use the best microphones. In FM, the engineer should have little or no control over the singer's performance after the microphones are satisfactorily located. He should not ride gain. Don't expect him to improve the quality of the singer; in AM, he was an important factor.

In group singing the object is to achieve a balanced ensemble, and this can best be done with the microphone suspended above the singers on a boom, or hanging from the ceiling. For larger choral groups the singers may be placed on risers. Their position will not vary to any extent from their position during rehearsal or concert. The melody should be distinguishable in whatever part it appears; it is a rule of good musicianship that all members of a choral group be sensitive to the nuances which make first one part and then another stand out from the rest.

Vocal Training

There is no longer any special training for the radio singer. The well-trained voice is the best voice for radio today. The student can best receive the fundamental principles of voice placement, vocal exercise, and proper breathing from a vocal teacher. Besides this, he can make a series of recordings which will allow him to hear for himself how he sounds to the radio listener. If these records are made using the same microphone that he will use for broadcasting, he will be able to experiment with his voice delivery and in placing himself before the microphone.

One of the essentials of the radio soloist is clean-cut enunciation that will carry words clearly to the listener. Proper speech training is vital. The vocal organs must be free of tension, yet fully under control. Sing before a mirror, but do not look into it for reflected beauty of features; rather listen for beauty of articulation and tone. Do not mouth words.

The acquisition of a good voice is a tedious job. It involves hours of lessons and practice. When one has acquired the attributes of a good singer for radio performance, these attributes must be put into practice until they become natural and easy.

Originality is the keynote to success in the radio showman. Consequently the broadcasting soloist of popular tunes takes liberties with the tempo of the song which will contrast with the rhythm of the orchestration. Nearly all singers of popular songs "pep up" their renditions. The radio has given the singer who lacks volume but who has singing ability an opportunity that the auditorium or theater never offered. But the voice of light volume must be true and the singer must have an individual style. Singers of the "blues," "torch songs," the so-called hit tunes, and hillbilly numbers are usually enhanced by the amplification offered by radio. Only fresh, unsophisticated entertainment will hold the listener.

Lucile Manners gave the following advice to radio singers:[1]

Fallacious ideas about "special radio technique."
1. Simply stand far enough away from the mike (at least 2½ feet), and sing as you would to any audience.
2. Do not get into the habit of "saving" the voice, but do your best in every performance.
3. Use free tone production and be as relaxed and natural as possible.
4. Radio will pick up "forcing" easier than you think.
Radio makes more exacting demands on the singer than either concert or opera, in many ways.
1. Radio singer depends on himself alone, that is, his voice. No stage or settings of any kind . . . nor pretty looks.
2. Repertoire is more exacting and can include less repeats. Learn to sing "on the breath."
Permit no breath to creep into the tone, however.
Do not use tones in public that do not lie naturally in your range.

[1] *Etude*, March, 1938.

1. Use tones that are resonated in the head in the cavities behind the nose, do not force.

2. Be careful of throat constrictions.

3. Writer uses "set" position for high notes; this, however, is different with each singer.

4. Always warm up the voice with scales and exercises before doing arias and demanding selections.

Need for a foundation of good musicianship.

1. One must be a well-rounded artist and work as hard for radio as one would for the concert stage or opera.

2. Even crooners today are increasing their musicianship.

Music and repertoire.

1. Theoretically the audience is always the "same" in radio, and singers cannot afford to repeat often.

2. There is a greater variety to radio repertoire than for concert or opera work. Lieder, opera, art songs, musical comedy, ballads, good popular music, and language songs are all to be mastered equally for success.

3. "Everyone" is in the radio audience, and an artist cannot sing specialized music too much.

4. A radio singer's greatest problem is to sing programs which contain something that everyone likes.

5. Such a list should include: a Schubert song, one of Liszt's, Stephen Foster, a Strauss waltz, a motion-picture hit song, etc.

6. Smooth, lovely melodies are best in the long run.

7. Don't be either too high-brow or too low-brow; all good music is welcome on the air.

Do not be a "prima donna," that is, be a "good fellow" and be reasonable in your relations with conductors and musicians in the station. Let your development, vocally and artistically, come slowly. Do not be in a hurry to be a "star"; this rating will come of itself in good time. Success will come as suddenly as failure has been persistent. *Above all, never allow yourself to feel that radio demands less than other fields of the vocal and musical arts!*

Instrumental Setup: Amplitude Modulation

If we remember that a microphone is merely a mechanical device which converts audible sounds into electrical impulses, it is only natural to expect that there must be certain definite rules for its placement with regard to the musical instruments whose music is to be broadcast. No general rules can be set down which will adequately treat all possible situations, but an understanding of the more important factors involved will enable the broadcaster to solve his own specific problems.

One of the greatest difficulties encountered with this electrical ear called the "microphone" is that it has no sense of discrimination and faithfully reproduces all the sounds that reach it. A person attending an orchestral concert can focus his attention on the musical sounds being produced and exclude most of the extraneous noises that may be present (coughs, sneezes, reverberation, etc.), but not so with the microphone. It hears all and tells all. Consequently, it must be placed so that it will hear only what it should, namely, the orchestra and its component parts. This means placing the microphone near the orchestra.

When the microphone is near enough to the orchestra to minimize unwanted sounds, a new problem arises—that of picking up just the right amount of sound from each instrument. This is what the engineer refers to when he talks about "balance"; in modern acoustically treated studios it is really the only problem of technique with which operators and producers must concern themselves.

The loudness of any instrument, as picked up by the microphone, depends upon three things: (1) its distance from the microphone, (2) its position relative to the sensitive face of the microphone, and (3) the loudness and directionality of the instrument itself. By directionality I mean that all instruments do not radiate tone equally in all directions. A violin does, but certainly the loudness of a trumpet depends upon whether one is in front of or beside the bell.

All microphones can be divided into three classes with regard to their sensitivity. They are unidirectional, bidirectional, or nondirectional. Most dynamics fall into the first classification. In the second are ribbons (or velocities). The Altec and the various condenser types make up the last group. A unidirectional microphone of the diaphragm type has its maximum sensitivity in a line perpendicular to its face, and as one goes around it the sensitivity falls off, so that at an angle of 40 degrees it is only 75 per cent efficient and at an angle of 60 degrees only 50 per cent efficient.

The proper height of the microphone can be determined only by experimentation. For a small orchestra, first try it at a height of 5 feet. For a larger organization, try it at a height of from 6 to 8 feet. In a live studio the microphone should be lower than in a dead studio, in order to cut down on reverberation. Also, where there is much reverberation, the microphone should be placed closer to the orchestra. The microphone is usually placed between the orchestra leader and his musicians, but to one side.

For piano solos a microphone should be set facing the piano and about 6 or 8 feet from the high-register side (Fig. 39). A separate microphone is provided if there is to be a piano solo. When the piano is used with an orchestra, it is located either far to one side or behind the musicians.

The bidirectional microphone has a double sensitivity pattern. There are two regions of sensitivity, on opposite sides of the microphone, each having the same general fan shape as that of the unidirectional type. If the musical group is on a stage or platform, the arrangement of instru-

FIG. 39. Microphone setup for piano solo.

ments already outlined can be used. However, there is always present the possibility that the opposite sensitive face will pick up unwanted noises from the audience or auditorium. The microphone may be tilted toward the orchestra to lessen the sensitivity of the back face. In broadcasting studios it is possible to set up the orchestra on both sides of the microphone, keeping the same relative distances that have been outlined.

When a nondirectional microphone is used, sensitivity is the same in all directions, so that the only factor that need be considered in placing instruments is that of distance, and this will, of course, depend upon the instruments and the acoustics of the room.

When an instrumentalist is to play a solo part with orchestral accompaniment, he will leave his position in the orchestra and play from a position nearer the microphone, so that his tones will stand out above the other instruments. This is also true of a small group in the orchestra who will rise when playing certain parts of the arrangement. In any studio which has a live end, the orchestra is placed with its back to that live end which acts as a shell for reflecting the sound.

The reader should bear in mind that what has been said here is a very general summary arrived at through years of experimentation by accredited broadcasters; it is not, by any stretch of the imagination, to be construed as a solution to all problems. These facts should aid in the preliminary setup of the orchestra or vocal group, but the final test is the quality of the program as it issues from the audition loud-speaker where the musical director is auditing the rehearsal. When special effects are desired, there must, of course, be considerable deviation from the general rules. Every leader has his individual effect to emphasize. Some will bring the violins close to the microphone, others the brass instruments.

Often a single studio orchestra must sound like three different orchestras upon different programs, with the result that the setup of the orchestra will be different for each presentation. There will also be varied musical arrangements. The final arrangement of the orchestra will depend upon the balance heard from the loud-speaker during rehearsal. The musical director is concerned with what the listener hears, not with how his orchestra looks in its radio setup.

Instrumental Pickup: Frequency Modulation

Perhaps one of the most controversial issues relative to musical pickups, whether in the studio or in auditoriums, is the single microphone versus the multiple microphone pickup. There are convincing arguments for each. In favor of the single mike pickup, it has been discovered that when several mikes are in use simultaneously the control-room operator becomes an associate musical conductor. If one microphone is located above and behind the director, the responsibility for the performance is not shared by the operator or the technicians, and the credit or blame for the performance is the director's, as it should be. From the studio standpoint, the experience has tended to indicate to date that single microphone pickups are much more desirable whenever possible than the multiple microphone setup being used extensively in AM broadcasting. The use of microphones such as the Stephens Tru-Sonic, the Altec, and the Electro-Voice, described briefly in Chap. I, is highly recommended for the single mike pickup of an orchestra.

Use a large studio for such instruments as the harp and the violin, or for piano solos, with the mike at a considerable distance from the performer. The separation should be about 15 feet.

There are musical programs which are produced best with multiple microphones such as those in which special accentuation is needed for soloists, for units within the orchestra, and quite frequently for dance-orchestra pickups. When in night clubs, etc., extraneous noises may require different microphone technique, in addition to special arrangements of muted instruments, guitars, and the like, for which accentuation is needed. The single-mike pickup is without doubt the best for a good orchestra, but for an amateur group it does not permit the operator to give greater strength to a weak violin section or to cut down upon an overly strong brass section. The balancing must be done within the orchestra, not by mechanical means.

High-fidelity

The past few years have seen a rapid growth in the number of people who have become more critical in their music listening habits. Instead of being content simply to listen to music, noting only its melody and rhythm, today's listener demands a quality in reproduction comparable to the quality in performance. No two people hear music in exactly the same way. Some prefer music soft, others loud; some respond to the shrill notes of the piccolo, others thrill to the roll of the organ. All music lovers agree, however, that most important is the need for "presence," the sense of feeling that the listener and the original performer are in the same room. This is the feeling that is the objective of the present-day "high-fidelity" system.

High-fidelity does not mean merely the reproduction of high notes or the topmost notes audible to the human ear. Every musical instrument has its own fundamental tones and its own special overtones which give it its own individual character. These go as high as human hearing (the extreme ranges of human hearing are 20 to 16,500 cycles). Without these overtones musical notes sound flat like some of the old phonograph records, which had top ranges below 5000 cycles. Thus, high-fidelity requires the extension of the top ranges in reproduction but requires also that they be properly equalized to match the original sound and accompanied by an extension of the bass range to provide proper balance. Attention to high notes alone can result in distorted reproduction with consequent dissatisfaction by the listener.

Ordinarily AM radio programs, especially network programs carried over telephone lines, are limited to 7500 cycles. In addition, AM reception is faced with the impossibility of overcoming noise from electrical appliances, hissing background noise on weak stations, or interference from adjacent stations.

In FM an entirely new method of transmission was developed which made possible the elimination of static, noise, fading, and interference by adjacent stations. Most important to the music lover, however, is the fact that FM can reproduce a full frequency range of 15,000 cycles. Thus, given a high-fidelity installation in the home, the music lover can have full "presence" of the performing artist, whether it is a recording played in the home, a live broadcast from an FM studio, or a broadcast of a recording played on professional equipment.

The Music Library

One of the most important divisions of a broadcasting station is the music library. The more music programs carried and produced by the station, the more important is the functioning of the music library. Where orchestras and other performers are employed by a station, the sheet music is purchased and filed by the music department. Also, recordings are bought, audited, timed, and catalogued. Programming of selections, preparation of music listings, and writing of continuity take place in the music library.

There are several different ways in which records and tapes can be catalogued, but the main test of the method chosen is whether it allows for a smooth operation in finding, "pulling," and refiling records. Sometimes a music department will have first to undergo a trial-and-error period in order to determine what system of cataloguing suits it best. One factor to be considered in setting up the catalogues is whether the music librarians will be "pulling" the discs for record programs, or whether the announcers themselves will be taking and replacing the records.

Programming of live and disc music programs will be prepared in the music library. This is usually done reasonably far in advance, with written notations made of the music to be performed, so there will be no overlapping or duplicating of selections broadcast within a short period of time.

Continuity written for music programs should be informal, accurate and interesting. Names of composers, compositions, etc., must *always* be correctly spelled, sometimes with the phonetic symbols written out. To help in the preparation of continuity, the librarian will want to have a comprehensive file of clippings, tear sheets and other information on composers and performers. These should be kept up to date and constantly expanded. It has been found that a satisfactory way to keep information contained on the backs of commercial record albums without having to file the cardboard bulk is to remove the record and then soak the cardboard jacket in a tub of water. The thin sheet containing the information is then easily removed, dried and filed in filing folders. This method of saving information is recommended for use when the cataloguing system requires the records to be removed from their commercial jackets and stored in plain, numbered sleeves.

The music department should be prepared to suggest ideas for new music programs, and should be able to carry these out. When the station policy permits the programming of serious music, it should be kept in mind that the music department has a certain responsibility for raising the general standards of music appreciation and understanding. The music department has a chance, then, to lead the way in the development of musical taste.

Music on Television

Some types of popular music programs have been transferred to television with outstanding success. The most notable example is "Your Hit Parade." To one who has seen this program it must be clear how much more difficult this program is on TV than it was on radio. Such a program is, of course, limited to high-budget network production. Some of the simpler music shows like the "Jo Stafford Show" have succeeded by building the program around a strong personality. A popular music show can also develop appeal where it is set in a specific locale, where a definite mood is developed, and where the music is interspersed with dialogue and dancing. These programs all utilize live music. TV has found no counterpart for the omnipresent disc jockey show on radio. Many different gimmicks have been tried, but I don't know of one that is in any degree as successful as a good radio d.j. show.

Operas, operettas, and musical comedies make excellent television fare, especially if they are staged and arranged for TV. A remote pickup of a stage production is less effective. The N.B.C. Opera Theatre has been eminently successful in bringing opera to television. They select operas that fit into the medium, and they have met with even more success when operas have been written especially for television. Gian-Carlo Menotti's Christmas opera, "Amahl and the Night Visitors," is perhaps

FIG. 40. N.B.C. spectacular production of "Naughty Marietta" being televised in color.

the best example. There are differences between the large stage of the theatre and the TV screen, but where these differences are accounted for, dramatic or semidramatic musical works can be shown on TV with great success.

The presentation of serious music on television involves more difficult problems. This is true whether the music is vocal or instrumental, solo or ensemble.

In the first place, what can pictures add to serious music? Is it true, as many have claimed, that pictures can add nothing, and in fact may be distracting? Well, let's think about it for a moment. People still go to the concert hall. It must be granted that the true music lover goes to the concert because it is only in this situation that he hears the music at its best. Despite the constant improvement, electronically amplified music is still a relatively poor substitute for the live sound. On the other hand, don't most people at a concert watch the performers as well as listen? Isn't the stage usually lighted to show the soloist or the orchestra to best advantage? Why, then, shouldn't the audience watch the performer on television?

It is indeed true that the TV picture can interfere with the music. By excessive cutting, use of weird angles, and other complicated TV effects, the director can take the audience's attention away from the sound. But "can" doesn't necessarily imply "does." Music can be presented on television in such a way that the visual and aural elements are not in conflict. The first principle to fix in mind is that in music the sound is of primary importance.

It follows, then, that the director's first job is to insure a good audio pickup. This must be done even at the expense of possible visual effects. The technique followed is the same as pickup for FM radio, since TV sound is broadcast by FM. Microphone placement, volume control, and similar subjects are covered in the radio section of this chapter.

All pieces of music have definite characteristics. They have a tempo, a mood, and a kind of dynamic personality. Music is written in segments such as measures, phrases, and movements. These factors determine how the director plans and cuts a music program. To do this it is necessary to plan and direct the show from the score. This implies that the TV director will have a sufficient knowledge of music to enable him to work in this fashion. The musically naïve person has no business trying to direct a music program, for once the character of the music has been violated by the camera the purpose of the music program has been lost. For example, it would rile the sensibilities of an audience if the director made rapid and violent cuts during a slow, legato piece of music. The visualization must be in keeping with the music. In this regard, as in the playing of music itself, there is no substitute for taste and musical experience.

When music programs are staged and directed by someone qualified in both music and television, they can be very pleasing. Experience tends to show that many people do like to watch the performers as long as the watching doesn't get in the way of the hearing. Trouble develops in putting music programs on TV when some inept soul tries to make something visually exciting where no such thing exists. He only succeeds in botching the job completely.

Another type of TV musical program that shows promise but is still in the experimental stage is the combination of music sounds and visual symbols. This method of programming also allows the use of recorded music on television. As examples, we can consider two programs prepared by Ted Hoffman and Jack Crist of the University of Illinois. In one program, three short works by Debussy and Ravel were played. Throughout the program the audience saw nothing but paintings done by artists of the French impressionistic school. Approximately 25 paintings were used, and they were carefully studied by the TV cameras. It was all worked out carefully with the mood and tempo of the music. The second program consisted of religious paintings from the Renaissance period viewed to the music of Bach's "Magnificat." This may sound like a simple procedure, but by the time the paintings are selected, their coverage rehearsed, and it is all fitted to the music, many hours of preparation have been used. The results, when well done, constitute a significant aesthetic experience.

Hillbilly, western, or country-style music fits into television with the greatest of ease. The performers are in costume. They are invariably accustomed to informal, easy presentations. They generate an atmosphere of fun and cordiality. The instruments played in this type of music lend themselves to interesting camera shots. A group of talented hillbilly artists can put on a good TV show with a minimum of fuss and planning, and on a very low production budget. Add an occasional bit of square dancing or a comedy routine and you have the makings of a highly appealing show. Again, this applies to live musicians, but in many parts of the country there is an ample supply of quite acceptable hillbilly talent.

As in the case of news, music programs should be offered on television because an audience that is watching television is not going to hear music played on radio, no matter how good that music may be. The continuing appeal of popular music indicates that a way will be found to use it on television. If you want a guaranteed career in television, just devise a program that will be the equivalent of the d.j. show on radio.

CHAPTER FIFTEEN

THE PREPARATION OF PROGRAMS FOR CHILDREN

It is not my purpose to enter into the controversy between child psychologists and commercial advertisers as to the validity of the contention that the majority of the children's programs now on the air are emotionally overstimulating and have undesirable effects upon the characters of the young listeners. It is more in keeping, in a handbook of this sort, to point out certain principles and techniques for the preparation and presentation of all kinds of programs directed toward an audience of children. Consideration of these principles will perhaps determine the program that the children themselves want, purposefully disregarding the preferences of commercial interests.

Writing for Children

The writer of children's programs must be well informed. He must know. If the script deals with current or historical events, it has to be true to underlying facts. If it is frankly fantastic and imaginary, it has to be conceivably genuine and not just fantasy used as an excuse for blood and thunder. Authenticity does not mean that the script contains all plodding details of everyday life. The writer must have a story, and it must move. Whether it is an original script or an adaptation of a literary classic, the writer may permit himself to telescope events and to select high points that keep interest in the program. A primary rule is not to pad a story. Trying to paint too complete a picture merely confuses the child and makes a story too long to hold his fickle attention.

In any case, the best interests of the child should be kept in mind and the choice of subject matter, the emphasis, and the play of good and evil should be such that the boy or girl who listens will like the qualities which we think make for happy living. We want the boys and girls to be attracted by all those things which build up mind, body, and spirit. We also want them to recognize the danger of opposite tendencies so that they will not fall into bad habits. In short, we want them to adopt and develop habits of self-control, self-respect, self-reliance, and self-culture.

What very young children, possibly from three to six years, want to hear over the air is difficult to gauge. Their listening tastes as well as their young minds are still in the formative stages. Thus children's scripts should make character building attractive. The Boy Scout laws of "trustworthiness, loyalty, helpfulness, bravery, cleanliness, friendliness, thrift, courtesy, and reverence" are a good standard for any writer to follow. Desirable activities should be stimulated, such as helping with the home duties, helping Dad, reading better books and magazines, and developing good hobbies. All these things may be inserted subtly into the script. With clever dialogue and easy style of writing, such things as lessons in safe use of matches and not talking to strangers are made highly palatable to the young listener.

It is entirely possible to combine the main objective of children's programs, wholesome entertainment, with a proper amount of instruction— not to be confused at any time with preaching. For example, there are morals in many of the classic fairy tales, and it should be noted that they are rarely exploited at the expense of the action of the plot.

Educational Programs

Much has been written and said about the value of more educational programs for children; programs which emphasize geography, history, mathematics, or other school subjects, programs which place the story as secondary with the education foremost. Education is very fine, but after a long day at school is the child not entitled to a little relaxation— listening to the programs he enjoys, instead of having adults trying to force some more book learning into his already overburdened head? As one children's director has said, "Don't forget that there is such a theory as a tired businessman of nine, and if history, geography, and botany have to creep into his listening hours, don't forget to let them creep."

Before attempting to write for children study them, their games, their reading habits, their comic-strip and movie preferences. Francis Pearson of Pennsylvania State College prepared a very helpful outline of the interests of children, based on age groups:

Children up to six years old like realism. They like to hear about the cat, the chicken, and the dog. Give such an audience stories of repetition, rhymes, and jingles. The stories must have quick action, rhythm, and familiar objects tinged with a bit of mystery. From six to nine, the child is always someone other than himself. It is the Fairy-tale period, and the child has passed from the realistic to the symbolical stage. This is a danger zone, for naturally if the symbols become real to him, sleep will be haunted with ogres and monsters. Yet such stories must be told, for to scorn the fairy tale is to scorn the source of our literature. It is well to be considerate to children in this age group by not offering them stories in which cruelty, revenge and bloodshed have a large part. If, however, in your approach to these topics you should encourage this group to listen, remember your moral-painting device and emphasize it.

Children from nine to twelve bring the barbaric, fighting instinct to the fore. Boys of this age, especially, are destructive out of curiosity. They demand action, danger and daring and are thrilled by physical bravery. Even with these children, you must be wary and use only stories that arouse ideals and fine aspirations. Robin Hood, so fearless and so kindly, is an excellent choice. Go to King Arthur, too, and you'll find a wealth of material. Keep to the realm of heroism whenever possible. And, until the boy begins to slick his hair and the girl to be interested in shades of lipstick, it will not be necessary to turn to the romantic.

Program Requisites

The first requisite for material to be used in a program for juvenile listeners is clarity—absolute clarity. No child will be interested in what he does not comprehend. Clarity can be achieved only through simplicity of language and construction and through simplicity of ideas. The first step is to decide the age group to which the program should appeal and then calculate as nearly as possible the ability of children of that age. Observation of a graded course of study for almost any grammar school will be helpful in determining what kind of material can be used for the different age groups. By knowing what they are studying in school, one can judge their ability to understand additional material.

Simplicity of language does not, under any consideration, imply baby talk. There is nothing quite so insulting to a child's intelligence as to be talked down to from the lofty heights of adulthood. Of course, a distinction should be made between talking to children and impersonating children. In selections like "The Raggedy Man," "At Auntie's House," and "Little Orphant Annie" by James Whitcomb Riley, the method is impersonation and the childish language is justified. Simplicity of language means the use of words understood by children of the age to which the material is directed, or, if any new words are used, the explanation of them in terms of words already known. It means, likewise, the use of simple sentence construction.

Clarity alone cannot insure a successful children's program. Equally important and much more difficult to achieve is interest. Children are even more impatient with the uninteresting than are adults. They cannot be induced to wait and see if something better will come later. They demand a story that holds them intent from the very first word to the last. They want fast action and plenty of it. Long explanations bore them, regardless of how beautiful the language may be. Therefore, anything that is not simple enough to be understood without explanation should be left out of children's stories. This does not mean that new and strange material cannot be used, but it should be introduced with simplicity.

Children's interests are aroused easiest by either the very familiar or the very strange. They like to hear the same stories over and over again, and they like to hear about boys and girls exactly like themselves. Or they like to hear about beautiful fairy princesses and giant killers, which are entirely out of the realm of actual experience, yet which are part of their world of imagination. So vivid and uninhibited are the imaginations of the young listeners that by concrete word pictures they can be lifted out of the present and from their homes to any place or era to which one may wish to take them. The instinct for hero worship can also be utilized to good advantage in the preparation of material to interest them. If they are able to identify themselves with an Abraham Lincoln or with a Babe Ruth and can hear the praises of those heroes, their interest is assured.

In addition to fast-moving action and image-arousing words, a further device for gaining interest is the use of direct address. By making the relationship one between the storyteller and each individual child rather than the group of children, the story becomes more important to each of them. Purely technical, but nonetheless important in holding interest, is the use of music and sound effects. Whimsical bridges and background music and appropriate and picturesque sound effects may be used to liven up the dramatic script.

During the past few years, there has been a decided tendency to neglect the fun-and-foolishness program and turn more to dramatic programs for children. This does not mean, however, that there should be no comedy in children's programs. Children love to laugh and be entertained the same as adults. They are ardent followers of comedians upon adult programs. For their own afternoon programs, however, they like drama.

These dramas should have some characters in them that are comical or at least suggest comedy. Comedy relief is needed in children's programs as well as in any other kind of program.

Characterization in a children's drama is of prime importance. Boys and girls will be the first to discover inconsistencies in young characters that are not true to the age they represent. The roles of all actors must be natural and true to life. They should not be too perfect. In fact, they should be endowed with both human weaknesses and human virtues. If they are too perfect, they might disillusion the child.

Don't attempt to emulate or imitate a program that is on the air. Test your stories on the neighborhood children; they will be sincere and severe critics. Don't leave the listener worked up to an emotional pitch; solve things, end the worry. Be sure to aim at a definite age group; constant shifting will result in confusion and the loss of any permanent listening audience. Avoid tragedy, psychological studies, wordy character plays, social drama, and sex. Above all, do not undertake to write for children if you don't like children and if you don't love to tell them stories.

Stage Plays Adaptable for Radio Use (for Children, Grades I–VI)

It is the tendency of the writer of children's plays to indulge in whimsy, to introduce the supernatural and unreal. There is also a very strong tendency to introduce into such plays a number of short acts with multiple settings and large casts. The director who broadcasts these plays encounters these difficulties and others. For example, the type of characters that populate the majority of plays for children are March hares and gasoline pumps, buttercups and maple trees, the North Wind, and spiders. There is no form of speech to enable the listener to distinguish between the speech of butterflies and of fish. To be sure, the speech of a dog may occasionally be punctuated with a bark and that of a cat with a "miaow," but this repetition would prove tiresome and not particularly interesting to the listener. For these reasons, then, be chary of those plays whose only characters are naturally speechless.

In regard to the setting of these plays, we are confronted by still another problem. While transition of scenes is easily accomplished over the air, it is necessary to remember that children's minds do not follow too many shifts with a great deal of ease. Therefore, it is wise to limit the number of scenes. A single plot, simply developed, is most easily understood and enjoyed. Then there are the time element; the lack of visual aid to arouse interest and understanding on the part of the audience;

the necessarily limited cast required for radio production—these and many other problems directors meet only too often.

Despite these numerous disadvantages, however, there still remain many plays that are admirably suited for radio production. It would be necessary, in the majority of instances, for the director to do some adapting to meet the principles of broadcasting as well as his or her own individual problems. For those directors who may experience difficulty in finding material suitable for adaptation, the following list of plays has been compiled. All plays listed herewith may be satisfactorily adapted for radio use. It will be noted that the number of characters in these plays has been omitted because with the necessary shifting and rearranging of parts the size and type of cast used for radio production would differ materially in individual cases. Asterisks designate plays especially recommended for radio use.

Auditorium Series, by Harriet, Alice Louise, and Florence March, The Auditorium Press, 2524 LaSalle Gardens North, Detroit, Mich. All rights reserved. (1) *The Bishop's Candlesticks;* (2) *Capt. Smith and Pocahontas;* (3) *Rumplestiltskin;* (4) *Rip Van Winkle;* (5) *The Boston Tea Party;* (6) *Robin Hood.**

Cross Your Heart, by Ann Clark, Dramatic Publishing Company, Chicago. Broadcasting rights on application.

11 Plays for Children, by Edith Lombard Squires, Fitzgerald Publishing Corporation, New York. All rights reserved. (1) *Donner and Blitzen;** (2) *Picnic Luck.*

Easy Plays for Children, Fitzgerald Publishing Company. All rights reserved. (1) *Please! Mr. Weatherman;* (2) *The Chocolate Bunny and the Sweetmeat Chick;** (3) *The Conceited Weathercock;** (4) *The Magic Word;* (5) *The Way the Noise Began.*

*The Emperor's New Clothes,** by Charlotte Charpenning, Samuel French, Inc., New York. Broadcasting rights by special arrangement.

Footlights Up!, by Louise Housman and Edward T. Koehler, Harper & Brothers, New York. Broadcasting rights by permission. (1) *Cap O' Rushes;** (2) *Dick Whittington;** (3) *The Three Citrons;** (4) *Man without a Country;** (5) *The Birdcage Maker.**

*Jack and the Beanstalk,** a puppet play, by Beatrice T. Lee, Samuel French, Inc., New York. May be broadcast with permission.

*Little Black Sambo,** by Hazel Sharrard Kaufman, Samuel French, Inc., New York. Special arrangements may be made for broadcasting.

Little Plays Told to the Children, by Lena Dalkeith, E. P. Dutton & Company, Inc., New York. (1) *Sir Gareth of Orkney;** (2) *The Princess and the Swineherd;* (3) *King Alfred and the Cakes;* (4) *Scene from Robin Hood.*

Nine Short Plays, collected by M. Jagendorf, The Macmillan Company, New York. Radio rights with permission. (1) *The Bean Boy* by Towle Adair;

(2) *Three of a Different Kind* by Eric Wolf;° (3) *The Dowry of Columbine* by Bertha Goes; (4) *A Tale from India* by Florence Bradley Moore.

The Pirate of Pooh and Other Plays, by Marjorie Barrows, Rand McNally & Company, Chicago. Broadcasting rights on application. (1) *The Pirate of Pooh;* (2) *The Clown of Doodle Doo;*° (3) *The Enchanted Door;* (4) *Santa and Son;*° (5) *The Brownie Bush;* (6) *Jack O'Lantern Inn;* (7) *The Prickly Prince;*° (8) *The Surprise Christmas;* (9) *The Wistful Witch;*° (10) *The Valentine Tree;*° (11) *The Pink Parrot.*

Poetry Programs for Children

Radio is perhaps the ideal way to present the wealth of good poetry to children. The child should think of poetry as something connected with leisure, fun, and entertainment, not as a subject in school, and at home the child seldom hears poetry read aloud after he outgrows the Mother Goose jingles. Few parents know the world's great treasury of poetry and so cannot lead and direct the child in his enjoyment. It is up to radio to help bring to youth the vast and fascinating world of poetry.

For children up to six or eight years, poems should stress rhythm and musical swing rather than meaning. The Mother Goose rhymes are ideal; their irresistible rhythm, their quaint verse form, and their whimsical nonsense delight children everywhere. They are a perfect basis on which to build an appreciation of poetry. (The musical arrangement of *Nursery Rhymes* by Pearl Curran is particularly interesting.)

The contact of many children with poetry stops when they have outgrown Mother Goose; however, there is a vast library of poetry for children of every age. The jingles and short verses pave the way for the poems of childhood, and these in turn should lead to the enjoyment of lyrics, epics, sonnets, and ballads. Only poems easily visualized and words easily understood should be used on the radio. Situations met in childhood, such as portrayed in "The Mortifying Mistake" by Anna Pratt, are very acceptable. Radio appeals to the child's imagination, inspires him to create mental pictures, and teaches him to observe the things about him.

> A birdie with a yellow bill
> Hopped upon my window sill.

Such short verses are remembered and are repeated by the small listener when a live bird is in sight. Good habits of diet may be represented in an interesting manner by members of a primary class broadcasting "Mary

Anne's Luncheon" by Dorothy Aldis. Many more programming ideas will be found in the wealth of poetry for children by Vachel Lindsay, A. A. Milne, Rose Fyleman, Walter de la Mare, Sara Teasdale, Robert Louis Stevenson, Eugene Field, and Lewis Carroll.

As the child develops into the adolescent stage he begins to enjoy serious as well as the lighter poetry. Inspirational poetry fulfills a growing need in the life of the adolescent. Examples include: "Abou Ben Adhem," "For Those Who Fail," "Lifting and Leaning." Another type of poetry popular especially with boys is the adventurous type: "The Ancient Mariner," "Gunga Din," "Lochinvar," and "The Explorer."

Performers for Children's Programs on Radio

In a consideration of the type of personality best adapted to the presentation of narrative children's programs, the most important characteristic is imagination. Not only must the performer have imagination, but he must be willing to forget his adult dignity and thoroughly enjoy the thrilling tales he unfolds for his youthful listeners. He must be able to speak their language and to enjoy speaking it. In addition to possessing this desirable personality, he must have the ability to project that personality through the single medium of voice. His interest in his audience will not be apparent unless his voice possesses vitality; while he may have sufficient patience, he may fail to make it felt by his audience unless his voice is smooth and his speech even and unhurried. A single harsh note creeping into the voice, because it suggests a lack of patience, may destroy confidence.

The conscientious reader will not only take great care in the preparation of each program but he will practice by telling stories in person to children at every opportunity. The effectiveness of his delivery will undoubtedly improve if he is able to incorporate the suggestions from and the preferences of this potential radio audience.

In a program that is strictly a dramatic presentation, acting ability is the important thing, but here again, as in the narrative type of show, the delivery will sound forced and condescending unless the actor actually enjoys his own particular role and the wonder and adventure of the script. A half-hearted characterization is readily apparent to the young listener, who resents such patronization. Performers in all types of children's programs should remember that it won't be fun to listen to unless it's fun to put on.

Television for Children

It may well be true that television's most faithful audience is the child population. The visual appeal of TV fills the vacuum left by radio and its essentially verbal appeal. When children can see the cowboys galloping across the plains in pursuit of the bad men, the make-believe is more real and fascinating.

It has become standard practice for television stations to devote the late afternoon hours, just before dinner, and a good share of Saturday morning to the children. There are many products that are sold largely through their appeal to children. Few parents care whether their children eat Wheaties or Corn Flakes for breakfast. If the advertiser can convince the youngster to ask for a certain cereal, or candy bar, or ice cream, he has usually made a sale. The right children's program on TV seems to accomplish this job.

The basic principles discussed in the early portions of this chapter apply to television. Programs must be clear and readily understood. They must contain elements that arouse a high degree of interest. They must move at a good pace. People on children's programs must be real, and that means real in children's terms, not adult terms.

Television has opened up a vast market for dramatic programs that appeal to children. Fortunately, however, not all sponsors and stations turn to drama. There are programs that depend on games, songs, comedy, and other devices for their appeal. There is nothing wrong with drama for children per se, but in the total programming structure some effort should be made to obtain participation from the viewing children. Too much emphasis on purely passive spectating is not st'mulating to the child's imagination and mental processes. Program formats that try to induce the child toward some activity offer a refreshing change of pace. Another opportunity that shouldn't be missed is the possibility of having animals, interesting objects, machines, and all manner of things in the studio for the children to see. This can be done, and good explanations made of the things being seen, without losing any interest. In fact, to the contrary, sometimes this kind of thing inserted in a children's show will become the major attraction. The world of everyday life holds many similar enchanting possibilities. A brief film visit to the local fire station, followed by one of the firemen in the studio with some of his equipment, is a typical example. None of this sort of programming need be thought of as education—to the child it is fascinating and fun.

It is probably safe to say that every TV station runs cowboy movies, almost every day at least. To those of us who remember making the regular Saturday trip to the cowboy double feature at the local movie house this isn't surprising. Most well-done adventure stories appeal to children, whether they be of the wild west, the Yukon, the jungles, outer space, or wherever. Children's hours on TV have opened a new market for Hollywood's vaults full of old cartoons, comedies, and melodramas. The TV screen offers circuses, puppets, marionettes, storytellers, folk singers, and a host of other talent trying to capture the fancy of the young fry. There have been, and continue to be, some outstanding children's programs on TV. Walt Disney has entered the field and his work always seems to have an enormous appeal. The Chicago-originated programs, "Ding-Dong School," "Zoo Parade," and "Mr. Wizard" have been outstanding. Productions of this latter type, and works like Barrie's "Peter Pan," follow the pattern of great children's literature; they appeal to children of all ages.

Television's programs for children have generated the same kind of criticism that has been leveled at radio. The truth of this matter probably rests at some point in between the critics and the broadcasters. Neither side is wholly right. There have been some excellent children's programs; programs which clearly prove that gruesome violence, raucous noise, distorted values, and salacious material aren't essential in an appeal to children. On the other hand, there have been children's programs which, at the very best, were anything but good, and at the worst were possibly very harmful.

Broadcasting is not like most other businesses. It is similar to the press in that it has solemn responsibilities as well as many privileges. It deals with human minds, and cannot be free to use any and all materials just because people will watch or listen. This is especially true in programming for children. Any broadcaster who is unwilling to assume his responsibilities toward children is not entitled to the use of a public license for profit. Fortunately, most broadcasters are aware of these responsibilities, and there is little on the air that can be established as downright harmful. Much of the controversy is a problem of tastes, and on this subject we cannot legislate.

Perhaps of more importance in this regard are the adult programs which children may watch. While broadcasters and writers of books about broadcasting may separate children's programs from adult programs, to the child it is all TV. The child will watch a horror story or grisly murder with as much relish as his parents. The question is, should he watch it? Broadcasters need to exercise care in seeing that programs which might be badly misunderstood by younger children are broadcast at hours when they normally aren't available to watch.

Still, the parents cannot hold the broadcasters responsible for the raising of the nation's children. A broadcaster can exercise normal care and restraint, but the parents must rear their own children. TV has had such a fascination for most children that it is all too convenient for the parent to abandon his duties to this electronic baby sitter. Experience shows that in homes where the parents take an interest in their children, some of this fascination dissipates after a short while, and the child resumes a normal life. At this stage, the child's consumption of television can be adequately controlled.

This same point is important in programming for older children. The home must exercise some control over the child. For the older child, TV affords many things of interest. The boys will like the baseball games and other sports. Both sexes like variety shows, comedies, romantic dramas, good historical dramas such as "You Are There," and many other programs. There probably will be some things that parents would rather their teen-agers didn't watch, but this may not be sufficient reason for taking them off the air.

CHAPTER SIXTEEN

BROADCASTS TO SCHOOLS

Those interested in the use of radio in education have recognized the opportunity resulting from the action of the Federal Communications Commission in setting aside frequencies in the FM bands for educational stations and in permitting low-power FM stations (described in Chap. II). At the beginning of 1956, there were 164 educational stations owned and operated by universities, school systems, and other educational groups and institutions. Of these 164, 34 were AM stations. Many are low-power stations which will develop into more powerful units by increasing their power. All of the stations owned and operated by school systems indulge in direct teaching by radio with their programs directed to the classroom. The majority of the AM-FM stations owned by universities and colleges have school programs as well.

This chapter is limited to an outline of methods that are successfully used in direct radio and television teaching. However, direct teaching is not the major purpose of educational broadcasting, for the majority of programs are designed to supplement or enrich the work of the local teacher, to stimulate the interest of the student, to demonstrate methods of teaching, or to provide a useful tool of instruction for school talent.

Despite the fact that teachers or those interested in education were the first to recognize the great opportunity offered to them by radio, they have not yet agreed upon a lucid definition of education by radio. Educational broadcasting should obviously include more than the presentation of such subject matter as is regularly taught in the various grades of school. In fact, adult education possibly has a greater value. It cannot be stated that every program emanating from an educational institution is educational, for there are many sports programs and dance-orchestra programs so broadcast. It is equally true that not all commercial programs can be condemned, for many of them possess educational merit. The following tests have been suggested to determine whether a commercial program is educational:

1. Does the program convey to the listeners socially desirable information which they did not possess before hearing the program? If so, the program is educational. But the significance of the term "socially desirable information" must not be overlooked. It means information which society at large would regard as being generally desirable for the average person to know, especially such types of information as tend to improve the individual himself and enable him to keep pace with the gradually rising level of social knowledge and culture. This would classify programs dealing with merely curious bits of information as being entertaining rather than educational.

2. Does the program discuss items of knowledge and give clear-cut directions for their practical application so that the listeners not only have a clear understanding of the items of knowledge but can make practical application of them as need or occasion arises? If so, the program is educational.

3. Does the program give a step-by-step explanation of how to do or make a certain thing with clear-cut directions as each step is covered so that the listeners can do or make the thing as need or occasion may arise? If so, the program is educational.

4. Does the program present a problem involving the exercise of judgment or constructive thinking in such a way as to bring out, in an impartial and dispassionate manner, all of the various factors involved in the problem so that the listeners are stimulated to make an intelligent evaluation and arrive at a logical conclusion? If so, the program is educational.

Program Types

Roughly classified, radio broadcasts can be grouped under the general headings: talks, directed activities, actuality broadcasts, conversations, debates, and plays. The different subjects demand different types of programs, which have been discussed in previous chapters. One of the most important factors of the successful program is the personality and attitude of the speaker. He must be friendly and courteous. His personality must be magnetic to such a degree that he can hold his unseen audience and make it receptive to his ideas. He must appear to be on the pupil's level, yet retain his own personality. His attitude must be one of cooperation. If the speaker feels his talk is somewhat serious for the juvenile audience, he should use stories from life to illustrate it.

It is through directed activity that nearly all radio teaching is done. Courses that are easy to teach in this manner are music, science, art, and arithmetic. Usually the students take notes or follow instructions during the broadcasts. Some teachers give short daily tests covering the material that has been presented. Other teachers encourage direct discussion, and still others use both oral and written compositions as a means of discovering just how much of the radio lesson the students have been able to retain.

Actuality broadcasts describe important events of public interest with the proper sound effects and commentaries. Broadcasts such as these aid the student in his study of current events. Actuality programs broadcast from a museum or art gallery, from the Senate Chamber, or from a courtroom are vivid dramas to teach the school boy or girl. Actuality broadcasts are sometimes exciting for the announcer as well as interesting to the listener. I recall that in one zoology broadcast a member of the faculty brought a 4-foot rattlesnake into the announcer's booth so that he might broadcast the rattle of the snake. In order to get the snake to rattle, the speaker had to annoy the snake. Another radio teacher brought a bear cub into the studio. I can assure you that in these cases there was plenty of interest upon the program, and the feelings of the interviewer were very obvious.

Conversation or dialogue on the air is interesting to the high school student. This procedure introduces new and different trends of thought and permits the student to tie his own ideas to those presented. The pupils hear the viewpoints of people who are well versed in the subject in hand. Thus the student's knowledge is increased and broadened.

The presentation of debates over the air is difficult. In the first place, the listener may feel that the station is biased. Then, too, the subject must be controversial, yet must not offend any of the listeners. The subject must also be interesting to a widespread audience. It is difficult to select a subject, do a great deal of research work on it, and then present it in such a way that the audience may grasp, in a limited period of time, the ideas that have been produced after weeks of work.

Plays for pupils should be short and the sound effects, while more numerous than in plays planned for the general audience, must be simple. Characters should be limited, and the contrast in voices should be marked. Special lines should be used to introduce each voice. Study the requirements set forth in the chapters on Writing the Radio and Television Play and on Preparation of Children's Programs.

Radio addresses can be used for all subjects but they must be short and attractive. Round tables for topics dealing with literature, civics, or current events give a varied viewpoint. In fact, every type of radio program should be examined, and the one best suited to the subject matter to be presented should be chosen.

Preparing the Program

It is wise to have a teacher gather the material, for accurate facts are essential, and then turn these facts over to the radio showman for development into an interesting presentation. However, the teacher and the broadcaster must cooperate in building the program because the former is better able to visualize the school audience while the latter is more familiar with the medium. The vocabulary level and the mental understanding of the young listeners should be determined by the educator. The subject matter, in conformation with the radio requirements, should be organized by the program director.

A limited phase of the topic should be chosen for each broadcast, for the listener demands a satisfying completeness despite the limited period allotted to the program. It is wise to create in each period an interest in the radio lesson to follow. A few points, illustrated clearly, make it possible for the pupil to retain what he hears. Start out with some interest-catching statement and work to an effective close. The requirements of radio style previously set forth should be followed—a friendly conversational style using strong simple diction. George M. Cohan wrote a song whose title contained good advice, "Always Leave Them Laughing When You Say Goodbye."

While interest is essential in the radio school program, it must not crowd out educational value. Frequently the drama type of school program has little left that is instructive after the music, sound effects, and plot have been discarded in the classroom discussion following the program. The school program, furthermore, should be planned to fit into the curricula of as many schools as possible. For this reason it is well to discuss such topics and presentations with education boards while planning them; do not broadcast programs on Shakespeare when the school children are studying O. Henry. Another general requirement is to arrange the program for pupils of a definite level and then inform teachers what grades are to listen. Be certain that the pupil in those grades will understand every word, follow every sentence, and be familiar with every allusion. While school programs must contain facts and information, no one will listen to learn those facts unless the programs are interesting. Try the continuity out on a group of youngsters before you send it into the air; otherwise it may just float away, bringing neither credit to the teacher nor knowledge to the listener. In order that teachers may call their classes to order and correctly tune their radios, the first 5 minutes should be either music or relatively unimportant material.

Listener Participation

A good program should conform to an outline that is easy for the listener to follow in note taking. Use all available means to create interest and cooperation by the student listeners, such as appointing secretaries, discussion leaders, class property men, and others with definite duties to perform in preparation for the broadcast or in following up the program. In selling his instruction, the wise educational broadcaster will adopt all the worthwhile ideas of the advertiser on sponsored programs. Contests, essays, the reading of "testimonials" from students—all these and other methods will enlist the interest of the audience. Some principals and teachers have only a limited number of their students listen to a radio program; these students take notes and report to the class, an excellent practice in listening and note taking. The broadcaster must learn when to pause so that the listener can take his notes or participate in other ways. The best idea is for the broadcaster to have a group of pupils in the studio with him where he can watch their participation and thus time his delivery. Listeners are frequently asked to repeat pronunciations of words, to answer questions, or to draw pictures; consequently the radio teacher must learn to give adequate opportunity for this participation. It is also wise to repeat essential material, but this should be done in such a way as not to bore the listener.

Music Instruction

Since Dr. Joseph E. Maddy was very successful in teaching the playing of wind and stringed instruments over the air from the University of Michigan, the procedure that he used is given in his own phraseology:

The procedure is simple. I use two adjoining studios, separated by sound-proof windows. In one studio I have a studio band, orchestra, or choir of university students or high school students. This group demonstrates for the pupils by sounding tones and chords to be repeated by the pupils at the receiving end of the lesson. In an adjoining studio I have a class of beginning students who sit facing a radio-receiving set, from which they receive their instructions. By watching these pupils I am enabled to synchronize the speed of the lesson with the average ability of the pupils taking the lesson.

Whenever I have a few spare hours I visit some of my radio classes for the purpose of ascertaining wherein I have failed to accomplish the objectives of the preceding lessons. I learn something from every class I visit, and in this way I believe I am improving my teaching technic week by week.

The first part of the first lesson consists in matching tones. The first exercise in the Radio Music Course uses three tones, do, re, and mi. The studio band sustains each of these tones while the pupils strive to match them. We take time to demonstrate to the pupils by tones which octave to play and give them some idea of how to read the fingering charts in their books.

We learn to play the first exercise by rote. The studio band plays the melody, then the pupils try to imitate the phrases as sounded by the studio band.

The first lesson is never complete until we have tried to play "America." It isn't necessary to completely teach the playing of "America," for they will learn it by themselves, even if they succeed in playing only the starting tone during the lesson.

If I can send every radio pupil home with the ability to play one tone and confidence that he will be able to learn to play "America" within a few hours' practice, my first lesson will have been a success.

Succeeding lessons follow a similar plan. The pupils learn to play two or three new songs each lesson, by rote, but they watch the notes for fingering marks and eventually acquire some ability in sight reading. The complete course is recorded so that the students may use the recordings at home between radio lessons. The recordings are harmonized so that pupils may harmonize with the recorded orchestra.

Vocational Guidance

As vocational guidance is becoming more and more important in our educational system, we see that the radio plays an equally important role in presenting adequate information about this subject to the schools.

The principal purpose of these programs is to provide high school boys and girls with information that will be helpful in choosing their vocations. Experience has shown that radio talks of this type have been received most favorably when the type of audience was kept clearly in mind in preparing and presenting the talk. A simple, straightforward, fairly informal style is the best.

What these young people want to know about an occupation is well indicated by the following outline, which has been prepared by specialists in this field. The main headings may be of assistance to you in preparing your radio talk.

1. *Importance of the Occupation.* A few sentences concerning its origin and development; society's dependence upon it; the number of people employed in it (men and women); supply of workers as compared with demand; distribution (in every community or in certain communities).

2. *Nature of the Work.* General character; divisions of the occupation (fields of specialization); what the worker does in the largest division or group (a typical day's work may be described). Is work routine in character or mentally stimulating?
3. *General Working Conditions.* Hours of work; slack and peak seasons; physical environment; social environment; health and safety conditions.
4. *Remuneration.* Average earnings at the beginning, after ten years, after twenty years; exceptional earnings; how paid—by hour, weekly, annually, by fees, etc.; pensions and annuities; vacation periods and sick leave; social recognition; satisfaction from community service.
5. *Opportunities for Advancement.* Possible lines of promotion; factors influencing promotion; opportunities to transfer to related occupations.
6. *Important Personal Qualifications.* Age requirements; physical requirements; mental requirements; temperamental requirements; personal traits needed; social aptitudes important.
7. *Preparation.* General education desirable; special education needed and where obtainable; cost of preparation; continued preparation after work begins and how secured; how occupation is entered.
8. *Teaching facilities.* Those available to one intending to enter this vocation.

Subject matter is the most important factor in the vocational program. The students are not to be entertained, primarily, but are in need of authoritative information about different vocations. A sheet of suggestions for utilizing each broadcast can be prepared to accompany each lesson, as well as a manual for teachers, containing supplemental questions and answers, based on the program, and a list of suggested readings.

Short plays are especially helpful in presenting the material to the student in an interesting way. These plays should take the child through the various experiences of choosing a vocation and show how the vocational adviser reaches his decisions in helping young people choose their work.

Interviews by students with men and women in some of these representative vocations make very successful programs. This type of program enables the students to get some firsthand information about various vocations, and as a result they are enthusiastic about learning all they can about the work in which they are especially interested. The problem is to avoid overstimulating susceptible listeners.

Elementary Science

The teaching of elementary science has been successfully conducted through the medium of the radio. It is vital for the teacher to humanize the subject, showing how its applications affect the individual. The programs, while being a form of direct teaching, are largely considered to be an incentive to further study and experimentation by the student. It is wise to choose class discussions in which there may be some sound effects to make for greater realism. The speech itself may be direct lecture, a dialogue between a student and his teacher, or a classroom demonstration. It is wise to tie in the experiment being performed in a period with what has been broadcast on a previous lesson, and at the close of the program to announce the equipment that the receiving student should have available to be used in the next broadcast. There are many devices that may be used upon these science programs to create interest, such as questions that have been sent in by students. The radio teacher must insert adequate pauses to enable the student in his home workshop to carry on the experiment that is being demonstrated in the broadcasting studio. In presenting this type of course, the teacher must realize the limitations of the home laboratory and select as equipment those things that the student can easily obtain. Radio lessons in science are being conducted in many school systems. The following is a script used in Cleveland.

SCIENCE—RADIO—POCKET NO. IV—ITEM NO. 400

ELEMENTARY SCIENCE RADIO LESSONS

Grades 4B and 4A

UNIT III—WHY DO LIVING THINGS NEED AIR AND WATER?

Specific Directions For Each Lesson

Lesson No. 18—Air: What is it? Where is it?
   Lesson No. 18: During this lesson the children learn by experimenting that air is real, air takes up space, air presses against things, and that air is everywhere.

To be Copied on the Blackboard:

Prove that:
1. Air is real.
2. Air takes up space.
3. Air presses against things.
4. Air is everywhere.
5. Air supports light things.
6. Air that moves is wind.

Materials Needed:

Please have the following materials on the science table:

1. a box wrapped attractively as a gift with fancy paper and ribbons

For Experiment 1:

2. a clean empty medicine bottle (Please remove the cap.)
3. a pan of water (about three-fourths full) Use the one for washing boards

    * * If the children are seated around a table, it would be advantageous for each group to perform this experiment.

For Experiment 2:

4. a pan of water (the same one used in Experiment 1)
5. an empty glass

For Experiment 3:

6. a paper bag (Please have a clean one with no holes in it.)

For Experiment 4:

7. a milk bottle (Either a quart or pint milk bottle may be used.)
8. a ladies' handkerchief—one that will fit over the mouth of the bottle
9. some string (enough to tie the handkerchief over the mouth of the bottle)
10. an empty can
11. a pitcher of water

For Experiment 5:

12. an electric stove

    * * JUST *BEFORE* THE LESSON, PLUG THE HOT PLATE IN. PUT THE PAN OF WATER ON IT AND BOIL THE WATER. DURING THE LESSON WATCH THAT THE WATER DOES NOT BOIL AWAY. ADD SOME WATER IF IT GETS TOO LOW.

13. pan of water (about one-fourth full)
14. a lump of soil
15. a glass of water
16. paper towels—to dry hands if necessary

Suggestions for after the Lesson:

1. Check the sentences on the board that were proved during the lesson. Tell how they were proved. Do experiments again if necessary to review the main points of the lesson.

Follow-up Suggestions:

1. Perform experiments to prove sentences 4, 5, and 6 on the board.

Suggestions:

Sentence No. 5—Air supports light things:

Hold a sheet of paper straight out and let it drop. The paper drops slowly, very often it flutters from side to side. It is supported by the air.

Every time you hold a sheet of paper level, you will find that it flutters in this way, supported by the air.

Sentence No. 6—Air that moves is wind:

Fan each other with tablet backs. When you make the air move, you feel wind.

2. Perform the experiment with the cork, glass, and pan suggested in the Fourth Grade Science Course of Study, page 68. Use slide 4A Pe. 1—Why Does Cork Go To Bottom—to check the experiment.

3. Perform many other experiments about air.

Teaching History

Perhaps the most successful method for holding the attention of the student and giving to him facts in history is the dramalogue. Many of the commercial programs that are presenting historical dramas are of value to the student of history and may be assigned for "collateral listening." The historical dramatization must be prepared in such a way that the romantic or fiction material does not overwhelm the historical facts. These facts must be accurate and gathered by an instructor in history who has conducted research in the particular time and event that are to be presented over the radio. While wars are considered of great importance in the teaching of history, it is generally conceded that history radio programs should not glorify war or arouse hatred for the enemy. It is better in such dramatizations to stress the lives of individuals and through these lives bring out historical facts. The authors must be familiar with the daily life of the time he is portraying, for the diction and the minor events are of vital importance as well as the major historical facts.

A method that has been found very successful is that of tracing history backward, taking some aspects of life today and tracing it to its origin. Such topics as transportation, banking, communication, and cooperative movements can be treated by this method, either through the dramalogue or through other methods of presentation.

The straight-lecture type of program may also be used by the instructor who has the research libraries of a university at his disposal. He will give enriching material to supplement the work of the local teacher, who has neither the time nor the facilities for such research. Bibliographies of collateral reading may be broadcast in connection with such talks.

Civics

Classes in civics will gain a clearer concept through an actuality type of broadcast. The teachers of civics courses should keep in touch with the daily-program schedules that are distributed by radio stations whose programs may be heard in their locality. They will discover many broadcasts such as those from the Senate Chamber, those by the President, speeches by the Governor, traffic-court broadcasts, and various series dealing with government which will be both timely and instructive to their students. In the majority of instances broadcasting stations are willing to send their weekly schedules to the principals of schools. These can be posted upon the bulletin board for examination by the teachers in various courses.

News broadcasts are frequently of value to the civics teacher, especially those programs which vitalize the study of government through the introduction of speakers who are in the day's news. The local station may cooperate with classes by conducting radio visits to various officials. The teacher should introduce the program, telling something about the man who is to speak and laying a groundwork so that the student can visualize the broadcaster. Unfortunately many of the programs of this type are prepared for adult audiences; consequently the local teacher must be alert to make notes upon any statement that will not be understood by her pupils and to clarify it at the end of the program. Explanations of civil government by officials who would arrange their material for the school level could do much in educating the future citizens.

Geography

Visual aids are essential in the teaching of geography by radio. A radio tour may be conducted from week to week, visiting various cities and countries. Maps and globes may be used by the students to follow the trips. Sound effects on the program will assist in making the tour more realistic.

The dramatic method is particularly good in such a series. Interest should be built up around a central character. Possibly a father with his son and daughter may be traveling around the world. Human interest will create a week-to-week appeal in such programs. Various modes of travel by rail, steamship, airplane, and even the rocket plane have been used to conduct the schoolroom travelers quickly from one part of the world to another. The speaker must be careful not to attempt to cover too much in a single program. Some limited phase of geography should be chosen for the series. The series might consider the famous art galleries, the industries of different nations, the people and the customs, or agricultural resources. Advance information concerning each broadcast should be sent out to the schoolteachers who are using the series so that pictures, maps, and other material may be posted upon the blackboards of the schoolroom to interest juvenile travelers.

Speech

Probably no single course is more extensively taught by radio than that of speech. In fact, every announcer is an instructor in such a course. Speech departments in nearly all the universities have presented radio courses. In most of these programs the instructor is assisted by students whose pronunciation, persuasiveness, arrangement of material, clarity, and speech qualities are criticized by the radio teacher. However, the programs should not be permitted to end until the student has corrected his delivery and material to conform to the criticism that has been made. For such courses mimeographed material is usually provided for the students who are listening from some distant point, or a textbook is assigned. The use of a public-address system in the local school in imitation of a radio program may be used as a tool to stimulate interest in speech instruction. I have always maintained to my students in broadcast speech that, if they were to accept positions in the teaching of speech in a town in which there is a local broadcasting station, they could build short programs to be presented by their pupils. The local broadcasting station could be induced to present these during the morning hours when sustaining programs are needed. Programs by the school children would bring a definite audience to the station, consisting of parents and friends of the children who participate. These programs will be interesting and will demonstrate what is being done in the classroom. Such an activity would strengthen the position of the teacher, since she would have all the parents enthusiastic about the work they hear over the radio. This project for the speech teacher in the elementary schools would also serve as a wedge to be used in breaking into the field of broadcasting. The radio is an excellent medium of instruction for speech and debating. All radio programs by public men and outstanding announcers enrich and supplement the work of the local teacher.

Other Radio Classes

Arithmetic has been successfully taught by the radio classroom method, using mimeographed sheets which are distributed to the pupils and which are corrected by the local teacher. Such a program must be given very slowly. The pupil activity will hold the attention of the distant students. Cooperation of the local teacher is essential in such a radio class. Both music and art appreciation have been extensively taught by radio. Visual aids are particularly helpful in the art-appreciation courses, in which familiar statues and paintings are evaluated. Foreign languages have been taught both on the broadcast and by short wave. Through these mediums accurate pronunciation may be brought to the student. The local student is usually provided with a textbook and follows the pronunciation given by the radio teacher. When such broadcasts are sent from a university or college, it is possible to bring a foreign student before the microphone to speak in the language of his native country and tell about the life of the youth in that country. Such programs must present speakers whose enunciation is precise and not rapid.

Teachers' Guides

All those who are actively engaged in teaching by radio and in broadcasting educational programs to the schools agree upon the vital necessity of preparing teachers' guides to be sent in advance of the program to the teachers who will be receiving the programs.

The Radio Council of the Chicago Public Schools, George Jennings, director, does an excellent job in the preparation of such teachers' broadcast handbooks. Each semester, 10 to 20 programs are selected as a "core" of broadcasting, and handbooks for teachers' use prepared for them, covering the entire series of programs. These handbooks are mimeographed and distributed to each school. In addition, a semester schedule is prepared which lists all program series by individual title, grade level, and subject area.

A number of different approaches to the problem of teachers' guides have been developed at the Radio Council. For "The American Heritage" broadcasts, one page of the handbook was given over to "suggested *series* activities":

THE AMERICAN HERITAGE

SUGGESTED SERIES ACTIVITIES

Learn the *Freedom Pledge.*

Review the *Four Freedoms* as set forth by Franklin Delano Roosevelt in his Message to the 77th Congress. State their meanings in simple, everyday language. Translate the meaning of lost freedom, particularly as that meaning has revealed itself in conquered countries. Discuss present-day influences that are working against democracy. Show the viciousness of any system that attempts to subjugate people to the rules and whims of a few. Point out that our freedom can be endangered by our neglect of our duties as citizens. Have students tell how they can help maintain freedom.

Plan a "Hall of Fame" display of pictures of "Heroes of Democracy" who have made noteworthy contributions to our American Heritage; collect such pictures for individual or group scrapbooks.

Review outstanding events in our country's struggle for liberty. Assign student committees for research and report-back-to-class on salient points of such documents as: The Mayflower Compact, The Declaration of Independence, The Preamble to our Constitution, The Bill of Rights, Washington's Farewell Address, Lincoln's Gettysburg Address, Wilson's Flag Day Address, and others.

Visit exhibits related to the broadcast content at the Chicago Historical Society and the Rosenwald Museum of Science and Industry.

Recall visits to the Freedom Train. Report on the Freedom Train motion picture, newspaper and magazine accounts.

Prepare an American Heritage assembly in culmination of listening to the broadcast series—dramatization or simulated broadcast. (Scripts for the programs of this series are available from the RADIO COUNCIL. Address: AMERICAN HERITAGE Program, Radio Council, 228 N. LaSalle St., Chicago 1, Illinois.)

Paint an "American Heritage" mural or group-composite painting; individual pictures of heroes and episodes that are most significant to you.

Listen to other "American Heritage" broadcasts: *LEST WE FORGET—The American Dream, ADVENTURES IN FREEDOM, HEADLINES FROM HISTORY, PASS IN REVIEW,* others (refer to RADIO COUNCIL weekly *Program Bulletin* and *Semester Schedule* for related broadcasts, dates—time—stations).

Supplement broadcast listening with playing of transcriptions and records: Norman Corwin's *LONESOME TRAIN* (Decca), *BALLAD FOR AMERICANS* (Victor), Corwin's *ON A NOTE OF TRIUMPH* (Columbia), others (consult the RADIO COUNCIL for additional suggestions); with related music: *"The House I Live In," "March of the United Nations," "God Bless America,"* Irving Berlin's *"Freedom Train,"* other songs; with related reading suggested by your librarian; with related films and slides.

Also, each program within the series was fully outlined with suggested word-study; pre- and post-broadcast activities; and supplementary film listing and bibliography.

In the "Nature Walks" series of science broadcasts, for third and fourth grades, the handbook presents a résumé of the content of each program, a suggested list of things to talk about and do, a vocabulary, and suggestions for keeping a "nature diary":

PROGRAM XIII—May 16, 1949   PLANTS INJURIOUS TO MAN

City folk run more risk of being harmed during a trip to the corner than they do during a whole year in the woods. Woodcraft is nice to know but a little ordinary common sense is all you need to make your outdoor excursions the most enjoyable days in the year. There are very few things to be afraid of. Learn to recognize poison ivy and avoid it. Some berries will make you sick. Do not eat ANY mushroom unless you KNOW by experience that it is harmless and edible . . . some are deadly poison.

Things to talk about and do: What wild plants contribute the pollen that, flying through the air, causes hay fever? Did you know that ragweed pollen which, of all of them, most readily floats through the air, can be carried hundreds of miles by high winds?

Do you know anyone who picks wild mushrooms and eats them? What kind do they pick and eat?

Do you know the common nightshade vine? Its shiny red berries will make you sick.

Words to talk about and learn:

Jack-in-the-pulpit	Poison	Cocklebur
Ivy	Jimson weed	Thorn
Nettle	Drug	Pollen
Cut grass	Ragweed	Nightshade
Horse chestnut	Pokeberry	

Nature diary: Make as long a list as you can of edible wild fruits and berries that grow in Cook County. What color is each one when ripe? Which are sweet and which are sour? Make a list of edible wild plants such as burdock, dandelion, and so forth.

It is most important that the classroom teacher know not only what the broadcast is about (from the teachers' handbooks), but when the program is coming, and if you really want some disappointed listeners, change a scheduled classroom broadcast, particularly after the teacher has followed all the handbook instructions for the preparation of her class.

Every possible aid is given the teacher. Maps, charts, art prints and reproductions, photographs, posters, and pamphlets, often are sent with the handbooks. In all handbooks, supplementary reading lists and film lists are included. In some instances, where they are available, lists of transcriptions or phonograph discs applicable to a certain broadcast are likewise included.

Teacher Training

A number of institutions are now offering instruction for preparing the teacher to receive radio programs. Teachers should know how to use their influence in guiding the listening habits of their pupils so that they will obtain that which is of value from both commercial and strictly educational programs. Naturally, radio programs should not be used in the classroom when other available means will better fulfill the teaching objective. Teachers must familiarize themselves with all the sources of information about forthcoming broadcasts and their value to the pupils. No program should be recommended until other programs in the same series have been studied or advance information from the broadcasting station has been examined from the educator's viewpoint.

An educational program has been defined by Franklin Dunham, chief, Educational Uses of Radio, U.S. Office of Education, as one "that has for its purpose the increase of knowledge, the development of skills, or the widening of appreciations of the worthwhile activities of life." However, the value of the broadcast depends greatly upon the course being taught by the instructor and the skill and ingenuity of the teacher. Commercial programs which do not come within the limitations of the above definition may be used in courses in salesmanship and advertising. Students in music appreciation may contrast swing music with symphony music. The teacher who assigns a radio program for study must have a justifiable purpose in doing so and a knowledge of the program assigned. In evaluating a program, consider the hour at which it is broadcast and whether it can be satisfactorily received in the locality. Determine whether the program is accurate in facts presented and free from offensive advertising. The program must accomplish an educational objective and fit into the course for which it is assigned. The teacher must determine whether it is suited to the mental age of the students. No program should be assigned which does not supplement the classroom work.

The broadcasting of educational programs to the school is seriously handicapped at the present time by the lack of cooperation between the receivers and the broadcasters. An effort should be made in the various states to organize boards made up of representatives of the state departments of education, superintendents of schools, principals, and teachers to determine what subjects can most advantageously be presented to the schools through the medium of radio. Inasmuch as it has been

practically impossible to arrange broadcasting schedules to conform to
the class schedules of the various schools, some periods during the day
should be set aside for the reception of radio programs that meet the
approval of the above unifying group. Such a plan would be helpful to
all. If a bulletin listing all the educational programs which are broadcast each week and which are available to the schools of the state could
be distributed to teachers, it would aid them in selecting those programs
which would be beneficial to their pupils. Such a listing should include
an evaluation of each program, the school class to which the subject
would appeal, and the mental level to which it would apply. It is further
suggested that the continuities of educational programs to be broadcast
to classes in the schools should be submitted to a board of the type suggested above to determine whether such instruction conforms to the educational policy of the state. If school broadcasting is to be developed beyond its present status, there is need for properly qualified and trained
people to carry it on.

Only those subjects should be taught by radio which can better be
taught by this medium than by the local teacher. The local teacher
should be convinced that such instruction will not supplant the local
teacher but will merely supplement her personal efforts.

Teachers are advised to set the class an example by listening carefully, making notes of words that will require explanation, of ideas that
are too advanced, or of links with other work that the class has already
done. Unless the broadcast is to teach note taking, the pupils will lose
the thread of the talk if they are required to make notes. After the broadcast, class discussion encourages the students to restate ideas that have
impressed them. This follow-up work is considered important and evidences the ingenuity of the teacher.

Television in the Schools

By early 1956 there were 18 educational television stations on the air.
A few universities and colleges operate commercial, or partly commercial,
stations. Other schools and school systems have working agreements
with local commercial stations. More and more, educators are finding
uses for television in adult education, in-school broadcasting, and for
after-school programming for youngsters. A new type of educational
television station has appeared, primarily because of the imposing cost
factors. In large cities, community television stations have been developed. These are not the same thing as the distinguished New York

City radio station, WNYC. The city owns and operates WNYC as a municipal service. Rather, in the community TV stations, a nonprofit corporation has been formed and all of the schools, colleges, libraries, and other interested agencies cooperate in the operation of the station. In this setup, the public school system, and frequently the parochial schools as well, are participating members. This affords them regular and frequent use of the medium at a fraction of the cost of operating a separate station.

As in radio, much of the programming done by educationally owned stations, and that done by educational institutions over commercial stations, is aimed at an adult audience. TV has brought to the public attention the tremendous potential of the broadcasting media in the field of continuing adult education. This movement has been gathering momentum and may in the near future become a force of considerable significance. However, as was mentioned earlier, this chapter is primarily concerned with broadcasting to schools for consumption in the classroom.

In-school programs can be roughly divided into direct-teaching programs and enrichment programs. The general principles outlined for radio apply to television as well, and to both types of programs. Teachers must have a strong hand in the planning and production of such programs. They must be geared to the curricula of the school system or systems. This is especially true of the direct-teaching program, but even the enrichment variety must fit into the manner and the time that the particular subject is taught. Teachers must be trained in the use of television and radio programs in the classroom. Teachers' guides must be carefully prepared and sent out well ahead of time to allow for adequate preparation. A television program in class is not an excuse for the teacher to take a ¼ or ½ hour of rest. Proper use of such material probably requires more effort and time by the teacher than the use of more traditional methods.

The differences between radio and television in the classroom are simply the differences between the two media. Television can handle those subjects where materials have to be presented visually. At the moment, children's attention is better when viewing television than when listening to the radio, but it isn't clear yet whether this is a temporary or a permanent phenomenon.

Subjects that can be efficiently taught by television readily come to mind; science, astronomy, geography, art, crafts, etc. Many opportunities will be available for enrichment programs. Art galleries, foreign lands, museums, and many other places can be presented—places that may never be accessible to the students in a particular school. It is also possible to use this type of program to stimulate interest so that pupils will use the local libraries, museums, zoos, and other informational and cultural agencies. Money, imagination, and determination to overcome lethargy are the factors that will determine the extent to which this new tool is used as an instrument for classroom teaching.

Another function which TV can perform admirably for schools is the bringing of the outside world into the school building. Many of the country's major events will be televised: events like the inauguration of presidents, the arrival of foreign dignitaries, hearings by congressional committees, important actions by state and local governments, major parades, and a host of other happenings that illustrate the life of America. These can be viewed in school. It is hoped that teachers will have the foresight to surround these events with information, concepts, and factors of appreciation so that they will take on added meaning for the young viewers.

There are educators who hope that television will help, in some degree at least, in solving the ever-growing shortage of teachers and classrooms. It is thought possible that some work can be offered over television in such a way that the gifted and trained teacher can be used to maximum advantage. Experiments are now under way to test these theories at all levels of public education; elementary, secondary, and college. This is a different kind of use from that which we normally think of in regard to television. It is not an attempt to develop new types of programming, but rather is a frank use of a communications instrument to help solve a very real and important problem. There is high hope that some such use will prove effective, but only time can tell.

CHAPTER SEVENTEEN

WRITING THE RADIO AND TELEVISION PLAY

The prerequisite for the radio author is primarily a story to tell, a fascinating story. It is the story that counts. But in addition he must have a thorough understanding of the medium for which he is to write. He must understand the limitations of the microphone, the psychology of the listener. He must study what has been accepted for radio—be an analytic listener. He must have showmanship, an indefinite term that includes a feeling for the dramatic, knowledge of what appeals to the public and how to make that appeal. Finally, he must be able to write, not only to portray live people accurately and to write realistic conversation but also to develop a plot. Then he must write and write, for while he may follow all the instructions for writing the radio play as set forth in numerous texts, it is experience that will be his best teacher.

Unfortunately, few noted writers for the stage have been attracted to the radio, and announcers and advertising men cannot be expected to create outstanding drama for the air. Because of the high pressure that has been placed upon its writers, the radio drama has not yet been considered a serious literary form. Conditions must be changed before great writers will undertake the work. In the first place they must be speedy producers, for they must write a new play each week. There are no long runs in the theater of the air. In the second place, the radio play must be written right the first time for there is no opportunity for a tryout and revision on the road before the first-night opening.

The radio play has only a first night unless it is put on tape for a replay. In either case it is not changed after its presentation. The author's name is just mentioned and he acquires little renown by dramatic critics. He is paid moderately for his script and only in case of a repeat performance does he get any royalty. While the play is presented on a single night to a greater audience than usually attends a long run in the theatre, the author does not enjoy the applause of a single stage presentation. When writers are willing to put aside their desire for leisurely writing, for wealth, for fame, for appreciation, then they will study the peculiar script requirements of the radio play.

While it is generally said that the radio playwright is writing for an audience that is blind, in reality he is writing for an audience that has mental images built upon remembrances of scenes and experiences which help it to visualize and create scenery. The writer must appeal to the eye of the mind and build sound pictures that may be even more vivid than the visual ones of the stage. Fortunately the radio writer is unhampered by the rigid prop restrictions of television. The radio script can go anywhere, into the jungle, to the ice cap, on an airplane in flight, even into the darkness of a coal mine.

The radio playwright must write for an armchair audience instead of for a theater filled with people who are keyed up to the right mood to receive his play. He must create an attitude, an atmosphere, which the theater has created for its audience. Allowing the audience greater freedom in the mental pictures of characters and of setting possibly will make the play more vivid for the listener, for he can pick out his ideal heroine and place the scene in a location with which he is familiar.

Plot

People go to the theater because it is a land of make-believe. It contains the relief of romance, the familiarity of realism, the thrill of adventure. The radio audience does not, however, want stark reality, does not care for dull, brutal, and tragic things. The radio drama is truly a form of relaxation; yet the characters must be intensely human and recognizable in order to appeal to the recollection and visual image created by the listener. The plot of the radio play should deal with human interests and mental conflict and yet have adequate action. It should be simple, not metaphysical. Melodrama is decidedly popular because it appeals to intense emotion and present thrills, but these qualities must not be impossible for the radio listener to conceive. While melodrama is a popular radio form, it must be somewhat Victorian in character, for the unseen audience will not permit the air to be polluted by profanity or suggestiveness. The most modest of Broadway plays would have to be expurgated before it could be sent into the pure country air.

The theater has certain requirements for its plays. The unity of action has been discarded by the radio; the sound effect of a train carries the action from coast to coast; a boat whistle or an airplane motor transports the scene to foreign ports. The unity of time has no place in radio. Unities of character and plot are observed because the radio audience is interested in people represented by their voices. Gossip proves that we are interested in people who do things. Front-page news of the newspapers deals with the conflicts of individuals with other persons, the elements, or natural obstacles. We are more interested in a sergeant who captures a squad of enemy than in the regiment that invades enemy territory because we can put ourselves in the place of the sergeant. It is hard to feel like an army. Of course, the character must live an eventful life, have adventures that we listeners envy or are thrilled by. These conflicts or adventures in radio are better created by persons than by things. A man with his dog team might fight the elements to deliver serum to a snowbound village in the northland and create a conflict with adequate suspense, but in radio this would result in pure monologue description, not dramatics.

Radio drama is inclined to be suggestive; that is, it suggests a play which is in reality acted in the mind of the listener. The author gives adequate hints and situations; the plot-conscious listener builds his own play. He is led to the desired climax by the author but is pleased by his own mind creation. Of course, the plot must not be too obvious; there must be conflict, a struggle between characters or between characters and a situation. The climax may be unexpected—indeed, the listener is pleased by the surprise ending of the O. Henry type.

While no dogmatic instructions can be laid down for the selection of a plot for the radio play, certain factors should be kept in mind by the author. While the audience is not attracted by the drama designed to teach, it does prefer a plot that develops an idea. The more universal the theme, the greater the audience. The plot with the greatest appeal is the one that touches the interests, the experiences, of the greatest number of listeners. The first thing to do, then, in writing a radio play is to study the lives of those who will constitute your audience. Find what there is in their lives that may form the basis for a conflict. Develop your ability to write dialogue by listening to the conversation of those about you. Where you find a human being you find material for drama. The fact that most lives seem rather commonplace is no deterrent. While "real life" may form the basis of the plot an interesting play is not merely real life. It is more like a series of crises encountered by idiotic characters who persist in getting themselves in trouble. Simplicity and catholicity of appeal have never been known to constitute a condemnation of a plot. Into the simplicity of the average life your imagination can insert a logical, a possible, conflict. The radio audience assists you by preferring stories with American characters, heroes and heroines in the middle class socially. A good script has purpose and familiarity—purpose to justify listening, familiarity to make it ring true. The radio requires simplicity, which has nothing to do with the intellectual level of the audience but rather is the result of the limitations of the single-sense appeal. The play must be directly communicable and easily assimilated. It must have a plot, a style, to attract the attention of the listener. The listener is interested in action and conflict.

On examination of the plot types that are popular for radio plays, however, one finds that the tendency is toward the thriller play, such as detective stories, spy dramas, ghost stories, and tales of the wild west. Even the historical plays that are popular are filled with excitement and thrills. Many programs are devoted to adaptation of stage plays and novels such as those of Dumas. If it were not for the limitation of copyrights, the short stories of O. Henry and Bret Harte would make excellent radio plays. Sex plots are dangerous, and the major networks have refused to present political sketches to be used as a part of a political campaign.

The majority of radio plays are sponsored by advertisers, and the commercial sponsor is inclined to select plays that will cater to the taste of the buying public.

Because of its brevity, the radio play should not contain too many scenes that cause confusing transitions, or have too many acts. There are, however, no positive rules for the writing of a successful radio play. The popular "Cavalcade of America" has had as many as 15 scenes in its 22 minutes of dramatic time. Each scene should be concisely set so that the audience will have a clear understanding of the action that is to transpire. Each scene should carry the plot forward and be essential to its development; otherwise the time requirement would demand its elimination. No scene should run longer than 3 minutes without the entrance of a new character or a new element in the plot. With a series of scene shifts it is essential that you do not allow the characters to increase in number and complicate the play even more. The problem may be brought out in the first scene. Each of the developing scenes should create or remove obstacles, and the final scene should solve the

problem. There should be no change of scene that is not clearly accounted for in the action of the play or in the lines.

There are six methods for changing scenes in a dramatic program—
silence, fade, narration, and sound effects, musical interlude, and a single
musical tone that is amplified and perhaps distorted through echo chambers and filter microphones and then allowed to die away as the next
scene begins. Each method has its drawbacks. The average scene transition requires from 10 to 15 seconds, and listeners lose interest if that
much dead air intervenes frequently between scenes. The voice fade
sounds forced; it takes away from the naturalness, from the reality of
the play. Sound effects are apt to become monotonous; in any case, they
must be always easily recognizable. Narration breaks the spell of the
drama. Music is often complicated and may spoil a simple play, and
suitable music is difficult to obtain.

Naturally there must be obstacles in the radio play, but subplots are
dangerous for they create too complicated a plot for the radio audience
to follow. The radio audience requires logical development with an
explanation of just how things happen. It must not be left in the dark.
Minor details, if of value, must be made clear.

Probably the radio drama has a greater opportunity to create suspense
in its unseeing audience than the legitimate stage play. A shot followed
by a scream gains suspense because the audience is not aware of what
has happened until it is told. The element of suspense is as vital to the
play as is characterization or climax. Of course, everything must lead
up to this climax, which must not come until the very end of the program. In radio there is no opportunity for anticlimax in the play itself.

A tragic or unhappy ending may be satisfactory if a moral can be de-
duced. However, the tragic ending is not popular with either sponsors
or listeners. The ending of the play must satisfactorily bring the play to
a close, all problems solved, all characters accounted for. The adult
audience is not critical unless something that is expected is omitted.
Make the ending definite. The curtain line at the end of the play is just
as important in radio as it is in the theater.

The Announcer or Narrator

The narrator's introduction is decidedly important, for he must set
the stage for the listener. He creates in the mind of the listener a setting
in which the play is to be performed. He must not be too positive in his
details, but should allow the listener an opportunity to visualize the

scene as it appears to him. The narrator will tell something of the costumes if they are essential to the plot development (particularly if it is a period play). He creates the entire atmosphere by his introduction and by the music that accompanies his description. He should be chary in his delineation of character traits that will be brought out by the speech of the characters themselves.

The narrator might act as a verbal scene shifter as the play progresses, but must not dominate the play. Whenever possible, the lines spoken by characters should take the place of the interrupting narrator.

The Beginning

The beginning of the play, whether it is in the words of the narrator or of a character or in some other form of introduction, is of vital importance. During the first moments the listener decides whether he wishes to remain tuned to the station, and he should be put in the right mood to cooperate in the reception of the plot that is to follow and be given a promise of action, for action demands attention. There are different means of attracting and holding the listener and of creating the desired atmosphere. The radio play, like that of the stage, may depend upon its overture to put the listener into the right frame of mind, to get tuned in or settled in his seat, or to attract an attention that is wandering over the dial. The author should consider his opening of vital importance and should write the beginning announcement or dialogue to attract and hold attention. The style, diction, and content should really introduce the play and create the necessary attitude or mood reaction in the listener. Some plays may be effectively introduced by expressive sounds in conjunction with speech, and, if the sounds are such as to bring pictures to the listener's mind, suspense may be created through them. The use of local color in the opening dialogue—the language of the circus, of the campus, or of the sea creates an atmosphere that attracts the listener's attention. In this case speech may be enforced by sound effects. When the play is written, go back and work over the opening until you are certain that it will attract an audience and will create without fail the mood required for the appreciation of the play that is to follow. One last word of caution—the introduction must move swiftly so as not to take time that is necessary for plot development. While the immediate establishment of an atmosphere is advisable, it must not be offensive to the listener.

The beginning of the play has a definite job to fulfill. It sets forth the purpose of the play. It creates a picture. Characters, setting, and situation should be established immediately.

The successful play begins with extraordinary swiftness and with economy of words. Immediate attention can be obtained by a rapid development of the situation, promise of action, conflict or threat, powerful atmosphere, striking characterization, an intriguing unusual setting, or an extremely familiar setting. In general, listeners prefer introduction through dialogue.

Characters

The author should write a play requiring a limited cast, for more than six voices of major characters are confusing to the listener since he cannot identify the characters by sight. Seldom should more than four individuals enter into a conversation, and they should have voice contrast or a vocabulary contrast to make them individualistic. If a character is given a personal speech style, it must be maintained throughout the entire script. While exaggeration is permitted in certain character types, the characterization must not be burlesqued. If the character is given a "sound" personality, the listener will create his own picture of the type, for he can visualize the character by what he says and how he says it, whether he is a minister or a West Side "tough." Characters in all radio dramas should be made real to the listener. People like to listen to and follow the adventures of their own kind, or of those whom they can recognize on the radio. Not only does a character's manner of speech portray him to the unseeing listener; the writer of the script must also make each actor act in the way that the character is supposed to act in real life. Whenever possible it is advisable to give to a character some characteristic expression of words that identifies him. Have one character repeat certain phrases, but be careful not to overwork these phrases. One of the most common criticisms of the amateur radio script is that the characters' lines are interchangeable. The listener should be able to tune in on the middle of a broadcast and tell from the words of a character whether it is Amos, Andy, or the Kingfish who is speaking.

Of course, it is impossible, as in real life, to keep the principal characters talking with one another all the time; consequently minor characters may be introduced when they are necessary to forward development. Characters should not talk to themselves. Someone must intervene to make the action lifelike. However, do not allow the minor character to become important; it is best not to name him; merely identify his position. Various methods may be used to cut down the number of characters; among these is the use of the telephone, letter, or telegram. The last two should be short and important if read. Messages which help in explaining but which are not exciting in themselves may be summarized by the reader. Telephone conversations frequently save scene shifting, create atmosphere, and make situations clear. They are generally shorter than face-to-face conversation and thus speed up the play. Sometimes it is essential that the radio listener hear the speech at both ends of the telephone line, but since this is unnatural it should be avoided if possible.

Dialogue

Since the radio audience cannot see the actors, making the characters speak in character is vital. Emotions must be brought out to the listener, not by the shrugging of shoulders or by the lifting of eyebrows, but by words, sentence structure, and delivery. All emotions have to be conveyed through the air by speech; people under terrific emotional stress are likely to say little, to use short sentences or fragments.

The theater audience can see the actor enter the scene, but when a radio character comes into the play he must be introduced by dialogue, "Well, here comes Harry now; let's ask him." This identification must be carried on throughout the play as characters enter and leave the scene. It is a wise policy for characters to be addressed by name in the dialogue. However, this must not be overdone. Not only does the dialogue introduce the character but it may describe some essential manner or condition of the person. Try to build this picture in the mind of the listener with a comparison, a single-word description. For instance, "Who's the Rip Van Winkle coming?" Such brevity allows the listener to visualize an old, bearded man with tattered clothes, unkempt and bewildered. In this way the dialogue appeals to the visual sense of the listeners and obviates the necessity of a description of the characters by the narrator.

The author, like the director and like the audience, must forget his stage and listen to his words as if he were blind. The characters are never seen but the words they utter are vital. They should speak with a clearness and directness that leave no uncertainty in the mind of the listener either as to their purpose in the play or as to which character is speaking. Speeches must be much shorter in the radio play than they are upon the stage because of the time limitation. There is no place for the soliloquy. However, jerkiness must also be avoided. Every speech must carry forward the action. It is not an easy task to write conversation, but it must be very real, very human, in the radio play. Practice writing the dialogue of all types of people at every opportunity. The speeches must be in harmony with the characters who speak them. They should be written so that they can be understood in the dark. When questions, exclamations, or whisperings are used, they must be natural and realistic in their phraseology. On the stage the facial expression will help in the understanding of certain lines, but radio dialogue must be more explicit. The microphone emphasizes affectations; consequently diction must be so natural that it sounds extemporaneous and casual, and yet it must not be slipshod.

The speech of the characters should portray the scene and the action as well as the thought. All action must be talked about. It is better to say, "Why did you come in the window when you could see that the door was open?" than to inquire, "Why did you come in that way?" because the audience cannot see the entrance. Stage business and sounds are explained by dialogue. It is wise for the writer to allow the producer to tell him how to instruct his actors in the matter of entrances and exits in order that he may get the proper impressions of distance and motion to appeal to his audience. As the same sound effects frequently may be used to illustrate different sounds, the dialogue must bring out what the sound means; otherwise the roar of Niagara might sound to the listener like the escaping steam of a locomotive.

The sentence structure used in the radio dialogue should conform to the rules that have been laid down for all radio speech. Sentences should be short, simple, clear. The radio script must be actor-proof—written in such a way that it cannot be misinterpreted. Do not allow the entire plot to hinge upon a single line, because the listener's attention may be diverted during its delivery, with the result that he will lose the entire plot of the story. Of course, profanity, immodesty, the belittling of any race, and the use of poor grammar, except in cases where it is necessary to bring out character, are bad. Humor must not offend anybody who may be a patron of the sponsor of the program. The use of such descriptive nouns as "wop," "Chink," or "nigger" is absolutely forbidden. Even the sports announcer describing a prize fighter refrains from using the word "blood." Here is a final caution under the heading of dialogue: do not allow the script to become too "talky." Radio characters should not be loquacious.

The speed of the radio play is constant. There can be no pauses of any length while actors ponder, none of the lighting of cigarettes so loved by the amateur, no quiet and thoughtful moving from one side of the stage to the other. The tempo of the radio play is fast. No episode can be padded with description. There must be a planned forward action. Any lag in a play is very quickly apprehended by a listener and must be tightened up in those loose spots. On the other hand, it may become staccato and hurried where leisure is desirable.

Effects

The dramatic writer for radio uses various devices to create moods and effects and to economize in time. While writing it is helpful to keep in mind the part music can have in creating the mood and increasing the pace. Some pattern of music may strike the writer as being just the effect he desires to create; if so, he should jot it down in the script so that the director may sense the feeling he intends to bring out. Sound effects and music used artistically and effectively make the difference between a first-class production and a commonplace drama. Music can provide an emotional cyclorama. Good effects may be obtained by the use of whispers, exclamations, and questions, but they should be used only if they would come naturally in an ordinary conversation. A trick frequently used for speed and economy is the montage. This is a series of flashes or bits of conversation which almost overlap each other or are separated by brief passages of music or sound effects. The montage type of writing is extremely interesting and effective; if it is overdone the effectiveness will be lost.

As the radio drama is intended for the ear, the author should depend upon various sound effects and insert them in his script in order to create a more vivid picture for his listener. Through these sounds he may appeal to various emotions and may obtain even greater suspense reaction than can the author of the stage play. The persons who are most familiar with the use of sound effects are the sound-effects man and the control operator; consequently the author should confer with them as to what effects may be obtained and how these effects can be synchronized with dialogue. Such sounds may be used to create mood, to maintain tempo, to create color and atmosphere. However, they should never be introduced for their own sake. They have value only in carrying forward the plot. The author may write in such sounds as he feels will give meaning to the situation, but the final determination as to whether these sounds will be used will be made by the producer. Sound is judged by the ears of the producer, not by what the eyes see in the script.

Production

The radio play must be timed exactly so that the tempo can be maintained and the actors will not have to speed up or slow down at the end. Radio plays are heard most frequently upon 15- and 30-minute programs; approximately two-thirds of the program period is the most that can be devoted to the dialogue. The balance of the time is taken up by commercials, the announcement of the narrator, musical transitions, etc. Probably the script will be cut during the rehearsal to its correct time limit. Much will depend upon the rate of speech of the actors. A too-long script is preferred. It is easier to cut than to pad a script.

Good Taste

Always in writing for radio it is necessary to keep in mind the standard taboos.

1. The Deity's name must never be used irreverently. It is not so much what you say on the air as how you say it. There was the Mae West Christmas burlesque of Adam and Eve that caused a national investigation. The script was found to be innocuous, but the way Mae West spoke her lines was a startling sacrilege.

2. Offensive statements about or references to religious views, political groups, and racial characteristics should not be used. We presented a radio version of "Green Pastures," in which the Negro preacher exhorts his congregation as "You niggahs." The program was condemned by Negro listeners, and the students who composed the Ethiopian Club protested to the university president.

3. Physical deformities should not be made humorous or emphasized. The "soap opera" serials have recently had an epidemic of blindness, an emotional appeal for characters who have to live in darkness. Parents and relatives have protested to the sponsors, pointing out that radio is the outstanding source of entertainment for the blind and the shut-in. Emotional scenes concerning blindness are debilitating; they have lost listeners for the sponsors and made enemies. No guest coming into the home would laugh at a blind or a crippled host.

4. Murder and suicide are discouraged. Neither the criminal nor crime may be glorified. The criminal must be caught, punished, and the play end with the moral "Crime does not pay."

5. Overemphasis on insobriety is not permitted. Of course drunks are not welcome in the average home.

6. The use of the word "Flash" is reserved for special news bulletins. This is the rule Orson Welles caused to be laid down after his "Invasion from Mars" scareflashes.

7. Sex dramas are forbidden, and one sponsor refuses scripts in which women smoke. In many instances a subject which would be banned upon a comedy program may be used in a domestic story. For instance, childbirth and the attitude of youth in relation to the facts of life are permissible subjects in a family show, whereas they would be in bad taste if presented by a comedian. Comedians recently have been taking slight liberties with risqué stories.

8. Unintentional interpretations and words and phrases with double meanings and those which through mispronunciation or careless listening may result in embarrassment should be avoided. In preparation for a nationwide broadcast celebrating the centennial of the University of Michigan, a script was prepared about the first woman desiring to enroll as a coed. In the skit the President of the University advised her to try attending a class. She was hissed and booed by the men. The President asked her if she weren't going to cry. She replied, "I am going to study for my education, not cry for it." The continuity editor of the network wired instructions to omit the words "cry for it" because they were too intimately associated with the advertisement of a children's laxative. In the same skit the young woman said she had tried to get into the boardinghouses in the college town but they had all refused her admission. In rehearsals the word "boardinghouses" sounded too much like "bawdy houses."

The Manuscript

The radio script should be double-spaced. It is best to place the name of the character delivering a speech in the center of the line above the speech he delivers. If the character's name is placed in front of the line, there is a possibility that it may be read by him. Copies of the script must be provided for each character, the producer, the sound-effects man, the musical director, and the control operator. In case the script is one of a series to be presented, the number of the script in the series and the date upon which it is to be given should be included in the manuscript. If possible, it is also wise to list the rehearsal dates and hours.

The author should list the cast, giving some descriptive material about each characterization—types, ages, voices, and personality.

Phineas (Union guard, around 40, given to airs; fancies himself as an actor and shrewd fellow).
Old Jesse (groom, Yankee, garrulous, given to religious philosophizing).
James Winter (Confederate spy, young, bitter humor, courageous).
Colonel (Yankee, elderly, formal manner).
Chaplain (Yankee, prayer-book murmur).

It is also good practice at the beginning of the script to list all the sound effects that will be required. Do not use adjectives or adverbs to qualify the sound cue unless such adjectives give instruction as to volume or pace.

Sound Effects

Jingle of harness.	Slow steps on wooden platform.
Marching effects.	Squeak of pulley.
Whinny and pawing of horse.	Slow drum beat.

The titles of music to be used in the introduction, close, and scene transitions should also be given, or a space left in which the musical director can fill in this information. Such listing will be helpful to the casting director, the sound-effects man, and the musical director.

EDDIE: Well, you've got the idea, then. The first sound we hear is an automobile. The camera swings around and catches this car—a big, powerful-looking roadster—as it swings into the driveway. . . .
Music starts to fade in as a background—something misterioso, preferably
EDDIE: . . . We see the headlights cut across the house. Then the car stops in front of a doorway; a young man climbs out and knocks on the door. He waits a few moments, and then . . .
Music fades up and out rapidly

Whenever necessary the writer should give in the body of the script the intonation to be used by the character in the presentation of his part, the inflection, voice changes, and attitude.

EDDIE (*with an air of finality*) Well, that's that. It's terrible, then.
MARIAN: (*slight pause*) What's the matter? Don't you feel like talking?
EDDIE: (*mock indignation*) Why, Marian! How can you say such a thing? Me? Not talk?

Consult with the production director or producer to determine the amount of stage direction necessary. If the actors are competent and can interpret their parts do not clutter the script with unnecessary instructions. Also in the body of the script it is necessary to show where sound effects are to be used and which sound effects are to be used.

JUDGE JAY: This court stands adjourned until high noon tomorrow.
(*Gavel—crowd noises*)

If, in the opinion of the author, it is necessary for characters to emphasize certain words, these words may be underlined. The use of dashes as punctuation helps the actor, giving him an opportunity to characterize his part and make full use of the pauses. When there is a scene transition, the musical selections to be used in that transition should be listed by name or mention the mood desired—lilting, ominous, etc.

Adaptations

It is generally felt that adapting a stage play or bit of literature is the easiest way of obtaining radio material. This belief is based upon the fact that so much of the better radio-show material is adapted from plays, novels, short stories, or pictures. This belief is based upon the fact that many excellent motion pictures are adapted from novels and stage plays. Furthermore, the unimaginative writer feels that such a procedure eliminates the difficulties of creating plot and characterization. Adapting eliminates the difficulties of creation; however, the technical difficulties are by no means decreased, for making a good adaptation in reality requires more technical skill than writing an original skit.

The problems of adapting plays and pictures are probably the least difficult, since the original material is already in the form of drama. Two things are necessary: conformity to the usual time limitations of radio, and the removal of the dependence on the visual. These visual aids and stage business, if they are essential, must be translated into dialogue for the benefit of the radio audience. A good test of this requirement may be made by closing the eyes during a motion picture and trying to create in the imagination the scene on the screen, using as a basis only the sound. Conforming to time is another problem. One-act plays lend themselves more readily to adaptation because playing time already approximates radio time units. Condensation of the longer plays requires more than the cutting of speeches and scenes. In many cases it requires a rearrangement in order to strengthen narrative structure, it requires the combination of characters in order to eliminate confusion, and it requires the simplification of plot and the speeding up of the tempo.

The adapting of stories is a problem somewhat more difficult than that of adapting plays. Here more creative ability is needed because stories often contain very little dialogue and much description. The adaptor deserves almost as much credit as the author because he has so much work to do in translating the story into radio requirements. He will probably need to simplify the plot and eliminate or unravel subplots. This is more likely to be true of the novel than of the short story. New dialogue may have to be invented to take care of essential description, or sound effects may need to be employed to give descriptive effect. Conformation in the matter of time is again more easily accomplished in the shorter story; in fact, the novel is often best presented as a serial. And, finally, as is the case with plays, stories will need to be consolidated and compressed. Almost all forms of writing lend themselves to adaptation but it must be remembered that only one sense is appealed to by radio; there is no aid from the visual, and neither is there any opportunity to check back and clear up any misunderstanding.

It should also be noted that the adaptation of comparatively recent material requires a copyright release from the original author or his agent. Seldom does a magazine or publisher grant such rights. In many cases the author has retained his radio rights and he must be contacted.

Submitting Manuscripts

While it is inadvisable to submit ideas to radio stations about plays and programs, some stations can be trusted not to steal the idea. These stations require the originator to submit the idea in the form somewhat like the following:

Date:————————

To Station ————:

I am submitting my idea, summarized or characterized below, about a radio program to you today with the understanding that you are wholly free to determine questions of priority and originality in connection with any identical or substantially similar ideas or suggestions, and that for payment, in the event of use, I will rely upon your own sense of fairness and honesty.

————————————————

Brief summary or characterization of idea:

————————————————————————————

————————————————————————————

————————————————————————————

————————————————————————————

Note: Station ———— is not responsible for manuscripts or other materials submitted. It is understood that the author is retaining duplicate copies.

As many stations and advertising agencies will not even open an envelope which obviously contains a manuscript, fearing that any future similarity between the submitted manuscript and a produced play may result in a copyright suit, it is advisable to put the release in a separate stamped envelope attached to the manuscript package. The young author would do well to write to the agency or station before submitting his manuscript and ask for the release form required and then submit his script with this form filled out as required. He will stand a better chance of having his manuscript read. He will find that when he signs the required release he signs away all of his rights.

Dramatic Writing for Television

Drama on television, like drama on any other medium, is primarily, and above all else, drama. If this statement sounds redundant to you, it is time you gave the matter a little thought. The art form known as drama is nearly as old as civilization. The form has changed and developed to meet different tastes in different times, but the basic ingredients remain the same. These ingredients, which are the same for all drama, are far more important than the changes needed to fit a drama into radio, on the stage, on films, or on television. The effect of drama is obtained through plot, character, and dialogue. These ingredients make up the cake, while the advantages of a particular medium constitute the frosting, and perhaps even the filling between the layers. The important thing is that the characteristics of the medium do not, and cannot, replace the body of the cake. It is true, of course, that certain types of stories and situations are peculiarly adapted to the film medium, others to radio, and still others to the stage. We will undoubtedly find that there are also some which fit well into television. However, the fact still remains that they are all dramas. If they are poor dramas it doesn't matter into which medium we put them. If they are good dramas they are made better by an artistic use of the characteristics of the particular medium.

To write plays for television you need three things. First, you must be able to write. Second, you must be able to write in the dramatic form, and have an understanding of this form. Third, you must know television thoroughly. The first two of these requirements are outside the scope of this book. So, we will make the overly optimistic assumption that you are qualified in these areas and merely want to transfer your talents to television.

The television writer must know television. He must know cameras, lenses, production routines, lighting, scenery, special effects, and all of the potentialities as well as the limitations. It is helpful if he also has knowledge of the business end of television, advertising, and the various agencies involved in the production of programs. This, of course, concerns live television dramas as contrasted with films made for television. Writing for films is one problem, and writing for live television presentation is another.

While there are differences between films and live TV dramas, there are also some very important similarities. In both films and live television the visual elements tend to have more impact than the aural elements. Both are photographic media. This implies the use of camera lenses which afford the director an extraordinary degree of selectivity. He determines most precisely what the audience is to see. The story unfolds in a rapid sequence of "scenes." A "scene" is any change in camera position, angle, or degree of closeness. These scenes are put together in a meaningful pattern of long shots, medium shots, and closeups. In both films and television the close-up is usually the most effective device that can be used. The pictures are accompanied by electronically amplified sound which frequently includes a musical score.

The similarities between television and films are important, and so are the differences. The TV play is seen at home on a relatively small screen. Even with future promise of much larger TV screens, it is unlikely that we will ever have VistaVision or CinemaScope in the home. This limits the use of expansive panoramic scenes, and the use of great mob scenes that adorn some of Hollywood's epics. It limits the number of characters than can be in a scene at any one time. TV is microscopic rather than macroscopic. Film, on the other hand, can be either. TV plays are performed continuously, except for pauses in which the commercials appear. This fact materially alters the actor's job. It also changes the shooting and editing technique. Each scene in a film is shot separately, with time in between to reset camera and lights. In TV, the scenes must be arranged to flow from one into the other without pause. In a motion picture, the editing is done after the film is processed, and the editor has a long time to study the sequences and to make adjustments. Anything that doesn't meet the established standards is reshot or cut out. In television, the director does the editing instantaneously while the scenes pass before his busy eyes. Any flubs or poor scenes merely become history. Once they are on it is too late.

It is useless to argue whether film or live TV is the more effective. There are advantages and disadvantages in each. They are similar, yet different. We can well leave the ultimate degree of effectiveness to future critics. The potential writer should see that television drama is more closely allied to film techniques than to radio or stage techniques. At the same time, it is necessary to realize that television is controlled by the same people that operate radio, and that it is used for the same purposes as radio. Therefore, the customs, the taboos, and the kinds of audiences available are very similar to radio. In a descending scale of freedom to choose subject matter and treatment we would need to list stage, films, and radio-television, in that order. As in radio, the author must remember that people at home tune in with good faith, and complete assurance that this faith will not be violated. The purposes of commercial broadcasting are best served by keeping this trust with the audience. So, there is no market in radio and television for the utter frankness of the printed page or the Broadway stage. This may impose certain artistic limitations, but it is a fact of broadcasting life.

The television writer visualizes his story in terms of television cameras. As he tells the story and writes the dialogue he must keep in mind how all of this will translate into a swiftly moving sequence of pictures. Only when the TV play is written in this way will it turn out right on the screens at home.

None of this is intended to imply that the TV writer is a solitary craftsman. Anyone who wants to be the sole creator should not write drama for any medium. A play is a finished product only when it is staged, and actors breathe life into the written characters. Television is no different. The production of a drama on TV is a highly cooperative affair, and everyone concerned has a hand in the final outcome. The author supplies the raw material. The director, the actors, the designer, and all of the others forge that raw material into consumer goods—a play on TV. Because of this cooperative nature, it is not proper for the writer to attempt to stage the production as he prepares the script. He will not indicate all of the cuts and the camera changes. This is the director's job, and he is probably better qualified to do it than the author. This doesn't alter the need for the writer to think in these terms as he writes.

There is no really standard form for television scripts. However, many are typed on a sheet divided lengthwise, with all the audio and business directions in the right-hand column, and the video in the left-hand column. Sometimes there is a third column for the director's instructions and cues. At times a facing page will be used for additional information.

The important requirement is that there be one column for the dialogue and related information, and another column for the camera and video information, or, at least, some method of quickly recognizing what is audio and what is video. The N.B.C. script format uses the left-hand margin for everything, but indents the dialogue two spaces. As usual, the business and sound cues are capitalized or underlined. This form is somewhat confusing to me, but probably works well for those accustomed to it.

In the example below, the printed information probably would be included by the writer. The additions of the director are in longhand.

DESTINY BY MOONLIGHT

MYRA MIDDLETON'S APARTMENT. A WELL-FURNISHED, BUT NOT LUXURIOUS, LIVING ROOM. THERE IS A SET OF THREE LARGE WINDOWS AT ONE SIDE OF THE ROOM. BILL WILKINS, DRESSED IN SLACKS AND A LOUD SPORTS SHIRT, IS RUMMAGING AROUND ON AN END TABLE LOOKING FOR A CIGARETTE.

VIDEO	AUDIO
Fade-in #2, Pos. C. 90 mm	**BILL**
SLOW FADE-IN AS BILL STARTS TO SING	(SINGING) Davyyyyyyyy---Davyy Crockett. King of the wild frontier......There must be matches here somewhere. (GIVES UP AND SEARCHES HIS OWN POCKET) Well, what. d'ya know. (LIGHTS CIGARETTE. LOOKS AROUND AND SAUNTERS OVER TO WINDOWS.)
Take #1, Pos. A - 135 mm	
Take #3, Pos. X - 90 mm	
	To marked position
THROUGH WINDOW DOOR IN BG *(after Bill reaches window)*	(SINGING AGAIN) Born on a mountaintop in Tennessee....greenest state in the land of the free........Wish I could forget that silly song.
(Shift focus slightly as Myra enters)	
	MYRA
	(ENTERS, SEES BILL. SLAMS DOOR.)
	Myra - to position A
Take #2, 50 mm	**BILL**
	(WHIRLING) Myra, baby. Where've you been ? (RUSHES TO HER)
Take #3, 135 mm	
	MYRA
REVERSE ANGLE-MYRA'S FACE	(COLLAPSES ON HIS SHOULDER) Bill. Oh, Bill. I'm scared.
	BILL
	Scared of what, baby?
	MYRA
	Someone was following me. He followed me all the way home.
Take #1, 90 mm	**BILL**
REVERSE ANGLE-BILL'S FACE	(PULLING AWAY FROM HER SLIGHTLY AND LOOKING INTO HER FACE.) Not a big fat guy? Was he a big fat guy?
Take #3	**MYRA**
	How did you know? Who is the big fat guy, Bill?
Take #2, 50 mm	**BILL**
	(WALKS AWAY AND SITS IN CHAIR. SHE FOLLOWS HIM.)

This script may represent the director's point of view. It is essential that all the information be available at a glance. There should be enough room for the director to put in the necessary camera notations. Every program series probably has a particular form that has been developed. If submitting a script for a particular show, it would be worth some effort to find out exactly what script format is used. If the script is being written on hope, then any form that meets all of the conditions will suffice. It can always be retyped. The important thing is to write a good show. If you do that no one will argue about having a stenographer type it.

CHAPTER EIGHTEEN

WRITING THE RADIO AND TELEVISION SERIAL

It is the object of any advertising scheme to arouse in the public an awareness of a product which the sponsor wishes to sell.

The radio serial, more than any other advertising means, makes this possible, because the story's running over a period of months or years has the cumulative effect of renewing or refreshing the appeal of the sponsored commodity. A successful serial will increase its circle of listeners, thus widening the potential consumer market. Because the increase of the market is in direct proportion to the increase of the popularity of the radio program, sponsors and agents are on the lookout for scripts which indicate that they will appeal to the radio audience.

Radio serials are designed for three separate audiences. The morning and early afternoon programs are written for women who are busy about their solitary household tasks or who are lonesome shut-ins. The sponsors are manufacturers of products which housewives buy in large quantities—food, clothing, and domestic supplies, particularly soap, which has given the name "soap opera" to this type of entertainment. Each program is built around some one lovable character (usually an older woman with whom the listener can identify herself), who is in a position close to Trouble. The troubles may be her own or those afflicting her loved ones and neighbors, but she must be kept in continuous difficulties.

The serial form of radio drama is written not only for the housewife but also for children and for a general audience. In the serials for children the tales center about some hero or heroine with whom the young listener can identify himself, or else they are written around a superior, adventurous adult who fills the roll of an idol to be worshiped and emulated. The best-known drama written with an eye on the whole family, "Amos 'n' Andy," must have an enormous audience of tired businessmen, because so many of their adventures poke affectionate fun at their ineptitude in financial matters. "One Man's Family" has a range of characters which takes in the whole household. And as the hands of the clock swing around, these homey adventures are replaced with the more harrowing scripts aimed entirely at adult audiences—the "episodic serials" built around several familiar characters who have a different, complete adventure in each installment.

Listen to the programs on the air and select the type of program you think you are best fitted to write. If you are a woman, the chances are that you are more familiar with the experiences and daydreams which appeal chiefly to the feminine audience. As a rule men write more convincingly the scripts of exciting adventure. When you have decided on the audience you wish to entertain, choose your chief character and put him or her in a setting which is familiar to you, one which allows for the introduction of a variety of minor characters and an infinite succession of troubles.

Let us assume that you have already learned that a radio drama is a story told in dialogue with appropriate music and sound effects to aid the listener in imagining the action. It should have a beginning designed to catch immediate attention, a build-up of suspense leading to a climax, a denouement, and a close. The principal ingredients are characters, setting, and plot, carefully sifted and creamed together, with a liberal proportion of emotion worked in to keep it from being flat and a nice flavoring of humor if you are good at that sort of thing.

In a single drama written for radio, the emphasis is on plot. There is not time in half an hour to work out more than a sketchy characterization of the actors, and the play must be kept moving every minute with action or laughter if it is to hold the attention of the listener. In a serial, however, the important thing is characterization. No radio-wise sponsor expects to get a heavy response from the first 13 weeks of a new serial, and calculations have been made that it takes two years to work up to maximum pulling power. One of the most successful radio programs is an episodic serial in which the plots are so slight that they can hardly be outlined; the setting is invariably the cottage across the street but the characters are sufficiently appealing to be held in affection by most of the radio families in the country.

Take time in choosing leading characters and become thoroughly familiar with them before writing a word of dialogue. Some writers find it useful to make a dossier of each one—name, age, physical description, likes, dislikes, traits of character, favorite expressions, and attitude toward other actors in the story. Once you begin working with your personnel you can add to this outline as the characterizations grow.

Naturally a personality from the middle classes has the heaviest appeal because the bulk of the radio audience is most readily identified with such people. Experience has proved that the hero had better be elderly or at least middle-aged. If you prefer a younger leading actor, then plan to make him strive against odds, fail, pick himself up with courage and determination until he has achieved success in a venture which only draws him on to another striving against odds and failures.

The listener cannot keep track of many invisible actors; consequently the number in any given scene is limited to five or six important people —two or three is even better. In the course of time, however, radio serials can introduce a great variety of people who have some connection with the central characters, and these can be picked up or dropped at will.

The balance of character in the standard legitimate drama is perfectly good for radio—a juvenile lead and an ingénue, a "heavy," and a couple of character parts. This provides a scattering of appeal to different ages in the audience and also takes care of voice contrast, which is very important over the air. A fan who follows any given program expects to know who is talking almost the instant the sound begins to register, and a newcomer can tell a motherly, middle-aged voice from a young girl's, even without the name tags which must be thickly sprinkled through all radio dialogue.

The setting is best when it is familiar to the author; however, a different, unique, or unshopworn one would attract attention. Cottages and palaces, hospitals and orphanages, boardinghouses and theaters, newspaper offices and airplane cockpits—these are ordinary. It costs no money to build a new set for a radio drama. However, if you cannot produce a novelty along that line, pick the one you know best. Familiar material can be handled more efficiently and plenty of material will be required.

If you can write clever, realistic dialogue, preferably of a whimsical nature, or if you have a neat hand with good clean humor, start on an episodic serial in which each installment is complete by itself. These have the advantage of entertaining the occasional listener as well as the regular dialer-in, but they are tricky to handle. The episodic serial is not very different from the single radio drama, except that it concerns itself with one or more main characters who appear in a series of shows, and a large part of its appeal lies in the creation of people so distinctively human that the fans want to hear more about them. If the fan misses one show, the next episode will be a complete story in itself.

It is easier, however, to write a serial which carries its suspense over from day to day. For the first installment it is better not to get deeply involved in plot, because it is going to take a while to pick up an audience and you will only have to repeat later. Arouse curiosity about your characters and the situation in which they find themselves, so that at the sign-off listeners will be eager to know more about them and what is going to happen to them. It is best to start each program, after the series is well started, on a relatively high note, relax the tension somewhat, and then climb up to a high point before the program goes off the air for the day. It is not at all necessary that episodes follow a day-by-day relationship. Thus two or three scripts appearing on three successive days may deal with action that takes place in the space of a few hours. Do not allow the story to become so complex that a great deal of exposition is essential.

The second and subsequent installments will start with what is known as a "leadin"—a brief reference to the previous broadcasts. Authorities agree that no attempt should be made to summarize the story to date, since this would grow increasingly difficult in the allotted time. Most scripts have a few sentences to reveal what is going on during the current sequence or to tell where the protagonists were left yesterday. If you have any doubt as to how this is done, turn on your radio and listen.

One of radio's most serious limitations is the time element. Most of the daily serials are 15-minute spots, with nearly a third of the time allotment taken by station breaks and commercial announcements. Nearly all serials are sponsored programs and those that are sustaining are only being nursed along until they have sufficient pull to interest a sponsor. The average 15-minute serial should have from two to twelve lines of leadin, be about 2000 words long, and end with a "closing tag" which poses the what-will-happen-next formula in from one to six lines. It is wise to write 1 minute more of continuity than the time allotment permits. It is always easier to cut than to fill. The 15-minute broadcast period contains an average of $2\frac{3}{4}$ minutes of commercial copy. Approximately $3\frac{1}{2}$ minutes of each program are devoted to theme, tie-up with the preceding episode, and a "come-on" for tomorrow. The average dramatic time is $8\frac{1}{2}$ minutes to a 15-minute program.

Most authorities suggest that in submitting a proposed serial to an advertising agency or script department, two or three installments should be written, with a synopsis of additional material sufficient to make up a 13-week series. It might be wise to write the whole first sequence before you venture to submit anything, even though the extra installments are laid away until they are needed. It takes more time, ingenuity, and energy to write five scripts a week than you realize until you have tried it. Furthermore, do not submit a synopsis, for not even a common-law copyright protects an idea.

The experienced serial writer is usually working with two threads of suspense in his story—a major suspense, which will build up to the nearest climax, and a minor suspense, which will become the major as soon as the current pressing problem is solved. This is valuable because radio serials differ from every other form of writing in one important respect. If they are good they may go on for years and years without an ending. Since this is true, a radio serial is built on sequences, rather than on individual, distinct plots, and it is always a good idea to let the sequences overlap.

It may be true that there is no substitute for good writing, but in the concoction of radio serials good writing does not mean fine writing. Reluctant though you may be to face it, a beautiful, poetic flow of language is not appreciated by the average soap-opera fan. Commercial radio does not concern itself with the minorities, the greatest possible audience is sought. The housewife and the casual listener are drawn to the program by the easy conversational writing in which the author avoids the stilted or the sublime.

Radio serials are the etheric counterpart of the pulp literature which burdens the newsstands, and the devotees want to know in advance that everything is going to come out all right for their favorite characters. They like to identify promptly the hero, the heroine, and the villain; they want the proper people to triumph and the wrong ones to get their comeuppance. Further, it gives them pleasure to be so familiar with the language of these people that they can almost say the words themselves.

Interest is aroused in the serial through the suspense that develops in how the problem is solved, and the interest is held by a flow of perpetual emotion. Remember, too, that the radio audience is more interested in people than in ideas. If you have any pet propaganda about social uplift or intellectual development, couch these ideas in homely language and let some sweet character already admired by your listeners receive the credit for having said something.

The theme, then, should have a tremendous appeal to the emotions of the multitude, but should be written in a way to hold the solitary listener. While millions of people may be tuned in, they are listening in small units of not more than five individuals, usually less. You may be as cozy as you please with them.

There is no use trying to be subtle, because the average fan will not get it. You should be careful that the whole point of your installment does not hang on one sentence, because perhaps the telephone rang at the moment that sentence was uttered and when the listener returned from answering the phone she was baffled about the story, which she doesn't like being. Be as sentimental as you can without gagging, and you may ladle out tragedy with a trowel, provided it is clean dirt and will all come out in the wash.

Juvenile Serials

In serials for children there has been a campaign directed toward more wholesome broadcasts. Cheap melodrama playing upon fear is frowned upon, but continuous action is necessary to hold the attention of children and it must be used in larger proportions than are encountered in real life. The story of the experiences of a pioneering family has received the approbation of parents and educators because it teaches many facts of history, nature study, and character development, while maintaining a thread of steady adventure. Care must be used not to talk down to the child, and the use of bad grammar to characterize juveniles is rarely successful. If you know what children like, there is a great demand today for good scripts aimed at the juvenile audience. The broadcasting companies are eager to keep the parents pacified, provided the script actually interests the young people enough to give the sponsor the reaction he demands.

Children are able to transport themselves without any embarrassment to any setting to which the radio may direct them. Imagination knows no limits. This very fact has given rise to problems in writing the children's radio story. It has become necessary to exercise the greatest amount of control and caution. In the early days of radio for children, writers literally ran away with themselves and failed to realize the power of the medium with which they were working. Children's programs took on the color of the macabre, and nightmares instead of peaceful sleep resulted for many too impressionable but normal children. Finally protests began to flood the studios. Mothers all over the country demanded less violent and disturbing stories. The networks established a list of policies that were to govern any future writing. "The exalting, as modern heroes, of gangsters, criminals, and racketeers will not be allowed . . . cruelty, greed and selfishness must not be presented as worthy motivations."

Actually, the establishment of the list of policies had little effect on the writing, because script writers had seldom been guilty of the violations that the policies warned against. Gradually writers did become aware of at least one thing; scenes of cruelty which might be acceptable in print became too vivid over the radio. Efforts were made to subdue scenes that might offend or disturb. The youngster's love of adventure had to be catered to, but it was not necessary to inject horror to meet the demands of action.

As far as the structure of the children's serial is concerned, there is little difference between it and the regular daytime serial for women. Daily, end-of-the-week, and sequence climaxes are all part and parcel of children's radio writing, but there is the exception. Long sequences are best avoided. Especially is this true where young children constitute the major portion of the audience. As the audience age increases, the sequence length may grow.

Dilemmas in children's serials are without exception less mental than those designed for women. A children's serial must provide the young listener with hazard-studded adventures. A writer very easily can work problems into his story that in being solved teach a lesson in any one of several educational fields. Natural history, geography, first aid, and many others may at some time in the story become the pivot around which an entire sequence revolves. It has been found that information is best retained when learned against an emotional background. In this way radio serials can be educational as well as entertaining.

The protagonist in a child's serial is usually one of two types. He is either a youngster of the same age as the oldest of the child listeners, or else he is an older man with the reputation for infallibility. Because the age of the listeners seems to be related to the age of the child hero, it is wise not to make the hero too young. Fourteen would seem to be a reasonably safe age. The sponsors of a children's program discovered that they were losing the patronage of thousands of potential listeners and purchasers because the hero was too childish.

Care should also be taken to avoid excessive realism. For example, in a western serial the ranch went broke and the place was converted into a dude ranch in order to recoup some of the losses. Letters started coming in asking how much it would cost to go to the ranch. This was proof of the effectiveness of the story. It was real to thousands of children and apparently to many parents. But when the answers to these inquiries were sent out and it was learned that the ranch was a fake, many loyal fans were alienated.

The writer of the radio serial for children should cater to boys' interests, for girls will listen to stories for boys but boys refuse to listen to stories about girls. If there are any girl characters they should be tomboys, and adults should retain their youthful interests and attitudes as much as possible. The real solving of any problems or difficulties should always be done by a youthful character. The characters should never be given a definite age as children prefer to believe that their heroes are but slightly older than they are themselves. The characters' action should be consistent throughout the series. Plenty of action and a good plot are demanded by children, as they revel in experiences and adventures of all kinds, but the young mind insists that truth be accurate and that fiction be consistent.

One of the faults of radio serials for children is oversimplification. Surveys show that children listen to and prefer serials prepared for adults to those expressly written for the child listener. The elements of the adult serial should be modified only slightly for youth. Children have to look to the adult program for humor, for amusing family experiences, for the realism of childhood problems, for character interest rather than a continued series of thrills. Allow the child listener to visualize himself in place of the radio character. The secret of writing for the radio child is to put the child listener into the play rather than in the audience.

Boys from eight to fourteen years prefer plots that are exciting, filled with adventure, action, and travel. Comedy also has its appeal but wild-west and cowboy tales fit into their games. Girls like excitement but they will listen to sentimental plays; the slightest mention of love scares off the boys. Mystery, crime, and detective stories maintain their appeal but gangster and horror dramas no longer hold high favor with children or their parents. Actual historical characters were introduced and geography, natural history, and zoology were skillfully worked into an exciting series of events. "The Lone Ranger" has a mysterious masked rider whose life is one of adventures in which virtue triumphs. Older children have expressed interest in travelogues; a serial could be written about a boy who accompanies Commander Byrd or Roy Chapman Andrews. However, it is not vital that adventures be about pearl diving, jungle exploration, or sea voyage, for there is plenty of adventure upon our rivers, lakes, railroads, and mountains. The N.A.R.T.B. code states that writers need not remove the "vigor and vitality common to a child's imagination but rather base programs on sound social concepts, presented with a superior degree of craftsmanship." Possibly there is the real problem in improving programs for children—stop considering them from the viewpoint of childless psychologists and enjoy yourself as you live and play with the kids.

When you have finished your first draft of the script, it is a good rule, as in all writing, to lay it away for a time to "jell." You will see it in a clearer perspective after a brief absence from it. In the meantime, read more scripts or listen to another round of serial broadcasts and you will probably get fresh ideas which will improve your own copy.

Do not try to write a sample commercial to go with your script. The advertising agency can do that better than you can. Besides, you do not know who the sponsor may be. Of course some serials are written with a tie-up to the sponsor's product, but they are written on order, under contract. Next to writing gag continuity for radio's big comedians, the pay in radio writing goes to those who turn out serial scripts; serial dramas are remunerative because they go on the air from three to five times weekly and because they go on forever.

From the writer's viewpoint, this perpetuity demands the constitution of an ox and the fertility of a guinea pig. The chief qualification is endurance, rather than artistry. It is true that Archibald MacLeish and Maxwell Anderson have written some fine dramas for radio, but they do not write them every day, nor even every week. A creative worker, be he painter, composer, or writer, has a limited amount of original material stored up within himself which he pours out into his creations, and when he has emptied himself he must rest until his reservoirs fill up again. If he doesn't rest he has a nervous breakdown, which ends his output temporarily, or else he drifts into producing machine-made drivel.

Furthermore, as has been already pointed out, the radio audience prefers factory-made fiction, and that is something else you have to take into consideration if you have cast your eye on the commercial profits to be made in this sort of writing, rather than on the artistic side of it. Excepting a few top-flight writers, most of the acclaimed scripts don't earn much money for the man who grinds them out.

Very few listeners give undivided attention to these serial programs, so pace your script slowly enough and make it simple enough to be readily understood by such divided minds. However, you must also take into consideration that someone somewhere is probably paying attention at any given moment, and if his pet prejudices are offended, he is more apt to voice his condemnation than he ever would be to write his appreciation. For this reason there are many strict taboos in radio. Profanity is carefully censored, even when it might realistically belong in a story. Guard against political, racial, moral, or religious controversies, since the vast audience is touchy about these things and unfavorable reactions are promptly registered with the sponsor.

In spite of the many restrictions which have been stressed, there are compensations in the writing of serial scripts. A writer who has only average ability and who is equipped chiefly with determination and good health can make a very decent living by writing for radio. While his name will rarely be published abroad, there are other rewards. It is sweet to know that 10 million people may become interested in the welfare of the characters he created, and if they do become so interested, his material rewards are not inconsiderable.

The broadcasting companies and the sponsors invest an enormous amount in these programs, and they will be happy to grab what you write if you can do a better show with an appeal to the masses. Styles change constantly, giving opportunities to newcomers.

Serials on Television

The radio serial, or soap opera, has been transplanted to television. It is not such a popular format on TV as it has been on radio. Perhaps this is owing in part to the decrease in popularity of the serial in general, for serials are not as common on radio as they were a few years ago.

Fundamentally, there is no difference between the TV serial and the radio serial. For television, account must be taken of the visual possibilities and limitations. The author must remember that the actors have to memorize the lines for each performance. They must be simply set to avoid overly-complicated production problems. Once these matters have been taken care of, we have left the traditional soap opera.

The serial, especially the daytime serial, was built for casual listening.

Casual viewing is somewhat more difficult to accomplish. It is doubtful that the serial will ever become the standard TV fare that it once was on radio.

Children's serials have also crossed over into television. Some of them attempt continued stories in the usual sense, such as "Captain Video." However, the most successful ones are only semiserial in form. They use the same characters, similar situations, and much the same gimmicks, but the story is more or less complete in each program. Among these very popular shows are "Roy Rogers," "Superman," "The Lone Ranger" and "The Range Rider."

CHAPTER NINETEEN

DIRECTING THE RADIO PLAY AND THE ACTOR

First among the essential qualities of the radio dramatic director is knowledge of the legitimate theater, a knowledge based upon experience. Experience on the stage gives the director an ability to sense character and a power to carry that perception to the audience. His own experiences teach him to visualize the scene and, since he often must teach the actors to visualize, an ability to do so himself is imperative. A dramatic script, as it comes to the director, is nothing more than a cold black-and-white story, a drama set down in symbols, symbols which mean nothing until translated in terms of sound. The director infuses into the script a certain liveliness and lifelike quality through the means of voice. He is the final judge in matters of conflict, characterization, motivation, and technique. He is both the critic and the listener. Although radio is essentially different from the stage, the theater director brings with him a quality which permits him to eradicate all impressions except those that can be produced and suggested by the voice of the actor to the imagination of the listening audience, aided and abetted, of course, by proper sound effects and music. The director of the stage soon learns to "feel" the play, to live and think in terms of the play, and he brings to the microphone this ability to cut a script and still retain the dramatic effect.

One of the greatest directors of stage drama in the country today has stated that it is always his purpose in the final production to create for his audience the same emotional feeling he had when reading the script. All good directors should strive to do this. Every play has a mood and an emotional experience to present. A clever and wise director will strive to give his entire production the benefit of these qualities. Actors should feel this idea of the play-as-a-whole. It is the duty of the director to inspire them. An uninspiring director is forced to rely upon mechanical devices for every effect. The radio actor cannot count on the glamour of the stage to fill him with emotion just before he walks upon the scene. Consequently, an inspiring director in radio is perhaps more important than one for the stage.

A quality second only to theatrical experience is the ability to teach. If a man knows all the tricks of voice, all the attributes and artistry of characterization, all the subtleties of emotion, but cannot succeed in training his actors to produce these effects, he can never succeed in artistically producing a show. The dramatic director in radio must be able to teach his casts radio technique. He will often have to teach the stage actor to be an acceptable radio character. The excessive preciseness of stage action, the voice throwing of the theater, the magnified or elaborate naturalness of the actor are not suited to the comfortable listener in his home. His work is principally with voices, and voice work requires voice training and a knowledge of voice science. He must realize that the spoken word is an inflammatory thing, that the human voice is the most potent conveyor of emotion, an instrument that appeals to the imagination of man. He must coach his cast and train himself to listen for flexibility of voice, variety of inflection, lack of affectation, and good, clearly understandable diction. He must be ever cognizant of the fact that diction includes more than mere pronunciation and articulation. He must remember that it also involves phrasing, stress, the placing of groups of words into spoken italics, and, above all, a command of pitch.

The mere fact that the director has produced plays and knows dramatic technique does not mean that he can effectively direct a radio program. The fact that he has been a teacher of speech does not mean that he will be able to produce his radio show in an interesting fashion. He must have something else. He must be one who has come to the realization that there is a very definite technique peculiar to radio directing, and he must have availed himself of every opportunity to study that technique in the various ways that are at his disposal. Actual experience on radio programs would probably be the best training. There he would have the chance to learn all the phases and to saturate himself with the atmosphere of the broadcasting business. The most effective radio directors are probably those who have gained their experience in this way.

The director must have the confidence of his entire staff, and the ability to lead them. Cooperation between the director and his many assistants is of utmost importance. The actors can give better performances if they feel respect for the director's ability. His treatment of them determines to a great extent the value of the actor's performance. Those directors who are most outstanding are accessible, open to suggestion, and tolerant. They know that they know their job; yet they are seeking constantly to increase the effectiveness of their work, for they know that there is much to be learned in the radio profession.

A knowledge of music is another valuable asset for the director. Music is an integral part of the radio dramatic performance. It has various and sundry uses. It may be employed as a framework or theme to mark the general outline of the show; it may supply an identification factor for the play or for a particular character; it may serve as a device to carry action from one sequence to another, or as a bridge from locale to locale, time to time, or mood to mood; it may be used to back a scene, that is, to play at a background level behind that scene and thereby enhance it by creating and intensifying a particular mood; it may subtly appear, or be realistically used, as a part of the dramatic scene or story; it may become an arbitrary studio device to lengthen or shorten the broadcast in the event that the running time of the drama does not fill the period or that overcutting of the script has created a need for filler. Finally, the music may be used as a sound effect which serves to interpret the particular action of the moment. In any case, the dramatic director must know his music sufficiently to be able to blend his atmospheric bridges into the thought of the play. But in his blending he must bear in mind that the ear of the radio audience is keen—much keener and more critical than the eye and ear of the theater audience, which has the added factor of scenery to help create the effect of illusion.

A proper and adequate knowledge of the use of sound effects is a further aid to the dramatic director. Most scripts are written with many superfluous sounds, and the careful director will eliminate these as his first step in production. Again, he must be certain that the sounds to be produced really achieve the effect that they are intended to achieve. This may entail modifying or completely altering the sound cue indicated in the script by the writer. Most studios have a sound-effect library of recordings—but these often are not so successful as sound effects that the director and his staff may concoct and execute manually.

Studying the Script

Too frequently young directors go into rehearsals without sufficient knowledge of the script with which they are to work. It is not sufficient merely to read the script; it must be *studied* and then thoroughly digested. The man who is the power behind the microphone must know each and every character and that character's value to the plot. He must first get the mood, the feeling, of the show. He must understand the locale, sense the rhythm of the drama. This he should get in the first reading.

Before any rehearsals, he must see to it that the script is approximately the right length—at any rate, not too short. If some part of the script is not clear to the director he should discuss it with the author, if he is available. The director might even suggest small changes in the script if he is certain that such changes will benefit the performance. If the writer is not available, these changes are made by the director himself, although it is much better to have it done by the original writer.

One reading is never sufficient, however. A good director is never quite satisfied until he is able to *hear* the script while he reads it silently. In his second reading he makes his notes, writing ideas into the margins, checking positions of actors in relation to microphones and arrangement of studio equipment to fit the play. The director decides on the best arrangement of the microphones to pick up the words of the actors, the music if it is performed live, and the sound effects. If he has six characters in conversation, he may place them on both sides of a bidirectional microphone; the use of a nondirectional mike will permit the entire cast to surround and speak into the mike. It is best to use a single microphone for the cast, although there may be additional pickups for the orchestra and for sound effects. Use the minimum number of mikes since additional instruments introduce additional problems of mechanically controlling unity, perspective, and balance. He checks on speeches to be filtered—the mechanical elimination of certain high or low frequencies to produce distorted sound as in telephone conversations or ghostly conversation; he jots down ideas for the sound effects man and the control operator; he decides on the incidental music which will be needed. It is wise to have at this time a separate sound rehearsal, since unsatisfactory or badly timed sound will ruin an otherwise good scene. The director decides whether recorded or manual sound effects give the better impression.

With these details, the director is now ready for the third reading. He now has an idea of his characters, of the sounds, and of the music. In his third reading he reads with his mind focused on actors who are to portray the parts, deciding on types of voices and vocal traits which will most properly create the aural picture he requires. He is now ready for his next step, the casting of the play.

Selecting the Cast

The dramatic director must ever be aware of the fact that the microphone permits no letting down in interpretation. There is no bodily movement to help emphasize and interpret the spoken word. The voice alone conveys ideas, and the voice must be such as to remove from the mind of the audience any sense of remoteness and must cause that audience to perceive living personalities enacting a portion of life. Since the actor's voice must give the character meaning, that voice must be accurately chosen. A poor cast can ruin a good script, and a poor script may sometimes be made into a fairly decent show with carefully chosen voices artistically blended.

If the dramatic director is fortunate, he will know his potential cast. Low-pitched voices should predominate. High-pitched or harsh, rasping voices are seldom welcomed on the air. The casting committee is concerned with two things—what comes out of the loud-speaker and what happens in the mind of the listener. In the commercial studio, there is generally a file listing names, phone numbers, and addresses of talent available "on call." The director knows the limitations and capabilities of each of his co-workers. He knows each person's voice qualities and each person's depth of emotion, and he knows which character portrayal each person is best capable of producing.

If the dramatic director does not know his potential cast, it is wise for him to hold auditions or tryouts for the various parts. Here he may carefully select each voice, in order to avoid any confusion of voices over the air. He will be certain to see that voices with similar characteristics over the microphone will not be brought together. Though auditions may play their part in casting a play, they are never wholly satisfactory, because the actor never feels that he has done his best and the director never knows what an actor can do until he has heard him work in a play. In any event, it is best to cast by hearing the voices over the loud-speaker. The director listens for the flexibility of the voice in displaying an understanding of the lines, in varying speed according to the material, in expressing emotion without shouting, in giving emphasis, and in throwing cue lines. He tries to find the voice to fit each character, whether youthfully exuberant, mentally sluggish, hard, worn, plaintive, or happy. There is a great danger of casting two voices which have the same qualities over the microphone; select voices which will be different in quality to the extent that the listener may be able to discriminate between his characters simply by the tones of their voices.

It is a good idea to hear the possible cast of each scene read the same material in teams of two, in order to find the voices which are most easily distinguishable. When casting, it is best not to watch the actors through the control-room window. Casting hastily can give the director a tremendous amount of trouble; unless he knows his actors very well, he should try many voices before deciding on the final cast. Sometimes the dramatic director wonders about the effect of a voice on other people; in this case he can ask other members of the studio staff to comment.

Casting for radio must be done by voice alone, taking into consideration, of course, that the ability to read with smoothness and meaning is one of the attributes of a good voice so far as radio is concerned. There is no excuse for read-yness on a radio program. By the term "read-yness" we mean that quality of unnaturalness in the actor or speaker which gives the listener the feeling that he is reading rather than talking.

Having decided upon his selection of players for the show, the dramatic director next must set the time for the first rehearsal. It is rather politic to allow the members of the cast to retain the copies of the script, after the initial read-through, or first rehearsal if the two are combined, for thus they can thoroughly familiarize themselves with the characters they are to portray and also gain an idea of the whole drama. Knowing the show well, the actor will be able to give a more intelligent reading of his lines and thus time will be saved in rehearsal. Since the ordinary dramatic director must work against time, each bit of time saved is valuable to him and to the organization for which he works. Each actor underlines the name of the character whose part he takes each time it appears, and, if a speech is carried over to the next page, "More" is written at the bottom of the first page. Every effort, however, should be made by the typist to avoid carrying a speech from one page to another. The director goes over unusual words and gives character descriptions to the actors. Having completed the cast, the director is ready for the next step—rehearsal.

Rehearsing the Play

Before going into the actual rehearsal for the play, the director's task first is to consult with the sound-effects man and to make all arrangement for proper sound routines. He also must hold a conference with the music director, or other music personnel, and outline the music requirements.

The first rehearsal is generally quite informal, merely a reading of the script without the use of microphones. The director explains *his* idea of the script and tells his cast the effect he wishes to create. The director will encourage the actor to interpret the part that has been assigned to him. Naturally the director will endeavor to guide the actor's interpretation but he should avoid dictating the characterization. He must make the character feel his part rather than tell him how to speak his lines. He gives the cast the picture as he desires it and places upon them the responsibility of the achievement. The first reading should be allowed to proceed without interruption by the director in order that the entire cast may sense the play as a whole by the end of the session. However, if during the initial read-through any misreading threatens to jeopardize the actual significance of plot or characterization, the director must intervene long enough to steer the violator back onto the course.

During the second rehearsal the director usually listens in the control room, from which he interrupts the rehearsal to give suggestions either by means of signals or through the talk-back microphone. He makes further suggestions concerning characterizations, interpretations, pronunciation, enunciation, and so forth. The actors are encouraged to use natural body movements, as they promote ease of interpretation.

The third rehearsal is held with the microphone and the entire personnel of the show is present. All the instruments and apparatus are in place and the members of the staff know their parts and their duties. There may be a certain amount of rearrangement, but never a great deal if the preparations are made carefully. Each time the director interrupts the rehearsal, he stops his stop watch or stop clock and starts it again when the rehearsal is resumed. The director and the engineer must cooperate; besides interpreting his script in terms of drama, the director must also interpret it in terms of sound level and volume. The engineer is the equivalent of the chief electrician in a stage production (a man who is capable of making or breaking the show); the dramatic director therefore listens to the suggestions he may make in regard to placement of actors, sound effects, and music.

Before the last rehearsal, the director has a fairly accurate timing of the program and he will know which parts can be eliminated without loss to the performance. Most directors time every page of the script, writing down the exact time at the bottom of each page. Additional notations are made at the conclusion of every scene and of the time used by fades, bridges, or pauses between scenes. This detailed timing is necessary for the perfect control of the time element while the program is on the air. Most dramatic presentations stretch slightly when they go on the air; therefore, it is a good idea to cut a script before the broadcast to allow for stretching. If cuts are made, the director will have to correct the timing notations on his script, following the place where each cut was made. By looking at these notations, the director can tell whether the program is running short or long. In larger studios, timing is done by the production man, or assistant director, but in smaller studios there is seldom both a dramatic director and an assistant director.

No exact rule can be laid down for a required number of rehearsals, for many factors enter into the determination of the answer: the script itself, the ability of the actors, the amount and degree of difficulty in musical transitions, and, above all, the efficiency of the director himself. Comedies require less rehearsal time than drama because rehashing of lines, dwelling on them, is apt to kill spontaneity. No *good* director will stop rehearsing until he is certain that his show has reached the highest degree of perfection which he and his crew are capable of attaining. The dress rehearsal constitutes a complete performance of the script, precisely as though the program were being presented for an audience; in fact, it frequently has its most important audience—the sponsor. Before dress rehearsal is started, the director should time the musical portions of the program—the curtains and bridges for scenes. Every music cue should be numbered in rotation straight through the script, and these numbers should be entered on the director's script and the engineer's script. Thus, if a musical number is to be cut out, it is necessary only to indicate a number to the orchestra rather than a complete title. It is vital to time the commercials because these must be given regardless of time limitations. Dress rehearsal must be exactly as the actual broadcast; there can be no lackadaisical, perfunctory reading of lines, no lax routine delivery. The director must be a good disciplinarian as well as director. He must demand, and *obtain*, strict attention for the business at hand. During dress rehearsal, the dramatic director should accurately time the whole performance, making notations on his script. This rehearsal should show the director exactly what is wrong with the show. He should take notes, and wherever corrections are necessary they should be given to the persons concerned. But no actor should be disturbed just before he goes on the air. It is best to hold the dress rehearsal some time before the broadcast and to record it so that dramatic deficiencies may be pointed out to the cast.

Timing and cutting the show is an integral part of every dress rehearsal and results in having every part of the show get off "on the nose." In order to accomplish a split-second finish, the director must cultivate a sense of time, a power to know how long it takes to say or do a given thing. He knows from experience and the studio logs the actual time allotted for the various periods on the air: the ¼-hour show allows 14 minutes and 30 to 40 seconds, the ½-hour show, 29 minutes and 30 to 40 seconds. A like allotment is made for the shorter periods. The remaining 20 or 30 seconds of each period is allowed for telephonic and engineering operations or sold for station-break announcements by local stations. It then becomes the effort of the director so to time and arrange his show (by cutting the script, by shortening or lengthening musical cues, by stretching or diminishing time for sound effects, by coaching casts to gauge their reading rate more accurately) that his show finishes on the second of the period. There should be some part of the show— music, sound narration, transition, or speech—which can be stretched and used as a cushion. Music may be faded or repeated, as the case demands, without damage to the action, thought, or idea of the program. An audience is less likely to be offended (and, incidentally, less aware) when a show is being stretched than when one is rushing the show to get in under a dead line. If the director is to have any definite idea of how long his show is to run, proper addition and subtraction of timings is essential. Slovenly timing will result in a haphazard show. The use of a stop watch is recommended, and a fairly high-priced, progressive type of stop watch has proved to be the best. Further, it has been proved that jotting the time on the script at 30-second intervals is the most effective practice. Timings should be placed over words on which they fall or in the right-hand margin of the script at the end of the line in which they occur. They should be written clearly and legibly.

The dramatic director may, on the other hand, time each page of the script and note the exact elapsed time at the bottom of each page, or he may mark the elapsing of each succeeding unit or scene on the script. However, it is essential that the director know the time consumed by musical curtains, bridges, fades, and pauses.

The question of pauses is another matter to which the director must give some attention. He must bear in mind that pauses make ideas stand out prominently. A pause may take place before or after any utterance in order to gain a desired effect. An idea can be made to stand out with special significance if it is both preceded and followed by a pause. Yet even these pauses must be carefully timed, for only in this way can the director be certain of the over-all time consumed by the broadcast.

Scene and act transitions are made in different ways by different directors. The gong has been used to denote a change of scene or lapse of time. Frequently a strain of music or a few measures will create the desired mood between scenes or acts. Sound effects, such as the automobile, a train, or an airplane, may convey the listener from one setting to another. More frequently the dialogue following a brief pause will show that the scene has been transferred in the play. The radio director takes a great many liberties with the time element, not delaying the play to allow exact time to elapse for various actions.

The final presentation of a program is the director's busiest and most nerve-racking moment, for this is the test of his ability. During the performance, the director must be constantly on the alert, cuing actors, music, and sound effects, making sure that each line registers at the proper sound level. He must listen for extraneous sound, as of rustling scripts and squeaking shoes, and, at the same time, he must watch his stop watch or clock and be prepared to signal the performers to speed up or slow down to conform to the perfect timing of the program. In reality, everything that he can do for the performance should have been done before the time of its final presentation—everything except one thing: his ability to remain the calm master of the situation. Radio has devised a set of signals which enables the actor, sound man, announcer, and musician to know exactly what the director in the control booth desires. Wild gesticulations, glaring, hair pulling—and sometimes pantomimic mouthings of directions—will only serve to upset further an actor who has made a mistake.

Studio Audiences

A studio audience has been found useful in improving the quality of the performance of a comedian who desires the necessary timing for his jokes. The preview idea is one that is somewhat new to broadcasting, but it affords the producer and the actors a magnificent chance to see what will be appreciated by the audience and what will not. It is usually held two or three days before the show is actually scheduled to go on the air and is a kind of testing ground for the material which has been written.

However, a closed broadcast is preferred when the program is in dramatic form, for the distraction offered by a visual audience often prevents a smooth performance. Another advantage of the closed program lies in the mystery surrounding presentations that never admit guests. It is a well-known fact that some people, after witnessing one of their favorite broadcasts, listen with less interest to future programs. Their illusions are smashed by the nondramatic manner in which some plays are broadcast from the studio. From the advertiser's standpoint, both methods have their advantages. A large studio audience is usually gathered by inviting distributors and dealers of a client to the program. This builds good will for the advertiser, and, if the program is very interesting to witness, it is an excellent low-cost form of advertising.

The Radio Actor

The success or failure of a stage play is primarily in the hands of the playwright. The eyes of the director are responsible for the outstanding motion picture. The vocal interpretation of the actor makes the radio drama. Early in radio history advertising experts, educators, journalists, politicians, and preachers seized the opportunity to use their natural element—the air; but until recently the dramatic stars have been contemptuous of the opportunity to shine in the night air.

In the early days announcers and station help doubled as dramatic artists; the station help still sounded like the station help, the announcer like the announcer. Only the radio-trained actor can lift the etherized play from its mechanical setting. The stage actor, however, is overcoming his mike fright and braving the indifference and cynicism of the commercially minded broadcasters. Perfection has not been a requirement of radio performance, but the sincerity, intelligence, and imagination of the artist will create the impression of reality. The stage actor must accept the challenge of justifying his art by his voice alone and must master this simple vehicle of his emotions and thoughts. He must put aside his temperament and submit to the sponsor's demands in the interpretation of hurriedly produced dramatic skits.

Yearly, a great proportion of radio actors are enlisted from the stage and motion pictures. In spite of the lack of applause and color, there is a fascination in playing to millions on a single evening. Great actors are selling their names to advertisers. There is no better training for the broadcasting actor than a few years in a dramatic stock company. From the lecture circuits come recitationists, humorists, and monologuists. In the smaller broadcasting stations amateurs are trained for the big league;

however, their dramatic directors must be efficient trainers, for poor training makes a poor actor. The "broadcast actor" who is not a stage actor, when he is successful, is often the most successful of all. Departments of radio dramatics in colleges and universities are providing graduates with excellent foundations for success. Commercial radio, like the theater, had an antipathy for schools, but today a high percentage of radio actors are college-trained because such teaching usually results in good speech; the broad cultural background which the college-educated person brings with him equips him to understand more profoundly the full values of each situation which confronts him in radio.

Ability to Read Lines

Experienced stage actors have to be trained for radio appearances, where the first essential is the ability to read lines so that no listener will suspect that they are being read. No radio dramatic directors require their casts to memorize their parts, because of the time limitation placed upon production. Reading also tends to destroy the actor's own illusion. Then there is the difficulty of concentrating upon one's own part in the script so that cues are not missed while the eyes are following the speech of another character. Frequently the dialogue lacks spontaneity because of this failure to pick up cues—an artificiality that is particularly noticeable to the radio listener.

In radio acting, cues must be picked up with greater speed than in stage acting, as there is no visual stimulus for the audience to fall back on. The speed of picking up cues, however, will vary, even in radio. Variation in speed of picking up cues, along with variation in the speed of talking, is a matter of pace. Pace is one of the most important elements of radio dramatics.

Radio has suffered from a mechanical reading of lines. The greatest asset of the broadcasting actor is the ability to read understandingly and, while reading, to express emotion. When one appears for a dramatic audition, one is usually given a reading test; there must be no stumbling over lines, no mind wandering. The reader must feel the part he is reading, must articulate clearly, must, through his voice, project himself as the character he represents through the microphone to the receiving set. It is distressing to have all the characters in a play walking around with Webster under their arms, and all determined to avoid variance in speaking even the most exotic words. While the time is too short for the lighting and smoking of a cigarette, as is frequently done on the stage, the radio actor should nevertheless recognize the value of short pauses in his media.

The Voice

The sole medium of conveying the actor's mood, his characterization, and his surroundings in his voice. It alone can create the desired effect upon his listener; hence he must project and color it to capture the listener's interest or otherwise his artistry will fall flat. The radio actor cannot depend upon gestures, stage business, or facial expression to aid in expressing thoughts and attitudes. Emotional crises and dramatic tensions are orally portrayed by one who cannot be seen. There is no give-and-take contact with the audience, no supporting scenery—just a finely tuned vocal instrument.

The radio actor must be a living personality who has experimented with emotional changes of the voice. Most radio voices sound insincere, and histrionism is greatly exaggerated by the microphone. The actor must control the volume of his voice before the mike, yet he must not fail to retain the emotion necessary for motivation. Another requirement is that the radio actor must not permit himself to adopt another player's emotional mood instead of observing his own.

If he puts sincerity into his part and individualizes his delivery, he becomes a living personality entering the living room through the loud-speaker. All impression of remoteness must be removed. Above all, words must be spoken clearly, without leaving uncertainty in the mind of a listener as to what the character really means.

Stage Diction; Radio Speech

The merciless microphone, by focusing attention on the audible to the exclusion of all else, records affectations so faithfully that the stage diction of an actor of the old school sounds artificial when heard in home surroundings. Underplaying a part, however, does not get across to the radio audience. The radio actor must punch certain words in his part. This seems somewhat inconsistent with the fact that radio is an intimate presentation, but unless there is some overemphasis the scene does not become alive. On the loud-speaker stage, an actor who strives to be precise or dramatic often appears to be mincing or ranting. The "sweet young thing" sours the listener. Unleashed joviality makes the character into a boisterous clown. Radio enunciation must sound natural to common folk in the home; yet it must be precise, with a colorful quality that marks the artist. The radio actor must not be slipshod in his delivery, his pronunciation, or his diction. The quality of naturalness is not easy to attain; in fact, it is difficult to convince an "artist" that he is not being natural. The best teacher is a phonograph recording of the voice of the speaker or actor before the mike, provided, of course, that the recording is accurate.

One of the outstanding dramatic directors in radio has summed up the matter thus. "What we most strive for in radio diction is the fine line between diction so precise that it will sound affected and diction so natural that it will sound too casual. Naturalness is at a premium on the air as nowhere else. . . . A child who is being just naturally 'natural' . . . is better on the air than is many an old-school actor who is studiously trying to be natural."

In a theater play, the actor is trained to throw his voice to the back rows of the balcony, but when he appears in a radio play he must learn to control the volume of his delivery. Otherwise the control operator will be forced to modulate artificially the actor's voice, which may spoil his tone quality. The radio actor or speaker is trained with a volume-level meter in front of him, on the dial of which the strength of his voice is indicated by a fluctuating needle. The trained radio speaker will keep his level of volume upon the dial within the limits where no adjustment must be made mechanically by the control operator: the best actor is the one who has trained his delivery so that modulating is not necessary by the control operator. An excessive throwing of the voice frequently results from the actor's being too conscious of the vastness of his audience. He feels that he must put on a particularly high pressure, which makes his speech sound, in the home where the receiving set is located, like a person shouting. It is not necessary for the radio actor to raise his voice where there are background noises, sound effects, or music, because he is always located closer to the mike and his voice will come through clearly over the sound effects. He may train himself to modulate the voice by turning on his radio to some musical program and speaking his part at the regular level, frequently increasing the volume of the music but keeping his voice at the same level.

Acting

The physical exertion of acting for the radio is just as great as that expended by the stage actor. Added to the tension incited by the time element, by the awful zero-hour silence, and by the vastness of the radio audience is the physical participation in the dramatization of the part. While the area of the stage is limited by the sensitiveness of the microphone, the actor should actually throw himself into his part. I have seen radio actors portraying a man and his wife fleeing from wolves. During their entire skit they faced opposite sides of a ribbon mike and went

FIG. 41. Actors' positions around microphone.

through the motions of running as they read their parts from the manuscripts they held. Meanwhile in the background a dignified imitator howled and bayed. The two actors really became breathless and every fine emotional shading was clearly picked up by the microphone. The use of a mike suspended on a boom permits greater freedom of movement by actors since no upright stands are in the way.

The dramatic reader who is presenting a reading from "The Deacon's Masterpiece or the Wonderful One-hoss Shay" will sit in a squeaky chair which he will work back and forth as hard as possible. He will chew on an imaginary "chaw" of tobacco. He will crack an imaginary whip, acting the part that he is endeavoring to portray as he recites the lines, while in the background sound operators will turn wheels in a gravel track and produce the sounds of the horse's hoofs. Greater realism is produced when actors really act their parts.

Microphone Position

In general, the radio speaker stands about 1 foot from the mike. If he is farther away, he is not, in theatrical parlance, "center stage." When distance is necessary to create the desired effect for the listener, the actor will back away from the microphone. If the performer needs to exceed conversational loudness, he must step back from the microphone for such passages. In exceptional instances he may need to turn completely away from it in order to avoid blasting. All entrances which are indicated as fading-in are made from about 10 feet away and on the beam of the microphone. The actor speaks at the same level of volume during his approach to the mike in order to convey the perspective of coming on the scene from a given distance. If the listener is to "see" this movement through his ears, the actor must speak all the time that he is moving. If he pauses in his speech, but keeps on moving, when his voice is next heard from a lesser distance it may sound like that of another person. Another difference between the regular theater and the radio theater of the air is that in the former an actor must use strength to be heard above the mob. Over the air the mob is put into the background and the speaker who is close to the microphone should not raise his voice. While the radio speaker acts his part, he cannot be weaving to and fro from the microphone, for this will cause distortion. His movements must be determined by the control engineer rather than by his emotions. By changing the position or varying the delivery, different attitudes may be projected. When the actor is excited, he will stand at some distance from the mike, raise the pitch of his voice, and speak more rapidly. Sympathy brings the actor in closer contact with the sensitive diaphragm, where he will raise his voice only slightly above a murmur. Ghostly laughter, so frequently heard over the radio, starts some feet below the microphone and comes up to it. It has been said that the impression of loyalty is best created by speaking in a quiet kindly voice close to the microphone.

The distance at which radio actors work from the microphone varies with the type of scene being played. If it is a scene with many characters the control operator increases the volume to the level necessary to obtain the desired perspective; under these circumstances actors may read their lines 3 feet from the pickup. On intimate scenes the speakers may come as close as 3 inches; thus the scene not only sounds but is intimate. When a filter mike is used for a telephone conversation the off-stage speaker talks within 1 inch of the microphone. The engineer will raise the volume according to the wishes of the director.

When acting before the microphone the actor must be paying attention to a number of things at once. Aside from a strong concentration on the characterization he must read the script, take care to be the right distance from the mike, watch the director for signals concerning sound cues, speed of delivery, and distance, and pay attention to sound effects incidental to the action of the play.

CHAPTER TWENTY

SOUND EFFECTS

Sound effects are to the radio play what scenery is to stage production. Of course, there may be radio plays that are produced without the aid of sound effects, just as there are plays in which scenery is not essential. Sound effects are largely dependent upon the listener's imagination and are presented in order to make him create a visual picture of the scene in which the play is being produced. Much of their value depends upon the psychological suggestion of mentioning what the sound represents to stimulate the listener's imagination. In the majority of instances it is quite essential that the actors in their lines allude to the sound so that the listener will form the correct visual image.

It is far better to have no sound at all than a sound that is a poor representation of the desired effect. Sound effects should never be injected into a radio drama for their own sake. They must be a valuable aid to the visual imagination of the listener or else they must not be included. It is true that the youthful audience desires more sound effects than the adult audience. In order to get the proper reaction, the sound effects must be timed perfectly. Consequently it is better, according to the American system, to present them in the same studio with the actors.

The sound-effects man should possess a good sense of rhythm and timing. His position requires finesse, artistry, and good judgment. He works closely with the director, keeping one eye on the script and the other on the director. He may ring his cues in the script with red pencil and indicate where the sound is to be peaked and where it is to be faded out. He must be willing to experiment for hours creating new effects and getting the presentation of other sounds just exactly right. An active imagination and ingenuity are also essential. He should also be what is called in the theater a "quick study." It is helpful if he can memorize cues so that no time will be lost. When he has 50 to 60 cues, this is not too easy! The sound man must be absolutely dependable, for the sound effect must come on time, at just the right level, and for just the proper duration. Before the broadcast he should arrange everything in the order that it is to be used, and everything must be close at hand so that he will not waste time getting it into the microphone. While the show is in progress, the sound man is given his cues by the director. He, after all, can hear how the show sounds, since he is in the control room. So the sound man must watch constantly in order that he may tell by signals if the volume and the quality of sound are correct. He should be resourceful, eager to experiment, know radio engineering and studio technique, appreciate dramatic values, and have a workable knowledge of music and rhythm. Added to all this he must have a pleasant personality to withstand the rigors of long rehearsals and tired radio directors. (I have used this masculine pronoun, but many sound operators are women.)

Recorded Sound Effects

By far the largest proportion of sounds used in radio dramas are produced by recordings which are made from the actual sounds. These records, which ordinarily cost $2.50 each, are manufactured by Standard, Speed-Q, Major, Gennett, and other companies. Over 12,000 sounds are available and the list includes such unusual items as closing a barn door, sounds in a bowling alley, cats fighting, chopping through river ice, corn popping, drilling an oil well, horse and wagon in the snow, snores, man walking and running, milking a cow, a camel crying, and an elephant trumpeting. A number of variations of a sound may be recorded upon one side of the record; for instance, on one side may be the sounds of an automobile starting, door slam, speeding up, and stopping, while on the other the automobile will run continuously. The company that manufactures these transcription effects takes its sound-recording equipment to the football game to record the crowd noises and to the lighthouse to record the fog horn.

In some studios the sound recordings are played in the control studio and are wired into the mixing panel without the actor's hearing them. Whether the sound-effects records are played in the studio with the actors or in an adjacent studio, a separate microphone must be used in order to have absolute control over sound levels. Otherwise, if the sound pickup is on the same mike with the cast, it is impossible to have proper control of the balance of sound in relation to speech. The larger studios have a multiple-turntable equipment which may be rolled into the studio in which the drama is to be presented. The multiple turntable is used in order to blend sounds. For instance, a play may be taking place in the interior of a freight car. One of the records being played will be the noises heard in the freight car while the other will be the noises of the engine and the train itself. In a ghost-story recording, one record may bring in the shrieking of wind while another record conveys to the listener the sound of howling wolves. Alert sound operators experiment in

Fig. 42A. Sound table. Four pickup heads, three turntables, mixers, record racks in the front, speaker set into recess at end of sound table.

the combining of records in order to create new sounds and the playing of existing recordings at different speeds in order to create desired effects. The sound of frying bacon and popping corn has been combined to create the effect of the breaking-up of a glacier. The playing of a recording of artillery fire at a slow speed has been used for thunder.

The noises on records must be rehearsed, since it is often their volume which is most important. For instance, the sound of a car skidding into a crash is recorded as one unit. The sound engineer must take into con-

Fig. 42B. Sound recordings upon the turntables. Notice how the recordings are held with the needle set upon the record, the turntable revolving, until the cue is picked up by the operator. The circular mat in the foreground is a stroboscope disc used to test the constancy of the revolving speed of the turntable. When seen by the light of a neon lamp from a 60-cycle current the outer circle of teeth will seem to remain stationary when the disc is revolving at 33½ revolutions per minute. The inner circle will appear stationary when the disc is revolving at 78.26 revolutions per minute.

sideration whether that car is right in front of the actor, whether it is 20 feet away, or whether it is down a block or two. Also, he has to notice if the car skids as it is going by the actor and crashes away from him, or whether the whole thing takes place away from him.

In addition to the recording of noises and sounds, special background music is supplied by these companies to be used in creating the right atmosphere for scenes of sorrow, approaching danger, underhanded procedure, quarrels, and love-making.

Manual Sound Effects

Not all sounds are created by such recordings. The expense of building up a library of sound records is too great for the smaller station; consequently experimentation must be conducted by the dramatic director or sound-effects man in the local studio. As he experiments in order to create desired sounds for his radio dramas, he adds to the equipment to be used for sounds in the studio. All manner of junk such as tin cans, bottles, and broken china, as well as good cups, saucers, and plates, silverware, rocks, a bag of gravel, whisk-broom, soda-fountain straws, and other things are gathered by the experimenting sound-effects man. In the studio there will be planks which may be laid upon the floor in order that the actors may walk upon them to create the sound of walking upon a stage. There will be creaky rocking chairs and squeaky hinges which are treasured by the sound-effects operator. A good reliable squeaky door is a treasure. Very simple things may be used to create sounds. The radio warrior selects his swords by ear; and every 6-foot length of chain carries a different sound picture to the listener.

There are some manual sounds which are as important today as they ever were. These have been retained because they synchronize with speech or suggested action. The following list of manual effects eliminates those made better by recordings or those made naturally.

The opening and closing of doors and windows, movement of furniture, and so on may partake of the character and mood of the persons in the drama at the moment they occur. For example, when a person is angry he opens and shuts a door in quite a different manner from that which he uses when he is being stealthy or feeling calm.

Automobile Door. The only way to get the sound of an automobile door closing is to buy a section of an old automobile door from a junk yard and mount it in the studio. It should contain the glass in the frame. Mount it on casters so that it can be slid out of the way into a corner.

Brush Crackling. Use broom straw; it is handy to have in the sound-effects storeroom. Work it between the hands, close to the microphone. An old broom may be cut apart and used, but it is inclined to be rather stiff. Sometimes it is possible to use heavy cellophane.

Bubbling Brook. Gently blow through a straw immersed in a glass of water. Test for volume. If you have a studio drinking fountain put some pebbles in the basin, turn on the water, and put the mike close to it.

Chopping Wood.
   a. An ice pick driven into a piece of soft wood.
   b. Use a large jackknife against a branch of a tree, quite close to the microphone.

Cow Being Milked. Squeeze two ear syringes alternately into a bucket. It is advisable to have an additional supply of syringes if the effect must last for a length of time.

Crash. Build a crash box, which consists of a wooden box filled with broken glass and light pieces of metal and tin cans. Nail on the cover, and simply by turning it over near the microphone you get a crash.

Crash Glass. Place some cotton or soft material in the bottom of a box and fill the box with glass. Then drop some heavy article on the glass.

Crash Wood. Splinter a berry box; crush it by pushing thumbs through the bottom. A supply of berry boxes is essential to the studio equipment.

Dead Leaves. The effect of walking in dead leaves can be created by stirring corn flakes in the top of a cardboard box.

Door.

The door that is used in broadcasting should be made solidly. It is advisable to use a standard door from a lumberyard and set it into a frame constructed of 2-by-6 kiln-dried oak. Have the construction dovetailed to avoid warping. Use heavy hardware—hinges, lock, doorknob, and catches, and put a knocker on the door. It is foolish to build a cheap door because it will always sound like a summer-cottage door on the air. A lighter-weight door may be hinged at the other side of the frame and a screen door between the two in order to get a variety of door effects from a single unit.

Echo.

a. Large studios usually have echo chambers to produce this effect. They are usually in some part of the building where a loud-speaker can be placed at one end of a long hall or cellar room and a microphone at the other end. The voice is fed into the room through a loud-speaker, and its echo is picked up by the microphone. However, if it is not possible to have an echo chamber, the same effect may be obtained by facing a directional microphone into a long fiber wastebasket. Throw the voice from behind the microphone into the wastebasket so that it comes back to the microphone.

b. In case you do not have a directional microphone, drop the wastebasket over the microphone so that the voice must go up into the basket and resound into the microphone.

c. Another method of creating an echo is to talk through or rather around an inflated basketball bladder, holding the bladder between the mouth and the microphone.

d. To give the voice a hollow ghostlike sound, place one end of a 10-foot length of 2-inch pipe about 2 feet from the microphone. The actor will then speak into his hands, which he cups over the other end of the pipe.

Explosion. Use an inflated basketball bladder with 15 to 20 BB shot in it. Get an old type of bladder that does not have a valve. Holding the bladder about 3 inches from the mike, suddenly give it an upward jerk, or hit the bladder soundly upon something near the microphone and hold it up to the microphone so that the reverberations will be heard for some time.

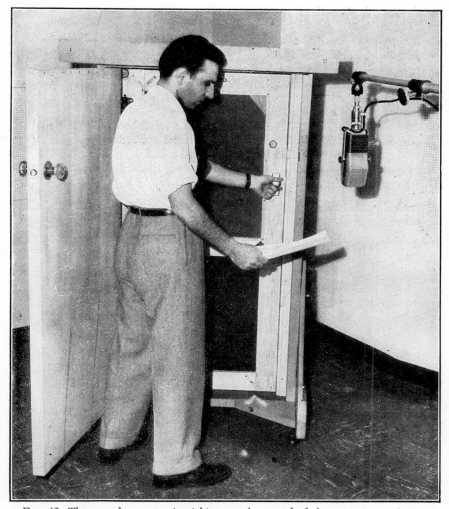

Fig. 43. The sound operator is picking up the sound of the opening or closing of a door with the microphone close to the door. Equipment shown is a combination of three doors: heavy outside door, screen door, inside door, all in one frame.

Fire. Lightly crackle cellophane between the hands, or crunch the heavy end of a bundle of broom straw. In case it is a forest fire, combine with the breaking of berry boxes.

Footsteps in the Snow.

   a. Grind thumbs into a cigar box filled with cornstarch.

   b. Fill two small sacks, not too full, with cornstarch. Tape them with electrician's tape to keep them from breaking and squeeze them with the correct rhythm near the microphone.

Ghostly Speech. Use the filter microphone (modern consoles have the filter installed in them), which removes the low-frequency vibrations. The effect thus produced is a hard and chilly tone. This may also be done into an echo chamber.

Horses.

  a. Use coconut shells with a little finger strap on the top so that the first finger may be slipped through the strap. These are used with the correct rhythm in flats filled with the proper type of soil.

  b. Another method to reproduce the sound of horses' hoofs is to use rubber plungers. They are held by their handles and rubbed across each other in the correct rhythm. This also gives a good effect.

Ice. Ice jam breaking up may be produced by twisting an inflated toy balloon close to the microphone.

Fig. 44. Marching men . . . pegs done in an end-to-end motion. (*Station WJR, Detroit.*)

Marching Men. The accompanying illustration shows the marching-men equipment. This consists of a wooden frame about 18 by 24 inches. Nine strong
cords are strung about 2 inches apart from end to end, and 12 cords are
strung from side to side. The ends of these cords are attached to a device
which will tighten them, a bolt which can be screwed out. From each
intersection of cords is hung a wooden peg, perpendicular to the frame.
A screw eye is inserted in the end of each peg and is tied to the cords;
this allows the pegs to hang loose. For the pegs we use round dowel rods.
As these pegs are lifted and pushed back and forth upon a large sheet
of paper or upon a wooden table top, the sound of marching feet is produced. It is advisable to sandpaper the bottoms of the pegs a little to
take off their rough edges before using.

Porch Swing. Rock an old swivel chair rhythmically.

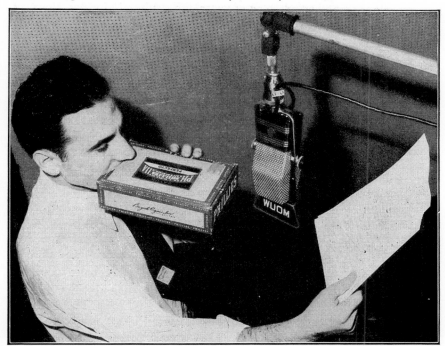

Fig. 45. Actor using a muffle box, which is a cigar box with a halfmoon cut out
of the end, to create the effect of a person speaking from behind a closed door or
of an off-stage voice.

Speech, Off-stage. When it is desired to give a muffled tone of a person speaking from inside a door, take a cigar box and cut a semicircle out of one
end, retaining the top, of course. This, held up to the mouth, allows the
person to speak into the closed cigar box, giving a muffled tone.

Splash. Simply drop a flat block of wood into a tub of water well off mike.
Be careful not to hit the side of the tub. Line tub with canvas to avoid
metal sound.

Squeaks. Rusty hinges or pulleys. A wooden peg twisted in a hole in a board may help, or turn a moistened cork in the mouth of a bottle.

Telegraph Keys. It is best to use a regular telegraph key. It must be attached to a battery. It is important to use an unintelligible message because the Communications Code prohibits the sending of intelligible messages. However, the Morse code should be used.

Telephone. It is best to use a real telephone for the click of the receiver. Discarded hand or desk sets are usually available from the telephone company. Rig up a board with a battery- or electric-current-operated bell and the buzzer to be heard while waiting an answer and when receiving a busy signal.

Telephone Conversation. Use filter system.

Water. If you want the sound of a paddle wheel in the water or a boat being rowed, or any other splashing of water, use a tub full of water. However, a metal tub filled with water will produce a metallic sound over radio; consequently if a metal tub is used, it must be lined with canvas, hung around the sides, to eliminate the metallic sound.

Window. The requirement for good window sounds in radio is the same as for good door sounds. Good solid frames and real sliding windows should be used. A shade can be attached to one side, and possibly a Venetian blind on the other side, in case you need either of these for an effect in a play. Both the door and the window should be mounted upon casters so that they can be rolled in corners of the studio when not in use.

Wood.

    a. Splintering: Use wooden matchboxes or berry boxes, or peach crates, according to the sound required.

    b. Chopping down a tree: Use a knife on a branch for the chopping sound. For the cracking sound, pull off a section of veneer from a piece of three- or four-ply wood. This shows that the tree is cracking and starting to fall. Jump into a berry crate to give the effect of the crash to the ground.

The operator must be careful that the equipment he uses will not break and cause a sound not desired. Furthermore, the control operator should be informed of the sound effect to be used and when it is to be used.

Natural Sounds

The sound-effects man should not neglect to experiment with the actual source of the required sound. Dishwashing is a sound that is difficult to imitate, so it is best to wash dishes before a microphone. Nothing sounds more like pouring water from a glass than pouring water from a glass. Try out the sound itself first if it is convenient. If it is not reproduced satisfactorily, then seek to create it by other methods. Other effects created best by the natural-sound method are footsteps, breaking glass, bells and chimes, kisses and slaps, gunshots, and coins.

CHAPTER TWENTY-ONE

DIRECTING THE TELEVISION PLAY

Directing a play for television involves two quite distinct processes. First, the director has to do much the same job as the director of a stage play. He starts by analyzing the script. He confers with the designer, and together they arrive at a ground plan from which the designer makes drawings for the settings. The director then blocks out the action or "business" with the cast, rehearses them on characterization, interpretation, line readings, and all the many details involved in wringing a dramatic performance out of a script and some actors. When this process is completed, the show is brought into the studio, and the complicated machinery of television is made to produce the desired effect on the screen.

These two steps are so closely interrelated that it is impossible to keep them entirely separate. In practice they are sometimes divided by having a staging director accomplish the first step and a camera director actually put the show on television. This is not, however, the common method. The action must be planned for the camera coverage, and the camera coverage must be in harmony with the blocking if the desired shots are to be secured. Because the staging and camera coverage are so closely related, it is generally much more efficient to have one director responsible for the entire production.

This chapter is principally concerned with the first part of the director's job, the staging. As in the actual directing of a show, it is impossible to keep the cameras entirely out of the discussion, but the emphasis is on what the director does before he and the cast arrive at the studio.

The director of any dramatic production starts by analyzing the script. What are the dramatic values in the play? What is the author trying to do? What effects should he try to create for the audience? If, for example, the play is a comedy, the director asks himself what the comedy is derived from. Characters? Dialogue? Plot? What kind of comedy is it?

Farce? Satire? Comedy of manners? This is as important a step in directing as any of the many duties that fall to this harried person. The ability
to analyze dramas and to put a finger on their essential values is not
easily achieved. It is developed through years of experience in reading
plays, working on them, trying things out, meeting success and failure
with the efforts. Students interested in becoming dramatic directors
should acquire all possible experience by working in plays of all kinds
and in any capacity. It is only by complete immersion in drama that the
real dramatic touch is developed.

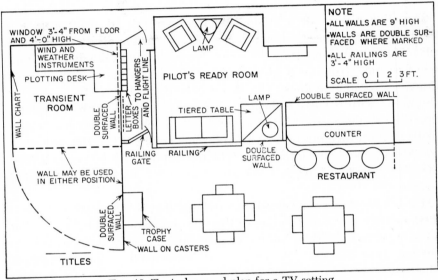

FIG. 46. Typical ground plan for a TV setting.

Ground Plan

While the director has been studying the script, the designer has also
been working on it from his point of view. The first problem, which is of
equal concern to both director and designer, is agreement on a ground
plan. The ground plan is a precise floor plan which shows the shape and
size of the set, location of furniture, and other major set props as viewed
from above, looking straight down to the floor (Fig. 46). It is of importance to the director because he must block all of the action and arrange
his cameras and microphones to fit the ground plan. In television, it is
also necessary to have a master floor plan showing the location in the
studio of the various sets, for few TV plays limit themselves to one set.
Even if there is but one set, the designer and the director must know the

exact location of the set in the studio. The ground plan and the studio floor plan are drawn to exact scale so that the locations can be dealt with realistically in the planning stage. Since the ground plan is so important to both the director and the designer, it is usually arrived at by mutual agreement. Once the ground plan is accepted, the director and the designer agree on a general style and tone for the production, and the designer proceeds with his job of dreaming up appropriate settings.

Casting

The director, meanwhile, is concerned with casting the show. In different productions the authority of the director in casting varies considerably. In some programs a producer handles matters of policy, budget, and major casting. In any event, the director will have a strong hand in the casting, if not complete authority. Casting is a product of the director's analysis of the play as seen against the available actors. It is another part of dramatic production that requires skill, experience, and insight. A play can be materially helped by good casting, and it can be ruined by faulty casting. There are many factors to be considered. Will the budget stand name actors? If it will, and if one qualified for a leading role is available, it is usually wise to use a name. The actor's appearance, experience, ability, voice, and his temperament are all important for television. Rehearsal time is drastically limited, so a director can ill afford to gamble with many beginners. Everyone has to be a beginner at some time or another, but the director should not put his show in jeopardy by casting a beginner in a key role. The camera is exceedingly revealing, so every member of the cast must look his part and his age. Where possible, tryouts should be used to aid in casting. This affords a chance to see different actors together, and sometimes the exact relationship between characters is important. Sometimes the director will want to see an actor on camera before making the final choice, for there are some people who do not look the same in real life as they do on camera.

The director cannot take too much pains with the problem of casting. Unless he has a suitable script and an adequate cast, there is little the director can do to make a show.

Planning the Action

The blocking of the action and the plotting of camera positions is worked out in detail by the director, using the scale ground plan. This is done well before he meets with the cast. In the production of a television play there is no time for the unprepared director to attempt to ad-lib his way through rehearsals. He has to know what he wants before rehearsals start.

As he reads a play over and over again, a kind of pattern will begin to form in the director's mind. This pattern develops as a series of shots. A

FIG. 47. Poor arrangement of furniture and ineffective blocking. Desk and actors are plastered against the back wall.

shot is the product of two things; the location of the characters on the set and in relation to each other, and the position of the camera and the lens used. It is almost like the old gag of which came first, the chicken or the egg. There is really no answer. The television director thinks, primarily, in terms of camera shots, but a shot cannot be obtained unless the action is properly blocked. He will also get ideas for other shots as he sees possibilities while the action is being rehearsed.

Working with the scale ground plan, the director begins, slowly and laboriously, to plot out the action. As each character appears on the scene, he marks down the basic movements. He keeps track of the general position of each character at all times. These are adjusted in terms of cameras which are also located at precise points on the ground plan.

FIG. 48. A better arrangement of the same scene as Fig. 47. Desk and actors are away from the wall and more interesting shots are possible. See Figs. 49 and 50.

There are devices available, such as the Bretz plotter,[1] with which the director can mark in the precise angle of view for his cameras. In this way he can check on paper exactly what is being seen at any given moment. Thus, the director blocks out the entire play. This prerehearsal blocking becomes a working blueprint. A highly precise, detailed plan

[1] See Class Project No. VI.

needs to be achieved by show time, and this preparation gives the director and the cast a logically conceived base from which to start.

Before he is finished with this stage of preparation, the director must also plot out the commercials, opening and closing credits, titles, and similar materials. Every detail must be worked out as exactly as possible on paper, and to scale, so that it can be duplicated on the floor of the studio. The director must depend on many other people to see to it that the studio setup corresponds to his plan. To do this, the plan has to be clear, accurate, and complete.

There are many more fine points about the characteristics of television cameras, and their relationship to the positions and actions of actors, than we can possibly discuss here. However, by investigating some of the more obvious characteristics we can gain some insight into this difficult problem.

It is necessary, first of all, to remember that television is a photographic medium. This means that it employs cameras and lenses with all of the advantages and all the disadvantages of cameras and lenses. Its main implication, for the director, is that it gives him an exceptional degree of selectivity. The audience sees no more, and no less, than the director allows it to see. This is an enormous opportunity for creative and imaginative directing, but at the same time, it imposes severe limitations and responsibilities. If we stay on a tight close-up of one actor when something else in another part of the scene is important, we have robbed the audience of its just due. On the other hand, the use of the close-up can be a potent weapon. It is relatively simple to emphasize whatever the director deems important through the close-up camera, and not always so easy on a stage. With imagination, the camera can be made more than a reporting instrument. It can be an additional tool of intrinsic artistic worth. It can be creative in the presentation of the story. To use cameras in this way, the director must have knowledge, experience, and imagination.

Camera lenses are not like the human eye. They do not see things in exactly the same way. They approximate the human eye. Lenses have certain characteristics that must be second nature to the director thinking of scenes viewed through these lenses. The following paragraphs treat of some of these characteristics and describe the ways that they affect the blocking of a show. Many of the results of lens characteristics are somewhat exaggerated by the fact that the final product is seen on a small rectangular screen.

It is necessary to reduce distances for television. Actors need to work much closer together than would be true on a stage. This is not to make them look closer together, but to make them look as though they were at normal distances. If we have two people talking face to face and want to shoot them more or less in profile, it is very awkward if they are so far apart that we have a large blank space in the middle of the picture. They have to work close together. In addition to how it looks on camera, this tendency toward reduced dimensions is furthered by the cramped space in studios, and the need to get sets, lights, cameras, mike booms, etc., in where they can be used. One general rule, then, is that you will use what seems like the least amount of space possible in blocking the action.

In a theater, the audience has only one point of view of the stage. In television, there are infinite views. Cameras can be placed anywhere, and can shoot from any angle. There are usually some practical limitations, but even with these there are untold camera positions and angles. The ground plan and the blocking should take this into account. Furniture and action should not be plastered in one dimension along the back wall, with all of the actors facing toward the front. There is no need for it. Make the arrangement and the patterns of movement real, meaningful, and artistic—then get a camera in the right place to show it. This allows for a roundness of setting and action that is impossible on a stage. It makes for more realism and a great many more opportunities for variety and originality. To be sure, it is necessary to be careful that severe changes in camera angle do not disorient the audience. This too, is a product of the high degree of selectivity. Never forget the possible confusion of a person who sees only what comes out on the screen.

There is an apparent exaggeration along the axis running through the length of the lens toward the subject being shot. The actual pattern seen through a lens is a cone. The television system reduces this to a two-dimensional rectangle in the proportion of three to four. Even so, if you visualize the scene as a cone, with the apex at the lens, you can see more readily the usable pattern. If you deploy a large group along the horizontal plane you are asking for trouble. The only way you can get them all in is to get an extremely wide shot. When you do this you are so far away that you have about a half mile of floor between the camera and the scene. By utilizing the conical pattern of the lens you can block much more effectively. This means that you use the long dimension of the cone more often than the wide rectangular pattern used on a stage.

There is an old saying, both in motion pictures and television, that lenses aren't made out of rubber. It is all too true. They have certain limitations, and no matter how hard you may try to stretch them, you are stuck with these limitations. One of these limitations is depth of field. When a camera lens is focused at a certain distance on an object or person, there is some distance on either side, both toward and away from the camera, in which other objects or people will also appear to be in focus (see Chap. XXIII). Thus, if you block your action in depth, you have to decide about such matters as focus. Say we have two people, one of whom is considerably closer to the camera than the other. If you want both of them to be in focus they will have to be within the limits of the depth of field. If one of them can be out of focus that is fine, as long as the cameraman knows which one is to be in focus.

The director must also decide from what angle he is going to shoot each scene. There are endless possibilities; from the side, from high up, from low down, from eye level, etc. Such choices are made for good reasons, not for arbitrary variety. Know why you pick a certain angle. There are also facial and bodily distortions to consider. Extreme angles of height or lowness introduce possible distortions which might be contrary to the director's purpose. Extreme camera angles have legitimate functions, but only when used knowingly. By choosing a high angle, you may make a lovely young lady look short and fat. Wide-angle lenses have an apparent distortion at the sides, and should you dolly in too close to a person's face, you might give him ears the size of a veteran wrestler.

Avoid thinking of action as seen from straight front. Attempt to picture a scene from the most advantageous position. To return to the example of two people facing each other; if it is a fairly long scene it might be useful to use reverse-angle shots (Figs. 49 and 50). Reverse angles are the combination of blocking action and selecting the best camera shots. Many ideas of this sort can be acquired by watching TV shows and concentrating on the action and how it is covered with the cameras.

Television employs many photographic techniques borrowed from motion pictures. The long shot—medium shot—close-up sequence is one of them. Just what constitutes a long shot, a medium shot, and a close-up is rather vague and relative. They have meaning only in the context of a specific sequence. It is well to remember that the sequential order of long shot, medium, and close-up is not an ironclad rule. It is a general guide, and one with a purpose. When a scene begins, it is necessary to orient your viewers. Let them know where they are, and what is going on. For this, you use an establishing shot, which means some degree of long shot. To jump directly from a long shot to a tight close-up is usually too abrupt. Hence, the medium shot is used as a buffer between the long and the tight shots. It is the purpose that is important, not rigid adherence to any

FIG. 49. Reverse-angle shot.

rule. Keep the viewer in mind. It is easy to see that occasionally you will have to return to a long shot or a medium shot to reestablish the scene.

This is relevant to our discussion here because action must be blocked to allow for these changes. What you are working toward is a series of shots that develops a pictorial continuity. It can only be worked out by integrating the action with the camera coverage. As a rule of thumb, you stay in as close as you can and still show everything that is important. Exceptions to the rules will be almost as numerous as cases that fit. It may be desirable to start with a close-up and gradually work back to an establishing shot. This isn't important. What is important is the need to develop the action and the camera coverage into a sequence with continuity and meaning. Don't settle for convenient reporting by the camera. Make every shot tell something important. In this way you are using the

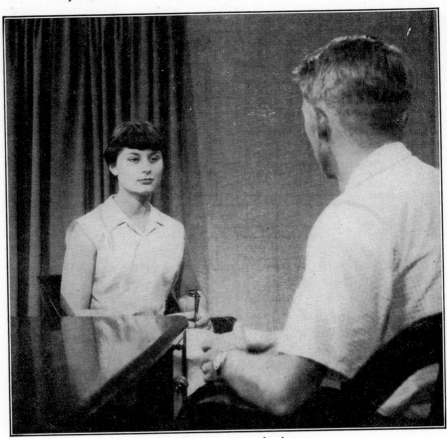

FIG. 50. Reverse-angle shot.

medium to advantage. Watch motion pictures and television programs with these thoughts in mind, and observe how skillfully the pictorial continuity is put together in the good productions. In a good show there are no meaningless shots. Every one is there for a purpose and is essential to the total meaning.

By now it should be quite clear that the planning of the action and the camera coverage is a matter involving optimum precision. Actors have little or no freedom to vary from the established pattern. On a stage it is frequently possible for the actors to feel their way during a performance and vary the rehearsed action somewhat. On television, if an actor is a foot out of position he may ruin a whole sequence of shots. Precision is a necessity. For many of the key shots, both the actor's position and the camera position are marked on the studio floor so that they will be sure to be there when the times comes. Nothing can be left to chance. Everything must be carefully planned in advance.

The Final Plan

Before finishing the planning stage of a show, the director confers with the designer, the costume designer, the lighting designer, the technical director, the audio engineer, and the music director. Sometimes, other specialists are needed as well as those mentioned. Each of these experts will look after his special area, but all of it must fit the general plan which the director has for the show as a whole. Many times these special areas have to coordinate their efforts with another member of the team. For example, the lighting designer can't plan the lighting until he knows where the microphone booms are to be located. The audio engineer can't place the boom till he knows what the set is like, and where the cameras are to be. What develops is a highly specialized team, and the director has to coordinate the work of all of the members.

As plans develop, all of the necessary information is entered into the prompt script. There are cues for cameras, lights, audio, music, sound effects, etc. There is the blocked action of the actors. All these many details the director must get into the prompt script. When the show is ready for the air, he has a working blueprint of every aspect of the show. *No memory is as dependable as a complete prompt script.*

Rehearsing the Actors

A good director has put in many hours of work before he meets with the cast for the first time. He has studied the script, met with the designer, blocked out the action, generally plotted his camera positions, has worked with the sound engineer on location of microphone booms, and has developed a quite definite idea about the ultimate production he wants to achieve. The tentative plan is complete, and the rehearsal period is devoted to making the plan come to life.

In starting work with the cast, the director has to keep in mind his most important function. The writer has provided the basic raw material for the show. The actors provide the flesh and blood which transforms that raw material into a living thing. The director must see the play with an over-all view. His is the hand that gives unity and purpose to the production as a whole. He cannot concentrate on one character, or one aspect of the play. He must see and hear it as the audience will see and hear it. Actors are primarily concerned with their own roles, but the director is concerned with the total effect produced by all of the cast acting in concert.

Cast rehearsals normally start with a reading while the cast is seated at a table. It is a good idea for the director to begin by telling the cast his interpretation of the show, and describing what he is trying to do. He will discuss the characters with the actors and help them fit their characters into the pattern of the play. Table rehearsal is devoted to characterization, line readings, subtle effects which might be obtained, and the over-all mood and impact of the show.

The director cannot be dictatorial in manner, and yet he must work with a firm hand. This is especially true in television because of the extreme limitation of time. The director is working with human beings, and often rather temperamental ones, not with automatons. He must have a deep understanding of people and of how to get the most out of them in a short period of time. If working with professional talent, the director assumes that the actors know how to act. He is, in this case, directing a play, not training actors. He will allow them to use their skills and give them ample opportunity to be creative. He guides them rather than fits them into a rigid, preconceived mold. If working with amateur talent, the situation might be completely different. Here the director might have to use different means because he is training actors at the same time. In either case, the director's job is one requiring infinite skill, patience, and understanding.

After the table reading, blocking rehearsals are started. These are almost never conducted in the studio. However, a scale ground plan can be drawn on the floor with chalk, and chairs and other simple props can be arranged to simulate the actual setting. It is important that this rehearsal set be shaped exactly to the size of the real set. Positions are critically exact in TV, and a few feet one way or the other will throw the camera coverage off. The first blocking rehearsals go slowly and painfully. Each movement and each position are blocked out with precision. Frequently it is desirable for the director to make clear to the actors why certain positions are selected. The actors have to be in a certain position so he can get the tight reverse-angle shot that is needed for the scene. The better idea the actor has about the camera coverage, the more willing he is to fix his positions, and the faster camera rehearsal will go when the show moves into the studio. The blocking stage of a play is tedious at best, and the director must be well prepared and remain calm and efficient through this trying period.

After the show is blocked, the cast can begin to play it. That is, they can begin to play for the dramatic effects outlined by the director. This stage of rehearsal is also used to establish the tempo and rhythm of the play. Fine points of characterization and interpretation are polished. It begins to look and sound like a production. The closer the director can bring this stage to a finished performance the better off he will be. Most of the tempo and rhythm, most of the dramatic effects, and much of the blocking will be lost in the first hours of camera rehearsal. The added confusion in the studio will override the previous preparation to a considerable extent. Moreover, the studio time is necessarily devoted to the task of getting the show on camera. The director is allowed precious little camera time, and he has to use it to full advantage. Probably not till dress rehearsal will the cast get another chance to really play the show. Thus, this kind of preparation must be done before the show comes to the studio.

During the prestudio rehearsals it is frequently desirable for the director to be able to see the scene approximately as it will look on camera. There are a couple of ways that this can be done. One of the easiest is to construct a Bretz box.[1] The director can look through this box and see a scene framed as it would be for any specific lens. There is on the market another gadget that will accomplish this same thing. It employs a changeable lens and is called a Dyson Televiewfinder. The director must always keep in mind the fact that the only thing that is important is what shows on camera. With the aid of a Bretz box or a Televiewfinder he can get a fairly accurate idea of what a scene will look like.

At no stage of the production process can the director approach his job with too much rigidity. He makes a definite plan in advance, yes. But as rehearsals start, he must be ready to change this plan to fit the situation. He may see somewhat different interpretations as the actors work on their parts. It may be necessary to change some of the blocking as it begins to take shape. It will certainly be necessary to alter and improve

[1] R. Bretz, *The Techniques of Television Production*, McGraw-Hill Book Company, Inc., New York, 1953.

things during the early camera rehearsals. So, the director's job is one of constant compromises. He has to have a detailed plan from which to work, but he must ever be ready to change the plan. He must always be alert for improvements, but he can never forget that when the clock is straight up the show goes on, so some possible improvements are never made. The pressure of time and the mass of details to be seen to are constant spurs to get on with the job as quickly as possible. Television directing is a job for the man of action, not for the daydreamer.

Directing Programs Other than Plays

This chapter has treated the directing of dramatic shows. This is not to imply that all shows are done this way, or that all directors do dramatic shows. However, the dramatic production illustrates the craft of directing at its zenith. For other types of programs the director uses as much or as little of this technique as fits the particular situation.

For example, directing a panel show like "What's My Line" is quite a different problem. There is very little movement, and what there is is much the same week in and week out. The format is fairly rigid, and the set is always the same. Little or no rehearsal is required for this type of show. The director's problem is one of timing the camera cuts and getting a camera on the right person at the right time. For quiz or other audience-participation shows, rehearsal with the participants is impossible. In this type of program the director depends on the emcee, or other permanent talent, to handle things in such a way that camera coverage can be obtained. The actual camera coverage must be accomplished "off the cuff." In a complicated show like "The Hit Parade," the problems and techniques are similar to the dramatic program. Here again all of the details are planned with precision.

The general rule is to plan as much as you possibly can considering the circumstances. Rehearse whenever it is possible and practical. Know what you are going to do before you walk into the studio control room. Always be ready to take advantage of situations as they develop. Remember always that the director's first job is to put on a good show in front of the cameras.

CHAPTER TWENTY-TWO

THE TELEVISION ACTOR

Acting is an ancient craft. It is a skill that is slowly developed through many years of hard work. To the casual observer, an actor's life may appear to be a bed of roses. On closer examination, however, it is readily seen that it is a precarious life, to say the least. There are years spent in preparation and training for a most exacting kind of work, and there is a very small mathematical chance that success will follow all of this work. It is indeed a tiny proportion of would-be actors that finally are able to make a living at their chosen trade. But, to the dedicated actor, no other life would be tolerable.

Television acting, like acting for any medium, is based on certain fundamental techniques. While our major purpose here is to consider the special problems of acting before the television cameras, it might be well briefly to review the more basic techniques. It cannot be said too often that an actor learns to act by acting. There is something to be gained from every acting experience, so the beginner should spend as much time acting as possible. Obviously, for television, stage experience is better than radio experience, but both are valuable.

An actor must be able to develop and project a definite and meaningful characterization. This ability implies knowledge and understanding of people and what makes them tick. The actor has to be an amateur psychologist. He must be able to lose his own personal characteristics and mannerisms and take on those of the character. Perhaps even more difficult, he must be able to make these new characteristics believable to an audience. Above all, the actor studies people. When called upon to play a certain character, he should be able to draw up from his memory examples on which to base his characterization.

The actor requires a trained and flexible vocal mechanism. Take all of the speech and voice work you can possibly get. Study singing, even if you never intend to sing in public. Use your voice for as many different things as you can find opportunity. A trained voice and speech pattern does not imply an artificial quality. If you are heading toward television you must be able to speak sincerely and realistically. You must always be believable.

Control of the muscular system is essential to acting. Participation in such things as athletics, fencing, and dancing helps to develop muscular coordination. Then, by performing in public it is possible gradually to

Fig. 51. Table-reading rehearsal at C.B.S.

acquire skill and grace so that movements are natural and un-self-conscious.

Probably the most intangible technique of acting, and certainly one of the most important, is a feeling for the dramatic situation and the ability to project it. This includes emotions, comedy, suspense, and all the other possible effects of which drama is capable. Ability to interpret dramatic effects is developed by study, practice, and keen observation and analysis of performances. If you see a show in which some actor's performance particularly impresses you, try to determine why. What made it an outstanding performance?

In short, the first step in becoming a television actor is to learn to act.

Once you have done that, the transition to television acting is relatively simple.

Television Acting

An actor making the transition from radio to television has much to learn, unless he has combined some stage experience with radio. The physical aspects of acting for a visual medium are, in many ways, more difficult to master than the reading of lines. The visual elements, plus the need to memorize lines, make television acting a much more difficult art than acting for the radio. Even the stage actor needs to learn many new techniques, because television cameras, the receiver screen, and microphones are quite different from a large stage in a theater filled with people. Assuming now that we are dealing with actors of some experience and ability, let's go on to discuss some of the techniques peculiar to television.

Perhaps the most important thing to learn about television acting is the scale on which to perform. In the theater, it is necessary to move, to gesture, and to read lines so that the people in the back of the auditorium will get the desired effect. On radio, since everything depends on reading of the lines, it is usual to slightly exaggerate the reading. Neither of these techniques is necessary in television.

It has been mentioned before that television is an intimate medium. This is true because of the characteristics of camera lenses, the relative size of the viewing screen, and the viewing situation. Together, these things make for less use of long shots and more use of medium and close shots. The combination of a normally closer view and the presence of the microphone scales down the reading of lines. The tendency is toward a more natural reading with less projection, and less exaggeration.

Only rarely is the television viewer given a shot that corresponds to the view of the theater patron in the back row. In the theater, the spectator sees the whole stage all of the time and selects for himself the precise center of his attention. In television, to a far greater degree, the director selects what part of the stage the viewer will see and on what his attention will be centered. In the vast majority of shots used in any play, the stage selected by the director is considerably less than the total. In other words, medium and close shots predominate over extremely long shots. This results in a scaling-down of the pattern of movements made by the actor.

There will be fewer gross movements such as crosses from one part of the set to another. Some such movements are necessary on the stage to avoid having the audience look too long at a static picture. This is no problem in television because of the ability to change points of view by changing cameras. Of course there will be such moves in a TV drama wherever they are motivated by the action. They do, however, tend to be fewer in number and smaller in scale. To the camera a little movement will be more meaningful than will a movement of comparable size on the stage. The same is true for gestures. A gesture does not have to be significant for the back row. It has only to be seen and to have meaning for the camera position, which is rarely further away than a front-row seat in the theater. Often a facial expression will serve in the place of a gesture or movement. Subtle facial expression is wasted on the back row of a theater audience. Not so on TV. Assume that one character says something that is quite shocking to a young lady. On the stage, the young lady might take a step or two back away from the other character and throw her arms up in a gesture of disgust. It might be staged the same way on television. Or it might be that the director would have the young lady stand still, have her reaction show in her face and cut to a reverse-angle shot showing her face close up. If the latter method is used, it is taking advantage of the potentialities of the medium and doing things in a way that is impossible on the stage. The advantage of TV is that frequently it can be done either way, and the director is free to make the choice. The result is that large movements are reduced in number, and all movement and gesture are somewhat reduced in scale when acting for television.

This is not to say that the body and the physical aspects of the acting performance are any less important. Clearly television uses many shots that can be called close-ups, but this doesn't mean that all you ever see is faces. The actor must perform with his total being. How the actor moves, stands, sits, reacts with his body, and gestures is vitally important. TV is a photographic and pictorial medium. Many times a shot will be a composed picture, a significant part of which will be the attitudes and relationships of the actors' bodies. A mobile face and the ability to read do not make a TV actor. He must be able to use to the fullest extent all of the resources at his command. The body and its appendages are important resources. The accomplished actor can portray a great deal about his character and about its relationship to other characters through bodily position and movement. A skilled director can heighten this effect with careful composition and camera work.

The actor, then, has his body, his face, and his voice to work as tools for him. Add to this the clever use of composition and camera coverage by the director, and you have an unlimited range of dramatic expression. As an actor, television provides you with a unique challenge. To realize a measure of success, you must think of the television camera as a device capable of probing deep into the heart of a drama and into the innermost psychology of the actors. If you are supposed to appear lifelike, discard any techniques that smack of the artificial.

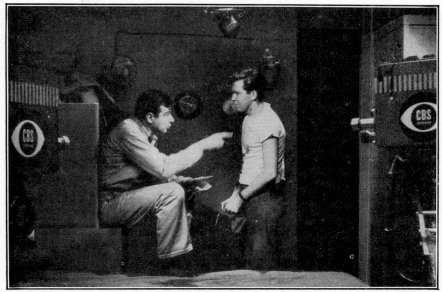

Fig. 52. A scene showing the limited space used in TV drama. (*Columbia Broadcasting System.*)

The finished product of a television drama is more like a film than either a stage or radio play. However, there are major differences in how that final product is achieved. The expansive kind of scene frequently found in films, such as the chase scene in a western or the amphitheater scenes in *Quo Vadis,* is impossible on television. The actor will never have to worry about this type of performance. Even more important is the fact that a television performance is continuous, except for the customary intermissions between acts. Films are shot in very short scenes over a long period of time. This is a crucial difference for the actor. In this regard, stage and radio experience help the actor to develop the ability to give a sustained and continuous performance.

The mechanics of television have a profound effect on the actor's performance. As was pointed out in Chap. XXI, the field of view of a lens is in the shape of a cone. The amount of usable space is considerably smaller than that customarily used on the stage. The actor must become accustomed to working in the smaller space and in positions and groupings that fit the scene as viewed through the camera. You do not have to be concerned about the audience's view, or turning your back on the audience, because the camera can see you from any number of

FIG. 53. Some of the equipment and crew that surround the actor.

positions and angles. The requirements of camera coverage are such that they impose an unusual degree of precision on the actor's movements and positions. The factor of time also imposes a necessary burden of precision. It is essential to be able to repeat the established tempo through the final rehearsals and the performance. In television, as in radio, when the second hand comes round the show is over, whether or not you have finished the performance. Actors in television must be able to learn and prepare their roles in a short period of time. The television play rarely has more than a week in which to rehearse. The performance is given in the midst of a mass of equipment and technicians constantly moving around the periphery of the set. The performer needs to be virtually immune to distractions. It is not possible for the television actor to be isolated so that he can summon his muse for inspiration.

The above are, in general, the problems that the actor needs to learn about to adapt his art to television. We can now examine some of the techniques used in more detail.

The Audio

In talking about television, it is common to stress the visual elements. It is true that television is primarily a visual medium, and it is the visual side that is different from radio. However, you can never overlook the audio, and certainly the actor must remember that a great share of his time goes into the learning and reading of lines.

A television dramatic series produces a new play every week, or in a few cases every other week. This tight schedule, together with the constant effort to reduce costs, strictly limits the amount of time that can be devoted to preparing and rehearsing each show. The television actor must be a "quick study," that is, he must be able to learn lines quickly and accurately. Television acting is, in many respects, similar to summer stock in the theater where a new play is produced every week. Summer stock experience is excellent training for the hopeful TV actor.

The ability to learn lines quickly is partly a native talent and partly a skill that is improved by practice. Begin learning lines by studying the play and the part you are to portray. Trying to learn the words by rote memory, out of context, is well-nigh impossible. Acquire a feeling and understanding of the character and how he fits into the play. This will make the ideas and thoughts which he expresses seem real and logical. Learn the thoughts first, and then gradually polish the words. Strive for as much exactness as possible, because the playwright has spent a lot of time trying to express the character's thoughts as effectively as possible. Start rehearsing without your script at the earliest possible moment. This helps develop assurance, and also allows you to connect the thoughts, ideas, and words with the action. You will probably find additional techniques that help you to learn lines. A dependable memory is essential since prompting on television is virtually impossible. Once the show starts, the actors are on their own. If you can't learn lines quickly and accurately, you had better stick with radio or films.

Since a microphone is used to amplify the sound, it is unnecessary, in television, for an actor to project his voice in an unnatural manner. A sincere, natural, easy style of delivery is best. Anything that sounds like reading or reciting must be avoided like the plague. You have to talk to people. Listen to what the other characters say and answer them in a conversational way. The ability to listen is as important as the ability to read, and in a medium as intimate as television, the actor who is never really in the scene sticks out like a sore thumb. The exchange of dramatic dialogue is a give-and-take proposition. Every time you speak a line you are responding to something that another character has done or said. Never allow the feeling to develop that you are giving a recitation which is periodically interrupted by speeches from other characters. Be in the scene at all times, and be a part of whatever is going on.

In television, as in radio, pauses are used for a purpose. There are no gaps between speeches except those that are deliberately put in for a dramatic effect. When the other character is through speaking, you start without pause. If a pause is put in, know why it is there. If this sounds unrealistic to you, remember that part of the actor's job, and only part, is to appear lifelike, not actually be lifelike. Dialogue that moves along with snap and a definite rhythm is effective, and nothing will kill a performance faster or more surely than gaping holes between cues. Planned pauses yes, accidental and meaningless gaps, never!

As you work on a part, keep in mind that the first and most important job in reading the lines is to get the meaning across to the audience. All else is lost if the audience has trouble picking out the meaning of what you are saying. The enunciation and other mechanical aspects of the voice are only part of the problem. You must shade the meanings, give emphasis to the important ideas and words, and make it clear in one reading exactly what is implied by the line. Basically, this is a problem of emphasis. Emphasis means more than stress, which has come to be associated with a kind of dynamic jumping on words or, as it is known in radio, "punching" a line. Emphasis can be achieved in a variety of ways, and punching is but one of them. It is possible to vary the rate of speech for emphasis. Pauses can be used both before and after a word or phrase. The inflectional pattern can be changed. Sometimes, rather than punching, it is more effective to emphasize an idea by reading it very softly. A capable actor can also charge words with emotional values and highlight their importance. The beginner should undertake to spend hours practicing these various techniques. Nothing will label an actor as a novice more quickly than an inability to bring out the meaning of his lines.

It is rarely necessary, in television, for the actor to be concerned about microphone position. Most of the time the microphone will be on a boom, and the boom operator will see to it that the microphone is in position for your lines. Sometimes the audio will be picked up by a microphone suspended in a fixed position. This will never solve all of the audio problems, but occasionally there is enough dialogue in one spot to justify the use of a hanging mike. Another possibility is the portable microphone set that can be used without a cable attached to it. The microphone is concealed on the person of the actor, who also carries a very small transmitting unit. This system permits a fairly stable microphone position but still allows for maximum freedom of movement.

On Camera

The first sign of a serious professional actor is his conscientious approach to rehearsals. He writes down what the director tells him, marks in his actions and business, and tries to follow precisely the same pattern every time, unless the director changes it. We have seen earlier how essential it is to end the rehearsal period with a precisely set pattern. When the director says he wants the actor in a certain position, he means exactly in that position, not a yard one way or the other. Frequently the key positions are marked on the studio floor, and it is the actor's job to get to these marked positions—to get there without it being obvious to the audience that he is looking for a mark on the floor. Precision, exactness, and repetition of the established pattern time after time; these are the things the actor must work for during the rehearsal period.

Normally, in dramatic performance, the actors should be unaware of the camera. Concentrate entirely on the other characters, except as advised by the director. Don't ever sneak glances at the camera. It cannot be done so that it goes unnoticed, and nothing looks worse to the viewer. Sometimes, as in the case of a narrator, it is necessary to talk directly to the audience. This is done by talking directly into the camera lens that is being used. Red tally lights on the front of the camera tell the talent which camera is on. The specific lens position will vary with the make of the camera. If you have to talk directly to the camera, do not hesitate to ask which lens is the one in use.

Ease, grace, and naturalness of movement are absolute musts for the TV actor. If a performer is ill at ease, awkward, and self-conscious about his movements, there is no way to hide this fact. You simply cannot appear and stand awkwardly on the set putting your hands in your pockets and taking them out, or twisting a handkerchief, unless it is a part of the show. What could be more distracting than a hand shaking with fright every time we see it in a close-up?

Actors learn to be graceful and natural in standing, sitting, walking, and moving about the set. Few people are born with this kind of ability. It is learned through long experience. Any kind of physical and muscular training is of value. Experience in performing before audiences is even more valuable. Concentrating your attention on the play and the other characters is the most effective insurance against self-consciousness. If you suddenly become aware of how you look, you have just dropped out of the scene, and you are no longer acting. If you are listening to what is said and concentrating on what is going on, you don't have time to worry about how you look.

Economy of movement is another essential in the TV actor's trade. When you make a cross, or a gesture, or any kind of movement, it should be done for a definite reason, and you should know exactly what the reason is. If there is no good valid reason, don't move. Don't become a scarecrow because you think you aren't acting if you aren't gesticulating and prancing about. Make every movement of the body count. Gestures and movements are of significance to the audience only when they tell the audience something concrete. Don't use movement and gesture to work off your own steam. They are among your most valuable tools, so use them wisely.

Facial expression is extremely important in television acting. The close-up is frequently the heart of a TV drama. If you aren't in character or aren't in the scene, you cannot hide it from the TV camera. Either your mind is in the show or the audience will be wondering what happened. In facial expression, too, economy is important. Make your face tell something. Don't grimace. Make your face reflect what is going on in your head and in your heart. If nothing is going on there, the close-up camera will so inform the audience, and you had better try scene design or some other field. There are movie stars, and there will be TV stars, who achieve stardom because of an expressive face. Theatrical arts are full of ways that enable performers to fool the public, but no one can deceive a tight close-up.

The physical aspects of acting are also important in delineating character. The actor must not only be able to use his body gracefully and naturally, but he must be able to move, to stand, to look like the character he is playing. Physical characterization is a deliberate and planned product. It is not dependent to a very great degree on inspiration. You stand a certain way, walk a certain way, gesture a certain way because you intentionally plan it that way. That is, if this behavior is to have any meaning you plan it. This stresses again the need to study and observe people. If you want to look like a certain type of person you must be able to visualize such a person and then adjust your behavior accordingly. Don't go into a trance and expect a character to emerge. It won't. The physical aspects of characterization are virtually never complete in every detail. You pick certain key movements or patterns, incorporate these into your performance, and they will carry the desired effect to the audience. Realize that this comes with working consciously for the desired effect.

An actor is never free from worry about his appearance. This is not meant to imply any self-consciousness about his appearance, but rather a concern that his appearance fits the role he is playing. In addition to the behavior patterns discussed above, there is concern with costume and make-up. For large-budget network productions, costume and make-up experts are available to help worry about these matters, but the actor needs some understanding of the requirements. The experienced actor feels comfortable and at home in any costume. The ability to wear clothes of all sorts with ease and comfort, and with a certain flare, is one of the trademarks of the actor. For plays in modern dress, pick a costume that fits the character you are playing, which may or may not fit your own tastes. Avoid excessive contrasts in color, especially black and white. Stick to the middle tones. If the actors are using their own clothes, they should offer the director some choice. Bring several possibilities to one of the final rehearsals and let the director select the best one. If the telecast is to be in color, it is mandatory to check all costumes in advance and get the advice of the technical staff.

Make-up, in television, follows the same basic principles as for the stage, but it must be more subtle. Stage make-up could never survive the penetrating close-up. Shadows, lines, and changes in facial features must be done with extreme care. Make-up, too, should be checked on camera before the performance. Because of the revealing nature of the camera it is generally not advisable to attempt to use young actors to play older character parts. The real thing just can't help looking more real. If the facial features do not need to be changed, frequently men can get by with very little or no make-up. Women can wear just slightly exaggerated street make-up.

Taking Direction

During the rehearsal period, there is but one person who has any kind of over-all view of the play. That person is the director. Since the total effect of the production is the desired end, it is necessary that the actors conform to the wishes of the director. The relationship between actor and director is a delicate one. We have discussed how careful the director must be in his relations with the cast. The actors, too, must realize the importance of the director and be willing to take his directions. The proper viewpoint is that the director is trying to make the best possible show, and that is why he is there. He is not there to criticize you as an actor. He merely wants to fit your performance into the show as a whole. This attitude of mutual understanding and respect between the actors and the director has become a tradition in the theater.

In television, the actor's relationship to the director is even more important. On the stage, when the curtain goes up the actors are pretty much on their own. The reverse of this is true in TV. The director, through the cameras, is very much in the final performance. He can do a great deal for the actor with good camera coverage. He can practically eliminate you from the show in the same manner. Since the director controls the cameras, the actors have no choice but to follow his directions. This is the practical side of the matter. Artistically, as well, the director is an important part of the performance. The team relationship between director and cast is extraordinarily close. If they cannot work together, or if any member of the cast cannot or will not follow directions, there is no way to produce a successful television show. The final fate of your acting performance rests in the hands of the director. This places upon his shoulders profound responsibility for the final product. It leaves the actor no choice but to cooperate fully with the director. If he is wrong the show will be a dud, but whether he is right or wrong the show is certain to be a dud if the actors do not follow his directions.

Throughout rehearsals, try to follow directions exactly. Make every effort to get things straight and to repeat them with precision. If you have a question, ask the director. For the most part, directors aren't whipcrackers. They serve more as guide than dictator. The nature of the medium insists that they assume a more important role in dramatic production than is true in the theater, but their interests and the interests of the cast are the same; a good show. If the actors are aware of the director's job, and the director understands the actor's problems, there should be no untoward friction.

The preparation of a television dramatic show is a somewhat harrowing experience. The process is complicated. Time is appallingly short. The pressures are many and powerful. A competent actor is a very valuable asset. A competent actor who is also calm and collected in the midst of TV confusion is nothing short of a blessing.

CHAPTER TWENTY-THREE

TELEVISION PRODUCTION

In order to understand the various jobs involved in getting a television program on the air, and to develop some skill in their performance, it is necessary to know something about the equipment used and the procedures followed. This chapter will cover the information usually implied by the use of the term "television production."

The Studio

The requirements of a television studio are considerably different from those of a radio studio. A room 50 by 75 feet would be a large radio studio, but it is a modest-sized television studio. The first requirement, then, is size. Television studios must be large. High ceilings are also necessary. Anything less than 20-foot ceiling heights introduces serious problems. It is desirable to be able to hang lights as high as 15 feet above the floor. If some kind of catwalk system is used for access to lights, we are past the 20-foot height by the time we put a man on the catwalk. Ceilings of 15 feet will work, but anything less materially hampers production. The floors need to be smooth, level, and of some relatively hard surface. Dollying cameras on rough, uneven floors is enough to give the crew ulcers, to say nothing of the audience. Carpeting is confined to the set area proper, and is never permanently installed. Some provision must be made for erecting scenery in any part of the studio. Facilities are needed for hanging lights. This may be accomplished with a grid of pipes installed 12 to 15 feet above the floor, by hanging pipe battens which may be either counterweighted or hung in fixed positions, or by specially designed systems that fit a particular installation.

Ideally, soundproofing requirements are the same as for radio. Because TV studios are large, and because the audio is less apparent than in radio, acoustical treatment is frequently accomplished on a minimal basis. In some cases nothing at all is done. The studio needs to be fairly dead, or at least have some provision for breaking up reflected sound waves, if usable audio is to be achieved.

Storage and shop space are vital to TV operation. At least as much space needs to be available for storage as is devoted to studios. Scenery, furniture, props, commercial supplies, and other materials accumulate

Fig. 54. Famed N.B.C. studio 8-H in Radio City, New York.

at a phenomenal rate. It is inefficient and uneconomic not to save much of this material. It is almost impossible to operate without fairly adequate shop facilities. This includes a carpentry shop for building scenery and properties, and an electrical shop for maintenance of electronic equipment and lighting instruments. When new stations are built, storage and shop space are frequently reduced to save money. This decision is always regretted after the station has been in operation for a year or two.

In addition to the normal needs for office space, reception room, and client's booth, television stations also require dressing rooms, art-department facilities, film-storage rooms, projection rooms, and announce booths.

The TV control room is normally located in one of the studio walls and somewhat elevated above the studio floor. The control room needs to be larger than the typical radio control room. It is desirable to be able to see the studio from the control room, but it is not essential. Visual signals and cues are almost never given from the control room and the

Fig. 55. A theater made into a TV studio. This studio is operated by C.B.S. in New York and is used to originate color programs.

director's main attention is focused on the camera monitors, so it is entirely possible to operate from a "blind" control room. Some stations have done so for years.

The over-all layout of the studio building is another aspect of design that demands careful consideration. The architect should consider the flow of traffic through the building, the moving of cameras and booms from one studio to another and to the shop, the moving of scenery from the scene shop to studios, and similar problems. Television studios should always be designed with the advice of persons who have had extensive experience in TV operations.

The Studio Crew

One director, an engineer, and a sound-effects man can do a fairly complicated radio show involving a good-sized cast. These three are just a start for the crew required to do a simple television show. The crew consists of: one cameraman for each camera (normally, a minimum of two), a floor manager, a microphone-boom operator, a video engineer, an audio engineer, a technical director or switcher, and the

Fig. 56. An N.B.C. color program in rehearsal with crew in working positions.

director. Sometimes, the director can do his own switching, but this is rather rare. This, you will understand, is minimum. We haven't provided for setting the stage, lighting, acquiring props, camera assistants to help dolly and move cranes, an assistant director, a projectionist, nor for any of the more specialized jobs like designer, make-up artist, title-card artist, etc. The more complicated the show, the more this awesome pyramid of staff grows. In this section we will consider the crew that works in the studio. A little later in the chapter we will discuss the control-room crew.

When we start to think about television, we naturally think first of the camera, and thus the cameraman. Being a photographic medium, television revolves around the camera and its operator. In most stations, the cameramen belong to the engineer's union. They may perform elementary maintenance on the cameras, but their chief specialty is operation. The cameraman moves the camera around the studio, aims it at the desired subject, frames the picture, and controls the focus. He may also

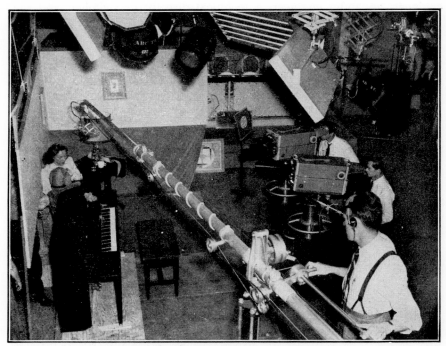

FIG. 57. A studio production at A.B.C.

be asked to adjust the iris setting, but the setting to be used is determined by the video engineer or the technical director. In television, the cameraman's job is not the responsible and creative job it is in motion pictures. In motion pictures, the head cameraman lights the scene, determines in a large measure how and from what angle the scene will be shot, and plays a much larger part in the final product than does the TV cameraman. However, do not get the idea that the operation of a TV camera is a simple job or one that requires no skill. Quite the reverse. You will probably never appreciate this statement properly until you try directing a show with inexperienced operators on the cameras. The job of television cameraman is one of considerable importance in the production of programs.

When crane cameras are used, or when a great deal of camera movement is necessary, assistants are required by the cameramen. The assistants, variously termed "camera assistants," "dolly pushers," and "cable pullers," are made available to help the cameramen move around the studio quickly, quietly, and with a minimum of fuss. Some camera

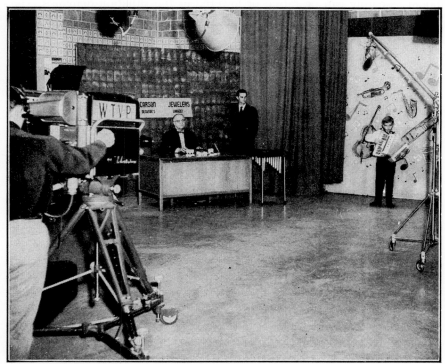

FIG. 58. A studio production at a local station, WTVP, Decatur, Illinois.

mounts cannot be handled without additional help. There is always the problem of keeping out of the way of cables, lights, microphone booms and other equipment. Sometimes space is at a minimum, and to get usable camera movement it is essential to have more than one operator for each camera.

The most common type of audio pickup in television is by means of a microphone boom. The same microphones are used as are found in radio. Probably the two seen most often are the RCA 77-D, and the Western Electric–Altec cardioid. The major difference between radio and television sound pickup is the way the microphone is handled. In addition to using booms, microphones may be hung in a fixed position, set upon a desk or table, or worn around the neck or on the lapel of the talent. More often than not, a boom will be used. The Mole-Richardson perambulator boom is the workhorse of the industry (Fig. 59). The perambulator can be moved to any convenient position near the set. The operator stands on the perambulator platform. The platform and the boom assembly can be raised or lowered as the situation demands. The

Fig. 59. The Mole-Richardson perambulator microphone boom.

platform can be raised and lowered separately from the boom assembly to adjust for operators of different heights. The operator has four directional controls over the microphone. He can raise and lower the boom arm by means of a cradle mount where the boom is fastened to the vertical pedestal. He can swing the boom arm from side to side. He can crank the telescoping boom arm out to a distance of 17 feet or in to a minimum length of slightly over 7 feet. Lastly, he can rotate the microphone on the end of the boom by means of a handle. With practice, an M-R boom operator can cover action and keep the microphone placed for a good audio pickup. One of the hardest things to acquire is a feeling for keeping the boom just above the frame of the picture being taken by the camera. Normally, when a mike boom is used it is desirable to keep the microphone out of the picture.

One of the most important jobs in television production is the floor manager. It is a job similar to that of the stage manager in the theater. The floor manager is the coordinator of the crew on the floor, and the director's representative in the studio. He receives all cues from the director through the intercom system and relays them to the talent or

Fig. 60. The R.C.A. black-and-white studio camera.

other members of the crew. The floor manager sees that props are moved, sets are ready, cameras are in position, title cards are set and in the right order. In short, he looks after all of the many details of production on the floor, and must always be ready to act quickly in emergencies. Since emergencies can happen with some regularity, a floor manager must have considerable experience in TV production and be familiar with everything that goes on.

The studio crew positions discussed thus far are essential to even a minimum operation. Frequently, in small stations, people do these jobs in addition to other duties, but if any kind of production, other than a person seated at a desk, is undertaken, the jobs must be done. The remaining crew jobs are usually absent from the small-station payroll, but increase in numbers and importance as the complexity of the station's operation increases. The work done is quite clear from the title of the position. In the larger stations we would find designers, coordinators, grips (or stagehands), electricians, lighting designers, prop men, special-effects men, and several varieties of flunkies. Of course, it is only at the network production center that all of these various specialized jobs are found.

Even in the small station, some of the above functions must be performed. If the station is going to use scenery, someone has to design and build it and set it up. In small-station fashion these jobs are usually done by the production crew. Typically, an employee might do a little carpentry work, help set up a show, set the lights, and then announce the show on the air. It is impossible to eliminate all of the functions, so what is found is a compound doubling of duties.

Television Cameras and Lenses

It is impossible to acquire any know-how in television production without a basic understanding of the medium's main instrument, the camera. An integral part of that instrument is the lens.

The present television studio camera is built around the image-orthi-

FIG. 61. The R.C.A. color camera.

con tube. The orthicon tube is a highly sensitive tube, capable of producing a picture with a minimum amount of light. It is also able to deliver a picture of high resolution. This means that an orth-tube camera can generate a picture that is sharp, well defined, good in gray scale tones, all with a practical amount of light. The orthicon camera can deliver a good, broadcastable picture with 35 to 40 foot-candles of light. This is considerably below the level normally used, between 100 and 125 foot-candles, but the picture can be used. It is not true that the television camera requires an unbearable amount of light. This was true when the iconoscope camera prevailed, but is not true with the orthicon tube.

An image-orthicon tube costs $1,200 and can be expected to give approximately 700 hours of service. Obviously, this becomes an important item in a station's budget. The R.C.A. color camera uses a matched set of three orthicon tubes. Nothing else needs to be said to indicate that some care should be exercised in the use of orthicon cameras. The tube is susceptible to damage of several kinds, thus a list of don'ts should be carefully learned by anyone that might have occasion to handle a TV camera.

1. Don't uncap a camera until permission is received from the video engineer.
2. Don't adjust any of the camera controls, except as specifically instructed by a qualified engineer.
3. Don't try to turn on or set up a camera until you have been trained to do so.
4. Don't keep an orthicon camera trained on a fixed subject for long periods of time. This results in the image being "burned in," and if enough time is allowed, the tube can be ruined. The burn-in characteristic gets worse as the tube gets older.
5. Don't handle a television camera carelessly or roughly.
6. Don't experiment. If trouble arises, or if you aren't certain what to do, call an engineer.

The camera proper is but one part of the total camera system. A "camera chain" consists of the camera, the power supply, and the camera-control unit. All three are necessary to the operation of each camera. A heavy cable, containing 24 circuits, connects the camera with the control-room units. Wherever the camera goes this large cable must accompany it.

Built into the camera is an electronic view finder. This provides the camera operator with a small television screen which shows him the

Fig. 62. The G.E. black-and-white studio camera.

Fig. 63. The G.E. color camera.

Fig. 64. The Du Mont studio camera.

picture which the camera is producing. If the equipment is properly lined up the picture seen by the cameraman will be approximately the same as that seen on the control-room monitors. The view finder is usually covered by a hood to keep ambient light from striking it. This

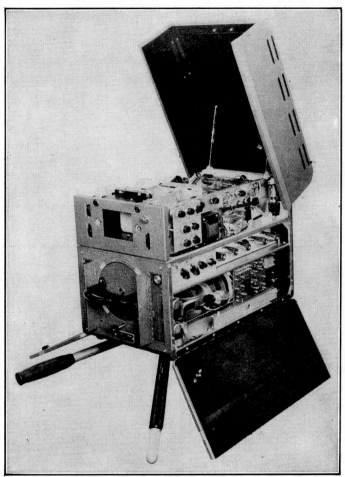

Fig. 65. The Du Mont camera open for maintenance.

is done to give the cameraman the best picture possible so that he can check on details and focus.

The modern television camera has a turret on the front end, on which can be mounted four lenses. On the R.C.A., G.E., and Du Mont cameras, this lens turret is rotated by hand. A handle on the rear of the camera is squeezed to release a catch, and the operator can then turn the turret to the desired position. On the G.P.L. camera, the turret is rotated by an electric servo motor when the operator punches a button on the back of the camera. The camera is so constructed that one of the lenses will be in front of the orthicon tube. This is the lens that is in use. The position of the orth tube, and thus the lens in use, varies among the different makes of cameras. On the R.C.A., it is at top center. On the G.E.,

Fig. 66. The G.P.L. studio camera, front view.

it is bottom center. On the Du Mont and G.P.L., it is in the lower right-hand corner from the operator's point of view, or lower left-hand corner from the talent's view. This position has significance when the talent is supposed to talk directly to the audience, which means into the lens in use.

Provision is made for some means of moving the orthicon tube back and forth behind the lens in use. As we shall see, in television cameras focus is achieved by moving the orth tube closer to or farther from the lens. A knob, or crank, is placed on the side of the camera to allow the operator to focus.

Cameras would be of little use if it weren't for the precision-ground lenses on the front end of them. In any kind of photographic device, the lens is of utmost importance, so lenses are important in television.

The function of a lens is to gather the rays of light reflected by the scene and to bring them to a point of convergence, or focus. The pattern of light admitted by the lens is in the shape of a cone. As the rays of light pass through the lens they are directed to a point of focus. The rays of light continue on to form a cone to the rear of the lens. The image

Fig. 67. The G.P.L. camera, rear view.

in this rear cone would, of course, be inverted (Figure 70). In a television camera, the orthicon-tube carriage is inserted so that the tube can be moved to the plane of focus.

While the pattern of light entering a lens and leaving it is cone-shaped, in television we are concerned with a rectangular, two-dimensional picture. Thus, we can momentarily forget the solid dimension and think of a vertical plane inserted into the conical pattern. On this plane the camera tube scans the rectangular picture. This process does not alter the fact that the actual light pattern is a cone, and this is very important in blocking action and knowing what patterns of movement best fit the TV camera. Since we use only the two-dimensional rectangle inscribed within the cone, it is easy to see that the resulting picture is determined by two angles, one horizontal and one vertical.

As far as television lenses are concerned, the dimension of primary concern is generally the horizontal angle. This angle determines the width of the picture that will be seen. The horizontal angle is a product of the focal length of the lens. Focal length is expressed in inches or in

FIG. 68. The G.P.L.–Watson Vari-focal lens.

millimeters. For all practical purposes, one can go on the basis that 25 millimeters equals 1 inch. Thus, 50-millimeter lens is the same as a 2-inch lens. The most common lenses used on TV studio cameras are the 50-millimeter, 90-millimeter, and 135-millimeter. On some makes of cameras, such as the G.P.L., the roughly equivalent 2-inch, 4-inch, and 6-inch lenses are used. The fourth lens on a studio camera may be a 7-inch, 8-inch, or some other slightly longer lens. For remote work, and other special purposes, lenses up to 30 inches focal length are available.

Fig. 69. The control-room components of the video system. The units mounted below the desk are the power supplies. Above the power supplies are the camera control units. The switcher is mounted in the desk and the master monitor is above it.

To give some idea of the horizontal angle viewed by lenses of varying focal lengths, some typical cases are listed below:

$$50 \text{ mm}—34°$$
$$90 \text{ mm}—19°$$
$$135 \text{ mm}—13°$$
$$8\frac{1}{2} \text{ in.}— 8°$$

There is a rule of thumb that soon becomes second nature to anyone spending time in a television studio. Assuming, of course, a fixed position for the camera, the shorter the focal length of the lens, the wider the horizontal angle of view, the smaller are objects seen, and the farther away the camera appears to be. By the same rule, the longer the focal length of the lens, the narrower the horizontal angle of view, the larger are the objects seen, and the closer the camera appears to be. In review, the focal length of the lens determines the horizontal angle of view. The horizontal angle of view determines the width of the scene viewed and the apparent closeness of the camera to the scene or objects viewed.

The vertical angle of view is no problem in television. In accordance with F.C.C. standards, television pictures must be transmitted as a rectangle with a 3:4 aspect ratio. In American television, the picture sent out is three units vertically by four units horizontally. Thus, the vertical angle is always three-quarters of the horizontal angle.

Television lenses, like all good lenses, are equipped with a diaphragm to control the quantity of light that is passed through. This diaphragm is called the "iris." The common method of designating the iris opening size is in f stop ratings. A fast lens might have a maximum opening of f/1.9. Other calibrations frequently found on TV lenses are: f/2.8, f/4, f/5.6, f/8, f/11, f/16, and f/22. Remember, the smaller the f stop number the larger the opening in the iris diaphragm; the larger the number, the

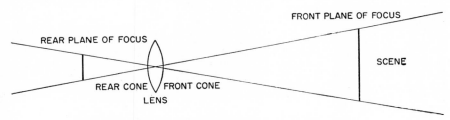

Fig. 70. The pattern of light rays passing through a lens.

smaller the opening. Each stop doubles or halves the amount of light entering the lens. For example, going from f/16 to f/11 doubles the amount of light admitted by the lens; f/8 admits four times as much light as f/16; etc. The same is true going the other way; each stop reduces the amount of light by half. In most cameras, it is necessary to set the iris opening by hand. On the G.P.L. camera, for the lens in the taking position, the iris is controlled by a gear system and a small electric motor. This allows the iris to be set remotely from the camera-control unit. Other manufacturers can supply this feature for a modest extra cost. The advantage of the remote iris control is that it gives the video engineer control over the iris setting as well as the electronic adjustments. It is the combination of these two that decides the final character of the picture.

The lenses of motion-picture and still cameras have a built-in means of focusing. You will recall that earlier in the discussion on lenses it was pointed out that at a certain distance behind the optical center of a lens there is a plane of focus. In photographic cameras the film is located at this plane of focus. For different distances, the lens characteristics are altered so that the plane of focus always coincides with the surface of the film. The reverse is true in the television camera. The lenses are fixed-focus, so that the plane of focus moves back and forth to adjust for the differences in distance. In order to achieve a picture which is in focus, the orthicon tube is moved back and forth behind the lens. In other words, the photosensitive surface of the tube is moved to the plane of focus. This is equivalent to a film camera in which the film would be moved back and forth to achieve focus.

Even the single aspect of focus, in the field of optics, can become exceedingly complex. From a practical point of view, there is but one application of focus, beyond a simple understanding of how to get the picture in focus, that is important in television. That is "depth of field." When a camera is focused on a given subject, there is but one plane of

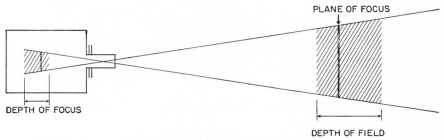

PLANE OF FOCUS

DEPTH OF FOCUS

DEPTH OF FIELD

Fig. 71. Depth of field.

true focus. However, there is a certain distance, both toward and away from the camera, in which objects will appear to be in focus (Fig. 71). The exact size of the depth of field is a rather arbitrary matter, since someone must decide in each specific case just what is acceptably in focus. In every case, however, there will be some spread which will be acceptable for most purposes. The depth of field is dependent on three things: the focal length of the lens used; the distance of the subject from the camera; and the iris setting. As a rule of thumb, you can say that the shorter the focal length, the greater the depth of field; the farther away from the camera the subject is, the greater the depth of field; the smaller the iris opening, the greater the depth of field. The only difficulty is that these three variables are interactive, each one affecting the others. So, while a shorter lens usually gives more depth of field, it does so only in consideration of similar iris setting and similar distance from the subject. All three factors must be taken into account.

Camera Mounts and Camera Movement

Television cameras are bulky and heavy, so an adequate means must be provided for making them maneuverable. Even with a turret of four lenses, mobility is highly important to smooth production.

The camera is fastened to either a friction head or a cradle mount (Fig. 72). This method provides a solid base on which the camera can rest, and it also permits up-and-down and side-to-side movement around

Fig. 72. The Houston-Fearless cradle mount.

the fixed axes of the mount. When the camera is pointed up or down, it is called "tilting." The operator tilts up, or he tilts down. When the camera is pointed to one side or the other, it is called "panning." The operator pans left, or he pans right. The friction head, or the cradle, is equipped with a handle to enable the operator to make these movements, and, logically enough, it is called the "pan-handle." It must be clearly fixed in mind that the above directions refer to the direction in which the lens is to be moved. If the cameraman gets the instruction to "pan right" he is to move the camera lens to the right. Since he is at the rear of the camera, this means that he must move the pan-handle to the left, in order to make the lens move to the right. The director isn't concerned with the operator's hands or the handle, but only with the direction in which the camera moves. "Tilt up" means that the camera lens is to be moved up. In both the friction head and the cradle there are drag controls for each direction, so that the operator can adjust the amount of force necessary to pan or tilt.

The friction head or cradle mount is affixed to some supporting structure. The simplest form is the tripod. For remote work it is often enough

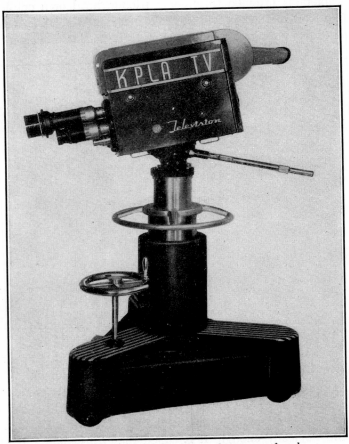

FIG. 73. The Houston-Fearless television pedestal.

to mount the cameras on tripods which can remain in fixed positions. However, in studio operations fixed-position cameras are almost never used. So, even when a tripod support is used it will be placed on a three-wheel triangular frame to allow it some mobility. The tripod-and-wheel mount is the simplest, but most inefficient, type of studio mount. It is almost impossible to use such a rig for camera movement on the air.

Nevertheless, it is adequate for making position changes between shots, and thus is vastly superior to a fixed camera.

One of the most common kinds of camera-mounting devices is the pedestal. Houston-Fearless were the originators of this type of mount,

Fig. 74. The PD-3 pedestal and the friction head mount.

and presently they offer several models. Both of the models shown in Figs. 73 and 74 have a heavy, three-wheeled base which can be steered, and can be moved smoothly for on-the-air camera movement. In the earlier model, variable height was available by means of a crank-and-gear system. In the later PD-3 model, height changes are possible by pressure of the operator's hand owing to a counterweight system on the center shaft. The ability to vary the height of the camera is a most desirable feature. With tripod mounts, you are stuck with a constant height. Other companies now make mounts similar to the pedestal, and most of them offer many advantages over tripod mounts.

There are three common types of crane mounts found in television studios. All three of them are manufactured by the Houston-Fearless

FIG. 75. The Panoram dolly.

Company. The smallest one is the Panoram dolly. The next larger is the TC-1 crane, or Sanner dolly. The largest one is the H-F Television Crane, which comes in several models. In the crane-type mount you have increasing flexibility of camera movement, but at the same time you have increasing complexity and difficulty of operation. The boom arm provides a great deal of flexibility in side-to-side movement and in height. The platform provides mobility around the studio. However, it can readily be seen that the more complicated the movement, the more the people that are needed to provide the movement. In the larger models of the TV crane, electric motors are installed to power-drive the platform, to raise and lower the arm, and to swing the arm from side to side. By this stage, we have passed beyond the budgets of all but large network centers.

As in the case of panning and tilting, movements of camera mounts have specific names which have become fairly standard in the industry.

FIG. 76. The TC-1 crane, or Sanner dolly.

The word "dolly" is somewhat confusing at first since it is used both as a noun and as a verb. The noun is used for any number of mobile mounts. The verb is used to describe movement of the camera toward or away from the subject being shot. "Dolly in" means to move the camera toward the subject. "Dolly out" or "dolly back" means to move the camera away from the subject. Dollying may be done while the camera is on the air, or between shots. When the camera is moved on a lateral line approximately perpendicular to the axis of the camera, it is called "trucking." Thus, a cameraman may be instructed to "truck left" or "truck right." Angular movements which involve both a lateral direction and a line toward or away from the subject are also used, and may be called by whichever direction is most important. Circular movements are also used, and these are usually referred to as "truck shots." For changes in elevation while using a pedestal type of mount, the usual instructions are "up on pedestal," or "down on pedestal." With the crane-

Fig. 77. The Houston-Fearless television crane.

type mount it is usually "boom up" and "boom down." To avoid confusion, some stations instruct crane operators "tongue right" and "tongue left" for sideward swing of the crane arm. You might hear "boom right" and "boom left" as well. The terms "up on pedestal," "boom up," and "tongue right" are not as widely standardized as "pan," "tilt," "dolly," and "truck." These last four are almost universally standard. As with most things in television production, some standard terminology is necessary so that instructions may be given clearly, simply, and quickly, and be readily understood.

Film Pickup Systems

The projection room is, in many respects, the busiest place in the average television station. It is here that all slides, films, and other projected materials are picked up for broadcast. Watch your local station for one evening and keep track of how many pieces of film, programs and spots, and slides, or other projected materials, are flashed onto the screen. They will include most commercials, nearly all between-program spots, all station-identification breaks, and many other slides and films. An efficient, dependable projection room is essential to station operation.

The projection room is normally located somewhere near the studio and control-room area, but not necessarily so. It can be anywhere, but it is more convenient if it is handy to the studio area. In addition to the pickup cameras and various projectors, the projection room needs storage space for films and slides, a bench equipped with film rewinds and a splicer, a video monitor, an audio monitor, and a dependable intercom system with the control room.

The whole operation revolves around the pickup system. There are three such systems in use. The oldest method employs the iconoscope film pickup camera. Many stations still use an ike, but few, if any, are being sold. There are some serious problems with the iconoscope tube that are avoided with the later systems. The second system utilizes the vidicon film chain. Operationally, this system is very much like the first one. It produces better results by virtue of technical improvements in the camera and the tube. The third method is radically different from the first two. It uses a continuous-motion flying-spot scanner. It has a number of advantages which we will discuss in a moment.

With both the iconoscope and the vidicon it is customary to feed several projectors into one film camera. The camera is mounted in a fixed position, and a multiplexing unit is used to relay the pictures from several projectors into the camera. In large stations and network centers, more cameras are used and less multiplexing is done. However, for reasons of economy, smaller stations crowd in as many projectors as possible. The film pickup camera operates in much the same way as a studio camera, except that it is especially designed to handle projected images.

The multiplexer is nothing but a system of mirrors that reflects the images from different projectors into the film camera. A typical arrangement is to have two 16-millimeter film projectors multiplexed in from the sides, one or more slide projectors, and sometimes an opaque projector, all feeding into the same camera. Only one projector is used at a time, unless it is desired to superimpose a slide over film. By using a multiplexing mechanism, an average station can get by with one film pickup camera.

Fig. 78. The R.C.A. vidicon film chain for black and white, multiplexing unit, and 16-millimeter film projectors.

In Chap. III it was pointed out that sound motion pictures are projected at the rate of 24 frames a second, and television operates on 30 frames per second. So, to avoid flicker, it is necessary in motion-picture projectors designed for TV use to incorporate some means of compensating for the difference in number of frames per second. In the regular type of projector each frame is flashed twice. In the TV projector every other frame is flashed three times. This is accomplished by either a modi-

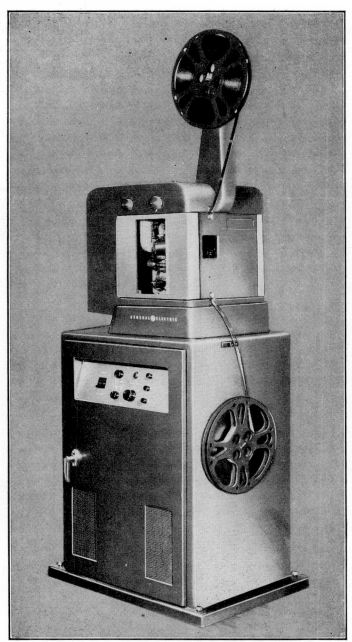

FIG. 79. The G.E. Synchrolite 16-millimeter film projector.

fication in the pull-down and shutter mechanism, or by using a pulsating
light. TV projectors operate only at sound speed, so all film used must
be shot at 24 frames per second. The most commonly used slide projectors are those handling 2- by 2-inch slides. Other types of slides are used

Fig. 80. The Du Mont Multiscanner pickup for film and slides.

at some stations, as well as opaques and other projected images. The TV
system will handle any projected picture that the station is mechanically
equipped to feed into the pickup camera. Both 16-millimeter film and
2- by 2-inch slides are available at all stations.

The third method of film and slide pickup is the electronic scanner.
In this system, the images are not projected in the usual sense of the

word. The frames are brought into an exact position and the image is electronically scanned. The scanning device will handle film, slides, and opaques. In the scanner system, a machine similar to a projector is used. The major difference is that the film is run through the machine continuously and at a constant speed. There is no need in this system for the pull-down shutter action found in the projector. As a result there is no flicker problem either, since it is relatively simple to build the scanner so that it scans 30 frames per second.

The last great advantage of the scanner is that it can be obtained, or be readily converted, to handle color. The problem of color pickup on films and slides is comparatively simple. With the iconoscope, color is out of the question. Several companies, including R.C.A., build a color vidicon film chain. This camera employs three vidicon tubes, and generally follows the same principles found in the R.C.A. color studio camera. Color pickup of films and slides presents fewer problems than color origination of studio programs.

The Television Control Room

As in radio, the TV control room is the nerve center of program production. It is in the control room that the whole process of production is coordinated, and commands and cues radiate out from it in a steady stream.

There is no standard arrangement for control rooms, but certain basic requirements must be met. There must be a position for the camera-control units so that the video engineer can shade and adjust the cameras. He must have both picture and wave-form monitors. An audio position is necessary, including the usual equipment found in the radio-control room: console, turntables, tape recorders, and an audio monitor. In addition, the audio engineer needs to be provided with a video monitor. There needs to be a place for the technical director and the switching equipment. This has to be where the T.D. can see the video monitors. The director's station should be fairly close to the T.D.'s position so that he can feed cues to the T.D. without any difficulty. The director, too, must have a good view of the monitors and be able to hear the audio monitor. Additional space is desirable since there are frequently assistant directors, agency people, or other supernumeraries in the control room.

The most common arrangement is to put the video engineer and the camera-control units at the front of the room at floor level. The director's and the T.D.'s positions are usually located behind the control units and elevated. Often, a second set of monitors is provided for the production personnel. The audio-control station is located in the most convenient position available, where the monitors can be seen, and where the operator can hear all cues.

The basic control-room crew consists of the video engineer, the audio engineer, the director, and the technical director or switcher. In larger stations, and for more complicated shows, additional persons will be added.

Fig. 81. Control room in studio 8-G, N.B.C., New York. Note that curtains cut off view into the studio.

The camera-control units are basically engineering equipment. They provide the video engineer with the adjustments necessary to control the quality of the picture. In some smaller stations, they also provide the only control-room video monitors. It is better if separate monitors are available for the production personnel.

The audio-control equipment is much the same as that used in radio. The only major difference is that circuits must be provided for picking up and amplifying sound from the motion-picture projectors. This adds a couple of knobs to the console.

All of the control-room equipment is important to the production process, but two items are of especial importance. These are the intercom system and the switcher. An efficient, dependable intercom system is essential to TV production. The director feeds a constant stream of instructions and cues to the cameramen and the floor manager, and calls to the projection room for film and slides. All of this operates on split-

Fig. 82. Control room of C.B.S. converted theater studio. Through the window on the far left can be seen the control console for the Izenour electronic lighting control board.

second timing. The control room must also be connected with the transmitter, master control, and any remote locations that are to be used. TV production lives and breathes through the intercom system.

The one most important piece of control-room equipment, as far as production personnel are concerned, is the switcher. The switcher is the device by which different cameras are put on the air, and through which special video effects are achieved. When a motion picture is made, the scenes are shot in many short "takes." The takes are later carefully and slowly edited together. In television, the editing is done continuously and instantaneously by the director. The switcher is the mechanism which provides the director with the means for editing the program.

There are three basic transitional devices used in television. All of them are borrowed from motion pictures. They are the "cut," the "dissolve," and the "fade." The cut is an instantaneous change from one camera to another. The dissolve was originally known in the film trade

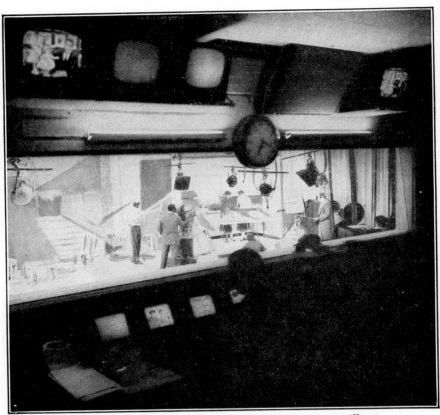

Fig. 83. Control room at a local station. WTVP, Decatur, Illinois.

as a "lap dissolve," which is descriptive of the process. One picture begins to fade out and at the same time another picture begins to fade in. Halfway through the process the two pictures overlap. Completing the transition, the old picture fades out and the new one fades completely in. The speed of the dissolve can be varied to fit the particular circumstances. Sometimes, as a special effect, the dissolve is carried halfway and left there. This is called a "superimposure," "superimposition," or commonly a "super." Care must be taken to prearrange the final effect of the super, but when it is properly used it is a worthwhile device in TV production. The fade is quite like the name implies. One camera is faded completely out, or "to black," as it is called. The new picture is then faded in. Again the speed can be varied to fit the individual circumstances.

To be adequate for studio production, a switcher must provide the means for cutting, dissolving, and fading. These are absolute minimums.

FIG. 84. Control room at WILL-TV, University of Illinois.

The typical switching system provides a row of buttons for cutting from camera to camera. The buttons are numbered to correspond to the cameras which they control. A pair of fading levers operates in conjunction with two additional rows of buttons, called the "effects rows." By punching the appropriate buttons and moving the fading levers it is possible to dissolve or fade. A very desirable addition to the switching system is a method of previewing. If a preview facility is incorporated into the switcher, it is possible to preview special effects or critical shots on the master monitor before they are sent out on the air.

If the budget permits, many stations add some kind of special-effects device to the switching system. Both R.C.A. and G.E. make such devices. R.C.A. calls theirs a "special-effects amplifier," and G.E. calls it a "montage amplifier." This equipment makes provision for horizontal and vertical wipes, split screen, insertions, wedge wipes, a rectangular irising effect, and other special video gimmicks. This is a very useful facility for commercials and for shows which can be enhanced by tricky effects.

No picture gets out on the air without first going through the switcher. Since the final video continuity depends entirely on how the switcher is

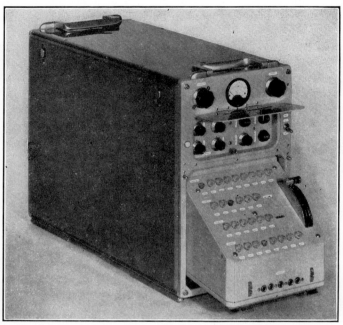

Fig. 85. The G.P.L switching system. The bottom row of buttons is the control bus. The two middle rows are the "effects rows" and work in conjunction with the fading levers on the right. The top row of buttons is for previewing.

used, it is essential that production personnel acquire a thorough knowledge of the switching system available in the studios where they will work.

Production Procedures

Television production revolves around the director. The process of production is so complicated, there are so many people involved, and time is so limited, that the only hope of cohesive organization is to channel all control through one person. In motion-picture production, which has many points in common with television, there is time to divide some of the responsibilities. In television, everything happens at once, and decisions must be made with split-second timing. The director makes these decisions.

The director is in complete control of the cameras. He instructs them where and when to move and what to cover. In many small stations he talks directly to the cameramen through the intercom system. In most network situations the technical director talks to the cameramen, relaying the instructions he receives from the director. When a technical director is used he also operates the switcher. He makes the cuts, fades, or dissolves on cue from the director. In some local stations the director can do his own switching, but this is not common because union contracts frequently require an engineer to operate the equipment. Another system is to have one person assigned to operate the switcher. In this method the switcher does not talk to the cameramen or exercise any kind of authority. He is simply a convenient set of fingers for the director. Whatever the system used, it must permit the director to exercise complete control over the use of the cameras and the switching equipment. It must also enable all of this to happen with the speed necessary to successful production.

The camera operators function entirely under the guidance of instructions from the control room. The basic rule is that the cameramen get the shots which the director wants. They do not get the shots that appeal to them and then let the director choose which one to use. There are exceptions to this rule. Frequently in unrehearsed, off-the-cuff shows a director will allow the cameramen to function in an informal way and to hunt for shots. The important thing to remember is that this is the director's decision to make. If he specifies particular shots it is the cameraman's job to get them as quickly and as smoothly as possible. The proper outlook for the camera operator is to make the director's job as easy and as trouble-free as possible.

Cues to the talent such as the cues to start, wind up, cut, and indications of time are relayed from the director by the floor manager. It is rarely practical to give cues visually from the control room. So, the director gives them over the intercom system, and the floor manager, equipped with headset, moves about the studio giving the cues to the talent. He uses the same signals that are used in radio. It should go without saying that the floor manager's job must be accomplished in silence. It is also his job to get in a position where the talent can see the cues and time signals without obvious movement. The director will also give the floor manager instructions and cues in regard to title cards and other special studio effects. Whatever the director needs to have done in the studio, other than camera operation, is accomplished by instructing the floor manager.

The audio engineer functions in much the same way as in radio. Cues for starting theme music or bridges, opening mikes, fades, and similar effects are given by the director. Frequently, it is necessary to coordinate the sound with the pictures, so the audio engineer must be able to see the video monitors. Often the director will prearrange with the audio operator for certain effects which are to be timed with the video, and the audio man will proceed on his own to carry out the desired effects.

The most important concept in relation to television production is that of teamwork. No one person can make a television program. Any member of the team can ruin one. Every job is vitally important. The director has the coordinating authority not because he is a kind of superman, but because the nature of the medium requires a single coordinating force. Every person engaged in production must depend on the other people to do their jobs, and to do them right. There are no unimportant jobs. All hands are members of a closely knit team, and the team must function efficiently and without friction.

Television Staging

Being a visual medium, television requires all of the trappings common to films and stage plays: scenery, properties, costumes, and other visual devices for establishing locale or mood. If the television program is a dramatic show, a musical comedy, or variety show, the general principles of staging which have been developed in the theater and in films apply to TV as well. There are, however, two important factors which make TV staging a unique field. Everything is seen through the television camera, which is not at all like the view of a stage and different from, though similar to, the view through a motion-picture camera. In addition, television stations broadcast many programs which are not dramatic, musical, or variety shows. For example, what kind of a set do you design for a show like "I've Got a Secret"?

There is a decided difference between dramatic-type staging and that employed for completely nondramatic programs. In the former, the *décor* may be described as representational. An effort is made to create the illusion that the action is in some specific place. The illusion is frequently described in terms of some degree of realism. Even when the setting is quite abstract, some kind of illusion is implied. For the nondramatic program what is required is a pleasing background that will allow for whatever action is involved, and which does not call attention to itself to the extent that it interferes with the content of the program. It frequently does help to create a mood or feeling, but without being too specific as to locale.

The characteristics of television cameras and lenses discussed in relation to blocking of action are important in staging as well. The high degree of selectivity possible with the camera is a vital factor in TV design. Many times it is possible to use just a corner of a room instead of designing and building the entire room. Since the audience sees only what you allow them to see they have no way of knowing that the room isn't complete. It is essential that the designer allow room for camera movement so that the action can be adequately covered. The cone-shaped pattern seen by the lens determines the general layout of sets. The color-response characteristics of the camera tube determine the colors and contrasts that may be used in settings, draperies, and properties. In short, the TV designer must learn all he can about the TV camera and its performance before he undertakes to design sets.

Because the walls, doors, windows, furniture, drapes, etc., are frequently seen in close-up, it is necessary that they look real. Canvas-covered flats, such as those found in the theater, are used in television, but more often the walls are covered with a more rigid, durable material like plywood. The walls are usually built in sections, or modules, to facilitate handling. A light frame of 1- by 3-inch or 1- by 4-inch stock, covered with ¼-inch plywood, is rigid enough for scenic purposes, but still light enough to be easily moved. Doors and windows are usually regular house-type doors and windows sufficiently well framed to be operated in the customary manner. The walls may be painted or covered with wallpaper. Details such as molding, baseboard, wainscoting, etc., are nearly always applied as they are in the real situation. They are almost never painted on.

Drapes and curtains frequently serve as background for television scenes. They may be hung on tracks or pipe battens which can be flown if space and facilities permit. One advantage accrues from the use of drapes in that they are rather neutral in feeling and can be used over and over. Good drapery material is expensive. Cheap materials always look cheap since they do not hang well. So, drapes are economical only when they are used frequently. However, at least one set of decent drapes is virtually a must for a TV studio.

Photographic devices are also used for sets in TV programs. Good photomurals make excellent backgrounds for certain types of situations. Photomurals are somewhat expensive to make, but when their cost is compared to other types of settings it is by no means prohibitive. Rear projection is another photographic device that finds frequent use in television. Special projectors shoot an image onto the rear surface of a transluscent plastic screen. The screens are available in a variety of sizes, and both still and motion-picture projectors are used. The cost of still-picture rear projection is not excessive. The cost of the equipment and the shooting of film for motion-picture rear projection is prohibitive to all but network centers. Where they can be used, motion pictures can create some very exciting backgrounds.

Properties must be appropriate to the situation, so thought needs to be given to their appearance, style, and condition. Whenever applicable, some thought must also be given to their practicality. Chairs and sofas cannot be of a type that makes it impossible to sit down on them or get up from them easily and gracefully. All furniture that is to be used must be thought of in terms of that use, and in relation to the person that will use it, as well as how it looks on the set. Items such as lamps, pictures, window drapes, pillows, and other materials used as *décor*, or set dressing, should be harmonious with the set and with the purpose and tone of the program. Normally, these things should be thought of in minimal terms. If a piece doesn't add anything, take it out. If something is distracting, take it out. Whoever is in charge of this aspect of production should watch the final camera rehearsal on a monitor and then adjust whatever is necessary before the show goes on. Set dressing can do a great deal to enhance the visual appeal and composition of the shots used on the air, but it can also make for messy, over-burdened pictures. As with so many things of this kind, there is no substitute for good taste!

Television Lighting

More often than not, the difference between good and poor television pictures is attributable to lighting. No other aspect of television staging creates so many problems as does lighting.

In the first place, lighting must be in accord with the characteristics of the camera tube and not the characteristics of the human eye. Thus, it is impossible to judge the adequacy of the lighting simply by looking at it in the studio. The TV system can handle only a limited range of brightness, and a limited scale of tonal values, both but a fraction of the range the human eye can see. It is extremely difficult to work in a studio with lights mounted anywhere but overhead. This creates disagreeable shadows on faces. Television is strictly a two-dimensional device, and only with the help of proper lighting can any kind of depth in the pictures be achieved. Then, when you have solved these problems, you find that you get bad shadows from the microphone boom, or some other piece of equipment. At this point, the lighting man is ready to get another job.

There are two basic aspects to lighting for television. It is necessary to provide enough illumination over the entire set area to enable the television system to reproduce a usable picture. When working through an electronic device the artist half of the lighting designer cannot forget the technical requirements of the equipment. In addition to this minimum illumination level, there are the artistic aims to be served by the lighting. It is by no means the case, but there should always be some artistic aim in the lighting used. Many small stations simply turn on enough lights to give a flat, even wash of illumination, and call it good. To be sure, this enables them to broadcast an acceptable picture, but it would look much better if some effort went into lighting the scene.

The image-orthicon tube will produce a picture with a minimum of 25 to 30 foot-candles. Far greater efficiency is achieved, however, with levels of 100 or more foot-candles. The over-all level of light bears on many related problems, which gives it added importance. For example, it governs the iris setting on the lens which in turn affects the depth of field obtained. It also changes the electronic adjustments of the camera. There is no standard light level that is in general use. It will vary from station to station, depending on how the engineers relate all of the variables involved. In this discussion, the levels mentioned are to be considered approximate, with the full realization that many stations will use different levels. The principles, however, remain the same.

There are three types of lighting instruments that accomplish the bulk of television lighting. There are countless others used for various special effects, but only three that are used almost universally. One is the slimline fluorescent bank. This is a large, rectangular pan-like unit containing six or more slimline fluorescent tubes, each with its own reflector. In the early days of television there was little agreement as to the effectiveness of fluorescent lights. The advantages of fluorescents are that they are cooler than incandescent lights, and they burn toward the blue end of the color spectrum, to which the orth tube is more sensitive. Thus, they are more efficient, in a sense. On the other hand, they are inflexible, cannot be dimmed, nor can they be controlled as to direction. Some studios do not use any fluorescents, and no studio uses nothing but fluorescents. They are useful when used in conjunction with incandescent fixtures. The second common instrument is the incandescent floodlight known as the "scoop," or "bucket." These floods use an ellipsoidal reflector and a pear-shaped incandescent lamp of from 500 to 2000 watts.

Fig. 86. The world's largest TV studio: the N.B.C. studio in Brooklyn, New York. It appears that several lighting instruments are used to light this mammoth studio.

The third instrument, and really the workhorse of TV lighting, is the fresnel lens spotlight. Fresnel lens spots are made by all of the companies that manufacture lighting equipment and come in the following sizes: the "inkie," 150 to 250 watts; 500 watts; the "keg," 750 or 1000 watts; the "deuce," 2000 watts; and 5000 watts. Some stations use all three of these basic instruments in lighting shows. Others use only the scoops and fresnel spots. Some designers light the entire set with spots alone. Perhaps the quickest and easiest method is to employ all three types, but it is certain that not all lighting designers would agree with this. Any combination of these instruments is satisfactory as long as the principles discussed below are followed.

The first rule of TV lighting is to avoid trying to set levels by eye. Good, consistent results are obtained only by the constant use of an adequate light meter. The meter should be of the incident type and read directly in foot-candles. The Norwood Director is an example of this type of meter. An experienced eye is still valuable in achieving good lighting, particularly in evaluating the results on the control-room monitors. In working out the levels to be used and in obtaining them regularly, the meter must be used.

There are five basic ways in which lights are used to fulfill specific functions. Of these, three are of primary importance. The start of the task of lighting a show is the "base light." This is an even wash of light over the entire set area. Its main purpose is to provide sufficient illumination to enable the cameras to function properly. Base light is most often achieved with fluorescent banks or scoops, or both. It can be done with fresnel spots. Base light is front light, in that it comes from the general direction of the area in which the cameras will be used.

Next comes "key light," "model light," or "accent light." These terms all mean the same thing and have come into use because of some confusion over the exact meaning of the term "key." The important thing to remember is the function to be served. More often than not you will hear the term "key light" used in this connection. Key light is supplied by spots which are used to highlight the talent, or objects, that are important in the scene. They are used from the front or sides. As one of the terms implies, they are intended to accent whatever is important. They cast some shadows on faces and help to get away from the flatness caused by the base light. The base light and the key light provide the bulk of the front light, and the level of this front light should be somewhere in the neighborhood of 125 foot-candles. It may be 100, or it may be 150, but it will almost always be somewhere within that range.

Following the base and key light, "back light" is added. The "back" has to do with the direction from which the light comes. Back light comes from the direction opposite to the camera positions and is usually spotted on the head and shoulders of the talent. Fresnel spots are normally used for back lighting. The purpose of back lighting is to separate the people from the background and to add as much depth as possible to the picture. The level of back light is normally from 1½ to 2½ times that of the front light. Thus, if your front light read 100 foot-candles you would use somewhere between 150 and 250 foot-candles of back light. For a start, the front-light reading can be doubled for the back light. Normally, 2:1 is a good ratio between front (1) and back light (2).

In addition to base, key, and back light, it is sometimes necessary to use "fill light" and "background light" or "set light." Fill light is supplied by floods or fluorescent pans and is used to fill in dark areas or to help eliminate undesirable shadows. Background or set light is used on the walls of the set to lighten the scene or to eliminate shadows. The need for these last two types of lighting is usually apparent after the base, key, and back lights are set.

No discussion of television lighting would be complete without some mention of shadows, particularly shadows cast by microphone booms. Do not start out with confidence that you are going to eliminate all shadows. It is impossible. Undesirable shadows are usually absent from motion pictures because the lights and camera can be repositioned for every shot. The shadows are there, but they aren't picked up on the camera. This is sometimes possible in television, but not always. All you can hope for is to avoid really heavy shadows, multiple shadows, and shadows which are recognizable in form. In short, you minimize the shadows and call it good. Since it is impossible to do most TV shows without audio, the lighting designer is frequently forced to light around the mike boom. If the boom gets into the beam of a spot you will have a recognizable shadow of it on the wall of the set, or worse, on a person's face. So, the designer must know where the boom will be throughout the program and light around it.

There are many kinds of special effects possible in TV lighting. Some of these require special instruments while others employ the standard instruments used in slightly different ways. Follow spots are commonly used in variety shows. Often an inkie, or other small light, is mounted on the camera and serves as a kind of fill light, perhaps to make an actor's eyes sparkle. Beam projectors are used to simulate a shaft of sunlight. One of the most frequently used special effects is the projecting of a pattern on a wall of a set or on a curtain backdrop. There are several ways of doing this, and again there is considerable confusion as to the nomenclature. These devices are variously termed "gobo," "cucalorus," and "fuddle." The principle is one that makes use of a cutout pattern which is placed in the beam of a spotlight so that a shadow of the pattern falls onto the wall. The pattern may be something specific like the bars of a venetian blind, a window, or a grating, or it may be a completely abstract design. Sometimes the cutout is simply hung in front of a light. There are on the market instruments, such as a Century Lekolite, which has a slot for holding cutout slides. Specially designed projectors are also available that will project patterns like clouds, foliage, etc., onto the set. Once the basic requirements of lighting have been met, there is ample room for experimentation and special gimmicks.

All well-equipped television studios have an adequate switch and dimmer system. As in the theater, the more control that is provided over the lighting the better the lighting can be. This indicates that lighting-control boards should provide the maximum flexibility and control. The same types of control boards are used in TV as are used in the theater. They may make use of resistance, autotransformer, or electronic dimming mechanisms. Some type of patching or multiple switching system is also included so that various circuits can be set up as the need requires. A good lighting-control board should be thought of as a necessity in a TV studio, but many small stations count this as one item that can wait. Actually, the result is the same as leaving a control board out of a theater. Shows can be put on, but poor lighting is always apparent. Good television requires good lighting.

CHAPTER TWENTY-FOUR

TELEVISION CAMERA DIRECTING

The job that is most typical of, and unique to, television, and the one that is the most difficult to master, is that of the control-room director, or as he is frequently called, the camera director. Elsewhere in this book it is pointed out that the staging, blocking of action, and organization are essential to a good show. They, too, are part of the directing job, but people have been doing this kind of thing for years, and many traditions and techniques have been developed. It has been but a short period of time that anyone has sat in a television control room and tried to wring a show out of a mass of complicated equipment and a swarm of busy, keyed-up people.

Television is like theater, like radio, like films, and yet—it is really not like any of them. In comparing TV production to films, for example, the television director assumes many of the duties of the motion-picture cameraman, director, editor, and head soundman. He not only does all of these things, but he does them continuously and instantaneously while the show is in progress. It is the camera director alone who can bring the qualities inherent in the television medium to bear on whatever material the show might contain. In his hands rests the translation of action taking place in a studio into action viewed on a television screen. It is not an easy task.

Directing is a job that requires steady nerves, quick reactions, and lightning-fast decisions. The director must know how to work closely with many kinds of people. He must be able to work under constant tension. He must possess good taste and sound judgment. He must have an appreciation for pictorial composition and artistic values. He must know what is important in the program and how to get the important things onto the television screen. Above all, he must be able to concentrate in the midst of confusion and keep his mind on several things at the same time. In short, it is a job that requires many talents and a broad background of learning and experience.

There are two major aspects to television directing. The director is, first of all, the coordinator of the many people involved in the production of a program. The many arts and skills that go into the program must be funneled into a concentrated effort. The director serves as the funnel. He is like the quarterback on a football team. He calls the signals and coordinates the effort, but he is not the whole team. The second half of the job is the creative one. The director conceives, before the fact, what the final show will be like. It is only in the director's mind that a specific show exists before the program is actually done. It is his concept of the pictorial continuity, combining all of the raw materials of the program, which is seen by the audience.

We can dispose of the director's chores in connection with the audio portion of a program rather quickly, since years of experience in radio are available to serve as a guide. The director cues themes in and out, cues bridges, opening and closing of mikes, and any special audio effects. He has the services of an audio engineer, the same as in radio, and a floor manager to relay cues to the talent in the studio. While most of our discussion will deal with the problems of the video side of a program, always keep in mind the director's responsibility for the audio. He must have an ear tuned to the monitor and be aware of what is going on in the way of audio. Beginning directors tend to minimize the audio, and this is wrong. The audio is always important and sometimes, as in a music program, it is most important.

Let's assume, for illustration, that a director is doing a show using two studio cameras and a film chain. A technical director is operating the switcher. There is an announcer available in an announce booth. The director's cues immediately prior to starting, and during the first 30 seconds of a program, might run like this:

Cameras 1 and 2 ready on opening shots
Ready with slides
Ready with theme
STAND BY
Hit theme—fade into 2
Super slide
Change slide
Theme under
Open announce mike—cue announcer
Change slide

Close announce mike
Wipe out the super
Ready to dissolve to 1
Open studio mike
Theme out
Dissolve to 1
Cue talent

After this flurry, the director is not free to collapse. He is just getting started. Now, we must go back and find out what this is all about.

The director has available a monitor for each camera in use. So, in our situation there would be a monitor for camera #1, camera #2, and the film chain. In addition, there would be a line monitor, or, as it is called, a master monitor. In most stations there would also be an air monitor. Frequently, there will be added an auxiliary monitor so that network feeds, remotes, etc., may be monitored before they are put on the air. In some situations, to avoid this multiplicity of monitors to some extent, a preview system is used. Several lines will be fed through a preview bus on the switcher, and thence to a single monitor. By punching the proper button on the switcher it is then possible to view whatever is desired. The important thing for the director is to be able to see all the picture sources that he will use.

The director's first job is to get the pictures that he wants. This is done by instructing the cameramen as to position, lens to be used, and precisely what the director wants framed in the shot. The technique is the same whether the director talks directly to the cameramen or relays his instructions through a technical director.

The cameras are positioned by using the most precise instructions possible. They are moved closer to or farther away from the set, to one side or the other, and raised or lowered, until the desired effect is achieved. Frequently, in scripted and well-rehearsed shows, exact positions are worked out and marked on the studio floor. When the show goes on the air, the cameras move from one marked position to another. In less formal shows, a general plan of coverage is decided upon, but the specific moves and positions are decided on the spur of the moment as the show develops. Lenses may be called for in one of two ways. Some directors call for specific lenses, such as "camera #2, try the 90," "#1, give me the 135," etc. Others simply ask for a wider shot or a closer shot. In some cases, it doesn't make any difference which lens is used, as long as the picture is satisfactory. At other times it does make a difference, because the possible perspective and the depth of field vary with lenses of differing focal length. It must be kept in mind that the shot is dependent on the camera position and the lens being used, so the two things must be thought of together. The last part of getting the desired pictures is to tell the cameraman just what should be included in the frame—in other words, on what precisely he is to focus. When these three things have been done, a usable picture results. This process should not be thought of as being static. Quite the reverse. A television show is highly fluid, and as soon as a shot has been used the camera is moved to obtain another one. It is a process that continues at a brisk pace throughout the program.

Once the desired pictures have been obtained it is necessary to get them on the air in some kind of meaningful order. This is done by instructing the technical director in the operation of the switcher. There are three fundamental transitions used in going from camera to camera. The routine transitions from shot to shot within a given sequence are normally made by cutting. The cut is, by far, the most frequently used transition. For more major transitions in subject matter, time, place, or mood, a dissolve is used. For still more major transitions, the fade is used. The director continuously watches all of the camera monitors, decides what pictures will be used and how the transitions are to be made. These decisions are passed on in a series of cues. Standard terminology has been developed to make the cuing simpler and more positive. Frequently, the cutting is rapid, and the cues must be given clearly, sharply, and without confusion. The cue to make a cut is "take #___." For a dissolve, "dissolve to #___." For a fade, "fade to black" or "fade out #___;" "fade in #___." It is better, when time permits, to precede these action cues with warning instructions: "Ready to take #___," "Ready to dissolve to #___," etc. This is particularly true of dissolves, fades, supers, and any other special effects, since it is usually necessary to preset the switcher to obtain these effects. Warning instructions are of value to both the technical director and the cameraman. The technical director knows what to expect for the next cue, and the cameraman knows that his camera is about to be put on the air. There is a little red light that tells the cameraman when he is on, but it is highly embarrassing to have a cameraman rack a lens or shift position just as his camera is punched up.

If film or slides are to be used, they are incorporated into the program in much the same way as another camera. Film and slides are available through one or more film chains, which are handled at the switcher in the same way studio cameras are. It is possible to cut, fade, or dissolve to and from film and slides. Film is cued to a specific number on a piece of society leader which is spliced onto the head end of the film. This allows a known number of seconds to elapse between the time the film projector is rolled and the time the film to be used actually appears. This makes it possible to cue film to very precise times. The director not only gives the cues for taking film and slides, but also must call to the projection room for the rolling of the projector and changing of slides.

As in radio, the director is responsible for starting and getting the program off on time. So, part of his attention must occasionally go to the clock.

Now, we have the director looking after the audio and giving all the cues necessary to smooth sound pickup. He is continuously instructing the cameramen in regard to movement, lenses, and shots to be obtained. He gives a constant stream of cues and commands to the technical director to get the various pictures on the air. He rolls film, changes slides, and gets them into the visual continuity at the right time. He is keeping time so that the program will get off on the nose. Can there be any doubt that the director is a busy person?

The greatest difficulty faced by beginning directors is the effort to gain a mastery over the mechanics of this involved technique. The mechanics are, of course, a secondary consideration. The primary function of the director is to put together a pictorial continuity that is the visual part of the program. The problem is that it is impossible to do this unless the director is in complete control of the mechanics. It is only when the mechanics become second nature that a director can really begin to accomplish his primary purpose.

During the preparatory and rehearsal stages, a program begins to take shape in the director's mind. The shape that it takes is a fairly rapid succession of shots which must be put together in a sequence and which will carry the desired effect to the audience. This pictorial continuity, common to both television and motion pictures, is not at all like viewing an action in a theater, or in any live situation. Because of the extreme degree of selectivity inherent in the use of the camera, the audience sees no more, and no less, than the series of pictures which the director gives him. It also sees these pictures in the order in which they are put together. This gives a photographic medium its peculiar character, and it is the effective use of this character that marks the skilled TV director.

There are really two separate parts involved in the use of the pictorial sequence. The director must show the audience whatever is important at any given moment. Sometimes this will make use of a long shot, sometimes a tight close-up, now a shot of this person, now that. Frequently, the director will arbitrarily decide just what is important, for it is often a matter of choice. He should always remember that if he doesn't give it to them, the audience will not see whatever is considered important. Continual use of the long shot is not the answer. To really show what is important, frequent close-ups are required. There results a constantly changing pattern of shot after shot.

The second phase of this technique is to add artistic values to the pictures presented. This is the quality that distinguishes the professional photographer from all of the duffers that snap pictures. It is the difference between an acceptable technician and a top-notch painter. It involves composition, the right sequence of shots, the right tempo and rhythm, and those intangibles that make an art. In sum, it makes up that ability, unique to the arts, to add values and meanings to whatever material is being presented.

This somewhat vague artistic contribution is the true test of a director's ability. The director who can use the medium of television creatively is the one in demand. He is the top banana. There is a place in the television industry for the good directing craftsman, also. A mastery of the mechanics of directing and a familiarity with the requirements of the industry are enough to insure a good job. It is not everyone who can fit into this exacting work. It is an unusually demanding craft. There may be jobs that require a higher degree of coordination, precision, self-control, and steeled nerves—but, if there are, they are unknown to this author.

CHAPTER TWENTY-FIVE

AUDIO AND VIDEO RECORDING

In the ten years following the end of the Second World War, advances in sound-recording techniques greatly changed many aspects of broadcasting. At one time, the more popular programs were always "live." Now, by way of contrast, recording them has become the rule of the day.

The stigma once attached to the broadcasting of recorded shows began to be dispelled when improved equipment and recording methods made it virtually impossible for the average listener to detect the difference between a recorded and a live program. Further, as the role of radio with respect to television became more defined, broadcasters sought to make the most efficient use of their facilities, and welcomed the savings in time and energy, as well as in money, that modern recording practices have made possible. The aspect of the listener being "on the scene" (live broadcasting) is desirable in many instances, but it is not all-important. The flexibility provided by tape recording, for instance, is often invaluable to the newscaster, who can take a 15- or 25-pound recorder to the home or office of an important person, or to the scene of some newsworthy event, in a matter of minutes. Once back at the studio, he can select the most interesting and meaningful portions of his recorded material and have it ready when the time comes for the next news broadcast. In terms of live broadcasting, many features now presented as a matter of routine would be impossible. One cannot always arrange for a train wreck or the arrival in town of an important personality several hours in advance. In other days, live broadcasting prevailed partly because one could not transport several hundred pounds of equipment around on a moment's notice.

At one time, radio productions were hovered over by worried-looking men with a battery of stop watches. Now, they have mostly all gone over to television, and with their salaries (or some portion thereof) the broadcaster has acquired machines which assure accuracy within a second or two in a half-hour. The program is "put together" and timed in advance . . . yes, by a production man with a stop watch, but at least he does not have to worry about actors' memory lapses, or embarrassing or offensive "fluffs"—they can all be edited out. The smoothness possible with careful and conscientious editing has enhanced the quality of many radio productions of today.

Tape Recording

The history of magnetic recording goes back over fifty years, the first wire recorder having been developed in 1900. Magnetic tape for broadcast use was largely pioneered by the Germans, who in the 1930s were using solid steel tapes. The close of the war in 1945 found many radio stations in Germany using plastic tape coated with a thin layer of magnetic particles (oxide), and getting high-quality results. These developments were continued rapidly in this country, and in 1948 and 1949 the major radio networks began to tape-record programs in advance, and to record the live shows for delayed broadcast to the different time zones.

It soon became apparent that this was a medium ideally suited to many broadcast needs. Tape recordings have low background noise and low distortion, they can be played many times without loss of quality, and when a recording has served its purpose, the electric impulses on the tape can be erased, and the tape itself reused many times.

Tape recording is an electromagnetic process, in which a varying field is induced on the thin magnetic coating attached to the plastic base. Magnetic tape commonly used for audio recording today is ¼ inch wide, and thin and flexible. It is wound on reels of various size, with some of the larger ones holding over a mile of tape. The recorder's mechanism pulls the tape at a constant speed past heads which the tape contacts. The heads are connected to the recording and playback amplifiers, and to the erase circuits. The erase head, which the tape passes first, removes the previous recording. Next, the tape contacts the record head, which is basically an electromagnet into which the varying audio current is introduced. The varying field, or flux, in the "gap" (a microscopically narrow slot) places permanent magnetic patterns on the oxide coating of the tape.

During playback of a previously recorded tape, the erase and record circuits are disconnected, and the signals on the tape are picked up by the playback head. This, like the record head, is an electromagnet, but it works "in reverse." The varying flux from the tape induces voltages into its windings which are amplified electronically, like the signals from a microphone.

Many machines, by means of internal switching, use the record head for playback, but most professional recorders have a third head for playback purposes, which the tape passes an instant after it passes the record head. This arrangement makes possible playback while recording,

Fig. 87. Tape recording and duplicating room. (*University of Michigan.*)

a valuable check for quality and helpful for determining continuity in editing and rerecording processes.

Speeds

The N.A.R.T.B. has standardized tape speeds at 15 and 7½ inches per second (i.p.s.). Certain higher and lower multiples are in use for work more or less critical than that encountered in broadcast practice. As a general rule, the higher tape speeds have higher fidelity, but more tape is used in a given time. Most radio stations accept 7½ i.p.s. as the satisfactory speed from a standpoint of economy and fidelity, while some studios may record at 30 i.p.s. to obtain the greatest dynamic range with low distortion. Machines intended for applications where fidelity is less important than longer playing time or economy may employ speeds of 3¾, 1⅞, or even 11⁄16 i.p.s. Recordings made at the higher speeds are easier to edit, particularly where words, syllables, or exact places in a musical score must be found.

Track Width

Half-track (sometimes called "double-track") recording was originally introduced as an economy measure for home machines, and is now encountered in professional work. On a half-track machine, the magnetic

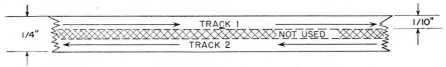

FIG. 88. Half-track recording on the "upper" half of the tape. When a reel is turned, track 2 is uppermost.

gap of the record head is 1⁄10 inch long, and is physically placed so that the magnetic path traced on the tape commences at one edge and covers slightly less than half the tape width. After the reel has been run through in one direction, it is possible to record another track on the unused half of the tape, either by reversing its direction and physically moving the head, or, when the heads are fixed, by reversing the reels.

The advantage of half-track recording is that twice the recording time is obtained on a given length of tape. Disadvantages are that it is impossible to cut portions out of one track without destroying the continuity of what may be on the other track, and also there is a slight increase in background noise, which decreases the dynamic range obtainable. Sometimes, on a machine which is out of adjustment, one track may be heard in the background while the other is playing (cross talk), although a small area (1⁄20 inch) at the center of the tape is left blank to prevent this.

A tape with two tracks recorded cannot be played back on a machine with full-width heads, as both recordings will be heard at once, one backwards. A machine with a half-track playback head will play either half-track or full-track recordings.

Buying Tape Recorders

There are numerous manufacturers making tape recorders. These vary in price from a hundred to several thousand dollars. In general, you pay for what you get. Most of the inexpensive machines costing under $400 have lower fidelity, or limited versatility, and are in the home-recorder class. Broadcast installations require machines that are reliable and can maintain peak performance under continuous service, and which do not require constant major repairs. Studio recorders must meet broadcast standards and be easily adaptable to the needs of editing and rerecording. Smaller portables are now being made with excellent fidelity and rugged construction; however, to reduce weight and size they generally lack large tape capacity.

It is of great importance to the broadcaster to know what to look for when buying a tape recorder. It is difficult to establish definite rules for this, particularly in view of the ambiguous specifications often published, but perhaps the following outline will be of assistance:

Speed: 7½ or 15 inches per second; preferably both.

Frequency Response: Plus or minus 2 decibels from 50 to 15,000 cycles per second at 15 i.p.s. Many machines will meet this specification at 7½ i.p.s.

Signal-to-Noise Ratio: The dynamic range should be at least 50 decibels by N.A.R.T.B. standards (where the distortion does not exceed 3 per cent). 55 to 60 decibels is preferable.

Distortion: 2 to 3 per cent at maximum modulation. This will be due primarily to the tape; amplifiers should contribute a negligible amount.

Wow and Flutter: No greater than 0.3 per cent; less is desirable because these effects are aggravated by successive rerecording.

Speed Regulation: 0.3 per cent is about 5 seconds in 30 minutes.

Tape Capacity: At least 30 minutes continuous playing time at the speed used most.

"Wow" and "flutter" are terms used to describe speed variations. They are measured in the percentage of pitch (frequency) change in a steady tone. A wow is characterized by a slow, recurrent change in pitch, while flutter is a more rapid deviation from constant speed and produces a garbling of the sound. Machines which do not hold a steady speed may record voices satisfactorily, but can ruin piano music.

Some of the above standards can be relaxed a bit in the case of light-weight portable recorders to be used for voice work. Portability is often much more important than a slight increase in distortion, but tapes made on the station's portable machines should sound good when played back in the studio. If editing is needed, tapes recorded slower than 7½ i.p.s. may be troublesome, and half-track recordings will have to be dubbed before they can be cut up.

Making the Recording

Most tape recorders are reasonably simple to operate, and anyone can soon learn to turn out quality recordings. Professional microphones and other excellent equipment are as important in making a tape recording as a trained technician. The studio or room in which the recording is to be made should be acoustically treated, and the microphone placement in relation to the speaker or musical group should be tested as carefully as it would be for a broadcast.

All professional recorders will have a meter for visual indication of the recorded level. The level must be kept below the point where noticeable distortion is present, but if it is too low the background noise will be objectionable. The dynamic ranges acceptable for FM or AM broadcasting are within the limits of the better machines and tapes.

Many machines require a second or two to come up to speed after starting, and should be allowed to do so before recording commences. Some recorders will run too slow near the end of a reel which has a very small hub. With these reels the last few feet of tape should not be used.

One precaution too often overlooked is that the surfaces which contact the tape must be kept free of dirt and tape oxide accumulation at all times. Traces of oxide often collect on the heads, and can seriously impair the quality of the recording if they prevent the tape from making good contact. The friction between the tape and these deposits may cause a mechanical vibration, like that of a violin string, which can ruin the recording. Clean the heads, idlers, and tape guides often. Use ethyl alcohol, carbon tetrachloride, or a solvent recommended by the machine manufacturer. Use a lint-free cloth or a Kleenex. Don't let the solvent contact the tape.

Sometimes, if oxide accumulates on the erase head, or if trouble develops in the erase circuits, a previous recording will remain on the tape, and cause annoying cross talk in the background. Some machines with weak erase circuits may not completely remove a recording made at high level. Bulk erasers (degaussers) are available with which tapes may be erased without even removing them from the box. These erasers create a strong alternating magnetic field, which destroys or "swamps" the sound recording. As the tape is placed in the field and *slowly* removed, its resulting magnetization becomes zero, in the same way that a watch is demagnetized by a jeweler. *Caution:* remove your own watch before using one of these degaussers.

Never let a metal object touch the heads on a recorder. Besides the likelihood that it may become scratched, the head can be left with a

Fig. 89. A full reel of tape may be cleaned all at one time with a bulk tape degausser (demagnetizer).

residual polarity if it is touched by a magnetized screwdriver or scissors. Sometimes the same effect is produced by recording a pistol shot or other sudden loud sound (transient) at too high a level. Residual magnetization can be removed with a head demagnetizer, which works on the same principles as the degausser. It is brought into contact with the head and slowly pulled away. Use the demagnetizer occasionally, and keep it a few feet away from recorded tapes. Turn the tape machine off first, to avoid damaging meters or speakers.

Tape recorders, like other high-quality instruments, require good maintenance as well as care in use. Follow the manufacturer's instructions as to lubrication. Poorly lubricated or worn bearings in motors or idlers will introduce irregularities into the tape motion, resulting in wow or flutter, or off-speed operation. Clutches or brakes that are too tight may cause the tape to stall, break, or stretch.

Fig. 90. Head demagnetizer, showing method of use.

A technician should check the heads occasionally for alignment and output, using a special tape made for this purpose. The heads should be replaced when worn, although they may last several thousand hours. A slot worn by the tape does not necessarily indicate the end of a head's useful life, but if there is a gradual loss of the higher frequencies it should be replaced.

Editing the Tape

Editing is the process of selecting or arranging recorded material for presentation, and can be done by a "cut and splice" method, or by rerecording, or both. Undesired aside noises or an actor's "fluffs" can be removed with a pair of scissors, or separate recordings or "takes" can be spliced together to make a finished program. Rerecording may be necessary or more economical at other times. If the governor makes a speech which must be used for rebroadcast, but the news editor wishes to use two or three of the governor's statements on an earlier program, the required sections of the original recording can be copied, in the order desired, onto another tape.

The techniques of editing are easy to learn . . . the most important assets are a good ear and the mastery of the manual skills involved. All

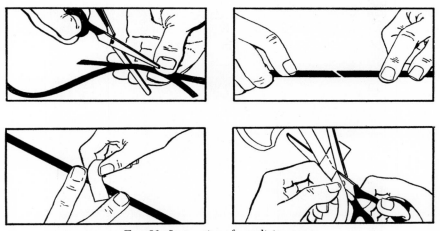

FIG. 91. Instructions for splicing tape.

splices are made on the shiny (plastic) side of the tape, and should be trimmed to be slightly narrower than the tape itself. Never use ordinary cellophane tape—its adhesive will flow under heat or pressure and contaminate adjacent turns on the reel. Use the pressure-sensitive splicing tape made for this purpose, which has a "hard" adhesive. Splicing blocks are available which hold the tape in alignment while it is cut (with a razor blade) and the splicing tape applied.

It is a good idea to demagnetize the scissors or razor blade to be used in editing. If these tools become magnetized in some way, there will be a noise on the tape where the splices are made. Use the degausser or the head demagnetizer.

A red grease pencil can be used to mark the tape (on the plastic side) where it is to be cut. When critical editing may be required, it is best to record at the highest speed practical, so that words or sounds may be located more exactly on the tape.

Special paper or plastic "leader and timing" tape is available, which can be spliced into a reel to identify selections or to make a pause, as between movements of a symphony. It can also be used to protect the beginning and end of a recording, where several feet should be used to take care of breakage in rewinding. This tape will have identifying marks every 7½ or 15 inches, so that the length of pauses can be made exact.

Some tape machines are more adaptable to editing than others. One important requirement is that the heads should be visible and accessible. In film editing, it is possible to pick out certain sounds by their appearance on the sound track, but the magnetic patterns on tape are not visible. To remove an extraneous noise, it is necessary first to locate it by its sound and then the tape can be marked where it contacts the playback head. Machines used for editing should start and stop quickly, and should not place a "pop" on the tape when the record circuits are engaged. It should be possible to play the tape and let it run directly into a box or onto the floor, if desired, rather than onto the take-up reel.

Duplication

One great obstacle that present-day tape recording has had to overcome has been the problem of large-quantity, low-cost reproduction, or duplication. On disc pressings, all the grooves are stamped out at once, but a duplicated tape must be run through a machine and recorded along its entire length.

High-speed duplication has made this process less time-consuming. Several copies are made at once, with the original, or master, and the duplicates run at speeds of up to eight times that at which the tapes will be played back. Specially designed heads and electronic equipment are required, since the highest sound frequencies will be shifted upward to 120,000 cycles per second at a speed of eight times normal.

The master is usually run backwards in the duplicating process, thus saving the time that would be required to rewind the copies. When half-track duplicates are being made by a duplicating process, both tracks are recorded at once.

The expense of duplicating machinery will not justify itself to the station or studio which is required to make a limited number of copies from many different originals, but time can be saved by taking advantage of the two speeds (7½ and 15 i.p.s.) available on most studio recorders.

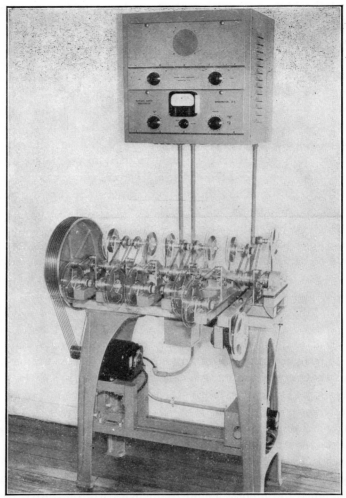

Fig. 92. Multitape system for quantity reproduction of recorded tapes. (*Rawdon Smith Associates.*)

Copies at 7½ i.p.s. can be made from a 7½-i.p.s. original by running all the tapes at 15 i.p.s.; the machines do not need to be modified in any way and should be operated just as if the original and the copies were 15-i.p.s. tapes. The sacrifice in quality is slight for most types of recorded material, and involves the frequencies which, when doubled, fall outside the range of the equipment. Most studio recorders in good working order can produce faithful copies by this method. It is easy to make 30 copies of a 15-minute program in one hour, or perhaps five copies each of six different programs in the same time.

Tape Storage

Tapes should be stored where they will be neither too dry nor too moist —40 to 60 per cent relative humidity is best. Excessive heat is bad, because the tapes may stretch or warp. It is wise to rewind the tape once before using if it has been stored for a long time. Tapes are available with the oxide coated on a polyester (Mylar) base, and these are not affected by extremes of temperature or humidity. Mylar tape is more expensive, but has the additional advantage of being stronger, and less likely to be broken because of careless handling.

Disc Recording

The acceptance of disc recording (instantaneous recordings, transcriptions, and phonograph records) has been universal in the broadcasting field for many years. While the newer medium of tape recording is preferable for many purposes, disc records have several inherent advantages and enjoy widespread popularity for use in the home and on the air. Improved recording and reproducing equipment and revisions of older recording standards (including speed and groove dimensions) make discs economical for mass production and convenient for storage and handling; with good playback equipment the fidelity from the best recordings meets the highest broadcast standards.

The earliest disc phonograph records were made by collecting sound with a horn; the pressure variations operated a mechanism which cut a groove into a thick wax-coated disc or cylinder. The groove "wiggled" from side to side (lateral recording) or up and down (vertical or "hill-and-dale" recording). Electrical recording was introduced in the late 1920s. The horn was replaced by one or more microphones, and the sound was amplified electrically and fed to an electromechanical cutter-head, which moved the recording stylus. The standard speed was 78 (more exactly, 78.26) revolutions per minute (r.p.m.), and the grooves, recorded laterally, were spaced so that about 3 minutes could be recorded on a 10-inch side, and about 4 minutes on a 12-inch side.

Recording on wax had the disadvantage that the disc coating was extremely soft, and direct playback was impossible without damaging the grooves. The wax master records had to be electroplated so that metal parts could be made to produce shellac pressings which were durable enough to withstand playing with the heavy pickups then in use. Instantaneous recording was introduced in the 1930s, in which era the grooves were cut on lacquer-coated aluminum-base discs which gave satisfactory results when played back with broadcast-quality pickups. This recording method provided radio stations with the means of making recordings in their studios, and made possible the first delayed broadcasts.

The radio industry adopted the use of 16-inch discs revolving at $33\frac{1}{3}$ r.p.m. (which were used for the first sound motion pictures) as standard for broadcast recordings; with the groove size and spacing chosen these discs provide about 15 minutes recording time per side. Although, strictly speaking, the term "transcription" refers to any recording not for sale and meant for broadcast use, the 16-inch $33\frac{1}{3}$-r.p.m. disc, because it was at that time the common means of radio recording, became known as a transcription, whether it was an instantaneous lacquer recording or a pressing. At one time vertical recording was thought to offer superior possibilities, and some transcription libraries still have vertical pressings; however, lateral recording eventually became the preferred method and is in use today for transcriptions and records.

Records

Commercially pressed records (and transcriptions) are produced by "silvering" and electroplating a lacquer recording and stripping it away from the metal, leaving a negative matrix, referred to as the master matrix. For a limited production run the master matrix can be chrome-plated and used to stamp the records; however, if it is not expendable it must be protected by an intermediate process, because the lacquer recording is often ruined in stripping it away from the master matrix and cannot be used again. The protection process includes making one or more metal "mothers" (positive matrixes) from the master, and then several stampers (negative) from each mother. The stamper is placed in a hydraulic press which may facetiously be compared to a waffle iron, where the record, or pressing, is formed from a hot viscous material. Although this series of functions is complex and exacting, the record industry has been refining the process for over 50 years; today's best pressings are exact replicas of the lacquer original, and are much more durable than an instantaneous record because the compound from which they are made is harder than the lacquer in which the grooves are cut directly.

Until 1948 the established speed for home phonograph records was 78 r.p.m. Microgroove recording was then introduced, first on the 10- and 12-inch records which play at 33⅓ r.p.m. and shortly afterward on the 7-inch records which play at 45 r.p.m. The 45-r.p.m. records are pressed with a 1½-inch center hole, so that they can be used with compact changers which have the dropping mechanism inside the supporting spindle. This construction also permits a considerable saving of vinyl by leaving out the center portion of the record, which would have no grooves anyway.

In microgroove recording and reproduction, the groove dimensions and spacing are reduced to approximately one-third those of former recording practice, a development made possible by the introduction of fine-grained record materials (Vinylite) which produce a far lower noise level on playback than did the older "shellac" compounds. Microgroove records are designed to be played back with a reproducer stylus which has a tip radius of $\frac{1}{1000}$ inch (as compared to the styli of $\frac{2}{1000}$ to $\frac{3}{1000}$ inch previously used for transcriptions and records); the stylus force should not exceed 6 to 8 grams (about ¼ ounce).

The two types of modern microgroove records (7-inch 45-r.p.m.; 10 or 12-inch 33⅓-r.p.m.) have become permanently established; each is used, depending upon the repertoire to be recorded. The 45-r.p.m. records, with a playing time of from 3 to 8 minutes per side, are easily adaptable for "pop" recordings, and the shorter light-classical and classical works. The larger 33⅓ records permit recording the longer classical works without frequent interruption; maximum recording time for the 12-inch LP records is over 30 minutes per side in many instances.[1]

Playback Equipment

Disc playback machinery represents a large investment for the average radio station, but justifiably so because a great part of the broadcast day usually consists of recorded popular and classical music, commercial spot announcements, and transcriptions. The equipment is fairly complex, because it must play four types of recordings (transcriptions; 33⅓-r.p.m. microgroove, 45-r.p.m. microgroove, and 78-r.p.m records) at the three different speeds. At least two types of pickup are necessary. The best available equipment should be purchased: the turntables should be

[1] Variable-pitch recording ("margin control" or "variable groove") is a process whereby the groove spacing can be varied while recording. During quiet passages the grooves are spaced closely, and for loud passages the spacing is increased. This permits maximum use of the record surface and a consequent extension of playing time.

large enough to accommodate 16-inch transcriptions, and preferably heavily weighted; they should run perfectly on speed without rumble. The starting and speed-change mechanisms should be simple and noise-free in operation, and the turntable should come up to speed rapidly. Separate pickups will be necessary for "standard-groove" and microgroove recordings. Many professional pickup arms have provision for interchangeable pickup heads which revolve by turning a lever, or which plug in as separate units. However, if microgroove and standard-groove records are often to be used together, it might be better to have a separate arm for playing each kind. Diamond styli are the accepted standard for nearly all radio use; they far outlast those of any other material and in the long run are cheaper to use.

It cannot be emphasized too strongly to students of radio and to radio-station personnel that the playback equipment and the records must be handled with the greatest of care. The moving mass in many modern pickups is less than $\frac{1}{1000}$ ounce; banging it around or dropping it on the record can do permanent damage to the pickup as well as to the record. Many stations use combination operators who must run the controls, read announcements, and cue up records (often hastily) at the same time. For this type of operation it may be best to use pickups in which the stylus assembly is replaceable, because frequent damage is inevitable; in this instance sapphire points will suffice if they are changed frequently.

The records must be handled carefully. Although Vinylite pressings are "unbreakable" they are not indestructible, and the surface is easily marred or scratched; pick the records up by the edges and keep fingers off the grooves. Dust is an enemy of microgroove records as well as lacquer instantaneous discs; foreign particles on the record surface cause annoying clicks and pops. Keep a camel's-hair brush or a record duster handy and use it on each record before playback. Keep the records in their protective sleeves when not in use—*don't* leave them lying around where they can collect dust and dirt.

Lacquer Recordings

Although lacquer disc recording has been in use since the 1930s, the techniques involved have never been easy to master for the beginner, and even professionals with years of experience have respect for the often-elusive difficulties which may detract from a recording. The stereotype of a recording engineer quietly muttering unprintable words to himself as he strives to get a clean, quiet cut is not a caricature;

it has a time-honored basis in fact. When tape recording was first introduced, it was not the compactness of the equipment that "sold" engineers and professional people on the new medium (some of the earliest studio tape recorders weighed ½ ton); the most important factor was that much more consistent results could be expected from tape recordings. Far less attention needs to be directed to the machinery in operation during the recording session, and more emphasis can be placed on correct microphone placement, levels, balance, etc.

Today there are relatively few applications where disc recordings are made from a "live" source; the record and transcription studios record all of their original material on tape. The tapes are then edited and timed before the disc is cut; an arrangement which takes much of the uncertainty out of the disc recording process and has helped to make the quality of the discs considerably higher. The applications of disc recording are fewer for general radio use than previously; and the operation of the equipment is exacting when high-quality results are to be obtained. Most disc recording is done by technicians who have experience gained under careful supervision, and who are completely familiar with the equipment.

The component elements in a disc recording system are a turntable, a cutterhead in which is mounted the cutting stylus, a lathe assembly which moves the cutterhead across the disc surface, and the amplifier which drives the cutterhead. Necessary accessories include a suction mechanism to dispose of the "chip" which is cut out of the record, a microscope to inspect the grooves, and a good pickup, monitor amplifier and loud-speaker with which test cuts and the recording can be checked for quality.

The cutting stylus consists of a carefully ground sapphire tip mounted in a metal shank. Properly used, it will last many hours, and can be resharpened when it becomes dulled or accidentally chipped. Diamond styli are not used for cutting because they would be too expensive to resharpen. For microgroove recording a "hot stylus" is generally used. The stylus is usually heated by a small coil of wire wound around the jewel tip, and the heat produced results in a quieter groove for any type of cutting stylus. The action is something like that of a hot knife cutting butter.

The lathe assembly may be automatic or semiautomatic, or may require manual operation to produce lead-in and lead-out grooves, bands, and lock-grooves. During recording, the feed mechanism is geared to the turntable, and moves the cutterhead across the record to produce the required number of grooves per inch.

Certain precautions must be observed in using the recording equipment: the cutterhead must be lowered carefully onto the record so that the stylus will not dig into the disc and contact the aluminum base; if the suction mechanism does not pick up the chip at once, a camel's-hair brush can be used to direct the chip toward the suction tube. Excessive vibration from the suction mechanism or from the turntable motor will place a visible "pattern" on the disc and will be heard on playback. Heavy walking or the slamming of doors may cause trouble. A correct cutting angle must be maintained, and can be checked by viewing the stylus and its reflection on the record surface. It should be perpendicular to the disc. If a stylus with a heating coil is used, the chip must not contact the wires; they are ordinarily heated to redness and will ignite the chip. Great care is required in the final disposal of the chip, as it is highly inflammable.

A calibrated microscope (in thousandths of an inch or mils) is essential in professional work to make sure that the depth and width of the cut meet the appropriate standards. The groove width at the top will be between 0.003 and 0.005 inch ordinarily, depending upon the number of grooves per inch ("pitch"). Usual practice is to record standard-groove transcriptions with a pitch of 112 to 136 lines per inch (78-r.p.m. records 80 to 104) and microgroove recordings with between 200 and 300 lines per inch. The bottom radius of the groove depends upon the type of cutting stylus used, and will be larger for standard-groove recordings than for microgroove. "V-groove" styli are available, and discs cut with them at the coarser pitches can be played back with a 1-mil or a 3-mil pickup.

A good pickup is essential in any disc-recording channel, as playback is the final judge of a recording. The arm should be mounted immediately adjacent to the recording table, if possible. A heavy pickup is definitely not recommended for this purpose; however, lightweight reproducers are available which will track reliably with a total stylus force of 1 or 2 grams and will not damage instantaneous recordings. Studios engaged in making lacquer master recordings for pressing generally do not let anything come into contact with the grooves, but rely on test cuts and visual inspection of the record for a quality check. It is always good practice to make a test cut before recording, to determine the condition of the recording stylus and the over-all fidelity of the system.

An economical way to file recordings for reference or for the station's archives is to make 16-inch microgroove discs. These can hold 30 to 45 minutes of material per side and are easily filed away for the time when they may be needed. If carefully recorded and played back with a good pickup, these or any instantaneous lacquer recordings give excellent fidelity and will last for many playings.

Transcribed Programs

Since every radio station relies to a great extent on records or transcriptions for its music, it builds up a large library of such records. In many instances, manufacturers of records will send "special purpose" records free of charge to be used on disc jockey programs. This is a form of advertising for the manufacturers and does much to build up the popular-music record library.

Many radio stations subscribe to one or more transcription libraries. There are several companies which offer this service. Some among them are World, Lang-Worth, N.B.C., Thesaurus, Sesac, and Associated. Such a subscription is generally for the period of three years, and special rates are given to noncommercial stations. When the station subscribes for this service, it receives, in many instances, large filing cases to hold the 16-inch transcription discs. These discs have recorded upon them some 2500 to 3000 selections. The contract usually stipulates that the transcription company will replace a certain number of worn records each month and provide from 15 to 20 new transcriptions each month accompanied by continuity and publicity material to be used in connection with such transcribed programs. The company also makes out schedules listing selections for music programs which may be used by the station if it does not wish to make up its own musical program. Each disc will have five or six selections recorded upon each side. There is a blank space between these recordings so that the musical librarian or engineer can pick out the selection desired.

Regulations of the Federal Communications Commission require that transcribed programs be announced as such. The wording of the regulation is as follows:

3.407 *Mechanical records.* Each broadcast program consisting of a mechanical record or a series of mechanical records shall be announced in the manner and to the extent set out below.

(a) A mechanical record or a series thereof, of longer duration than 30 minutes, shall be identified by appropriate announcement at the beginning of the program, at each 30-minute interval, and at the conclusion of the program: *Provided, however,* That the identifying announcement at each 30-minute interval is not required in case of a mechanical record consisting of a single, continuous, uninterrupted speech, play, religious service, symphony concert, or operatic production of longer duration than 30 minutes.

(*b*) A mechanical record, or a series thereof, of a longer duration than 5 minutes, and not in excess of 30 minutes, shall be identified by an appropriate announcement at the beginning and end of the program.

(*c*) A single mechanical record of a duration not in excess of 5 minutes shall be identified by appropriate announcement immediately preceding the use thereof.

(*d*) In case a mechanical record is used for background music, sound effects, station identification, program identification (theme music of short duration), or identification of the sponsorship of the program proper, no announcement of the mechanical record is required.

(*e*) The identifying announcement shall accurately describe the type of mechanical record used, i.e., where an electrical transcription is used it shall be announced as a "transcription" or an "electrical transcription," or as "transcribed" or "electrically transcribed," and where a phonograph record is used it shall be announced as a "record."

Television Recording

Television recordings are made on a machine called a "kinescope recorder." This machine makes a sound motion picture, taking the picture from the face of a special kinescope tube. The tube is much like other kinescopes except that it operates at a considerably higher voltage, and has a phosphor on its face that causes the picture to have a bright bluish cast. At one end of the recorder is the kinescope tube, enclosed in a housing, and at the other is a motion-picture camera. The camera and the tube are mounted on a cabinet which contains several special amplifying units (Fig. 93).

One of the first problems that had to be solved was the difference between the 24 frames per second of films and the 30 frames per second of TV. You will recall that in projecting films for TV use the 24 frames had to be stepped up to 30 frames. The reverse of this is, of course, true for the recording process. An electronic blanking system in the circuits of the kinescope tube causes the camera to see 24 frames instead of 30 frames per second. Apart from this, the transfer of the video to film is a straightforward photographic process. The major difficulty is the resultant loss in definition and quality. The starting point is a television picture which is relatively low in resolution and brightness. This picture is transferred to motion-picture film. Prints are made of this original film with additional loss in quality. These prints are then shown through another TV system which introduces still more loss. The total effect is a quality that is considerably inferior to live TV or good films.

Fig. 93. The G.P.L. video recorder.

The original recording may be either a positive or a negative. The polarity of the kinescope tube can be reversed by simply throwing a switch. Since the photographic process reverses the polarity of the original scene, by having the kinescope tube positive a negative film results, by having the kinescope negative a positive film results. If more than the one print is desired it is necessary to make a negative recording.

The sound is recorded directly off an audio line. The sound may be recorded either single system or double system. In the single system, the sound is recorded on the same film as the picture while it is running through the camera. In the double system, the sound is recorded separately and kept that way until the final prints are made. The advantage

Fig. 94. The video recorder with the cabinet doors and the light hood removed.

of single-system recording is that you are concerned with only the one piece of film, thereby saving time, trouble, and money. Positive recordings always employ single-system sound. It is only when making negative recordings that the decision has to be made on whether to record the sound single or double system. The disadvantages of the single system, both overcome by use of double system, are that it makes optimum quality impossible, and it eliminates the possibility of extensive editing.

The processing requirements are different for picture and sound track if the optimum quality is to be achieved for both. In single-system recording, the two obviously have to be given the same processing. On a sound motion picture, the sound track runs considerably ahead of the picture. This will be clear to you if you look at a projector. The picture is projected through the film gate behind the lens, while the playback head for the sound is located some distance away. This should make it obvious that the picture and sound do not run along side by side. This being the case, it is impossible to make extensive editing changes in a sound film. A single-system recording is a sound print. On the other hand, in the double system the sound is separate from the picture, so either, or both, can be changed. They are later matched and printed together in the final prints. So, if highest possible quality or extensive editing are factors to be considered, it is necessary to use double-system sound.

In double-system sound the original recording may be made either on optical film or on magnetic tape. One system in common use is to make a single-system recording, but at the same time make a magnetic double-system track. If the single-system track is satisfactory, the magnetic track may be erased.

In April, 1956, at the annual N.A.R.T.B. meeting in Chicago, the Ampex Corporation demonstrated its new video tape recorder [VTR]. For the first time a television program, both picture and sound, could be magnetically recorded with almost the same ease as radio programs are recorded. This development is having, and will continue to have, profound effects on the industry.

The Ampex VTR records television programs on a magnetic tape two inches wide traveling at a speed of fifteen inches per second. Four revolving recording heads are used, and the travel of the heads is such that the recording is done across the width of the tape rather than along its length, as is the case in $\frac{1}{4}$-inch sound tape. The machine will record and reproduce a minimum of 320 lines, which is better than the performance of home receivers. The typical home receiver will develop approximately 275 lines. As a result, to the viewer the picture looks as good as a live pickup. It is infinitely better than any known system of kinescope recording using motion-picture film.

The machine, in its present form, will not record or reproduce color—only black and white. There is some difference of opinion as to whether a magnetic tape system can adequately record color. Some engineers believe it can and that it is only a matter of time before tape recorders will be available for either black and white or color. Other engineers believe that for color the answer lies in some highly developed film-recording system, possibly using lenticular film.

Regardless of the future method of recording color, the television industry now has a recording system which will serve the same basic purposes that tape recording has served for radio.

CHAPTER TWENTY-SIX

THE BUSINESS OF RADIO AND TV ADVERTISING

I have no intention in this handbook of tracing the history and development of sound advertising from the town crier, who rang his bell in the city streets, to the network whose gong announces that this is the National Broadcasting Company, or from the advertisements of the United States Gramophone Company in 1894, offering to record any musical selection with a sponsor's advertising announcements, to the modern electrical transcription. Suffice it to say, the contention of the Gramophone Company that "nobody will refuse to listen to a fine song, or concert piece, or an oration—even if it is interrupted by a modest remark: 'Tartar's Baking Powder is the best'" has proved to be true. In 1923 Station WEAF announced that 10 minutes of its time on the air could be purchased by an advertiser for $100. Today on WRCA (formerly WEAF) the same period will cost the sponsor $1200. It was estimated that sponsors in the United States paid broadcasting stations $498,428,000 in 1954 to advertise their products over the radio. This amount does not include what was spent for talent, for writing the continuity, and for advertising the programs but is merely what was spent for the use of facilities and the air.

The radio salesman must be aided in his job of selling time to a potential advertiser by his own station management. In other words, the station must sell itself in order to sell itself to others. It is not enough to be on the air; the station should also grasp every opportunity in other media to attract listeners. Advertisements in newspapers, on the motion-picture screens, on billboards, and in window displays should not be neglected. The station is advertised by its audience-participating shows, its monthly schedule releases, and by stage contests in the movie houses. That's sales promotion. Intelligent selling is dependent upon a businesslike management. The salesman's job is half done if management has made the station outstanding in the community. A public-relations man is the best salesman a station can have even though he never sells an announcement.

The station whose staff is well informed, through surveys concerning the coverage of their station and everything about the market it is offering to the advertiser, is most likely to succeed. The salesman should have a coverage map and understand upon what basis it was made. He should be able to justify his station's rate card. He should be familiar with the programs presented by his station and their popularity rating. His surveys should enable him to give information to the advertiser about the age level, sex, and economic status of his station's listeners. He must be able to prove the effectiveness of radio advertising for other advertisers who have used his station. He must be familiar with his competition and the relative cost per person reached. From the viewpoint of the radio time salesman and the sponsor, "size of the audience" is the yardstick used to measure the relative worth of competing stations. In commercial radio, a radio program is a medium of advertising. If radio advertising is to be effective, there must be an audience. Since people listen only to programs that they like, the more enjoyable the program is, the larger the audience will be, and the commercial message will be heard by more potential purchasers. A radio program is considered successful when its listening audience is shown to be large enough to satisfy the advertising aims of the sponsor.

Radio stations, advertising agencies, and special agencies conduct surveys to determine the popularity of programs, presentation types, and stations. These surveys not only concern themselves with the preference of the listener but also with his economic and social status and his intelligence. The listener's habits and his activity while listening are also discovered by surveys. This information is sought to determine whether the program is reaching the audience to whom the product advertised will appeal. Surveys of this type are made by mail questionnaire, mail response to broadcast offers, personal interview, or telephone questions. The interview survey by a trained staff brings the most satisfying results. Devices which attach directly to the radio receiving set and which record electrically the stations tuned to are being used experimentally at present. These electric recording devices have a stylus, resting upon a tape, which is connected to the dial.

The Service of the Agency

The listener tuned to a star program being broadcast over the network is thrilled by the glamour and romance of broadcasting and desires to gain a position in the key station. The listener does not realize that the staff of the broadcasting station has about as much to do with the nation-wide sponsored program as the owner of a theater has to do with a play presented upon his stage. The key station merely leases its air rights, its facilities, to the sponsor. The advertising agency is the sponsor's agent in making the lease, the sponsor's booking agent in signing up the star performers, the dramatic director for the cast, the author of the commercial plugs, and the agent through whom the script is purchased. If one desires to observe the origin, development, and evaluation of a big program, one should seek a position in the radio department of the large advertising agency.

The client must give the agency all the information concerning the distribution of his advertising budget so that all media can be coordinated. In most instances a single agency will be in charge of the whole campaign: outdoor, newspaper and magazine, mail, window displays, and radio. All these must be unified in their purpose. Different media may be used for direct selling, for education, and to create good will.

In order to select the most efficient broadcasting stations, the agency should know the location of distributors and of wholesale and retail outlets and where purchasers are most likely to be reached. The client's methods of merchandising are considered, even the distinctive package, its size, its shape, and its color. If there is a special offer, a bargain package, or a product to be pushed, this information is essential to the agency in planning the campaign. Such items as the counter, display cards, and window streamers, also usually designed by the agency, are considered in the composition of the radio continuity.

A superficial knowledge of the product is not sufficient. While the agency should know how it is manufactured and what its ingredients are, the really important thing is what the product does for the purchaser. The listener is not interested in anything except how the product will aid or affect him.

In order to build a program designed to appeal to the potential purchaser, the agency must know whether the product appeals to the rich or the poor, the man or the woman, the child or the adult, the rural or the urban. The agency is also interested in the seasonal appeal of the product, in order to include it in the radio programs planned for certain seasons.

These are but a few of the facts that must be gathered before anything is done about the radio program. From these facts the agency will determine whether to recommend radio as an advertising medium, what stations to use in the campaign, whether a network or spot program is to be used, whether to have live talent or to use transcriptions, and for what type of program and commercial continuity to plan.

When the use of radio is decided upon, the agency contracts for time, either with the network or with various local stations. In the selection of stations the agency is indispensable. The agency, to perform efficient service for the advertiser, must possess information as to actual station coverage, type and schedule of programs being carried, the approximate number of receivers in the locality, as well as the percentage likely to be tuned to the station at a certain time, and the purchasing power of the listeners within the area. All such information is based upon surveys made by special agencies. The agency books time with each station for a period it considers best for that particular locality. A big advantage of the transcribed program is that the agency can select times without regard to a nationwide hookup, thus obtaining the best time in different parts of the nation.

The agency should consider the type of customer that presents the greatest potential market and should build a program to appeal to that purchaser. A program should be arranged which is expressive as a unit of the sales message and of the character of the sponsor.

Generally speaking, recognized stars are handled by individual agents or bookers, and the advertising agent and client deal with these representatives in endeavoring to build a program. There is an exchange arrangement between agents which permits the employment of stars by competing companies. The advantages of prestige, proved acceptability, and free newspaper publicity which big-name talent will bring to a program are obvious. On the other hand, the incorporation of the name of the product in a pseudonym for the artist is another opportunity to introduce advertising.

The agency usually goes to a client with a general idea of the radio program. After the client has approved of the general idea, which includes the type of show, type of music, name of the star, master of ceremonies, etc., the agency begins working with the network production department or an independent producer, or does all the work in its own production department—building and rehearsing of the production. This finished program is then auditioned by the client, usually the president, sales manager, and other interested persons. It is at this time that they accept or discard the plan. After the client has approved of the show, the proposition goes to the dealers and distributors, with the purpose of "selling" them on the sales value of this new operation.

The commercial announcements are a matter of pure advertising, the first purely advertising copy, in fact, for the radio department of the agency to write.[1] When the artists are employed, the script for the entire program accepted, the musical numbers chosen, and the entire program rehearsed and timed, then the sponsor is invited to a dress rehearsal.

Before the program is broadcast, there is conducted a tie-in campaign, consisting of the distribution of window streamers, show-cards, publicity to newspapers, and in some instances a direct-mail tie-in to customers. The merchandising campaign is conducted by the agency alone, the agency in cooperation with the client's field force, the agency in cooperation with the radio chain's sales department, or by any combination of these three. Dealers are notified of the coming broadcast. A big factor in the success of the radio advertising program is the advertising of the broadcast program through other media. Spot announcements are sometimes used in advance of the program to announce a forthcoming series. In the merchandising campaign the retailer is contacted to learn if his stock is adequate to take care of the anticipated demand, to give advice concerning the display of his stock, to furnish him with samples if a sample offer is to be made over the radio.

The local station performs the same services for the local store or sponsor that the agency does for its national and larger accounts, only on a smaller scale. The local station often goes to greater effort to give personal services.

The Radio Time Salesman

A position in the sales or commercial department of a radio station carries a better income than does a position in nearly any other department. In most instances the salesman is on a basic salary, but in many stations he receives a commission above his salary on his sales of time. The hours of labor are more satisfactory because the salesman should

---

[1] Refer to Chap. XXVII, Writing Commercial Continuity.

be diplomatic in selecting the hours when he will call on prospects. There is not the glamour that one enjoys before a microphone and having a contact with listeners; but there is the realization that without the salesman the local and the independent stations could not exist. A person who goes into radio sales must have a personality that will appeal to the purchaser of time. He must be an excellent salesman; he must have a thorough knowledge of the medium; he must have endless imagination and pep, a good educational background, and be a pleasing conversationalist.

The salesman should study his prospect and his prospect's business or product before approaching him concerning the purchase of time. He must know of the prospect's program likes and dislikes. He must be aware of the sex, economic status, and interests of the audience to whom the radio sales appeal will be addressed. He must be fully cognizant of the competition of other media and of radio programs sponsored by his prospect's competitors. It is easier for a local man to make good not only because he will be known by the merchants he will approach, but because he knows local conditions. The salesman for the station must have a thorough knowledge of the medium and of the station that he represents, understanding its opportunities and its limitations. He must have a fertile imagination to conceive and build programs that will appeal to the prospect and the listener. He must keep abreast of program ideas that are used in other localities and originate proposals of his own.

Ideas are the greatest asset of the radio salesman. It is hard work thinking up something original. Then in presenting the idea to the prospect, the salesman should spend his efforts in selling himself on the idea. Don't think about the prospect; if the salesman can sell himself, he will sell the merchant. When he has sold the sponsor, then he must deliver the goods; justify the faith of the purchaser. Even though the salesman neither writes, produces, nor announces the program, he and only he is responsible to the sponsor. Therefore, he must check up on the program's effectiveness and see that it comes up to the forecast he presented while selling it. If he does not deliver what he has promised to deliver he has lost his contact, he has lost a permanent customer. The salesman is the liaison man between the station and its supporting client. He must not promise what he can't deliver and must deliver what he promised.

The radio advertiser generally relies upon the advice of the agency or the time salesman of the local station in determining the length and type of his commercial announcements, the number of announcements per day, as well as the over-all length of the radio advertising campaign. Nearly all stations sell commercial time on the same basis. The evening periods and late Sunday afternoon and evening are the most expensive (Class A); the morning and afternoon periods cost a little bit less (Class B); the very early morning sunrise times are still lower (Class C); and the periods between midnight and dawn are the least expensive (Class D).

Each station has a different method of classifying the time which it sells for commercial plugs. These range from (1) station breaks, chain breaks, or spot announcements which generally run about 15 seconds, announcements of from 20 to 50 words, the 1-minute or usually 100-word spot; (2) 5-minute commercials; (3) ¼-hour programs; (4) ½-hour programs; and (5) 1-hour programs. Stations which are considerate of their audiences limit the minutes of commercial time on ¼-, ½-, and 1-hour programs. The price for each of these different commercial periods differs in accordance with the potential audience of the station, with the survey rating of the programs presented by that station; with the economic status of the listeners of the station; and other factors which are taken into consideration in determining the worth of time upon that station to the advertiser. Each station gets out a rate card upon which is listed the price of all types and periods on the basis of use of one time, thirteen times, twenty-six times, fifty-two times, etc. The more frequently time is used, the cheaper the rates become. In addition to the time periods, stations have specified rates for commercial plugs that are inserted in many programs that are given in connection with weather reports, time signals, and upon different participation programs such as disc jockey programs and programs for women. Two participating programs by the station may have different rates depending upon the popularity of the two programs. The stations have special rates for the presentation of transcribed announcements, and some stations refuse to put on transcribed commercials or singing commercials. In case there is the slightest bit of dramatic effort or effect—such as the announcer being required to cough while plugging a cold remedy—a talent fee is also charged in addition to the cost of time. This is true also when sound effects are ordered by the sponsor. As a comparison of rates, I have selected below three different stations located in the same city (Detroit). Because of potential audiences, rates in smaller communities would be much less.

RADIO AND TELEVISION BROADCASTING RATES
EVENING PERIODS—CLASS A

Watts	1 hour	½ hour	¼ hour	5 minutes	1 min. or less spots and breaks
Amplitude-modulation rates:					
250	$ 250.00	$ 150.00	$100.00	$ 50.00	$ 25.00
5,000	450.00	288.00	192.00	72.00	54.72
50,000	750.00	450.00	300.00	150.00	135.00
Frequency-modulation rates:					
20,000	140.00	80.00	50.00	22.50	12.50
Television rate:					
	1700.00	1020.00	680.00	425.00	140–350.00

Commercial Aspects of Television

It was pointed out in an earlier chapter that from the business and management point of view television and radio operate according to the same basic principles. So, much of what has been said about the business side of radio applies equally well to television. The place of the sponsor, the agency, the time salesman, and the rating surveys is just as vital in television as in radio.

There are two major differences between radio and television advertising. The costs of television advertising are several times the costs of advertising on radio. The characteristics of the television medium are such that it is much more difficult and expensive to prepare good commercials, but, at the same time, these identical characteristics make television a more effective advertising medium than radio. At least this is true in many instances.

As was mentioned earlier in this chapter, the purchase of a segment of time does not cover the costs of program production. When an advertiser contracts for a certain time period, he gets the technical facilities, the air time, the basic studio and control-room crew, and a limited amount of rehearsal time. At the local-station level most sponsors will settle for these facilities and add only the talent costs, scripting, and preparation of the commercials. Frequently, they will even bypass the agency to avoid the 15 per cent agency fee which is standard.

For high-budget network shows there are many costs added to the price of the time. It is a rare exception when a network program is done without the help of an advertising agency. Such a program will want the services of a particular director, perhaps a producer, designer, choreographer, announcer, all in addition to the talent. These people must be paid, and the better known they are the more they are paid. A network show will also want sets, costumes, and other trappings which are all over and above the time price. Networks and large stations are prepared to provide these services to a sponsor, but they must be paid for them. A complicated show cannot be done with the minimum allowable rehearsal time. So, extra rehearsal time has to be purchased. This is logical since a large show will completely tie up a studio for two or three days. The talent, too, must be paid extra for rehearsals beyond the established minimum. The result is that the cost of a major network show is fantastically high. The fact that there is virtually no unsold time on the major networks bears eloquent witness to the effectiveness of television as an advertising medium.

The high costs have given rise to some advertising practices which have been rare in radio. Many network television shows are jointly sponsored, or are sponsored by different concerns on alternate weeks. An excellent example of this is "Your Hit Parade," which for years has been sponsored by Lucky Strike, on both radio and television. To help beat the costs of this expensive program, Lucky Strike permits a cosmetic company to sponsor it every other week. This approach is undoubtedly a sound practice. Advertisers are practical men of business, and when they spend a dollar they are reasonably certain that it will bring in a return. Even on an alternating basis, television can produce that return.

There are three ways in which a television commercial can be done. It can be live in the studio, it can be on film, or it can use still pictures or slides with audio. The use of slides with audio copy is the cheapest and easiest TV commercial. For most purposes, it is also the least effective. It is quite similar to the radio commercial, but with the added emphasis of the visual elements supplied by the slides. The slides would include such information as the brand name, price, address, or phone number. This type of commercial is intended to hammer one main idea on a repetitive basis, and for this purpose it serves very well.

For many kinds of products, the live commercial is a golden opportunity. Appliances and other gadgets can be demonstrated. Before-and-after effects can be shown. Because of the intimacy and close-up detail possible on television, a genuine sales pitch can be made. Thus, TV becomes a real sales device as well as an advertising medium.

More television commercials are done on film than in any other way. There are a number of advantages to film commercials. You know in advance that everything will go exactly like it is supposed to. This precise quality is one of great value in many instances. There are also many special effects possible on film which aren't possible, or aren't dependable, live. Animation is perhaps the outstanding example of this kind of effect. Where animation is called for, nothing else will serve the purpose as well. Film spots can be distributed to many stations as part of a national spot campaign, and the advertiser knows that the message will be presented as he wants it given. Simple film commercials are not exorbitant in price, but the more fancy and tricky they become, the more expensive they are. A well-done, animated spot can run to several thousand dollars for a 30-second film.

There are two special types of commercial that require some mention. Some large concerns have found it desirable to prepare informative film shorts dealing with their products or services. For example, General Electric might make a film about the designing, building, and use of jet engines. Such a film might run 3 or 4 minutes. While it is a kind of institutional advertising, these shorts are informative and interesting There is little doubt that over a period of time they enhance the prestige of the company. Another commercial possibility in television is to place the sponsor's product, or the brand name, somewhere on the set. In this way, there is a constant reminder before the eyes of the viewing audience. By putting a drawing of a bottle of Stopette, or a Remington shaver, on the front of John Daly's desk on "What's My Line," the advertiser is certain that the audience will not forget who is sponsoring the program.

The field of television advertising is one of enormous opportunity for a person with imagination and a willingness to learn about it. Apart from high-priced name talent, people in the advertising end of television broadcasting are probably the best paid. The way to success in this field is built on imagination, hard work, and a serious approach to the business of advertising. Advertising is a huge business. It is increasingly being based on research, factual knowledge, and serious study of the results obtained. So, a person interested in such a career should study business, economics, and advertising, as well as radio and television.

CHAPTER TWENTY-SEVEN

WRITING COMMERCIAL CONTINUITY

In the American system of broadcasting, the commercial sponsor is the angel for the broadcasting station. Without the money he pays for the presentation of his advertising continuity, the commercial broadcasting station could not exist. The sponsor is interested only in the entertainment value and the appeal of his program to the extent that they will attract and hold a large enough audience to make the delivery of his commercial copy profitable. Consequently it must be written to comply with the general requirements of the psychology of advertising and the rules of grammar. By the term "commercial continuity" I refer to all types of advertising plugs: the 20-word station break; the 100-word commercial announcement, which is frequently sold as a 1-minute announcement; the 5-minute commercial program; and the advertising portion of longer entertainment features.

In writing the commercial it is wise to keep in mind that people do not buy things, they buy uses. They buy the skin you love to touch, not soap. They buy kissable lips, not lipstick. The Simmons Mattress Company doesn't try to sell mattresses; it tries to sell sleep and comfort. Thus it is the result of the purchase that should be spoken of rather than the product itself. Here are some emotional motives that can be played upon in the commercial:

1. Self-preservation from harm or danger, which includes care of health.
2. Satisfaction of appetite; pleasing taste.
3. Romantic instinct.
4. Care of children and family.
5. Ambition and advancement, economic or social; intellectual desire for advancement.
6. Desire for securing comfort, personal comfort or comfort in the home.
7. Desire for entertainment, pleasure, leisure.
8. Cleanliness. This is a deep-seated instinct.

9. Pride—in appearance, in one's home, in one's family, etc.

10. The expression of artistic taste, which takes the form sometimes of the selection of gifts.

On the other hand, the rational motives for buying are handiness, efficiency in operation or use, dependability in use, dependability in quality, durability, economy in use, economy in purchase. By comparison, it may easily be seen that the emotional motives far outweigh and outnumber the rational motives.

The continuity writer is concerned primarily with writing copy expressly for the purpose of advertising a product. In order that he may write such advertisements well, he should be thoroughly familiar with the product that he is to advertise. It is wise for him to visit the plant where it is made, see the conditions under which it is made, talk with people who have used the product, and sell himself thoroughly before attempting to sell the radio audience. Only when he has had such a thorough working knowledge can he enthusiastically portray the product's worth in words. However, such an investigation should not result in the writer's viewing the product from the manufacturing point of view instead of from the point of appeal to the buyer. An interview with the sales manager or someone who will recommend the product is usually of value.

The continuity writer must have all the originality, new ideas, and new methods that are to be found in the capable advertising man. Because of the innumerable commercial programs that are on the air, methods of presenting commercial plugs soon become hackneyed and trite, and the man who conceives new styles becomes a leader in this field.

The reading of advertisements is fine training for writing them. The writer must have a sense of both dramatic value and newspaper-writing principles. When the writer lacks these qualities, his commercials will strike the radio public as deficient in grace, tactless, or uninteresting —hence unproductive.

It must be remembered that only a small proportion of the commercial continuity that is heard from a broadcasting station is written by the staff of that station. Most of the programs that advertise national products are bought directly from the writers by advertising agencies, who also cast the shows and turn to the broadcasting network for the purchase of time on the air. Furthermore, many of the advertising agencies prepare the short commercial plugs for their clients. The larger advertising agencies have their own radio departments with continuity writers who are experienced in the writing of advertising copy. In every instance the broadcasting station endeavors to work in harmony with the advertising agency and to suggest changes in style and content in the continuity that is to go out over its facilities. The station advertising department, however, must use great tact in suggesting changes, because the copy may have been written by the sponsor, or the advertising agency may have submitted the copy to the sponsor and would feel that its services were being belittled if the copy were criticized and changed by the station's experienced continuity writer. Ordinarily the work of the continuity writer of the broadcasting station is offered free to the advertiser who purchases radio time. He works directly for the studio, writing copy that is used to bring in revenue to the organization.

Great care should be exercised in the placing of commercial credits in the longer type of commercial programs. The best times are shortly after the opening and, if the program is to be a full-hour program, at the half-hour break; if the closing announcement is employed at all, the commercial plug should be brief and to the point and should precede the actual closing of the program. The style and form of these three commercials should be varied, for nothing so annoys the radio audience as unnecessary repetition, especially if it is of a descriptive character.

Subject Matter

Commercial continuity should always attempt to create good will and friends for the product. The copy must have a style that will attract attention and through this attention make its sales appeal.

There is a favorable reaction to the type of continuity in which the sponsor makes himself known indirectly, possibly by naming the orchestra after his product. Such names connected with artists create a lasting impression, which is the main objective of the advertiser.

While advertising continuity must not be too sweetly appealing, it should be persuasive. There are various methods of making an idea persuasive, which include appeals to patriotism, to the property-owning motive in human nature, to the desire for power and superiority, to health as a means of achieving power, and to the affection instinct. The sex motive looms large in advertising, and an indirect sex motivation can often be found in products. Frequently, if the program is a local one, the injection of a bit of local news or interest will make the appeal more personal. Nearly every subject permits an appeal to some kind of human fear, which is always effective, or an appeal to human desires, which are equally or more important. Primary motives are food, shelter, and ornamentation or luxuries. Over 60 per cent of our national income is expended for things or services under the classification of ornamentation or luxury. Ordinarily, therefore, any advertising appeal should be addressed more to desire than to fear or necessity.

False or questionable statements and all other forms of misrepresentation must be eliminated. The Federal Trade Commission acts as the watchdog for accuracy in radio as well as in other forms of advertising. It is interesting to note that the percentage of criticism for radio is less than that for other advertising media. It is ill-advised to belittle the product of a competitor. All stories and pictures of an unpleasant or a disgusting nature should be avoided. Make the copy pleasant because it may be received during a social event or a dinner party and would create a bad impression for the product if it were not in good taste. It is human nature not to like to hear or to discuss disagreeable things. Questionable and risqué stories, songs, or jokes should be forbidden; and, of course, general broadcasting principles eliminate profanity, sacrilegious expressions, and all other language of doubtful propriety. Statements or suggestions that are offensive to religious views, racial consciousness, and the like are to be avoided. If testimonials are given, they must reflect the genuine experience or opinion of a competent witness who speaks in an honest, convincing manner. When dramatized commercials are used that involve statements by doctors, dentists, druggists, nurses, or other professional persons, the lines must be read by a member of these professions reciting actual experiences, or explanations must be made by the announcer that the scenes enacted are fictitious. There must be no misleading statements concerning price or claims of the product; and comparison with other products is not diplomatic.

The radio public objects frequently to the amount of advertising included in a radio program. The continuity writer should therefore use discretion in determining how much continuity to include in his period. High-powered salesmanship, undue repetition of price, and the excessive use of superlatives are not in good taste.

It must be recorded that these cautions against the use of questionable claims, superlatives, unpleasant ideas, the imperative tense, and disparagement of competitors—while undoubtedly for the good of commercial radio and its advertisers as a whole—are being conspicuously violated, principally by local stations, for the immediate advantage of individuals. The networks seem to have higher commercial ideals.

The continuity writer should see that there is no conflict between the broadcast announcement and the sponsor's advertisements for the same product in other media. All types should coordinate. It is good policy to mention the names of local dealers of a product in order that they may appreciate the value of the radio advertising.

Style

The two main faults of beginning writers in preparing copy for radio announcements are (1) that the copy is written to be read, not heard; and (2) that interest-seeking writers use unjustified methods of attracting attention. Commercial writers are inclined to use a newspaper-headline style instead of the conversational form. Sentences are inverted; words are left out; the advertisement is prepared to be seen, not heard. When a reader sees the same copy in a newspaper or magazine, he unconsciously fills in the missing words, but when this copy is heard over the air the incomplete statements are meaningless. Possibly this style results from the limitation imposed by broadcasting stations on the number of words in certain types of commercial plugs. Conciseness and simplicity are major requisites, but nevertheless clearness is essential. The continuity writer should explain his points in simple, direct language. He should be concrete, not abstract. Large figures are not easily followed and may be misunderstood. Percentages are confusing. The use of similes and vivid figures of speech is desirable.

The style of the radio announcement should be simple and personal, for the announcer is talking to an individual, not to thousands. He should never be "high-hat," no matter how expensive the product he is advertising. In writing copy never visualize the radio audience as a tremendous number of people seated together, but rather as a family group or an individual. Material that is presented in a personal way is given more attention than material that is presented objectively. The listener should be made to feel that he is buying a product from a friend, from one who has taken the trouble to entertain and to help him. Talk with the listener in the second person; be chatty, intimate, and persuasive.

While the listener may be addressed in the second person, the announcement should never make the announcer a member of the firm that is advertising. He should not say, "Come down to our store," because his voice is known as that of an announcer connected with the broadcasting station. Such a style would be misleading and, moreover, would constitute an endorsement of the sale or article by the station.

Facts and products are most easily popularized through an engaging personality, and the words of the continuity must create this character. The radio listener reacts better to a modest and unobtrusive approach. If the words are shouted at him, there is no opportunity for the speaker to emphasize certain vital words and facts. The writer should examine his copy to see if it is in the same form and has the same content that he would use if he were calling upon and talking to the listener personally. It is very good practice for the continuity writer to test out his copy by putting it onto the office dictaphone and then playing it back to see whether it sounds friendly and convincing. Probably a better practice would be to have someone read the announcement back to the writer, who may be surprised how one who is unfamiliar with the sense intended by the writer may interpret the copy. Write so that only one interpretation can possibly be given to the message. Make the continuity for your sales talks as attractive as you would endeavor to make your application when seeking a position.

The tendency of certain advertisers to introduce their commercial announcements with interest-catching devices such as "Important news flash" or "Calling all cars" is bad, because such an introduction is misleading and is inclined to offend the listener rather than appeal to him. Announcements can be interesting without being heralded as "news," so that such introductions are a waste of words. To "soft-soap" the listener is bad, to plead is worse, and to bully is the worst of all. The program should be appealing, but not commanding. Mechanical methods of approach do not make for vital, attractive, or inoffensive continuity.

A short announcement, to be effective, should contain not more than one idea. If you wish to make a lasting impression, do not have more than one request for action in a single short announcement and do not arouse conflicting appeals; to describe vividly the gnawing on a chicken leg overshadows the appeal of a tooth paste. Place the name of the product advertised and the point to be impressed early in the announcement; then, if the listener turns off his radio, you have at least introduced your product to him. If the continuity includes an offer, it should be stated simply and clearly without any involved or prolonged explanation. A well-centered climactic sales script is better than one that has many cheap and obvious climaxes. While repetition is used to drive home a point, the same phraseology should not be reiterated to the point of annoyance. Trade names and addresses should be given a number of times, but the form of delivery should be changed. The most productive way to obtain direct-mail response is to have replies sent directly to the broadcasting station, for the call letters of this station will be heard a number of times whereas the address of the sponsor can be heard only upon that immediate announcement.

Dramatized Commercials

The inclusion of the commercials in the continuity of the variety show is desirable, for programs should be knit closely together. The director must bind the program into a unified production instead of shoveling it out to the audience in unrelated parts. There is no excuse for a break of movement or a shift in the tone of the broadcast. The most successful programs on the air today build the announcers into the structure of the show and make them human and appealing characters who carry weight in their own right. This simplifies the task of putting human interest into the selling, and often the commercial hardly seems to be a selling announcement. If the show has been properly constructed, it will hold the listeners' interest throughout, and they will listen right through the commercial without knowing that they have invited a salesman into their homes. The best announcement is that which becomes part of the entertainment and follows the spirit and the tempo of the show.

The straight commercial announcement no longer is so effective as the dramatized commercial. More and more advertisers are realizing the wisdom of dramatizing their announcements as part of the entire show. A radio show cannot be allowed to lag or it will lose the listener. Careful attention is paid to this requirement during the entertainment part of the show, and there is no reason why all this effort should be nullified by permitting the commercial to change the tempo. After all, this is the most important part of the show to the sponsor, and he should take care not to lose the listener to some other program because of dull announcements.

When the announcement is given, it should be right in step with the rest of the show. The product, however, should not be dramatized. A dramatic situation should be created, and the solution achieved through the agency of the product. The more natural the solution, the more believable the dramatic situation.

A great variety of forms are used today in radio advertising, which may be traced back to an early phase in the history of broadcasting. The commercial theme song came first for promoting the sales message. In 1920 it was used as the main selling factor in many advertising campaigns, and no sponsor in those days was too dignified to make use of the theme song. It did have a valuable purpose, too—that of associating a product with a hummable tune, creating a melodious slogan.

During the twenties the continuity writer wrote his product into the introduction of the musical numbers. This practice has developed into the incorporation of advertising with the regular script of the show and now is used in most comedy shows. The product is usually worked into a gag and draws a laugh and oftentimes applause. The listener does not object to such advertising, and yet at the same time the sales talk is being put across.

In the dramatized commercials, the writer has a wide variety of devices from which to choose. He can use lyrics, dialogue, or straight selling. His dramatization may be one, two, or three episodes, all linked, if necessary, by swift narration. But whatever devices he chooses to use, his commercial must have three basic divisions, (1) the teaser, (2) the message, and (3) the compulsion.

The teaser must create an appetite for the message. It decides whether the listener will listen. Its job is much like the illustration, color, or catch line in the printed ad. The teaser can employ many techniques to seize the immediate interest. The play can be on (*a*) timeliness, season, holiday, special events, etc.:

ANNOUNCER: Now that warm weather has come, no doubt many of you are planning many delightful outings for the beautiful week ends to come, just like the Smiths are in this little scene . . . (*Fades into:* skit in which the Smith family agrees that the sponsor's product is necessary for a perfect time.)

The public is always eager to use the latest gadgets and devices on the market, and the idea of (*b*) newness will catch the ear:

ANNOUNCER: Are you burdening yourself with the old-fashioned ways of working around the house? Mrs. Darwin isn't; she's enjoying an afternoon at the club with her friends . . . (*Fades into:* women chattering at club, talk of scores, shots, and putts.)
MRS. A: You played a wonderful game today, Jane.
JANE: Yes, my game has steadily been improving, but that's because I've been able to get more afternoons off to play golf.
MRS. A: However do you manage it? Why, I had so much ironing yesterday I was almost too tired to come out today.
JANE: Oh, that hasn't bothered me since I got a new Whizzo Ironer. Why they're just too (etc.).

Appeal directly to the listener is often made in order to give the commercial (*c*) personal touch. This suggests the heart-to-heart talk between announcer and listener:

ANNOUNCER: (*Sneezes loudly; talks through nose as if he had a bad cold*) Ladies ad geddlemen (*Sneezes*) . . . Ads I wads zaying (*Sneezes again*) . . .

ANNOUNCER B: (*Interrupting*) Say, Jim, you can't make an announcement in that condition. Ladies and gentlemen, you will please excuse my fellow announcer, but as you can see he is in no shape to go on the air. Evidently he hasn't heard about Dr. Zilch's famous cold remedy. *You've* heard of it no doubt—of course you have—that's the remedy with zenoexytol, the latest discovery of science for fighting off colds. Well, I'm sure you'd want me to tell my friend Jim about it so that he can be back on the job tomorrow, and then he can tell you what was on his mind.

Flattery (*d*) is often an effective appeal to catch the listeners' attention, although it should be used with discretion. The announcer says: "Every intelligent person knows," etc., etc., or "No really wise buyer will spend more than," etc., etc.

The best means of attracting attention is that which will immediately bring some sort of emotional reactions. An emotional receptivity for the coming message is more desirable than the mere creation of mental curiosity. This is the specialty of the dramatized commercial, for drama more quickly than any other approach can mold our emotions. The idea is to create a situation in which the listener imagines himself to be and from which the only escape lies in the purchase of the advertised product. But care must be taken to picture the outcome of the use of the product not as shiny white teeth, a clean body, or sweet breath, but a successful romance, a happy life, or a good job.

The actual message is merely a description of the product often laid down by the advertiser in his own phraseology. The script writer has little opportunity for ingenuity here; his task is merely to link together, in the smoothest way possible, the sponsor's favorite phrases.

The compulsion line is usually as terse and as compelling as possible. These lines run: "Don't wait, it may be too late! Buy yours today," or "Go to your nearest dealer and have him show you the latest model cleaner." In this final and important phase of the commercial is included: "Save the coupon on the back, it may be used to obtain valuable premiums." One of the most popular methods today is the contest; compulsion lines in such campaigns run: "Visit your nearest Gaso dealer and get your free entry blank for the big $10,000 contest!"

A further modification of the use of dramatics in advertising is the personification of products, with all the emotions of humans. Such stunts as a vacuum cleaner humming and singing as it cleans and the almighty dollar shouting that it is being stretched too far are of this type. It is a vulgarization of dramatics, a burlesque, but it nevertheless is an example of radio advertising in forms other than the usual straight announcing.

In the limited dramatic skit used in dramatized commercials, sound saves time without depriving the ad of any of its desired effects. The sound of a car saves the wordage a straight commercial would use in setting the scene. The same sound can give the impression of speed, progress, or other similar effects without using a word. Sound effects will catch the listener's ear more quickly than an announcement. A shrieking siren or clanging bell will take the listener's mind off whatever he is doing more quickly than will a human voice. Wherever possible, sound effects should be used in the dramatized commercial in order to obtain the most effectiveness in the least time.

Length

The advertising man appreciates the value of white space in the layout of a magazine or a newspaper advertisement, but inconsistently he endeavors to fill every second of a radio announcement with copy. This is a mistake. White space in entertainment—in the form of brief pauses —has just as much value in radio copy. Nearly all advertising continuity is too long, and the principal reason for this is that the writer does not seek vivid words to take the place of groups of words. Verbs and adverbs are neglected for adjectives. The advertising story should be told quickly. Condense and intensify. Give the salient qualities of a product, its trade name and slogan, its price, and where it can be purchased.

The apparent length of a commercial depends a great deal upon the interest it can arouse. Many an interesting announcement has taken up twice as much time and seemed only half as long as most uninteresting ads. When the advertising message has been completed, stop before you become an obnoxious salesman.

Diction

Words used in radio commercial copy should be simple, dignified, and in good taste. The announcer does not make friends if he attempts to use high-flown words or to display an extensive vocabulary. If it is necessary to use a technical phrase, define it. It is a well-recognized fact that words of Anglo-Saxon origin are stronger than those with foreign base. Do not use any words that may have a double meaning. Because his entire impression on the audience is made through the sense of hearing, the radio writer must be even more careful than others to write in words understandable to the audience. The person listening to a speech cannot stop to look up unfamiliar words without losing a part of the message. Furthermore, a startling or unusual word will attract attention to itself, rather than to the commercial message. Choose language that expresses big ideas rather than that which displays big words.

Advertising copy should be addressed to the level of those people to whom the sponsor expects to sell his product and to the audience expected to listen at the particular time—juvenile, adult, feminine, masculine. The writer of copy addressed to adults must adjust his vocabulary so that all his listeners, who, of course, have varying degrees of education, may be reached. His speech must be understandable to the least learned as well as to the most learned. The successful writer always selects words that will be within the scope of his prospective listeners.

While good usage is considered essential, certain programs allow some liberty. Slang and sport phraseology have a place only on certain types of programs. Trite and hackneyed expressions are offensive; foreign derivatives should never be used; figures of speech should be carefully chosen. In the preparation of copy a thesaurus (Roget), a book differentiating between synonyms (Crabb), and a good dictionary are most useful.

Writers of radio commercials have some standard ideas on the subject of diction, according to a survey of 303 commercials made by David L. Thompson, graduate student researcher of the University of Wisconsin School of Journalism. The word most used is "you"; it appears eight times a commercial on the average. "Wonderful" is next in popularity, a total of 167 times in the 303 commercials. Then come, in order, "new," "good," "better," "fine," "best," "effective," "natural," "big," "fast," "finest," "great," "efficient," "improved," "nice," and "favorite." However, the words that the writers thought listeners like the best—just for the sound when they are spoken—are these: "pleasant," "sparkling," "beautiful," "lovely," "refreshing," "perfect," "delightful," "loveliest," "pleasure," and "pleasing."

Thompson found that radio writers have an array of favorite words for use in specific instances. To establish a congenial atmosphere the announcer addressed the radio audience with "you," "ladies," "folks," or "families." The time for action is "today," "now," "tomorrow," or "daily." Listeners are most often commanded to "try," "remember," "get," "buy," "enjoy," "use," "serve," "take," and "taste."

Do not use words that don't add color or motion. Don't even write "the" unless you mean "the." Edit all words that gray (the) color or clog (the) motion. Don't use (the word) "and" unless you (actually) need to emphasize the impression of adding (something).

Sentence Structure

The structure of the sentence plays a great part in the clearness of the material presented. If the thought is obscured by complicated and involved sentence structure, the audience can do nothing to rescue itself from wandering. The best way to be sure of sentence clarity is to use simple and compound sentences and to avoid complex forms. If the listener does not understand every sentence as the speaker utters it, he immediately loses interest. Avoid the use of adversative and coordinate conjunctions. Break your sentences in two, but, on the other hand, do not let them be of the same length, for in that case the delivery will have a monotonous melody. It is not always easy to make short sentences beautiful, but they will have force and drive home the idea. Do not fail to read aloud each sentence to see whether it clearly states the idea, and be sure that it cannot give any other than the desired idea; you cannot rely upon your announcer's delivery.

While short, glowing sentences are most successful, certain statements demand longer sentence structure; but where this is the case, the sentence should not be involved. Each successive phrase and clause must clearly unfold the thought. Sentences should be built up to an important word or idea. They must not flow downward. Of course, in general, grammatical rules must be obeyed; nevertheless speech permits some liberties. The chief concern is, Does the copy read well? Is it easily understood when heard?

Rhetoric

Correct grammatical rules are not always followed in this type of writing. Occasionally it becomes suitable to change and deviate from rules in order to give the copy a unique and forceful style. However, strict attention should be given to accurate grammatical relationships, such as the agreement of verbs with their subjects, pronouns with their antecedents, and pronominal adjectives with substantives, and the agreement of tenses. A grammatical error in any of these catches and holds the attention of the listener whom you wish to impress by your sales talk. The use of the imperative is rather irritating to the listener, who would prefer to be permitted to arrive at his own decision rather than to be dictated to by the announcer. The use of questions is an old device for demanding attention, but the writer must be very positive that no humorous answer or no antagonistic answer can possibly be given. He must be certain that the only answer possible is the one that he desires. One of the oldest axioms of successful advertising is to pursue a positive lead of the listener's or reader's thought; this is immediately defeated when the writer asks a question. Therefore it is obvious that the safer course to pursue is to omit the question element entirely. Tongue twisters should be avoided, for the most experienced radio announcer may become nervous and make a slip, regardless of how well he knows the material. Certain methods of arrangement and phrasing of material help to secure effectiveness in a radio message. Suspense may be created by allowing the listener to be conscious that you are working toward an objective, an interesting objective. The placing of emphasis upon certain words by the announcer may be assured by placing these words following pauses indicated by marks of punctuation.

In many instances the copy writer is so intent upon making a point that he fails to see that what he has written will make a different impression from that which is in his mind. This is often caused by misplaced modifying clauses, stringiness, or poor construction. A few illustrations of careless writing heard over the networks and the stations are: "See Harry Applebaum for that new pair of Sunday pants, open evenings and Sundays for your convenience"; "Don't wait until you have a headache; ask for it today"; "Thank you for feeding your dogs and cats Thrivo and we want you to recommend it to all your friends and relatives"; "Thousands of people who have listened to this program have headaches right now"; and "When I see a lady who does her own housework and dishwashing and who has soft, pretty hands I know she has been using her head." How would you retain the intended ideas and correct these announcements so that the announcer could not go wrong? You must not rely upon an announcer to say what you want him to say unless you write the announcement so that he cannot possibly give a misinterpretation.

Commercial Announcements, F.C.C. Regulations

The F.C.C., as you are aware by this time, completely oversees the activities of the radio station, even regulating commercial announcements.

Sec. 317. All matter broadcast by any radio station for which service, money or other valuable consideration is directly or indirectly paid, or promised to or charged or accepted by, the station so broadcasting, from any person, shall at the time the same is so broadcast, be announced as paid for or furnished as the case may be by such person.

The rules and regulations of the Federal Communications Comm'ssion (Section 3.409—Announcement of Sponsored Programs) read as follows:

(*a*) In the case of each program for the broadcasting of which money, services, or other valuable consideration is either directly or indirectly paid or promised to, or charged or received by, any radio broadcast station, the station broadcasting such programs shall make, or cause to be made, an appropriate announcement that the program is sponsored, paid for, or furnished, either in whole or in part.

(*b*) In the case of any political program or any program involving the discussion of public controversial issues for which any records, transcriptions, talent, scripts, or other material or services of any kind are furnished, either directly or indirectly, to a station as an inducement to the broadcasting of such program, an announcement shall be made both at the beginning and conclusion of such program on which such material or services are used that such records, transcriptions, talent, scripts, or other material or services have been furnished to such station in connection with the broadcasting of such program; provided, however, that only one such announcement need to be made in the case of any such program of five minutes' duration or less, which announcement may be made either at the beginning or conclusion of the program.

(*c*) The announcement required by this section shall fully and fairly disclose the true identity of the person or persons by whom or in whose behalf such payment is made or promised, or from whom or in whose behalf such services or other valuable consideration is received, or by whom the material or services referred to in subsection (*b*) hereof are furnished. Where an agent or other person contracts or otherwise makes arrangements with a station on behalf of another, and such fact is known to the station, the announcement shall disclose the identity of the person or persons in whose behalf such agent is acting instead of the name of such agent.

(*d*) In the case of any program, other than a program advertising commercial products or services, which is sponsored, paid for or furnished, either in whole or in part, or for which material or services referred to in subsection (*b*) hereof are furnished, by a corporation, committee, association or other unincorporated group, the announcement required by this section, shall disclose the name of such corporation, committee, association or other unincorporated group. In each such case the station shall require that a list of the chief executive officers or members of the executive committee or of the board of directors of the corporation, committee, association or other unincorporated group shall be made available for public inspection at one of the radio stations carrying the program.

(e) In the case of programs advertising commercial products or services, an announcement stating the sponsor's corporate or trade name or the name of the sponsor's product, shall be deemed sufficient for the purposes of this section and only one such announcement need be made at any time during the course of the program.

DO'S FOR COMMERCIAL WRITERS

Continuity should
 Attract attention.
 Arouse interest.
 Create desire.
 Impregnate remembrance of product name.
 Suggest action.
Develop new ideas, new approaches.
Make the commercial palatable.
Think and write in the positive—adds strength.
Write "do" copy.
Use "go," "do," "remember," "buy."
Descriptive words should describe and speak that description.
Use words that have character, life, sparkle, meaning.
Be choosey in your diction.
Use only selling words.
Test every word for ear value to impress name and action.
Make it clear.
Write copy in plain simple terms.
Follow the verb with its object.
Strong verbs are better than weak adjectives.
Use active verbs in the present tense.
Avoid superlatives.
Brief copy to avoid wasted time.
Avoid stating the obvious.
Eliminate unnecessary "the" and "that."
Avoid the close repetition of a word.
Make copy "sayable."
Use a practical language that listeners understand.
Use short sentences.
Remember that too many thoughts confuse the listener.
Watch for inconsistencies in copy that make for humor or misunderstanding.

Cut all material from copy which distracts from the product's name.

Leave adequate white space for emphasis to grasp effectiveness.

Indicate pronunciation of names.

A store name is always singular. Stofflet's *is.* . . .

Speak the truth—state facts—believable facts.

Be concrete.

Seek personal contact through person to person conversation.

Create good will.

Use repetition when emphasis is to be placed on one outstanding point such as slogans, addresses, prices, etc.

You may sum up what has been said.

You may begin and conclude with the same thought.

Eliminate anticlimax.

Repeat good copy.

Commercial Continuity for Television

A brief look at television is enough to indicate that the traditions, techniques, and principles of radio advertising have been carried over into television. The only differences arise out of the visual possibilities of television.

In general, when writing for a visual medium, it is better to visualize the message first, and then add the verbal accompaniment. There are two good reasons why this isn't always done in television advertising. TV advertising is an outgrowth of radio advertising and is much affected by the glowing verbosity of the style developed for radio. Furthermore, advertising people are aware that if the audience's attention wanders it is apt to be during the commercial. They know that it is easy to divert the eyes from the TV screen, so by adding good strong audio they are increasing the possibility that some of the message will get across.

The best TV commercials are not prepared by taking audio copy and attempting to add pictures to it. The better approach is to decide what can be shown about the sponsor's product, and then to give these things verbal emphasis. In the short spot announcement, it is frequently difficult to say whether the audio or the video is more important. In the live demonstration, and the film commercial, the video must definitely take the lead. If an appliance is to be demonstrated, for example, this will need to follow a certain order and will consume a certain amount of time. Only when these things are determined can the audio copy be written. It would be foolish to write the copy and expect the demonstration automatically to fit it. This is not to say that the verbal portion of TV commercials is unimportant. Far from it. It is simply a matter of giving primary attention to the visual elements when preparing material for a visual medium.

The best training for the preparation of television commercials is experience in writing radio continuity. However, the transition is not always easy to make. It requires some reorientation to conceive of ideas primarily in visual terms, rather than in verbal. Such a change in approach is necessary if good TV commercials are to be produced. Apart from this basic change, the same principles apply.

CHAPTER TWENTY-EIGHT

THE LAW AS IT AFFECTS BROADCASTING

In 1909, Enrico Caruso sang into a megaphone, with a vibrating diaphragm at its apex, located upon the stage of the Metropolitan Opera House in New York. A telephone line carried his voice to Lee B. De Forest, in his laboratory on the bank of the Harlem River. He took the telephoned music from the first remote-control wire in history and put it into the air. Wireless operators on ships reported that they had heard fragments of Caruso's voice through their earphones. For nearly ten years after this initial broadcast anyone who wanted to could set up broadcasting equipment upon any wave length desired. However, shortly after the Armistice the government was induced to take over the control of the air—to allot wave lengths and to control their use. The Department of Commerce had been commissioned to control radio under the Marine Act of 1912. This act broadly covered the regulations for the use of wireless in the United States and placed the licensing power for the transmission of broadcasts with the Secretary of Commerce. A controversy arose, however, as to whether the Secretary of Commerce had the right to regulate the time that the stations he licensed were to be on the air. This question was submitted to the Attorney General of the United States, and his opinion concerning the Act of 1912 was that it was a "direct legislative regulation of the use of wave lengths," and that the Secretary of Commerce did not have the authority to regulate the amount of power a station might use, the time it might operate, or the frequencies it might occupy.

The government realized the need for a unified system of regulation of radio, and therefore the Radio Act of 1927 was passed and the Federal Radio Commission established. The source of authority was found in the Constitution, which conferred upon Congress the right to make treaties with other nations and to carry them into effect by appropriate legislation, to establish post offices and post roads, to declare war, and to regulate commerce with foreign nations and among the several states. It was decided by the courts that the transmission of intelligence is commerce. Early cases decided that the national government had exclusive jurisdiction over radio and that state or local governments could not tax receiving or transmitting equipment.

The Radio Act of 1927 functioned quite efficiently, but with the growth of the industry a new law was needed which would be more explicit in its regulation of broadcasting. The Radio Act of 1927 was designed primarily for the regulation

. . . of all forms of interstate and foreign radio transmissions and communications within the United States over all the channels of interstate and foreign radio transmission: and to provide for the use of such channels, but not the ownership thereof, by individuals, firms, or corporations, for limited periods of time, under licenses granted by Federal authority, and no such license shall be construed to create any right beyond the terms, conditions, and periods of the license.

The Radio Act of 1927 also provided for the creation of a body of five members, to be known as the Federal Radio Commission.

Briefly, its duties were to (1) classify radio stations; (2) prescribe the nature of the service to be rendered by each class of licensed stations; (3) assign bands of frequencies or wave-lengths to the various classes of stations, and individual stations, and determine the power which each station shall use, and the time during which it may operate; (4) determine the locations of stations, or classes of stations; (5) regulate the kind of apparatus to be used with respect to its external effects and the purity and sharpness of the emissions of each station and from the apparatus therein; (6) make such regulations not inconsistent with law as it may deem necessary to prevent interference between stations and to carry out the provisions of this act.

One of the first acts of the Federal Radio Commission was to assign the region in the radio spectrum from 500 to 1500 kilocycles to commercial broadcasting; later it made three high-fidelity channels available for a combined experimental-commercial use—1530, 1550, and 1570 kilocycles. It also divided the country into seven radio zones and decided what frequencies and powers should be available in those zones. The following classification of radio stations has now been established: (1) clear-channel, consisting of frequencies on which only one station may operate; (2) high-power regional, which is usually not less than 5000 watts and shares frequency with some other station in a distant part of the country; (3) regional, not less than 250 watts and usually 1000 watts at night and 2500 in the daytime; and (4) local, having 50 to 250 watts. The commission may also give the following time designation to stations: (1) unlimited, (2) limited, (3) daytime only, and (4) sharing time with another station.

On June 19, 1934, the Congress of the United States approved the Communications Act of 1934, which broadened the scope of Federal control over communications so as to include telephone and telegraph as well as radio communication. This act also provided for certain changes in the commission itself, but left the radio laws essentially as they were defined by the Radio Act of 1927. The Communications Act of 1934 was based upon three fundamentals: first, the air should be public property; second, the radio industry should be privately owned and operated; and third, free speech on the air should be preserved. These principles were incorporated in Title Three of the Communications Act of 1934.

Although the Radio Act specifically says that the Federal Radio Commission is to exercise no censorship over broadcasting, the commission has been able to exercise a large degree of censorship. This is because of the requirement that a station must be operating in the public interest, convenience, and necessity before its license can be renewed. Thus, if a station has not lived up to the requirements placed upon it by the commission, when the station wishes to renew its license the commission can decide that the station is not operating in the public interest, convenience, and necessity, and so deny the application for renewal. The commission has been upheld in cases involving this very point.[1]

There was a provision in the new law, as there was in the old one, that in the case of national emergency, all the wire and radio services could be taken over by the government. (This was done after the United States had entered the First World War.) The President was given the power to take over these services but was required to give the employees just compensation for their services.[2]

The 1934 act provided for the Federal Communications Commission to be composed of seven men appointed by the President with the advice and consent of the Senate, each serving for a term of seven years. The stipulation was made that no more than four of the men on the commis-

---

[1] See *KFAB Broadcasting Association* v. *Federal Radio Commission*, 47 F. (2d) 670; and *Trinity Methodist Church, South,* v. *Federal Radio Commission*, 62 F. (2d) 850; 60 App. D.C. 311.

[2] Now covered by CONELRAD F.C.C. Rules and Regulations Part 3, Subpart G

sion should be members of the same political party. At the inception of the act the members of the first commission were appointed for staggered terms so that only one member of the commission would retire each year. One of the changes that the later law made was that of authorizing the commission to issue radio licenses for a period of three years instead of six months, as had been allowed under the act of 1927. The act also forbids the conducting of lotteries over the radio.

The first duty of the F.C.C. is to supervise the granting of licenses to applicants for radio stations, in order to assure good, strong radio signals, tolerably free from interference, to all sections of the United States. This involves the assignment of the number of electromagnetic waves sent out per second over the air by a transmitter, commonly known as frequencies. This is an engineering problem and requires the applicant to prove to the commission that its requested frequency will not interfere with any other station using the same wave length. Surveys are made by engineers employed by the applicant and the results are considered by the technical staff of the commission. This power to regulate the granting of licenses is probably the most important duty of the commission.

The Communications Act of 1934 applies to all interstate and foreign communication by wire or radio which originates in the United States or which is received within the United States, and to the licensing and regulation of all radio stations. Not only does the Federal Communications Commission regulate the standard-broadcast stations, but it also has control of those that are designated as relay, international, television, facsimile, high-frequency, development, and noncommercial and educational stations.

In connection with this supervision of the technical details, the commission has the power to approve or disapprove proposed mechanical equipment to be used by a station and the location of the antenna, and it may require the use of directional antennas in the case of interference. Application forms for the different types of broadcasting are obtained from the commission and they are very penetrative in their technical requirements. Various prerequisites are set down for good standards which must be complied with by the station.

In receiving application for a station, the F.C.C. requires a vast amount of data. Not only does it insist that the applicant set forth all the equipment that will be used by the proposed station, but it desires to know about the location of the transmitter and the property rights of the applicant in the ground upon which the antenna and transmitter are to be located. The applicant's profession or occupation must be thoroughly outlined, particularly because no alien is permitted to be the owner of a broadcasting station. If the applicant is a corporation, all the facts concerning the incorporation, stock, sales, etc., must be set forth. It must be shown that the station will be self-supporting; consequently, even before the license is granted, tentative contracts must be entered into between the applicant and local concerns which agree to broadcast commercial programs. A complete statement of the anticipated income and the cost of operation must be submitted. Typical program schedules for a week are required. Before the application will be accepted the necessary funds for the building and equipping of the station and for its maintenance must be placed in escrow. The applicant must submit its proposed wave length or frequency and request a power assignment. Letters are generally obtained from all civic bodies pointing out that the proposed station will serve public interest, necessity, and convenience. The population of the city in which the station is to be located must be given, together with its annual sales and bank clearances. Surveys must be made of ground conditions in the location where the transmitter is to be built, because these affect the signal. Other stations which are on the same frequency are permitted to file exceptions to the granting of the application. At present it is extremely difficult to obtain a license for a radio station in the standard band. Approximately the same procedure must be followed in applying for a frequency-modulation station or television station either in the commercial or in the educational band.[1]

The broadcast field for AM is not open to everyone in any practical sense. At the end of 1955 there were 2804 AM stations on the air, which was close to the capacity of the broadcast channels. It is very difficult to find an available channel in most areas. There are nearly 5000 communities with populations of 1000 or larger which have no local radio station. Over 100 of these communities have populations ranging from 20,000 to 300,000. In January, 1956, the total number of FM commercial stations broadcasting was 536. In addition to these commercial FM stations there were 130 in the noncommercial classification. The number of television stations on the air was 454.

There are two ambiguous phrases which really are the basis of radio law: first, "power to determine whether or not a radio station is acting

---

[1] See Federal Communications Commission "Rules Governing Radio Broadcast Services," Part 3, Federal Communications Commission, Superintendent of Documents, U.S. Government Printing Office, Washington 25, D.C.

for public interest, necessity, and convenience," and, second, "no person within the jurisdiction of the United States shall utter any obscene, indecent, profane language by means of radio communications." If it is found by the commission that the area which should be served by the proposed station is already well served by other stations, public necessity and interest would not demand the establishment of a new station. It must be shown by the applicant not only that commercial programs are to be broadcast, but that there will also be public-service programs of interest to the particular locality. Just what types of programs satisfy public interest and necessity is not known. The terms "profane" and "indecent" have been far from positively defined by the courts, legislature, or commission, much to the dismay of broadcasters. Whether words such as "damn" and "hell" and expressions such as "My God!" are considered to be profane depends much upon the way they are uttered and used.

The power of the F.C.C. to prohibit the use of obscene, indecent, and profane language over the radio comes from the police power which Congress has over interstate commerce and exercises through similar prohibitions in the use of the mail. That the Federal Radio Commission has the right to prohibit the use of obscene language over the radio was established in the case of *Duncan* v. *U.S.*[1] Matters of indecency in many instances depend upon the presentation. Stations are inclined to lean over backward in order to avoid censorship in these respects. The commission is a quasi-judicial body, and all complaints against any broadcasting station in the United States are referred to it. These complaints most often come in letters from the listening public or from the field staff which the commission maintains for this particular purpose. When a complaint is received, if it does not demand immediate attention, it waits until the six month's period for which the station is licensed has expired and the station in question has come up for relicensing. When such a hearing is held, the legal staff of the commission sits as judges to decide whether or not the license should be refused, or what action should be taken. The decisions of the commission may be appealed to the Court of Appeals of the District of Columbia and then to the Supreme Court of the United States. This, however, is very seldom done for the simple reason that the industry has adopted the attitude of peace at any price.

The commission considers applications for licenses, for the renewal of licenses, for the modification of such licenses, and for the transfer of a

[1] 48 F. (2d) 128 (1931).

license. It has laid down regulations for the use of facilities by candidates for public office. It requires a station to make clear that broadcast matter of a commercial nature is paid for by the advertiser. It grants separate licenses for mobile service. The commission determines whether material may be originated on a foreign soil and carried by remote control to an American station to be broadcast, as well as whether such material may be taken across the border from the United States and broadcast by a foreign station. It does not permit a station to pick up a program being broadcast by any other station and rebroadcast it without the written consent of the originating station and of the commission. It has the power to determine whether programs in other than the standard band may be of a commercial nature. All operators obtain their licenses from the Federal Communications Commission.

In connection with the condemnation of the content of the commercial program, the advertising matter is considered by the Federal Trade Commission, which is not a part of the Federal Communications Commission, but is a separate governmental agency supervising the truthfulness of advertising material. If the station is found to be giving commercial programs which do not conform with the standards of advertising set down by the Federal Trade Commission, its license may be revoked. This happened in the case of a doctor who used a radio station to give medical advice of doubtful value over the air.

In September, 1945, the F.C.C. issued a set of rules and regulations for television stations that were substantially the same as those for FM.[1]

Since the reception area of FM and television stations is limited, generally, to the "line of sight" from the transmitting antenna, there is a limited radius of efficient transmission. This raises the question of whether the broadcast area was entirely within the state. If it is, the station theoretically becomes subject to state law through being in intrastate commerce. The courts, however, probably would accept the idea that all radio broadcasting was amenable to congressional control and immune from state control except for its police powers. They could seize upon the fact that it cannot be said that reception outside the state is impossible.

Another facet of the problem of controlling television is the "censorship" of television broadcasts. There the difficulties are similar to those of the movie industry with regard to the scantiness of costume, length of embraces, types of characters portrayed, etc. The F.C.C. uses its

[1] See footnote 1, page 418.

power to refuse a license renewal, to exert a moral persuasion on the station, to examine the script, and thus to insure against the broadcasting of objectionable material. A somewhat different problem arises in television broadcasts made from a public area. There is the danger of involvement with the rights of privacy of those who are portrayed accidentally on the screen. If an individual is singled out for special treatment or commercial exploitation, without his permission, then his right of privacy has been infringed upon, with the broadcaster's resulting liability for damage.

Radio Libel

There have been two types of laws concerning defamatory remarks. These may be classified as libel and slander. The main distinction between the two is that libel is written and slander is oral defamation. Libel is considered the more serious of the two. For libelous utterances a man can, in most states, be held criminally liable, while for committing slander he is accountable only for civil damages. These laws have their basis in the old common law, and at the present time every state in the Union has legislative statutes concerning slanderous and libelous remarks.

With the advent of the radio, a whole new field was made available to which the laws of defamation could apply. The first case for defamation by radio did not arise until twelve years after the introduction of broadcasting on a commercial scale in the United States. In 1932, Station KFAB, located in the state of Nebraska, allowed a political candidate to speak over the radio. The station had been compelled to allow him to speak by a provision in the Federal Radio Act of 1927 which made it mandatory for a station to give to each of rival candidates an equal opportunity to speak over its facilities. KFAB had allowed Mr. Sorenson, who became the plaintiff in the subsequent suit, to speak, and it therefore had to permit Mr. Wood, who became a codefendant with the radio station in the suit, to speak also. This same provision in the Federal law prevented the radio station from exercising any censorship over Mr. Wood's speech. Mr. Wood spoke and uttered defamatory remarks about Sorenson, who thereupon sued both Wood and the broadcasting station.

In the case of *Sorenson* v. *Wood and KFAB Broadcasting Co.*,[1] the Supreme Court of Nebraska applied the same defamation doctrine to the

[1] 123 Neb. 348, 243 N.W. 82 (1932).

radio station that applies to the newspapers. It held that the station was jointly liable with the actual defamer. In this connection the court said:

The publication of a libel by a radio to listeners over the air requires the participation of both the speaker and the owner of the station. The publication is not completed until the material is broadcast.

This is exactly the same doctrine that applies to defamation by publication in newspapers. The court also declared at the same time that, as in the case of newspapers, defamatory remarks over the radio constituted libel and not slander.

The fundamental principles of law involved in publication by a newspaper and by a radio station seem to be alike. There is no legal reason why one should be favored over another or why a broadcasting station should be granted special favors as against one who may be the victim of a libelous publication.[1]

In the answer to the defense of KFAB that the Federal statue prevented the station from censoring the speech of Wood, the Nebraska court held that this statute merely prevented the station from censoring words as to their "partisan or political trend," but did not give the radio station the right to "join and assist in the publication of a libel." The significance of this decision is that Sorenson v. Wood declared that defamatory language broadcast by a radio station is libel rather than slander, and that, as is true with newspapers, due care and honest mistakes do not relieve a broadcasting station from liability for libel. While radio defamation is oral in its inception, it is more akin to the common-law libel action, for in the preparation of a program a great deal of deliberation is required and a broadcast results in a very wide dissemination of the defamatory material. The fact also must be taken into account that many programs are now transcribed before going on the air and many are cut directly from the air, thus making it possible to retain the defamatory matter in permanent form to be disseminated at will.

The next important case along the same line was that of Miles v. Louis Wasmer, Inc. et al.[2] In this case, Louis Wasmer, Inc., the owner of Station KHQ, had sold time on the air to an organization crusading in the interest of prohibition. In the defamatory remarks, read by an announcer of KHQ, it was strongly implied that the local sheriff had been confiscating stills and then reselling them at a very low price, thus allowing other

[1] 123 Neb. 348, 243 N.W. 82 (1932).
[2] 172 Wash. 466, 20 Pac. (2d) 849 (1933).

"moonshiners" to start up cheaply. Miles, the sheriff, brought suit against the radio station, the announcer, and the author of the defamatory passage. The Washington court, in awarding the decision to the plaintiff, quoted approvingly the principles declared in *Sorenson* v. *Wood* and added:

It seems to us that there is a close analogy between the words spoken over the radio station and libelous words contained in a paid advertisement in a newspaper. The owner of the station furnished the means by which the defamatory words could be spoken to thousands of people.[1]

The third suit of importance on the question of defamation is that of *Coffey* v. *Midland Broadcasting Co.*[2] In this case the Midland Broadcasting Co., owning Station KMBC, had broadcast defamatory remarks against Coffey. KMBC was an outlet for the Columbia Broadcasting System and had broadcast these remarks as part of a chain program sponsored by Remington Rand, Inc. The defamatory remarks had been spoken into the microphone in New York by an employee of Remington Rand, Inc., and carried over telephone circuit to KMBC, from where they had been sent out over the air. All three participants in the program were sued. This suit was also decided in favor of the plaintiff. This decision carried the case one step further than *Sorenson* v. *Wood* and *Miles* v. *Wasmer* and placed the liability on the outlet chain station—or rebroadcaster—as well as on the station where the defamatory remark originated.

The law has recognized a distinction between remarks written into the script, and thus submitted to the radio station ahead of broadcast time, and the uttering of extemporaneous remarks which depart from the prepared script. The latter is what was done by the defendants in *Summit Hotel Company* v. *National Broadcasting Company*[3] and *Josephson* v. *Knickerbocker Broadcasting Company*,[4] and the courts involved held that public policy could best be served by relieving the radio station from liability in instances of unpreventable defamation. In these forward-looking decisions, the courts held that where a station takes the necessary precaution of examining, prior to broadcasting, the prepared script, it should not be held liable for defamatory material interpolated without warning into the broadcast. However, a radio station cannot arbitrarily prohibit a broadcast, under the ordinary contract for the leasing of

[1] 172 Wash. 466, 20 Pac. (2d) 849 (1933).
[2] 8 F. Supp. 889 (1934).
[3] 336 Pa. 182, 8 Atl. (2d) 302 (1939).
[4] 38 NYS (2d) 985 (1942).

broadcast time, on the ground that some of the material in the script "might" be defamatory. In *Rose* v. *Brown*[1] the court held that the station was bound by the existing contract to allow the material to be broadcast unless the script actually contained slanderous matter.

There is a legal tendency to establish a distinction between broadcasts which are extemporaneous and those in which the speaker reads from a script (reading aloud has been considered libel since 1610). The most apparently unjust cases of liability are those that result when a speaker to whom air time has been rented departs from the previously submitted and approved script and utters defamatory remarks. It would seem that a radio station should be protected if due care is used, but this doctrine can be invoked only when the courts depart from the application of libel and slander to broadcast defamation and this they have not seen fit to do.

As to defamatory remarks uttered by a party who is speaking extemporaneously or ad-libbing, whether they are true or not, the station's liability seems definite, for, say the courts, the station is negligent in not having demanded a script for examination before the broadcast. Absolute liability, based upon the same reasoning, also follows when defamation overlooked by the station is included in a previously submitted script. In those programs which are essentially impromptu, such as current events, sporting contests, parades, etc., the station's liability also exists.

The sponsor of a commercial broadcast is liable, as are each and every other person and station which participated in the defamatory broadcast.[2] One of the difficulties in prosecuting a defamation action, as shown in the Boake Carter case, is to effect service on the proper parties. In this case the broadcast was heard in New Jersey and the plaintiff attempted to sue jointly a nonresident news commentator, a nonresident sponsor, and a nonresident network system, all of whom were domiciled in different states. The plaintiff would have to sue only certain defendants or start a suit against each separately.

The so-called rules of privilege and fair comment are important in political campaigns. A statement must be recognized as comment and not a statement of fact.[3] Criticisms may, under these rules, be made of authors and their works, composers, public officials, candidates for public office, and other persons in the public eye. Such broadcasts, however,

[1] 58 NYS (2d) 654 (1945).
[2] *Hoffman* v. *Boake Carter*, 187 Atl. 576 (1936); *Locke* v. *Benton & Bowles*, 165 Misc. N.Y. 631; 1 N.Y. Supp. 2d 240 (1937).
[3] *Foley* v. *Press Publishing Co.*, 226 App. Div. N.Y. 535 (1929).

must not go beyond the limits of criticism and opinion by attacking the motives or character of such persons.[1]

An interesting question involving the conflict of laws arises in virtually every case of a defamation by radio broadcast since it may be heard in several states simultaneously. There is sufficient "publication" wherever the broadcast is heard, as well as where it originates, to support a lawsuit, but the problem arises as to which state's law is applicable. The apparent solution that it is permissible to bring an action in several states for one defamation offends the principles and practice of the courts, so the only answer appears to be that there is needed a new rule of conflict of laws applicable to radio broadcasting.

The F.C.C. has control over defamation by radio through the refusal to renew the license of the culprit station when it has a record of many defamatory utterances, on the basis that such actions are contrary to public interest. It also has refused to permit construction of a new station when many of the residents of the area affected had complained of the applicant's present predisposition toward defamation as indicated by his newspaper utterances.

In addition to the court decisions declaring defamatory remarks over the radio to be libel, several states have statutory provisions that do this.

Music

A number of years ago, in a case having nothing to do with the radio, that of *Herbert* v. *Shanley Co.*,[2] the Supreme Court decided that a performance of a musical composition or any other copyrighted article was a performance within the meaning of the law so long as it was performed with the purpose of gaining some profit, whether that profit was gained directly or indirectly.

The first case concerning the violation of the copyright laws by a radio station was that of *Witmark* v. *Bamberger*[3] in 1923. In that case the court decided that the broadcast of a copyrighted song by a radio station constituted a public performance for profit. In 1924, Jerome H. Remick & Co. brought suit against the American Automobile Accessories Co.[4] for using its copyrighted songs, unauthorized, over the air. In this case the

---

[1] *Irwin* v. *Ashurst,* 74 P. 2d 1127 (1938) Ore.

[2] 242 U.S. 591: 61 L. ed. 511.

[3] 291 Fed. 776 (D.C.N.J. 1923).

[4] *Jerome H. Remick & Co.* v. *American Automobile Accessories Co.,* 5 F. (2d) 411:40 A.L.R. 1511.

musician was an employee of the station, which was owned by the defendant. The court held that broadcasting a copyrighted musical composition by an artist employed by the broadcaster was an infringement of the copyright laws "where the purpose was to stimulate the sale of radio products."

In 1926, in the case of *Remick & Co.* v. *General Electric Co.*,[1] the application of the copyright laws to radio was carried still further. In this case the court decided that the station was liable even if the performer was not an employee of the station, that is, the station was liable on the ground of contributory infringement, it having contributed to the performance by transmitting the composition over the air.

The most important and significant decision, however, in the realm of copyright laws and the radio was that of *Buck et al.* v. *Jewell-LaSalle Realty Co.*,[2] decided in 1931. The defendant in this case was the owner of a hotel that had installed radio loud-speakers in all its guest rooms. These loud-speakers were connected with a master receiving set in the hotel. This master set picked up the broadcast of a radio program on which were broadcast compositions whose copyrights were owned by the American Society of Composers, Authors, and Publishers. The radio station had not been authorized to broadcast these compositions; and Buck, acting for the A.S.C.A.P., had repeatedly warned the radio station against doing this and had also warned the hotel against distributing the programs over its loud-speaker system. When the broadcasts continued, Buck brought the action. In a historic decision, the Supreme Court of the United States held that:

> The acts of a hotel proprietor, in making available to his guests, through the instrumentality of a radio receiving set, and loudspeakers installed in his hotel and under his control, and for the entertainment of his guests, the hearing of a copyrighted musical composition which had been broadcast from the radio transmitting station constituted a performance of such composition within the meaning of the copyright laws.

It is on this case of *Buck* v. *Jewell-LaSalle Realty Co.* that the A.S.C.A.P. bases its present policy of control over the copyrights that it holds on musical compositions.

The American Society of Composers, Authors, and Publishers is an unincorporated organization made up of music composers and a certain

---

[1] 16 F. (2d) 829 (S.B.N.Y. 1926).
[2] 283 U.S. 191: 51 Sup. Ct. 410: 75 L. ed. 971: 76, A.L.R. 1266. *Buck* v. *Jewell-LaSalle Realty Co.*, *supra.*

number of music-publishing houses. The individual members and publishers in this voluntary society own the copyrights and merely assign the performing rights to the society. The society negotiates for the sale of licenses to use the music and takes care of the collection of fees and other details of making available to orchestras and other performers, including radio stations, the music held by the society's members. The American Society of Composers, Authors, and Publishers has worked out a price scale that has proved, in the main, satisfactory to all concerned.

The amount of the royalties, or license fees paid, is based upon such factors as the wattage of the radio station, the surrounding population of the city where the station is located, and the extent to which the broadcasting station commercializes its facilities in selling commercial advertising programs, and subject to restrictions as to certain song numbers.

The fee is usually for a blanket license. All noncommercial educational, municipal, and religious stations enjoy complimentary licenses ($1.00 a year) from A.S.C.A.P. and S.E.S.A.C. and have used this music royalty free for years; even those educational institutions not owning their own stations but broadcasting over commercial stations are licensed for the nominal fee by A.S.C.A.P. B.M.I. also grants privileges to educational institutions. The purpose behind such centralized authority as A.S.C.A.P., B.M.I., M.P.P.A. (Music Publishers Protective Association), and S.E.S.A.C. is excellent, for its existence obviates the necessity of dealing with individual copyright holders.

To constitute an infringement of a copyright of a musical selection, three elements must exist: (1) there must be a performance, (2) it must be public, and (3) it must be for profit, either direct or indirect.[1] Any substantial portion of a selection constitutes a violation of the copyright. This is generally accepted as being over four bars of a musical number. The common-law copyright applies to music.

The remedies for infringement of copyright are: injunction, recapture of profits, and damages for the infringement.[2]

The question has arisen as to whether music played over a station operating on a nonprofit basis is a performance for profit. The defendant in *Associated Music Publishers* v. *Debs Memorial Radio Fund*[3] was a nonprofit corporation organized for educational and civic activities. Its

[1] *Air Law Review,* 1933, p. 316.
[2] *Ibid.*
[3] 141 F. (2d) 852; cert. denied, 323 U.S. 766; 65 Sup. Ct. 120 (1944).

radio station was operated primarily as an open forum, but some revenue was derived from advertising. The court held that even though there
was no intent that the defendant company, or its station, should show a
profit there had been no contention raised that it was a public or charit-
able corporation. One-third of the station's time was devoted to commercial programs, the court found, and extended the rule affecting
commercial stations to apply to this type of station. The court recognized as well settled the rule that the playing of a musical composition
on a sustaining program of a commercial station is an infringement of
the copyright.[1]

Noncommercial stations may broadcast and record music but never
for profit. Reproduction even in song books requires releases. If rebroadcast by a commercial station, that station must have a release. Arrangements come under the same regulations as new music. It is wise to get a
release from young composers even if they be staff members. The test is
performance for profit.

Copyrights

The broadcaster desires to know what written material of the present
day or of the past may be adapted for radio or be used in its original
form. The writer desires to know what novels, short stories, and plays
may be adapted for radio and television. The broadcaster and the writer
are equally interested in the protection of their original material—the
broadcaster in protecting scripts prepared by his employees, the author
in protecting his original manuscripts. There are two types of copyrights,
the common-law and the statutory copyright.

Common-law Copyright. N.B.C. places the following notice upon the
flyleaf of all its sustaining scripts:

This dramatic work is the property of the National Broadcasting Company,
Inc. It is fully protected under what is known as a common law copyright and
damages may be assessed for unauthorized performance thereof or for the
making of copies thereof.

An author of a literary or other artistic work is granted exclusive ownership thereof.[2] His common-law rights are protected until he has permitted the content of his work to be communicated generally to the pub-

---

[1] *Radio and the Law* by J. G. Moser and R. A. Lavine (1947).
[2] *Morrill* v. *Smith et al.*, 271 Fed. 211.

lic. The present copyright law expressly provides that the statutory law does not in any way annul or limit the enforcement of common-law rights, either in law or in equity. However, when the owner of a common-law copyright avails himself of a statutory copyright, he thereby abandons common-law rights. Until publication, therefore, intellectual creations are protected perpetually at common law in the form in which the author has expressed his originality. The duration of such common-law rights is perpetual so long as the work is unpublished, but publication terminates all rights.[1] This, of course, vests exclusively the right of first publication in the author. There is no legal procedure, no registering of the manuscript, no filing of the copy on the part of the author to obtain a common-law copyright. It is his by virtue of his writing the original manuscript.

The physical transfer of an unpublished manuscript does not divest the author of his common-law rights. An author may transfer a manuscript with reservations limiting the extent of common-law rights granted. For instance, he may give his ownership of a manuscript for motion-picture production and retain his common-law copyright for radio production. If such a work is published without the authority of the author, this does not divest him of his common-law rights. The distribution of copies need not be for profit. Mere printing without circulation, however, is not publication. The courts have usually held that the typewriting or even the mimeographing of a limited number of broadcast scripts for the purpose of making the work available for several potential program producers should not alone divest the author of his right at common law and dedicate the work to society at large.[2]

To have a publication at common law you must always have a concrete tangible form by means of which the work can be communicated intelligently to the public. The actual presentation of the work to the public by an unrestricted performance, reading, or expression thereof has been held not to constitute a publication. The performance of a play,[3] the rendition of a musical composition by an orchestra, and the public delivery of a lecture or other address[4] have been held as not constituting an abandonment of the work by an author so as to constitute a dedication thereof to the public. As was held in the now famous case of *Uproar*

---

[1] *Caliga* v. *Inter-Ocean Newspaper Co.*, 215 U.S. 182; 30 Sup. Ct. 38.

[2] *Macmillan* v. *King*, 223 Fed. 862.

[3] *Ferris* v. *Froman*, 223 U.S. 424; 32 Sup. Ct. 263.

[4] *Nutt* v. *Instit. for Improvement of Memory*, 31 F. (2d) 236.

Company v. *The National Broadcasting Company,*[1] this theory was extended to radio broadcasting by holding that the rendition and performance of a work publicly by means of the facilities of a network of broadcasting stations or by one broadcasting station is not an abandonment of ownership of the work or a dedication thereof to the public at large. However, if the manuscript is sold, absolutely and unconditionally, the common-law rights are lost. Such common-law rights are terminated by publication, which means the act of making a book, writing, or other work offered or communicated to the public generally available in the sale or distribution of copies. Such distribution need not take place in the United States. When one or more copies of a work have been prepared and made available to the general public there is publication at common law, and as a result the author loses his common-law rights. If the work be leased or loaned, the author's rights at common law will be barred because the work has thereby been made generally available to the public.

The author of a creative work may secure damages at law for any unauthorized use of his property; and a court of equity will issue an injunction to restrain any unauthorized use and will decree an accounting of profits derived from such use. Suits of this sort are properly lodged in the state courts. A common-law work may not be copied, mechanically reproduced by any device whatsoever, arranged, translated, adapted, or performed by any means or through any media, without the consent of the owner of the work so protected.

The time element is of importance in establishing a common-law copyright. It is always possible for someone to claim that his manuscript was written previously. Consequently, authors have adopted the practice of sending to themselves by registered mail, a copy of their manuscripts; when the manuscript is received, they do not open it but keep it sealed so that, by placing a sealed envelope with its postmarked date in evidence, they can establish the date upon which their manuscript was completed.

The writer of a letter has a common-law copyright in his missive.[2] The writer has the right to make copies of the letter, although it has been sent to its recipient. The person who receives such a letter, be it testimonial or comment, owns no literary property whatsoever in the letter, and its use without the consent of the writer is a violation of the common-

---

[1] 81 F. (2d) 273 (1936).
[2] *Folsom* v. *Marsh,* Fed. Case No. 4901; 2 Story 100.

law copyright, unless from the terms of the letter or from its implications the author extends such permission. The sender of a telegram has the same literary property in his telegram. In many ways it seems that the common-law copyright is adequate protection for the author, but the proof of his common-law right is probably more difficult, inasmuch as the original manuscripts or artistic creations have not been filed for reference.

Statutory Protection. Article One, Section Eight, of the United States Constitution provides that Congress shall have the power: "To promote the progress of science and useful arts by securing for a limited time to authors and inventors the exclusive right to their respective writings and discoveries." This grant of power to Congress did not divest the several states of jurisdiction to grant authors judicial protection at common law of literary and intellectual property, but copyright was thereby placed in the domain of Congress exclusively, so that the states now have no power to pass substitute legislation in this field.

The first United States copyright act in 1790 provided for a period of protection for fourteen years and a renewal period of the same duration. By the Act of February 3, 1831, the original period of protection was extended to twenty-eight years, but the renewal period of fourteen years was not changed. Under the Act of 1909 a period of twenty-eight years of original protection was granted and a renewal period of the same length was permitted, provided that the application for such renewal should be made to the Copyright Office and duly registered therein one year prior to the expiration of the original term of copyright. The periods for such protection run from the earliest date when the first copy of the best edition is placed on sale. In the case of default of renewal or failure to renew from any other cause, the work falls into public domain. If such renewal is made according to the legal requirements, the work falls into the public domain at the end of the renewal period. A work which was copyrighted previous to the 1909 act, it would seem, should have a renewal period of only fourteen years because that period was allowed at the time the original copyright was taken out. However, according to *Silverman* v. *Sunrise Picture Corporation*[1] and *Southern Music Publishing Co.* v. *Bibo-Lang, Inc.*,[2] a renewal of copyright is a new grant of copyright, and the rights which accrue to the owner of such a renewed copyright are the rights granted under the provisions of the law which is in effect at the date of

[1] 273 Fed. 909.
[2] 10 F. Supp.

the commencement of the renewal term. The renewal of a copyright depends upon the validity of the original copyright, although it is considered as a new grant of copyright.[1]

A renewal may be obtained by the author, by anyone to whom he has sold his copyright privilege, by an employer for whom the work was made for hire and who secured the original copyright, or by the author's heirs or administrators. Under this act an employer of an author who is hired not as an independent contractor, but on a stated salary basis, is considered the author thereof and is himself entitled to a copyright of the work in question. For instance, those employed by a radio station to write scripts ordinarily have no copyright privilege in what they write, but the copyright lies in their employer. However, the mere fact that the author is an employee does not necessitate the conclusion that the copyright privilege to all said author shall produce shall be in his employer, the determinate being the intent of the parties with the presumption in favor of the employer, unless the author-employee is a so-called independent contractor, in which case the presumption rests upon the side of the employee.[2]

An author employed to write a series of scripts or a serial for a sponsor, an author employed by an advertising agency, broadcasting station, or network to produce scripts, a gag writer who originates jokes for a comedian—in each of these cases the author has no copyright privileges in what he produces unless his contract with his employer so specifies. The copyright lies in the employer. If, on the other hand, the author is considered to be an independent contractor not directly in the employ for the purpose of writing, the copyright exists in him. It is very hard to differentiate at times as to whether the author is an employee or an independent contractor. The most logical rule was laid by the New York Court of Appeals in *Beach* v. *Velsey*,[3] where it was ruled, "The test as to whether an author is an employee or an independent contractor lies in the extent of the control and the amount of direction of detail, etc., that the so-called or alleged employer exercises over the progress of the work." It is usually said that if the producer contracts for the script itself and says nothing more about it, the script writer is an independent contractor, but if the author is dominated throughout the process of completing the work, the author is usually said to be an employee.

---

[1] *Wheaton* v. *Peters,* 33 U.S. (8 Pet.) 591: 8 L. Ed.; 1055 (1834).
[2] *Uproar Co.* v. *National Broadcasting Co.,* 81 Fed. (2d) 373.
[3] 238 N.Y. 100–103; 143 N.E. 805.

Section 11 of the Act of 1909 expressly extends copyright protection to designated works of which copies are not produced for sale. Among the specified classes of work are various types of material for broadcast purposes, including lectures and addresses, dramatic and musical compositions.

Under treaty regulations, benefits of copyrights on substantially the same basis as those granted to citizens of this country are extended to approximately fifty nations, the first agreement having been made with Belgium, France, Great Britain, the British Possessions, and Switzerland in 1891.

The broadcast program script is a comparatively new form of literary expression, and it is still a controversial matter as to whether the entire program script may be copyrighted as such, or whether it needs to be copyrighted in parts. In the vernacular of the industry the two terms "script" and "continuity" are often used interchangeably. However, the law seems to make the following distinction between the two. A script is material prepared for performers, announcers, speakers, and others whose voices are broadcast and who must have before them in written form the words they intend to use in the broadcast. Continuity, on the other hand, is more like a timetable or a chronological development of the contents of the program. A continuity is necessary in order to plan and control the use of the time within the broadcast period. The continuity is the shell of the program and the script the substance thereof. A single program, therefore, may be composed of many scripts, those of the announcers, the actors, and so on.

In determining whether a broadcast script may be copyrighted, it is necessary to make a detailed analysis of it; although the Copyright Act was passed before the radio industry came into being, Section Five of the act specifies with some generality what works may secure copyright protection, and although, of course, the broadcast script is not specifically mentioned, such script may secure protection under the general classification therein. Of course those scripts which are not published are protected at common law. Authors of scripts embodying lectures, addresses, and so forth, may obtain statutory protection under Section Five-C, which provides parenthetically for registration of works prepared for oral delivery.

Continuity is the sum total of all materials and scripts in a specified program. If such continuity is coextensive with a complete dramatic program, it may be separately registered and receive copyright protection.

However, to be eligible for protection, continuity and scripts must have unity. This is a question of fact to be decided by a jury.[1]

If a script is copyrighted as a dramatic composition, the copyright owner has the exclusive right to make other forms or dramatizations thereof[2] or to convert his work into a novel or other known dramatic compositions. If the script or continuity is sold outright, this includes all the rights which the author had. It is advisable, however, in the sale or the purchase of such material, to specify definitely what rights are transferred.

If a script is registered for copyright as a dramatic work, it may not be broadcast without the consent of the copyright owner. Broadcasting is a public performance despite the fact that broadcasts are not publications under common law. It makes no difference whether such a broadcast is for profit or merely is a sustaining program, such a broadcast would violate the copyright privileges, and both civil and criminal proceedings may be instituted in such a case.[3] If the author has transferred all his rights in the script to the producer, it may be changed or altered in any way, except that it may not be distorted to the extent that it will injure the reputation of the original author. The grant of the right by an author to use a script in one particular broadcast program does not give the producer the right to use it in any other broadcast program.

If a statutory copyright is to be obtained, the author, his assignee, or employer should write to the Library of Congress, Copyright Office, Washington, D.C., and request form 12. This application form lists the various types of creative effort for which copyright may be obtained and enumerates the forms that must be filled out to obtain final copyright. When the application has been forwarded to the Library of Congress, another form is obtained to be filled out for the type of material on which a copyright is desired. This is returned with a specified number of copies of the first and best publication, together with the specified amount. The act provides that the registrar of a copyright shall receive, and the author or owner of the copyright shall pay, the following fees. If a play is to be copyrighted and to be published, it is necessary to send two copies of the play, together with $2, to the Copyright Office. The case of *Marx* v. *United States*[4] was one in which Groucho and Chico

---

[1] *Seltzer et al.* v. *Sunbrock et al.*, 22 Fed. Supp. 621.

[2] *Fitch* v. *Young*, 230 Fed. 743.

[3] *Associated Music Publishers* v. *Debs Memorial Radio Fund*, 141 F. (2d) 852; cert. denied 323 U.S. 766 (1944).

[4] *Marx* v. *United States*, 96 Fed. (2d) 204.

Marx were convicted of infringing and aiding and abetting infringement of a copyrighted radio script. All that had been done by the author was to register the script under Section U of the Copyright Act of 1909 which grants protection where no copies of the works are reproduced for sale, the only requirement being the depositing with the Register of Copyrights of a copy of such works together with a claim of copyright. (Section U only protects lectures and similar works or a dramatic, musical, or dramatico-musical composition.) The authors of the script in question had placed the script with an agent who mailed the script to Groucho. A conference of authors, Marx brothers, and gag writers was held, but no action taken. Years later, the defendants broadcast a script in which was included altered but recognizable material from the copyrighted script. The Marx brothers claimed to have forgotten completely about the original and claimed that the gagmen had been paid for the script used. The court held the defendants guilty of "piracy." The copyright ran for twenty-eight years from the date of depositing the script with the Register. If statutory protection is desired for a speech which is not to be published, the registration requires only one copy and costs only $1. No attempt is made on the part of the Copyright Office to scrutinize the work, except to ascertain that it complies with the laws prohibiting the publication of obscene matter, etc.

Infringement of a copyright exists where the defendant has appropriated copyrightable material. Once such appropriation is thoroughly established, a question of fact exists for the jury in determining whether a substantial and material portion of the plaintiff's work has been appropriated. The whole work need not be appropriated; it is sufficient that the labors of the author be substantially appropriated by another.[1]

Before using published material, such as books, novels, short stories, poetry, and other narrative material, the broadcaster should examine the copyright notice. It is generally accepted that unless the material was originally written for oral delivery it is not protected against public delivery for profit, which means broadcasting. Such material is protected, however, against the making of physical copies, dramatization, or alteration. Most copyright notices today add restrictions concerning the use of the material in the movies, on radio, and on TV. If it is not so stated they may be broadcast in their original form. The assigning of voices to parts of a dialogue might be considered dramatization. A li-

West Publishing Co. v. Edward Thompson Co., 169 Fed. 833.

cense is required for all types of plays, monologues, and other material designed for the stage or other public presentation.

The idea of the work, or, as it is customarily termed, plot, is not copyrightable, but where the expression of the fundamental theme is appropriated infringement takes place.[1] An idea is protected under the law of unfair competition. In *Fisher* v. *Star Co.*, 231 N.Y. 414 j 132 N.E. 133 (1921), the creator of "Mutt and Jeff" was protected against the defendant "passing off" as his own the idea embodied in a continuing series of cartoons.

The courts are not always quick to protect ideas, however. In *Grombach Productions* v. *Waring*, 293 N.Y. 609, 59 N.E. (ad) 425 (1945), the court refused to protect an idea submitted to an agent of Fred Waring on the grounds that the disclosure was "gratuitous" and therefore no implied contract in relationship of trust was created. This decision is difficult to accept in the light of the actual situation, since an author who submits an idea rarely does so merely seeking advice or praise.

The courts will protect ideas under the theory of an implied contract. In *American Mint Corporation* v. *Ex-Lax, Inc.*, 31 N.Y.S. (2d) 708 (1941), the plaintiff had, at the request of the defendant, given its advice, suggestions, and ideas on the manufacture and packaging of a new product. Recovery was allowed though there was no mention that the ideas had been communicated in written form. Some courts, however, will require that an idea be reduced to concrete form. The court in *Stone* v. *Liggett & Myers Tobacco Co.*, 23 N.Y.S. (2d) 210 (1940), refused recovery even though the plaintiff had submitted, at the request of the defendant, a rough script adapting her radio continuities to motion pictures and the defendant thereafter used the plaintiff's suggestions in producing some advertising motion pictures.

In *Yadkoe* v. *Fields*, 66 Cal. Opp. (2d) 150, 151 P. (2d) 906 (1944), the plaintiff submitted to W. C. Fields, by means of letters, certain ideas of humorous incidents and stated in his first letter "Whatever you think the enclosed radio script is worth is O.K. with me, Bill." Fields thereafter made use of portions of this material. The court rendered judgment for the plaintiff, saying that the circumstances raised an obligation to pay for the material used, and that ideas embodied in the material cannot be taken and used with impunity just because the concrete expressions of the author were not employed.

[1] *Simonton* v. *Gordon*, 2 Fed. (2d) 116.

In 1949 a California State Supreme Court affirmed a judgment against a network for the misappropriation of a radio program idea. The network was found to have committed plagiarism.

The result of the action and not the intention of the actor is the thing that determines the question of infringement. Where the infringement of a copyright is established, intent is immaterial.[1] If the infringement is proved, the intent to infringe will be presumed; nor does the infringing act need to be for profit.[2]

In a few limited instances a copyrighted work may be used without constituting an infringement. It was held in *Chapel & Co.* v. *Fields*[3] that the imitation, mimicry, or parodying of a copyrighted work is a fair use thereof. However, it is essential that good faith serve as a basis for the imitation and that due acknowledgment be made to the author or to the copyright proprietor. While damage awards under the statute are controlled under detailed regulations, it will suffice to say that in addition to injunction relief from infringement, the author is also entitled to damages and all profits derived from said infringement. According to Section 35 of the Act of 1909, damages for such infringements must be assessed by the court of not less than $250 nor more than $5000.

Under existing copyright laws, the scope of copyright protection to both dramatic and musical compositions and the exclusive right to produce such work mechanically is vested in the copyright holder. The right of recording or transcribing a copyright program script for broadcast purposes exists in the name of the copyright holder only. However, works in the public domain may be freely transcribed, modified, or transformed with impunity. Care should be observed, however, that a copyright arrangement of a public-domain tune is not used. In checking the availability of a selection, one must know the author, composer, publisher, and arrangement.

According to this ruling, it is a violation of the copyright to record a broadcast program, picking it up from the receiving set, or to rebroadcast such a program, to send such a program over telephone or electric-light wires, or to present it over public-address equipment or upon a television screen in a theater.

Copyright runs from the time when the first publication is made of a work to the end of the original copyright period, plus the renewal pe-

[1] *Altman* v. *Newhaven Union Co.*, 254 Fed. 113.
[2] *Pathé Exchange, Incorporated* v. *International Alliance,* 3 Fed. Supp. 63.
[3] 210 Fed. 864.

riod, if such renewal is obtained. If a compiler at the present time gathers into a single book a large number of short stories or plays and obtains a copyright for the compilation, he does not extend the copyright period of any one of the plays or stories contained in the book. His copyright is upon the compilation, the collection, rather than upon the individual contents of the book. It is safe to assume that anything written fifty-six years ago is in the public domain and may be used or adapted with impunity. Otherwise the consent of the copyright holder should be obtained before adapting or using such material.

Literary Works

Well-known authors retain legal agents to check up on radio violations of their copyrights. There has been some difference in judicial opinion as to whether the copyright law, which specifically lists "a lecture, sermon, address or similar productions, a drama or musical composition," applies also to poems and dramatizations of short stories and novels. One court has held that the recitation of a poem did not constitute a violation; however, the tendency is toward a liberal construction of the copyright law to entitle the creator "to any lawful use of his property whereby he may get a profit from it."

In 1952, a bill was introduced in Congress by the Authors League to require consent of an author before reading or quoting from any copyrighted work as a part of a radio or television program or any other public performance. Under this bill, the author shall have the exclusive right: (1) to deliver, authorize the delivery of, read, or present the copyrighted work in public if it be a lecture, sermon, address, or similar production, or other nondramatic literary work; (2) to make or procure the making of any transcription or record thereof by or from which in whole or in part, it may in any manner or by any method be exhibited, delivered, presented, produced, or reproduced; (3) and to play or perform it in public for profit, and to exhibit, represent, produce, or reproduce it in any manner or by any method whatsoever; provided, however, that the use of any extract, quotation or paraphrase from the copyrighted work used commercially or otherwise in a manner substantially noncompetitive with the copyrighted work shall not be construed as an infringing use. In brief, if a profit is involved or if the program will reduce the income of the copyright holder, get his consent.

Noncommercial or educational stations are treated with much greater liberality than are commercial stations. Literary works may be read in whole or in part, but the form of the original must not be changed by dramatization. Music background or multiple voice does not constitute dramatization. Solo reading may be safely given. However, the foregoing applies only to noncommercial television. All dramatic performances, commercial or noncommercial, must be cleared; this applies to musical comedies and film. A reading, however, is not a dramatization except in television.

News (Unfair Competition)

While a newspaper item is not ordinarily copyrighted, the newspaper may sue the radio or television station which reads verbatim a news item taken from a newspaper, under the laws relating to unfair competition. A commercial station may not appropriate the results of the efforts of a competitor, whether that competitor is another station or a newspaper. A commercial station may not read from a newspaper copy which might interfere with the sale of the paper without first securing the consent of the publisher.

Recording

Most commercial and educational broadcasters possess recording equipment and in some instances desire to make recordings for public sale. The law provides that the copyright holder of a musical selection such as a college song or march may license a manufacturer of recordings to record his selection and file notice of this license in the Copyright Office. Thereafter any other person can make recordings of the selection upon serving notice upon the copyright holder and upon paying him 2 cents for each record manufactured. Until the copyright holder has granted such an initial license no recording can be made without his consent. However, the copyright on a musical selection does not prevent the recording of adaptations and arrangements of that selection. The right to public performance of such recordings requires the consent of the copyright holder. It is dangerous to cut records of a broadcast from the air unless permission is first obtained from the holder of copyrighted selections being performed.

Special Legal Problems in Television

Television is subject to the same laws, F.C.C. regulations, and court decisions that affect radio. Licensing procedures, laws of libel, copyright protection, etc., are the same. There are, however, some problems which arise in television and are not found in radio. While not all of the problems have been completely solved by court findings, certain trends are in evidence.

Television stations use motion pictures in their program schedules. It has been decided that motion pictures, of all types, are dramas, as far as legal protection is concerned. This means that they are protected in the same way that dramas are, and permission must be obtained for their use, whether or not the performance is for profit.

Courts have held that any broadcast by a commercial station is a performance for profit since it enhances the prestige of a profit-making concern, even though it may not bring a direct financial return. Broadcasts by noncommercial, educational stations are not performances for profit. The "for profit" test affects such things as music and nondramatic literary works, but does not change the protection afforded the holder of a copyright on dramatic, musico-dramatic, or film material.

The special problems of recording rights, unfair competition, right of privacy, and contractual obligations are well treated in a pamphlet written by Professor Frederick S. Siebert, Director of the School of Journalism and Communications, University of Illinois, and published by the National Association of Educational Broadcasters, 14 Gregory Hall, University of Illinois, Urbana, Illinois. With permission, the sections on these subjects are quoted below:

IV. *Recording Rights*

A RADIO OR TELEVISION PROGRAM CONTAINING COPYRIGHTED MUSIC AND/OR NON-DRAMATIC LITERARY MATERIAL, MAY BE RECORDED ON TAPE, FILM OR KINESCOPE WITHOUT CONSENT OF THE COPYRIGHT OWNERS. SUCH RADIO OR TELEVISION PROGRAM MAY BE REPRODUCED FOR BROADCAST OR FOR OTHER PURPOSES PROVIDED SUCH REPRODUCTION IS NOT A PUBLIC PERFORMANCE FOR PROFIT.

1. The above statement does not apply to programs containing "dramatic or dramatico-musical" copyrighted works. Such works must be cleared for *all* types of performances.

2. Anyone may make a recording (transcription, film or kinescope) of copyrighted music or non-dramatic literary material so long as the purpose of such recording is not "public performance for profit."

3. A broadcast of such recording by a licensee of an educational station is not a "performance for profit" and does not require clearance.

4. A broadcast of the same type of program by a *profit-making* organization

or institution requires clearance. (It is still questionable whether a non-profit educational institution holding a commercial license must clear the above type of programs.)

5. The use of such recording for other types of presentation by non-profit organizations such as in schools, etc., does not require clearance.

6. The right to use tapes, films or kinescopes set out above may be limited or restricted *by contracts* between the broadcaster and a source of program material and also by contracts or arrangements between the broadcaster and performing artist.

7. *All* broadcast stations are required to comply with the Sec. 325a of the Communications Act of 1934 prohibiting rebroadcasts without the *express* consent of the originating station.

V. *Unfair Competition*

The law of unfair competition applies to a situation where two or more media are competing for the same audience or the same advertising revenue. It is doubtful that the courts would consider a non-commercial educational station as engaged in competition. A commercial station, however, may not appropriate the results of efforts of a competitor, whether that competitor be another station or a newspaper. For example, a commercial station may not read news from a newspaper which might interfere with the sale of the paper, without first securing the consent of the publisher.

VI. *Privacy*

Television stations, both commercial and non-commercial, are facing an entirely new set of problems in the area of privacy because of the visual presentation.

All types of stations undoubtedly have the right to broadcast pictorial material about news events and persons in the news. This right, however, does not guarantee to the station the privilege of access with cameras and recording equipment to all types of news events. News events occurring in public places may be reported both by camera and recorder. Public places include streets, parks, and other sites to which every member of the public has access without payment or restriction.

Most news occurrences, however, take place in what might be called semi-public places, such as government buildings, sports arenas, or controlled-admission halls. Television stations may report events occurring in such sites only with the permission of the authority controlling admission to the site.

The right of the individual to protest televising his person depends on whether or not he is currently newsworthy and on whether or not the camera-man has legal access to the site. For example, an educational station may not televise the picture of a person without his consent unless he is in the news. The station, however, if given permission to televise a football game, does not have to get permission from each individual player or from each member of the audience who might appear on the screen.

VII. *Contractual obligations*

A television or radio station is bound by the contractual relations which it enters into with its employees and others furnishing program materials. In the absence of a specific provision in the terms of employment, the station acquires complete rights to all materials produced by its employees for the station.

Where a station subscribes to a program service, it must comply with all conditions placed on the use of such service. If an educational station accepts a film for presentation on its station, it cannot delete the commercial announcements in the film without including a provision for such deletion in the original arrangement for the use of the film.

CHAPTER TWENTY-NINE

RADIO AND TELEVISION AS VOCATIONS

The N.B.C. lists in its "Job Inventory" in the fields of radio and television 60 classifications with 75 subheadings. The wages and salaries vary greatly between localities, and depend upon the size and income of stations, and the ability of the applicant. Some stations are unionized, resulting in an established wage scale. Therefore this chapter is concerned only with the abilities and duties of employees.

The Studio Staff

A number of factors affect the composition of a radio-station staff. In some cases, the staff personnel may be so versatile that a minimum number is necessary to operate the station. In other cases, a greater emphasis upon live programming and announcing will result in a larger staff. Among network stations of the same size there may be considerable variations in staff size depending upon the extent to which they do originating. Essentially, the size and composition of the radio station staff are products of the individual station. Each station adjusts the size and composition of its staff to its market, its income, and its program and operational policies.

The Announcer

In launching into a discussion of radio as a vocation, the logical place to start is in the studio, with the employees who come into more direct contact with the listening public. Of these persons probably the best known is the announcer. As is still the case in practically all branches of radio today, the supply of announcing talent far exceeds the demand.

The mistake that is made by most persons who desire to enter the radio profession is that they attempt to start in the more important stations.

The networks require an announcer to have had experience with an outlet station. The larger outlets suggest that the radio speaker gain training
in the small local station. The ideal way to break into broadcasting is to
start with a local station, where the work of all departments of the station may be studied. Here there is also opportunity to try out types of
programs, writing dramatic skits and continuity, and selling advertising
time. If the neophyte is successful, he may be called to an outlet station;
at least he will have a background of experience when he applies for a
position.

A few of the more fortunate beginners may find employment in the
network outlets, but such cases are rare. The place to start is at the bottom and learn the task thoroughly, so that you may be able to do not only
the job for which you have been employed but someone else's too—
for that is the way advancement is obtained. Too many beginners take a
job with a small station feeling that in such a job they will hear of other
jobs that they can try out for. This is the wrong attitude. Make a business of getting a job, and after securing one make a business of keeping
it. Do not make a business of employment seeking. Appreciate your affiliation with the small station; it has all the ramifications of a large network, only on a smaller scale and with fewer people to engage in them.

Auditions

Applications for an audition may be made in person, by telephone, or
by mail. The applicant must be persistent and not easily discouraged.
Although he may take an audition and although his name may be placed
upon record, the applicant who happens to be in the studio when a position is open usually gets the job. Some stations, in order to discourage
the applicant, will give him a pronunciation test to read such as sent
out free by the G. and C. Merriam Company, publishers of *Webster's
New International Dictionary*. In every instance the applicant will be
given sight reading and may read copy he has himself prepared. In the
outlet and local station an applicant who can double as a singer or an
actor as well as an announcer has an advantage. Some stations, over-
whelmed by applicants, refuse personal interviews or auditions and
merely listen to the voice over a telephone. If the voice is pleasant, the
applicant is invited to the studio for an audition. Many applications are
received by mail, and the writer is judged by his letter; however, he is
not employed until he has passed a studio audition.

The following is an outline of the Announcer's Test used by N.B.C.:

1. Knowledge of foreign languages. Frequently used names of foreign operas, arias, and composers. Italian, French, German titles of songs and arias. Some Spanish.
2. *a.* Verbal ad lib. To test presence of mind. Descriptions as in special event. Patrick Kelly, chief announcer, assigns subject at time of test.
   b. Mr. Kelly at time of test frequently gives list of musical numbers to aspirant and asks him to ad-lib as though program were on the air.
3. Candidate is given sample of commercial announcement to read in order to demonstrate both sales ability and diction as announcer.

Those who are intent upon becoming radio announcers should not neglect backdoor methods. Any job in a radio station is a steppingstone to the microphone. Many announcers who began in technical work have become radio personages. Important sponsors are frequently able to place capable friends in a station, and, if these friends prove their worth, they are on the job when a permanent position is open. The ability to get along with other people is first among the qualifications sought in an announcer. When one realizes how, in a radio studio, everyone is thrust into close and informal contact with others on the staff, this becomes immediately apparent. An announcer must also have that quality commonly known as "horse sense." He must be able to think quickly and clearly upon occasions, for, while things usually flow pretty smoothly, one can never tell when some split-second decision will have to be made, and he must be prepared to make it. The announcer must be able to work the switches that control the microphone. He must be calm in a pinch and able to vary the tempo of his speech in order to end a program on time.

An applicant with a university degree is given preference, and a degree is nearly a prerequisite when you consider how many college graduates are applying for radio positions. The university training gives to them the broad background required, for the radio announcer should "know a little about a lot of things and a lot about many things." He has to be versatile enough to shift from poetry to pugilism. He must know sport and musical terminology. He must have a personality that makes him a master of ceremonies one hour and enables him to introduce a religious program the next. He must be able to pronounce the names in the news, music, and art. To prepare himself for this he should have covered as much ground as is possible during his four years upon the campus. He should not have overlooked physical development, because he needs a healthy body for the fatiguing grind of a life composed of split seconds, and his body must be healthy to make his voice sound that way. The N.B.C. expects its announcers to have a speaking knowledge of several languages as well as a good background in music.

With the development of the radio receiver to its present status, where it can reproduce the sounds almost exactly as they leave the studio, the importance of a particular type of voice is not so great as it once was. Sponsors, however, demand announcers with "commercial voices," that is, voices that command attention in a friendly and unassuming manner. It should be said, however, that a pleasing voice, a "voice with a smile," is a decided asset to any radio announcer, and the lack of it is a decided handicap. In addition, the announcer must be capable of reading fluently at sight. He must speak clearly and without affectation. He must have a pleasing personality and be able to project it through his voice, as well as conform to all the requirements set forth in previous chapters for the radio speaker.

Additional qualifications for the announcer include the command of a good English vocabulary; confidence, initiative, and quick thinking to describe a program; the ability to give an impromptu talk if the emergency occurs; a good sense of news values and the ability to describe news, sports, and other special events. The ability to use a typewriter is a decided asset.

The announcer may be called upon to perform his announcing duties at any time of the day or night, and he must be willing to subordinate other interests to his job. The quality of punctuality is essential. Radio is not looking for men who make excuses. There is a certain amount of routine in the announcer's work, but, on the whole, with its irregular hours and variety of programs and artists, it is far from a routine job. Among his many qualifications are the ability to write continuity and take complete charge of a program, acting as producer or dramatic director when necessary.

Among the various tasks that may bring additional income to the announcer is that of preparing the daily schedule for the announcers, showing what programs and what standbys they are to take. In some stations the announcer who takes upon himself this task is given the title of "chief announcer." It is his duty to see that the requests of sponsors for particular announcers are satisfied, that the voices are varied upon successive programs, and that the announcers are on the job at the required times. In a small local station, it may also be his job to direct and produce the dramatic and special musical shows put on by the station, casting from members of the staff when necessary, rehearsing the sound man, cast, and music.

Next comes the announcer who is in charge of traffic, sometimes called "program director," whose duty it is to oversee the work of everyone in the studio and to see that everything runs smoothly. In many radio stations he also assumes the function of planning what will be broadcast during the intervals between commercial programs. In this capacity he receives daily-program announcements in advance from the network with which his station is affiliated, and, combining these offerings with the facilities at his immediate command, he must so arrange and organize each day's broadcast that a variety of entertainment will be provided, taking into account the types of programs that are to be presented by the network through his outlet as well as commercial programs and those sponsored by his local advertising clientele. He will be the connecting link between the artistic side of broadcasting and the business department. He will keep his finger on the public pulse and induce artists and those who are in the day's news to give personal appearances over his station. His greatest task is to keep putting originality into his day's entertainment.

The announcer may obtain his position with a local station as the result of an audition for the dramatic, vocal, or announcing field; or as the result of some connection with a sponsor or advertising agency. His first advancement in the local station is either to become assistant production manager or into sports; if he is good he steps into the chain gang. If he goes into production he advances to become local production manager, where he hesitates long and uncertainly, hoping to become manager of the station. His chances are slim. If he goes into local sports he can advance to network sports, where he finds himself stymied unless he pays the forfeit of going back into announcing for the network. The network announcer may work up to be program manager. Seldom does the announcer rise higher than production manager for the local stations or program manager for the network.

Radio Writers

The copy that the announcer reads on the air is prepared by another member of the staff, the continuity writer. For the local station usually one or two continuity writers are sufficient to handle all the work to be done, especially if that station is affiliated with a network from which it can draw programs. The continuity writer must be able to express messages in clear, concise English, and type his own copy. Since research is often required in locating and organizing material, college training or its equivalent is desirable. It will be of value if, while in school, the writer has covered a broad range of subject matter and acquired an extensive vocabulary.

The continuity writer must be able to imagine just how the announcer assigned to a particular program will read the copy, so that he or she can prepare copy best adapted to that person's manner of speaking. This author prepares commercial copy as well as announcements for sustaining programs. The continuity writer has frequently worked into radio writing from a newspaper or an advertising agency and has a knowledge of writing principles.

There is a decided shortage of good dramatic scripts written for the radio. Many try their hands at it, but in most cases they lack the natural ability to write good plays. When once a playwright's reputation is established through his products for the legitimate stage, he will not risk it on radio plays.

Writers for radio are placed in three classes, those on the staff, those under contract, and free-lance writers. Staff writers do not make so much as contract writers but they have a definite salary and work during definite hours. Staff writers prepare continuity, talks, announcements, interviews, special-occasion scripts, original plays, adaptations, and often station publicity.

Dramatic writers also sell their plays to electrical-transcription houses. A single script can be sold to a number of different local stations in widely separated parts of the country. There does not seem to be any line of advancement for the continuity writer except that he may become a better continuity writer. He is in a blind alley.

The best-paid continuity writer is one who writes for the radio comedians. Frequently he is employed by the comic for whom his gags or situations are created, while in some cases his scripts are syndicated by concerns which furnish continuity to widely separated local stations. Humorous writing is divided into situation writing and gag writing. The former consists of connected comedy, the latter of jokes. The situation writer builds skits that run for months, even years; the gag writer lives from program to program or supplies only a small portion of a single program.

The gag writer has a difficult task, for constant broadcasting has nearly exhausted the joke book, despite the fact that the gag writer usually has a huge file of jokes that have been used for centuries. Celebrated comics require as many as 50 gags for a single program. Consequently there is a demand for good writers who can be relied upon to supply both quality and quantity. Few can maintain the pace. The neophyte must establish a name for himself, submit to the comedian gags styled especially for him, and continue to write regardless of discouragements. Gags may be sold to the comedians, to advertising agencies, to syndicates, or to broadcasting stations. They must be original. The gag writer must have boundless energy, talent, persistence, and material in addition to experience and contacts before he can anticipate steady employment or a living wage. Those who can write fresh material which creates laughter and which is acceptable in both Pine Center and Boston have "names" in radio that result in excellent incomes but in little publicity.

Musical Staff

There is, of course, always the possibility of working into radio as a vocalist or musician. The musician must be versatile and capable of playing everything from symphony to jazz music. Studio orchestras are usually very carefully chosen and contain excellent musicians. They frequently make special arrangements of selections and write musical bridges and theme music, as well as background music.

The music library is a very important part of the broadcasting station's equipment and must be in charge of a capable librarian. He must have various types of indexes; the selections must be timed and classified for different kinds of programs. He will also be in charge of transcriptions and sound-effect recordings.

The Producer

The production director is sometimes called the "dramatic" director; however, production is a more inclusive term, for the producer puts together the musical program, the variety show, the dramatic performance, and in fact all productions. He generally has had dramatic training as well as experience in all the radio departments. His qualifications have been enlarged upon in a previous chapter. In local stations he may be an announcer as well as director and frequently does a bit of dramatic writing. Job advancement for the production director consists of moving into a network position. With additional features, such as commercial dramatic announcements, he has opportunities for outside income and frequently serves both a station and a transcription service. Program manager of a chain is about tops in advancement. He may be employed by an advertising agency with a production department or by one of the many agencies that specialize in production to put on a show.

The Actor

The station may have a nucleus of a dramatic staff on its regular pay roll but the majority are on call. The radio actors' training and requirements have been discussed in a chapter devoted to them. They come from dramatic schools, from stock companies and vaudeville, from motion pictures, and even from the opera. Unknowns do leap to fame after auditions. Recently a network production chief noticed a lack of available talent and developed a training department; candidates were selected from six colleges and were instructed in radio techniques and twice each week required to attend the theater, opera, concerts, motion pictures. Most radio actors belong to A.F.T.R.A. (American Federation of Television-Radio Artists). Many advertising agencies employ their own actors, and name characters are under contract. The announcer who is "a voice" in a play becomes an artist and is entitled to additional pay. Pay always includes a stipulated rehearsal period.

The sound-effects operator has been discussed in the chapter on sound effects. Frequently he is drafted from the technical staff. There is no logical advancement from his position.

Many stations operate Artists' Service Bureaus to secure employment for artists upon sustaining programs and for personal appearances. The management of such a bureau collects a commission upon the remuneration received by the artist.

Technical Staff

Each station has a staff of about six or seven licensed technicians working in shifts in the control room in connection with the studio; where the transmitting station is located away from the studio, as is becoming more and more the case, a staff of at least four men is required at the transmitter.

A licensed radio operator must be in charge of the transmitter and the S.T.L. at all times that it is in operation. Licenses for operators are granted by the F.C.C. upon the successful completion of a written examination, which must be taken at any one of several of the commission offices. This examination is highly technical and is designed to test the applicant's knowledge of the care and operation of the transmitter within broadcasting transmission laws. Such licenses are granted for a period of three years but under certain conditions may be revoked by the commission.

The qualifications for such positions have been set up as follows:

1. Foresight, judgment, resourcefulness, industry, and cooperation.
2. Knowledge of radio engineering and associated branches of electrical engineering and detailed knowledge of plant he supervises.
3. Knowledge of radio laws and regulations and possession of a radiotelegraph and/or a radiotelephone operator's license.

With the development of highly technical phases of radio, especially television, the demand for college and technical school men is rapidly increasing. The F.C.C. restrictions are becoming more rigid, thereby further increasing the need for highly trained personnel.

A college education in engineering is not essential to the radio operator. A high school background of mathematics and physics, coupled with a flair for radio and four to six months in a training school, is usually enough to enable him to get a license. The designing of radio apparatus is a different field entirely, and for it a college degree in electrical engineering is important.

In the local station the technician usually comes from a trade school to become an apprentice. He works up to chief engineer and has a better chance of becoming the station manager than anyone outside of those on the business staff. In the network setup there are monitors, field engineers, control-room head, and operations chief. Here again the engineer can rise to an executive position in the chain.

Advertising or Sales Department

The business of the advertising sales department of the broadcasting station is to sell the radio medium to buyers of advertising media in coordination with other media. All forms of advertising are worked into a unified campaign to sell a product. Broadcasting stations are going back into the business of selling direct to advertisers, adapting the radio medium to the advertising program of the sponsor. Frequently the radio merely focuses attention upon the product while visual media are used actually to sell it. Television offers both audio and visual contact. The radio station cooperates with the advertising agency, and often it is unnecessary for the sales department of the station to make the original contact with the advertiser. Practically every large broadcasting station has its central sales representatives in New York, Chicago, San Francisco, and Detroit.

The ideal salesman for the station is one who has had a university education or at least a high school training. He should also have had actual experience in selling advertising, and the training received in an advertising agency is of great value. The salesman's personality is important. The turnover in the sales department is very low. A promotion manager creates the trade for the salesman by advertising the station in trade periodicals. A few years' service upon the staff of a small newspaper is excellent preparation for radio sales work. Native ability and deftness in the turning of phrases are steppingstones.

The radio salesman must have business ability, selling ability, and showmanship. He must be familiar with all advertising media. He must have originality and imagination to create commercial programs that will attract purchasers. He should be honest with a prospective client and refuse business or programs that will be unproductive; this will result in fewer cancellations and more good friends.

In this department, also, commercial programs are planned. For example, when an advertiser has been contacted and has agreed that radio advertising would be valuable to him, he informs the sales department that he has a specific amount of money to spend and asks what he can get for that amount. What seems to be a good program is outlined, and if the client likes it the details are completed and the deal is consummated.

If you want to get to the top either in local stations or in the networks, join the sales staff. The salesman is very likely to advance to sales manager, business manager, and then to station manager. The accountant and the financial secretary are also in this line of march, according to surveys made of different stations.

Station Promotion

All major stations and networks have persons on the staff responsible for channeling information about programs, personalities and services to the public and to actual or potential sponsors. The commodity which a broadcaster has for sale to sponsors is an audience, and it becomes the function of the publicity staff to attract the largest possible audience to his station by the means at his disposal.

The publicist frequently aims at the columns of newspapers. This may be done by advertising in which the station pays for a certain amount of space and fills it with a carefully phrased message, or by creating and disseminating "news" which merits space free because it is of sufficient public interest. News is always subject to editorial rephrasing in the newspaper office; advertising is not.

The publicist constantly and aggressively must seek to contact new groups of people to whom he can transmit his message. He may use billboards, posters, car cards, magazine articles and an unending variety of "gimmicks" designed to keep the name of his organization before the public. He may even attempt to launch a word-of-mouth campaign, which is also an impelling form of publicity, but one of the most uncontrollable and dangerous forms, and one best left to the very adept.

More often than not, the publicist must create his own news. By far the greatest number of stories which you have seen or heard about broadcasting operations started as an idea in the mind of some promotion man or woman. Hence, the work requires someone with a good "news sense," a feeling for what the public wants to know and what they will read. He does not limit his activities to *reporting* what goes on at the station or network in the sense that a newspaper writer reports events, but he must have the imagination to ferret out interesting details and build them into a news report. He must also make things happen that will be worthy of reporting. Some writers have described a publicist as "a news engineer."

It is often the responsibility of the publicist to employ his own broadcasting station to publicize itself. This is referred to as "on-the-air publicity." The stock-in-trade of on-the-air publicity is the spot announcement. Referring to some future program, these spots are judiciously placed in the broadcast schedule to attract the interest of audiences at different times of the day. Another important, if less prevalent, method is to arrange for two regular programs to plug each other. One of the classics in this style of promotion was the Jack Benny–Fred Allen "feud" some years ago in which each hilariously insulted the other and the audience leaped from Benny to Allen to hear the rebuttals: publicity, simple and effective.

Staff Turnover

Since the studio routine in each station is somewhat different from that in any other, an effort is made to keep the staff, which has been trained in the routine, intact. However, as must be the case in a profession closely allied with the entertainment business, where an effort must be made to satisfy the ever-changing tastes of both the public and the advertiser, there is likely to be a moderately rapid turnover, especially among those persons directly connected with actual broadcasting. This is particularly true in the case of the smaller stations in the larger chains. The high turnover on the smaller stations arises from the fact that their talent is continually looking for something a little better, so that these stations become practical training schools.

If a person wishes to become connected with an industry which, without doubt, is still in its infancy and is rapidly growing, and one which will not soon be outdated, he can make no better choice, I think, than radio and TV—that is, if he is willing to sacrifice the glory of the public eye and take a place behind the scenes for permanence and stability of employment. If, however, he is interested in the actual broadcasting of programs, he must risk the danger of a shorter period of employment and prepare himself for some other profession to keep him alive after he has outlived his period of usefulness to broadcasting. Broadcasting has not yet discovered what to do with the weathered old voice. The considerate station owner is perplexed by his loyal old employee.

Training for Radio

In addition to the foregoing employees there are in a large station accountants, a legal staff, guest- and station-relations personnel, and a large number of secretarial and clerical employees.

In a survey recently conducted by the University of Kentucky,[1] 29 commercial stations said radio instruction was valuable for the following, in this order of importance: (1) announcing, (2) writing and commercial copy, (3) studio engineering, (4) sales, (5) news writing and reporting, (6) studio production (nondramatic), (7) dramatic production, (8) acting. The same stations rated the following courses as being important for the radio student, in this order: (1) journalism, (2) merchandising, (3) speech and the theater, (4) music, and (5) commerce.

Some comments from commercial stations are as follows:

Ninety-five per cent of all applicants for announcing work are unable to be natural, unable to project personality into their voices.

Please teach [students] to talk *TO* people—not *AT* them.

We rarely find a person who can read the news well.

[1] *What Every Student of Radio Should Know*, University of Kentucky, 1955.

College graduates can make more money for themselves if they are more "sales conscious."

Students need more down-to-earth, small-station training and thinking.

At a short-staffed, busy, heavily commercial small station, short cuts must be taken to get the job done . . . and it is absolutely necessary that every staff member be adaptable.

One of the chief shortcomings in most of the new employees we hire is lack of initiative and ability to make rapid decisions.

Suggest that you imbue all students with the importance of being rapid typists.

Suggest all liberal arts are important to study.

Women in Radio

Women in radio, like women in every other profession where men predominate, have to be twice as keen and work twice as hard as a man, under the same circumstances. They may resent this fact, but those who have forged ahead in radio have accepted it and acted accordingly. Radio has opened its doors to many women and has found them to be particularly adept at public service and as continuity writers, publicity writers, musical directors, and script writers. Advertising copy writing offers scope to the woman who can qualify, but the field of announcing and conducting radio programs has been very limited, as far as women are concerned. This has been due to several influences, among them, the reaction of women themselves to women on the radio. Only in a very few instances have women announcers been successful. Not because they were not good, nor again because their voices were not satisfactory, but because they could not physically stand the strain of day-long and night-long announcing.

Some stations hire many women and like them for many varied and interesting positions. They feel that women bring much to radio and stress the fact that women have great ability for detail and a wealth of imagination. The principal fault of women is their lack of perspective, since their ability to concentrate on details often makes them blind to the over-all picture. They do not always analyze an idea completely but, in cooperation with men who can do this well, women have proved very successful radio workers.

The training for women in radio is much the same as for men, and the requirements vary but little. However, women have one handicap which men do not have, and that is, high notes or tones in the speaking voice.

A high-pitched voice or shrill laugh will bar any woman from radio as far as working before the mike is concerned. A cultivated, low voice and pleasant, vibrant tones are a necessity for a woman in radio. Resonance is more necessary for women than it is for men. Women who plan radio careers should have frequent recordings made of their voices and should listen to them carefully and critically, to correct faults of shrillness, tone quality, and diction. Other than that, the field is open to women if they want to put the effort behind it. Television has opened many new fields to women and it is possible that this may be the opening which they have needed. Women in radio are there to stay, but they must work harder, longer, and without displaying their intelligence too much to their masculine counterparts. They must be alert, keen, and adaptable. The dictates of good taste and genuine business ability will be sufficient to assure them success in the field of radio.

Early in the life of radio, women entered into the fields of acting and singing and later into writing, but it is only recently that we find them directing, taking charge of advertising, and occupying other positions of responsibility. There is a very definite place for the ideas and suggestions of women, especially since the radio audience is largely made up of women. From early morning until dinner the majority of the listeners are women, and these women must be pleased.

Many positions in the radio field are not open to women; it might be better to say that it is difficult for women to enter certain branches of the work. Few women are engineers in radio stations, partly because most station managers prefer a man in a position of this kind. The small number of women announcers is to some extent due to the fact that they are not physically able to endure the long hours of work. However, many women would enter this type of work were it not for the prejudice the public has against women announcers. There are without doubt many programs that should be announced by women. Programs that advertise products for women are among these. By stressing voice culture and training, women may overcome the faults that often keep them from entering the field of announcing.

On the other hand, women are better able to do secretarial work in the broadcasting station than men. Many young college graduates who wish to go into radio as a career begin as secretaries and eventually work up to executive positions. Every station uses women as singers and actresses. Many stations have hostesses who meet the visitors and conduct tours through the studios. The young woman who wishes to be a hostess must have a charming personality, must be attractive, must enjoy talking with and meeting people, and must know the fundamentals of radio so that she may answer questions intelligently.

Besides acting in these capacities, women act as telephone operators, publicity writers, directors of children's programs, studio librarians, and traffic managers. Those women who actually get before the microphone give talks on household hints, fashion revues, recipes, child training, etiquette, and other subjects that are closely associated with the home and the women. Movie chats and reviews of plays are often given by women, and programs presented for the entertainment of small children are usually written, directed, and given over the air by women.

The filing and recording of fan mail is another important task performed by women. All fan mail that comes to a station must be examined, since a program is to a certain extent judged according to the fan mail it brings to the station. It is through this public reaction to radio programs that many decisions are made as to what programs and artists are to be kept before the microphone. The work of the studio librarian is also important. All scripts, music, and any other written material must be filed under every possible heading so that it can be found at a moment's notice. A file is kept of all the phonograph records and transcriptions. Dictionaries of books on pronunciation, poetry, and biography make up an important part of the studio library, and it is up to the librarian to have these ready for use at all times.

It is much less difficult for a woman to become a radio writer than an actress or a singer; and a woman in a little town or even on a farm can learn to write and send her manuscripts to the city. The small-town writer has the advantage of coming into contact with many types and many dialects. All the small-town girl needs to do is to open her eyes and ears to what is going on about her, and she may not only create plays with real live characters in them, but she may write plays that will be unusual in plot, thus making her chances for success much greater.

Today, with the increase of radio advertising, many women who have been educated with the thought of going into advertising agencies are changing their minds in favor of radio advertising. Writing advertisements for the radio and for the magazine and newspaper requires the same psychological attack, that is, appealing to the people's likes and avoiding their dislikes; the difference lies in the use of words themselves. The woman who desires to write radio advertising copy should have a good vocabulary of picturesque words and should know how to use it.

How can I get into radio work? This is the question the young woman who is interested in this field asks. The best way is to ask for any kind of job in a radio station, even if it is far removed from what she wants. The main thing is to get into the station and to learn everything possible about the profession. Girls who are willing to work at a minimum salary for the experience often eventually get good positions in the studio and make themselves indispensable to the station. Breaking into radio work is difficult but it can be done by hard work, ability, and lots of enthusiasm.

With expansion in the radio industry there are more and more places being made every year for women who have the ability and the interest in broadcasting. As women make a definite study of broadcasting as a career, more successful members of the feminine sex will be found in radio work.

Jobs in Television

Jobs at a television station include those found in a radio station. In addition, there are a number that are peculiar to television.

In the production field there are such jobs as floor manager, make-up artist, scenic designer, production coordinator, studio supervisor, film procurement, film-production supervisor, and script girl. As was mentioned for radio stations, the number and variety of jobs to be found in any given station varies considerably, depending on how much live programming is originated.

The floor manager is the director's assistant in the studio. He gives cues, and coordinates the production operation on the floor. It frequently is a steppingstone to the job of assistant director or director. A make-up artist is, of course, a specialist in make-up for television. Experience in make-up and related fields would be necessary for employment in this area. The scenic designer is an artist specializing in the designing of sets. Most scenic designers are graduates of schools specializing in this field or they have had extensive experience in stage or film design. Because of the tremendously complex procedure of getting large TV productions on the air, a production coordinator is necessary. His job is to coordinate the efforts of all the many departments concerned; director, lighting, engineering, design, scene shop, properties, etc. This requires accurate scheduling and constant checking to insure that everything will be ready when the show moves into the studio. This kind of work requires extensive experience in all phases of television or stage production. The studio supervisor is a kind of foreman who supervises the studio crew of grips, stagehands, property men, etc. For this job, too, experience in television or stage production is essential.

Nearly all stations have someone in charge of film procurement. Frequently he is called the film director, at least at the local-station level. His job is to handle the traffic in films and film programs. It is exacting work and requires a high degree of organization and the ability to look after many details. Larger stations will also engage in some film production. A film-production supervisor will be in charge of all aspects of filming programs or commercials. In smaller stations he may be a one-man film unit, even operating the camera himself. In network centers he may be in charge of a complete motion-picture crew. In any case, some experience in motion-picture making is required. Many of the larger stations supply directors with an assistant, frequently called a script girl. She will serve as a combination secretary, handywoman, fetcher-of-coffee, and will follow the script and feed the director cues during rehearsal and broadcast.

Additional technical jobs in television include: kinescope-recording engineer, who specializes in the operation and maintenance of kinescope-recording equipment; video-control engineer, who shades and controls the cameras in the control room; camera engineer, who operates and performs simple maintenance on television cameras; technical director, who serves as chief studio engineer and operates the switcher; camera assistant, who helps operate cameras by pushing cranes, handling cable, etc.; and microphone-boom operator. There are other technical jobs not strictly broadcast engineering: lighting director, who is responsible for lighting television shows; projectionist, who operates 16-millimeter and/or 35-millimeter film-projection equipment, slide projectors, and similar equipment; and motion-picture technicians such as cutter, editor, and laboratory technician. These technical jobs require extensive experience and training in the specialty. In addition, holders of these jobs are usually union members in all but the smaller markets.

GLOSSARY

THE SIGNALS, SLANG, AND ABBREVIATIONS OF RADIO AND TELEVISION

Radio Signals

During the presentation of a radio program it is impossible to instruct the artists or speakers by spoken words. Consequently a system of signs has been developed for conveying instructions. Each director, control operator, and conductor has his own "handies." A great deal depends upon the ability of the individual to convey instructions by pantomime and facial expression. The following, however, are rather well established by broadcasting stations:

If the program is moving too slowly, the production director uses a circular motion of his index finger indicating that he desires the tempo speeded up.

If, on the other hand, he desires to slow down the program, he makes the "stretching out gesture," drawing his hands apart as if he were stretching a rubber band between them.

Signs are used to direct the artist to come closer or to move back from the mike; the director uses one hand as though pulling the artist closer to or pushing him away from the microphone.

Lifting the hand, palm upward, means that the voice, the music, or the sound effect should be louder. The opposite sign, palm downward, means that it should be softer. Some directors use both hands instead of one for these signs.

At the beginning of a program the man in charge will lift one hand, as if giving a benediction, which means to stand by.

Bringing the hands slowly down, palms downward, and then spreading them apart indicates that the director desires to have the music or sound effect faded out and then "cut" or ended.

An upraised fist means that the selection is to be played right to the finish.

Crossed wrists, hands extended, indicate that the rehearsal is to be stopped so that instructions may be given over the talk-back.

Lifting the left hand and forming a circle with the thumb and index finger indicates that the director considers the program to be perfect.

Placing the index finger on the tip of the nose means that the program has ended on time or "on the nose."

Another sign indicating that the program must be cut or the musical selection

461

ended is made by drawing the hand across the throat as if the production director were cutting his throat.

To begin a scene, sound effect, or musical number, the production director frequently points his finger directly at the person involved.

The control operator or announcer will frequently show by the number of fingers the number of minutes left in the program. Crossed fingers or hooked fingers show that there is less than 1 minute.

TV Signals

In television, the same signals are used for cuing the talent. The floor manager, rather than the director, gives these signals to the talent. The director relays the information to the floor manager through the intercom system.

In addition to hand signals in television, the floor manager will frequently use cards, with letters of sufficient size to be easily read, giving time cues, wind-up, cut, etc. It is difficult always to have a clock where the talent can see it without a movement of the body or head which is quite apparent on camera. The floor manager can usually get into a position where the talent can see him without undue movement.

Basic Studio Expressions

Radio and television phraseology is decidedly local. While there are certain expressions that are used by those who are in broadcasting, in general the broadcaster and technician speak approximately the same language that is spoken by the average layman. However, there are some words and phrases that are not in the layman's vocabulary.

across the board—a program presented five days a week at the same hour.
angle shot—a camera technique in which a subject or scene is shot from an unusual or extreme angle, such as an abnormal side view, or looking down from a high boom level, or looking up from a low boom level. The angle shot is usually used for dramatic effect. [TV]
aspect ratio—the 3:4 rectangular shape of the television picture, required by F.C.C. regulation. [TV]
audio—equipment such as microphones, amplifiers, cables, and lines used in the transmission of a sound program up to but not including the transmitter. It also is used to designate the range of audible frequencies.
background—sound that forms an atmosphere behind the speech of an actor.
balance—the arrangement of musicians, sound, and speakers so that the correct impression of the location of such participants is clear to the listener; a blending of sounds to create a natural effect.
balop—a projector used for projection of opaque pictures. [TV]
band—a range of radio frequencies within two definite limits and used for a definite purpose. Thus, the standard broadcast band extends from 550 to 1600 kilocycles.
batten—a pipe suspended above the television studio flood and used for hanging lights or scenery. [TV]

beard—an error made by an announcer, such as that of the announcer who was introducing the "Early Bookworm" program: his fluff, or beard, resulted in his announcing "Burly Hookworm" program.

blasting—putting too much volume into the microphone. This formerly threw the equipment off the air, but now it is taken care of by automatic methods.

blocking—the process by which the director of a TV program arranges the movements of actors, plots positions on the set, and relates these to camera positions.

bloom—the condition of bright illumination in a picture or a portion of a picture on the picture tube, obscuring picture details. This occurs when an area of white bounces light; for instance, the white bosom front worn by a man with his black tuxedo may cause the picture to bloom and obscure the details of his face. [TV]

board—the control panels through which the program passes from the studio control board to the master control or the transmitter.

boom down—the lowered position of the camera dolly boom and consequently of the camera. The dolly boom is lowered, thereby lowering the camera, for a head-on shot or a tilted-up shot. [TV]

boom microphone—a microphone suspended from a boom which can be lowered or raised, extended or retracted by an operator to keep the microphone over the performers as they move about the stage set.

bug—some intermittent trouble in the equipment which is not easily found.

call letters—the initials assigned by the F.C.C. to identify a station. Many applicants try to get call letters that are appropriate. For instance, Battle Creek has WELL, a laundry company WASH, a lumber concern WOOD, Ohio State University WOSU, etc.

cans—the headphones that are used by the control operator.

carrier (or **carrier wave**)—the radio wave produced by a transmitter, which may be modulated to carry signals, voice, music, or pictures.

chain (camera chain, film chain)—a complete set of the camera components, including camera, power supply, and control unit. [TV]

channel—a band of frequencies assigned to a transmitter. In standard broadcasting the channel is 10 kilocycles wide—5 kilocycles on either side of the carrier frequency. In television the channel is 6 megacycles wide.

cheat—an acting technique in which the performer changes his normal body position in relation to other actors or objects within the scene, creating a more balanced picture for the television camera. [TV]

clear channel—the frequency upon which no other station in the United States is operating.

clearance, music—the obtaining of releases from the copyright holders of music or ascertaining whether the station, as the result of contractual relations with organizations holding copyrights, is privileged to present a musical selection, or whether the station is restrained from presenting a selection because it is restricted by the copyright holder or his agent.

clear a number (*see* clearance)

close-up (CU)—a camera view of a subject consisting of a head or head-and-shoulder picture, or a close view of an object. [TV]

coaxial cable—a specially designed cable which will carry picture or high-frequency signals. It consists of two concentric electrical conductors (a cylindrical conductor with a single wire centered along its length) which are separated by an insulating medium. [TV–FM]

cold—the opening of a radio program which begins without a theme, announcement, or introduction of any kind.

continuity writers—those who prepare the entire program, which includes entertainment or dramatic features, commercials, musical introductions, and the listing of music.

cover shot—a camera shot employing a sufficiently wide angle to include all of the action in the scene. [TV]

cross-fade—the gradual dimming of the volume of one sound and the increasing in volume of another sound.

cross talk—extraneous conversation picked up by the microphones which leaks in through some transmission fault.

crystal (*abbr.:* xtal)—a material, usually natural quartz, which vibrates at a fixed frequency, depending on the size to which it has been ground. It is used in radio transmitters to maintain accurate frequency and stability, and in radio receivers to improve selectivity.

cucalorus (**gobo, fuddle**)—a device used to cast shadow patterns on the wall of a TV set. [TV]

cut (**take**)—the instantaneous change from one camera to another. [TV]

cutting head—the part of a recorder which cuts the sound grooves on a phonograph disc.

dawn patrol—those announcers and engineers who open up the studio and put on the early-morning programs.

dead end—the end of the studio in which there is very slight reverberation.

dead mike—one which is not connected or is out of order.

dead spot—an unintentional silence on the air.

dissolve—a control technique by which a picture on a second camera is merged with the picture being televised, so that the second picture comes clearly into view as the original fades. [TV]

dolly—the movable stand or base on which a television camera or other apparatus is mounted. [TV]

dub, dubbing—to transfer material from one record to another or from tape to disc or vice versa.

echo chamber—a room with a great deal of reverberation which is used to create hollow effects.

f/stop—a rating scale for controlling the iris opening in a lens. Each stop doubles or halves the light admitted by the adjacent stop. [TV]

fade—(1) decreasing of volume or (2) in TV, decreasing intensity of the picture until it disappears.

fading—variation in the intensity of a received radio signal, caused by changes in transmission paths.

fading in—(1) increasing the volume in such a way that the music, sound, or speech seems to come in gradually or (2) in TV, slowly coming in from a blank screen to a picture.

feedback—the return of a sound from a loud-speaker to the microphone in which it originated—a whistling sound.

feeding—the delivery of a program over a telephone line, either to a network or to some other station.

filter—an electrical device which, under ordinary circumstances, eliminates the low or high frequencies—generally used to create the effect of a telephone conversation being heard by a person in the studio.

flat light—lighting a scene for television with over-all brightness, as contrasted with the use of modeling lights or highlighting which bring out the contours of actors and objects. [TV]

foot-candle—a measure of light intensity. The amount of light from one standard candle, at 1 foot distance, on 1 square foot. [TV]

frame—a single complete television or motion-picture scene. On a television screen 30 frames per second are shown, whereas 24 frames per second are generally used in motion pictures. [TV]

frequency response—the degree to which radio equipment responds equally well to various tones.

gain—the control of volume used in transmission.

ghost—a secondary image appearing in a television picture due to signal reflection by mountains or large buildings near the receiving antenna. [TV]

gray scale—a stepped gradation of tone from white to black, used to control the tonal quality of the picture. [TV]

high fidelity—the accurate reproduction of musical tones and equipment used to reproduce music.

iconoscope—the tube used in the first television camera to convert the light and shadow of a scene into electrical impulses. [TV]

ID—station identification—**film ID**—announcing that the program televised is or was reproduced from motion-picture film. [TV]

ike—short for iconoscope, the tube in a television camera in which the light and dark of a scene are converted into electrical impulses. [TV]

in the beam—that territory where speech is most effectively picked up by the microphone.

iris—the diaphragm in a lens which controls the amount of light which is allowed to pass through the lens. [TV]

jacks—the sockets into which the plugs of a patch cord are pushed.

jamming—transmitting radio signals in such a manner as to interfere with the reception of signals from another station.

jumping a cue—an actor has come in earlier than he is supposed to.

key station—the point of origination or the first station in the network.

kine—short for kinescope, the picture tube which transposes electrical impulses into an image in the television receiver. [TV]

kinescope—the cathode-ray or picture tube which may be used in television receivers and at monitor positions in control rooms. [TV]

kinescope recording—a sound motion picture made from the face of a special kinescope tube.

leader—(1) blank tape at the beginning of tape segment for cuing purposes or (2) blank film at the beginning of a motion picture. [TV]

level—the amount of volume noted upon the meter of the control board.

limbo—the use of a dark background for a TV program. The appearance is that the action is taking place in a void.

line—(1) a telephone wire used for the transmission of the program or (2) a single trace of the electron beam from left to right across a television picture screen. At the present time there are 525 lines to a complete picture. [TV]

live mike—a microphone through which current is flowing, sometimes called a "hot mike."

live program—one in which live performers take part, in contrast to the transcribed program, which consists in playing electrical transcriptions or recordings. In television, an "on-the-spot" program rather than the transmission of film material.

local program—one that is put onto the air by the station's own transmitter.

long shot—a camera shot that uses some degree of wideness in the horizontal angle. Differentiated from a medium shot and a close-up. [TV]

loop—a two-way circuit or line connecting the broadcasting location with the control board. A telephone line connecting a small group of stations, forming a part of a network.

master control—the control board to which all studios are connected and from which programs are sent on the transmitter.

middle break—a station announcement or identification in the middle of a program.

mixer—the panel for control and blending sound picked up by various microphones.

mobile unit—a truck with all the equipment of a television or radio station which may be driven to the scene to be televised or broadcast. It relays picture and sound back to the main transmitter.

monitor—(1) the control of the volume level by the technicians. (2) Control of picture shading as well, in the transmission of a television program.

montage—(1) the superimposing of three or more pictures by means of dissolves or (2) in radio a series of abbreviated scenes and musical bridges which give the effect of time passing.

multiplexer—a set of mirrors used to feed the output of several projectors into one film chain. [TV]

musical bridge—a musical transition used in a radio play or production of any sort.

network—a network program is one that is released over two or more stations connected by telephone lines. A network is a series of stations regularly joined by lines.

off mike—the instruction to an actor to turn his head away from the mike or speak his part at a distance from the mike to create an effect.

on mike—speaking directly into the microphone at the proper distance.

on the air—the period when a program is broadcast.

orthicon—the main picture tube used in modern TV cameras. [TV]

panning—taking in additional portions of a television scene by turning the camera to left or right in a horizontal plane. [TV]

patch cord—an emergency hookup of electrical impulses, merely a short utility cord of insulated wires used in the control room.

peak—the maximum amplitude of sound in electrical energy formed while passing through a circuit. It is the highest point reached upon the volume indicator.

picking up a cue—beginning one's lines immediately after the last word of the preceding speaker.

picture noise—spots and other irregular patterns on the television receiver picture, caused by interference signals. [TV]

piping (see feeding)

platter—a record for the phonograph, an electrical transcription, a sound-effects record, or any other disc.

plug—a short commercial that is more or less jammed into the program and given in a hurried manner, sometimes called a "blurb."

primary area—that area in which the signal of the station is heard with assured regularity.

radiator—that part of an antenna from which radio waves are emitted.

rake—used in connection with stage scenery. To rake a set is to shift its position. To strike a set, on the other hand, is to dismantle it. [TV]

read-y—an actor is reading his part rather than interpreting it.

rebroadcast—picking up a radio program from the air and rebroadcasting it over the station's transmitter. A delayed broadcast.

relay station—a station used to receive picture and sound signals from a master station and to transmit them to a second relay station or to a television station transmitter. [TV–FM]

remote—a program that is picked up from some point outside the studio. Such programs originate in dance halls, hotels, churches, educational institutions, mobile trucks, athletic fields, etc.

remote control—a program which originates outside the studios of the station.

reverse angle shot—a shot toward an actor's face from the approximate position of another actor. For example, if two actors were playing in profile the camera might shoot over the shoulder of one into the face of the other. The cut might be to the reverse of this.

riding gain—the control of the volume of a program by the engineer previous to putting it on the lines to the transmitter.

round robin—the telephone line that connects stations on a network returning to the key station.

satellite television station—a station which is programmed in whole, as far as live talent is concerned, from a network. It may supplement its program schedule by local newsreel films or remote pickups. Such a station may serve a community outside the service area of the master station. [TV]

scanning—the process of deflecting the electron beam in a camera or picture tube so that it moves at high speed from left to right in a sequence of rows or lines from top to bottom, thus changing light and shadows of a scene into electrical impulses to form the image on the receiver tube. [TV–FAX]

schematic diagram—a diagram of the general scheme of an electrical circuit, with graphic symbols representing components.

selectivity—the degree to which a radio receiver can accept the signals of one station while rejecting those of all other stations on adjacent channels.

signal—any sound that may be picked up from a station's transmitter.

society leader—film leader which is numbered at precise intervals, and is used for cuing films. An adaptation of the motion-picture industry's academy leader. [TV]

sound man—one who creates by original methods or recordings the sounds that are required in a program. He is often called a "pancake turner" if his work consists in using recorded sound.

split focus—adjustment of a television camera midway between two objects when one is in the foreground and the other in the background. Usually done in two shots to give each subject dramatic value. [TV]

sponsored program—a sponsored program is one that is an advertising program for which the station received remuneration.

station break—the pause in a network program to permit outlying stations to identify themselves.

stand-by—a program that is relied upon in emergencies, that is available when a program for an allotted time has been cancelled or, because of technical difficulties, cannot be picked up. Such a stand-by is sometimes necessary when a speaker is taken off the air because of inappropriate remarks or speech. In a case of this sort, a stand-by pianist or other performer must be on hand to fill in. **Stand by** is also the instruction given by a production manager to a cast to be ready to go on the air in less than a minute.

static—noise heard in a radio receiver caused by electrical disturbances in the atmosphere such as lightning, northern lights, etc.

stock shots—short films of people or objects which have been filed for future use. Portions of newsreels and motion pictures may then be used in the televising of studio programs. [TV]

stylus (Pl.:**styli**)—the needle used in recording sounds on recorders; usually made of sapphire.

super (**superimposure, superimposition**)—the blending of two TV pictures. [TV]

sustaining program—a sustaining program is one that is presented by radio stations without profit or income of any sort.

switcher—the mechanism used in the TV control room to cut, dissolve, fade, and super. [TV]

sync—the synchronizing pulses generated by the synchronizing generator. [TV]

tag line—a line in the copy that must be "hit" or given emphasis. It may either be the gag that ends a short scene or the climax spoken before a musical transition.

tears—a noise disturbance in a television picture which makes the picture appear to be tearing apart. [TV]

telecast—a television program, or a television broadcast. [TV]

telecasting—broadcasting a television program. [TV]

televiewers—the spectators or audience watching a television show on a receiver. [TV]

terminal—a fitting to which electrical connections are made.

test pattern—the linearity chart consisting of lines, circles, and a gray scale transmitted by TV stations. [TV]

tie-in—a commercial announcement given by the local announcer immediately after a break in a network program or at the end of a network program. It generally takes the form of naming the local merchant who sells the product that has been advertised upon the main program.

tilting—the up and down movement of a camera along the vertical axis using the friction head or cradle mount. [TV]

transition—moving from one scene to another in a dramatic presentation. A transition may be effected by a musical bridge, by fading out the speaker, by the use of a sound effect, or by some other method devised by the director.

trailer (*see* tie-in)

truck shot—a technique of dollying the television camera along a line of subjects in a scene (a chorus or group of actors) while it is on the air. [TV]

ultra high frequency (*abbr.:* UHF)—standardized to refer to frequencies of 300 megacycles and above. Waves of this frequency are called "microwaves."

very high frequency (*abbr.:* VHF)—standardized to refer to frequencies of 30 to 300 megacycles.

video—the electric currents and other equipment used in transmitting the television picture. A loose synonym for "television." [TV]

vidicon—a television camera tube found in industrial cameras and in film chains. [TV]

volume indicator—the dial on the control board on which the volume is shown.

wrapping it around the pin—means that if the speaker shouts, he will send the needle to the very top of the dial. This results in blasting.

zoom—a fast movement toward or away from the subject being photographed. May be accomplished by a rapid dolly, or by a zoom-type or vari-focal lens. [TV]

There are many other expressions that are used in the studio, but the majority of them are strictly local.

Abbreviations

The call letters of a station are written in capital letters, but, as they are not abbreviations, no periods are placed between these letters. However, there are quite a number of abbreviations in radio and television.

A.B.C.—American Broadcasting Company.

A.F.T.R.A.—The American Federation of Television and Radio Artists.

A.S.C.A.P.—The American Society of Composers, Authors, and Publishers.

This abbreviation has been generally accepted in radio fields as a word, "Ascap."

AM—amplitude modulation.

A.P.—Associated Press, News Service.

B.B.C.—British Broadcasting Corporation.

B.M.I.—Broadcast Music Incorporated.

C.B.C.—Canadian Broadcasting Commission.

C.B.S.—Columbia Broadcasting System.

ERP—effective radiated power—the resultant power determined by the rated gain of the antenna multiplied by the final amplifier power input.

ET—electric transcription.

FAX–FACS–FX–Facsimile. Fax is a trade name.

F.C.C.—Federal Communications Commission.

FM—frequency modulation.

F.T.C.—Federal Trade Commission.

I.B.S.—Intercollegiate Broadcasting System.

I.N.S.—International News Service.

I.p.s.—inches per second (tape recording).

Kc—kilocycles.

Kw—kilowatts.

LP—long-play records, microgroove.

M.B.S.—Mutual Broadcasting System.

Meg—megacycles.

Mm—millimeters.

M.P.P.A.—Music Publishers Protective Association.

N.A.R.T.B.—National Association of Radio and Television Broadcasters.

N.A.E.B.—National Association of Educational Broadcasters.

N.B.C.—National Broadcasting Company.

P.A.—public-address system.

R.C.A.—Radio Corporation of America.

R.p.m.—revolutions per minute (of a record upon a turntable).

STL—studio-to-transmitter link.

T.D.—technical director for television, sometimes called "video operator."

TV—television.

UHF—ultra high frequencies.

U.P.—United Press, News Service.

VHF—very high frequencies.

V.I.—volume indicator. This is a delicate instrument or meter on the control board which indicates the amount of volume or sound that is being fed from the microphone.

VTR—video tape recorder. First introduced by the Ampex Corporation.

V.U.—volume units (in place of decibels upon the V.I. indicator).

W.B.S.—World Broadcasting System. Frequently, in a studio, this abbreviation (W.B.S.) is made into a word "Wabus," which means that electrical transcriptions furnished by the World Broadcasting System will be used upon a program.

SUGGESTED CLASS PROJECTS

PROJECT I

WIRED WIRELESS OR GAS–PIPE STATION

Students in radio classes in many universities and colleges do not have adequate opportunity for radio experience. In some instances, the institutions do not have their own radio stations and present a limited number of programs

Fig. 95. Wired 5-watt radio transmitter. (*University of Michigan.*)

over commercial stations. In others, the radio station is a separate unit, and students are only acceptable when they have reached the graduate level.

Therefore, it seems to me that wired wireless offers a grand opportunity to students in speech departments to have the same experience that they would have upon a regular broadcasting station. This, of course, would only be possible where there were dormitories to which wired programs might be fed.

In Chap. I, I have given an outline of the cost of a wired wireless station; however, it is possible for students with an interest in radio, electricity, and equipment to build their own transmitters at very low cost. Such a project, I think, is most valuable for preparing for a future career. The best studio control operators that I have have come through such training in the maintenance and building of equipment for radio classes rather than from the electrical engineering or the electronics courses. Of course, some equipment such as a microphone, a turntable for playing records, and an amplifier would, of necessity, have to be purchased. I am presenting a schematic drawing of the wired

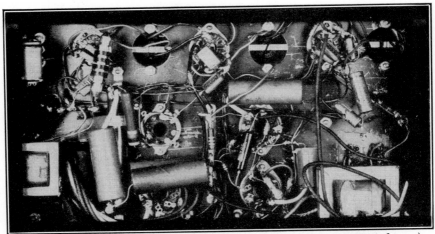

Fig. 96. Wired 5-watt radio transmitter—bottom view. (*University of Michigan.*)

wireless transmitter together with a list of materials and parts to be used in the construction of the transmitter, and also technical data for building such a transmitter. I advise a group interested in this project to get in touch with the Intercollegiate Broadcasting System, 3107 Westover Dr. S.E., Washington 20, D.C., and also to write to the Federal Communications Commission for all regulations concerning wired wireless. Go through the list of radio stations in your area and pick a frequency for a local station not being used near by; be sure to pick a frequency that will not interfere with any station that might be heard in your locality.

Here is the approximate minimum cost involved in the construction of a wired-wireless setup. Because of the variations from campus to campus of buildings and dormitories, this estimate is incomplete.

A 5-watt transmitter (Figs. 95, 96) including monitor can be built for approximately $200 to $225. The parts required for this transmitter, together with schematic (Fig. 97) and technical data, are as follows:

MATERIALS AND PARTS FOR CONSTRUCTION OF WIRED RADIO TRANSMITTER

C1	250 MMFD	R1	390	½W
C2	250 MMFD	R2	7500	10W
C3	250 MMFD	R3	0.25M	½W
C4	250 MMFD	R4	390	½W
C5	250 MMFD	R5	22,000	½W
C6	250 MMFD	R6	0.25M	½W
C7	250 MMFD	R7	390	½W
C8	250 MMFD	R8	22,000	½W
C9	250 MMFD	R9	1000	½W
C10	250 MMFD	R10	0.25M	½W
C11	250 MMFD	R11	50,000	½W
C12	10 MFD	R12	0.25M	½W
C13	.01 MFD	R13	400	½W
C14	8 MFD	R14	10,000	½W
C15	8 MFD	R15	50,000	50W
C16	8 MFD			
C17	8 MFD			
T1, T2, T3	600 Kc IF transformers			
T4	500-ohm line to grid			
T5	10,000-ohm to 10,000-ohm modulation transformer			
T6	600 v, 5 v, 6.3 v, 150 ma. PWR transformer			
CK1	5 henry 50 ma. filter choke			

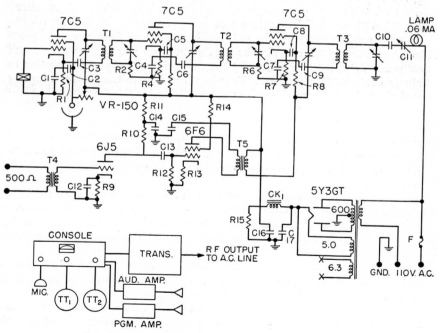

FIG. 97. Wired radio transmitter—schematic diagram.

WIRED RADIO TRANSMITTER

(Technical Data)

This transmitter is basically a crystal-controlled, high-level modulated radio-frequency amplifier which is coupled to the 110-volt alternating-current power line.

Tube complement:

(1) 7C5 crystal-controlled oscillator

(1) 7C5 buffer amplifier

(1) 7C5 radio-frequency amplifier

(1) 6J5 speech-amplifier driver (class A)

(1) 6F6 modulator (class A)

The speech and modulator unit is resistance-coupled and fed through a 500-ohm line transformer. Maximum input for 100 per cent modulation is 4 decibels. Input level is controlled by any conventional mixer amplifier unit preceding the transmitter. The radio-frequency portion comprises a crystal-controlled oscillator with a 200-kilocycle crystal tuned to the third harmonic or 600 kilocycles. This is fed to a buffer with tuned circuits at 600 kilocycles. The buffer output is fed to the radio-frequency amplifier with plate and screen modulated simultaneously. Any desired frequency may be achieved by selection of the proper crystal. One stage is provided between the oscillator and amplifier to provide isolation and to prevent interaction which might produce carrier shift with high percentages of modulation. The oscillator is stabilized with a VR–105 tube regulating the screen voltage.

All parts used to construct the unit can be purchased from any radio parts distributor. The crystal can also be purchased from war surplus at a much lower price. Tetrode tubes are used throughout the radio-frequency section to eliminate neutralization problems. Tuned grid and plate transformer coupling is used throughout. Transformers are not available for this frequency but can be easily made by removing about 40 turns from each winding of standard 456-kilocycle IF transformers. The revision is made simpler by the use of an L–C checker to find the correct ratio of inductance and capacity. If a higher frequency is desired, some of the capacity will have to be removed to maintain a high enough "Q" in the circuit. The cost of all parts is approximately $85.

Components are mounted on a 12- by 7- by 3-inch chassis. Care must be taken to keep the power transformer away from the 500-ohm line input transformer. Mount it below chassis or at right angles to prevent hum pickup. If the second and other even-order harmonics prove troublesome, the output circuit should be series-wave-trapped to eliminate them.

No ground is necessary. After the transmitter is installed, and all transformers peaked, it is ready for operation. If it is moved to a new location, the coils must be repeaked to match the new line antenna.

Radio-frequency output is between 3 and 5 watts with a radiation pattern of 262 feet radius at 600 kilocycles, ample to cover a large building, but within legal limits. Field-strength measurements should be made to confirm this.

In addition to the transmitter, the station should have:

2 microphones, one with desk stand and cable.......each, $95 to $120
2 phonograph turntables ....each, $50 to $100
2 phonograph pickups ....each, $25 to $75
2 preamplifiers, mixer, VU meter.................each, $50 to $175
2 monitor amplifiers, one for program, the other for
  audition ....each, $100 to $200
2 monitor speakers in brass reflex enclosure.........each, $80 to $150

The probabilities are that some member of the group will have an AM receiver, AM–FM, or FM receiver so that you can pick up programs and rebroadcast them. One great advantage is that you can pick up an FM program and broadcast it by wire on an AM frequency so that students in the dorm with only an AM portable can receive the FM programs.

This cost estimate does not include studio sound treatment. No provision is made for recordings. Borrow them from fraternities, students, and the record shops and give the shop a commercial plug. When you start putting on dramatic shows you will need sound effects. If you plan to pick up man-on-the-street programs or athletic events, you will need a remote amplifier. These bits of equipment can come later. Some student groups sell time to local merchants and earn money to buy additional equipment.

PROJECT II

VISUAL AIDS

Here is a pleasant project. Have some parties. No broadcaster is really good unless he enjoys people and is a pleasant conversationalist. He must enjoy life in order to make his listeners enjoy themselves. The playboy makes a good emcee just as long as he doesn't mix pleasure with business. However, this project is more than a social activity, for it is planned to introduce visual aids. All members of the class will be interested in the project, but a small group should be assigned to carry it out—arrange for a sound projector, borrow films, find a meeting place, etc.

Here are the available motion pictures and filmstrips, the motion pictures being identified by "MP" and the filmstrips by "FS." Names of producers —and of distributors, when producers and distributors are not the same—are also given in abbreviated form. These abbreviations are explained in the list of sources at the end of the list of visual aids. Unless otherwise indicated, the motion pictures are 16-millimeter sound black and white and the filmstrips are 35-millimeter black-and-white silent. The length of the motion pictures is given in minutes (min), that of the filmstrips in frames (fr). Most of the films can be rented from the local or state 16-millimeter film libraries.[1]

[1] A nationwide list of local film sources is given in *A Directory of 2660 16mm Film Libraries* available for 50 cents from the Superintendent of Documents, Washington 25, D.C. For other films one can also consult the latest annual edition and supplement of *Educational Film Guide* and *Filmstrip Guide*, published by the H. W. Wilson Co., New York. The *Guides* are available in most school, college, and public libraries.

Basic Principles of Frequency Modulation (MP, USA/UWF, 31 min) Describes what "FM" is in radio communication, how it is used, and what its advantages and limitations are.

Best in Television (MP, IVT, 10 min) Sequences from television programs including a meeting of the Assembly of the United Nations, Missouri River flood, Arturo Toscanini, baseball, Groucho Marx, and others.

Four Ways to Drama (MP, UCLA, 33 min) A short dramatic episode is presented in four different versions—for stage, radio, television, and motion pictures—using the same plot and characters. Illustrates the requirements of each medium as a contrast and comparison study.

Go Slow on the Brighton Line (MP, Kinesis, 6 min) A camera in the locomotive of a train from London to Brighton shooting at two frames per second compresses the 51-mile trip into four minutes at an apparent speed of 750 m.p.h. Produced by BBC Television.

How Color Television Works (FS, McGraw, 45 fr) Explains the basic principles of color television, and describes TV cameras and the transmission of color TV scripts. Produced by Popular Science Publishing Co.

How Television Works (MP, UWF, 10 min) Explains the elementary principles of television by following, mostly in animation, the path of a TV show from the studio to a family living room.

Independent Commercial Radio Station (MP, USIA/UWF, 18 min) Shows the day-by-day operation of a local commercial radio station in the United States.

It's Time for Everybody (MP, Movies, 16 min color) Story of radio's importance in America's changing economy. Animated cartoon sponsored by the Columbia Broadcasting System.

The Movies and You (MP series, TFC) Series of films, 10 min each, depicting various phases of the motion-picture industry. The following ones are applicable to the production of television programs:

> *Art Director*
> *The Cinematographer*
> *Screen Actors*
> *Screen Director*
> *Screen Writer*
> *Sound Man*

Naturally It's FM (MP, GE, 17 min color) Explains in nontechnical language the differences between AM and FM methods of radio broadcasting.

NYU Television Workshop (MP, USIA/UWF, 9 min) Depicts the work of a television workshop at New York University; describes the various crafts required in the production of a dramatic television program; also shows students at work in one of New York's commercial television studios.

Radio Broadcasting Today (MP, McGraw, 19 min) March of Time review of radio entertainment and the radio industry.

Television Is for You (MP, NPAC) Four films, 15 min each, showing the principles and practices used in teaching television to extension specialists and agents.

Part 1. Illustrates what television can do in adult extension education programs.

Part 2. Illustrates types of shows extension workers can do.

Part 3. Demonstrates tips on planning and presenting TV shows.

Part 4. Stresses the "you" element and demonstrates action, motion, and conduct before the TV camera.

Test Films (MP, SMPTE) Number of films produced by the Society of Motion Picture and Television Engineers to test the performance of projection and sound equipment. List of titles available from SMPTE.

Tune in Tomorrow (MP, Movies, 13 min color) Points out the influence which advertising, including radio, can have in continuing America's economic expansion. Animated cartoon sponsored by the CBS Radio Network.

PRIMARY SOURCES OF FILMS

GE—General Electric Co., 1 River Road, Schenectady 5, N.Y.

IVT—Institute of Visual Training, 40 E. 49th St., New York 17, N.Y.

Kinesis—Kinesis, Inc., 54 W. 47th St., New York 36, N.Y.

McGraw—McGraw-Hill Book Co., Text-Film Dept., 330 W. 42nd St., New York 36, N.Y.

Movies—Sterling-Movies U.S.A., 205 E. 43rd St., New York 17, N.Y.

NPAC—National Project in Agricultural Communications, Michigan State University, East Lansing, Mich.

SMPTE—Society of Motion Picture and Television Engineers, 55 W. 42nd St., New York 36, N.Y.

TFC—Teaching Film Custodians, Inc., 25 W. 43rd St., New York 36, N.Y.

UCLA—University of California, Los Angeles 24, Calif.

USA—U.S. Dept. of the Army, Washington 25, D.C.

USIA—U.S. Information Agency, Washington 25, D.C. (Films distributed in the U.S. by United World Films.)

UWF—United World Films, Inc., 1445 Park Ave., New York 29, N.Y.

PROJECT III

AUDITIONS

If a radio station is seriously considering employing an announcer, it will give the applicant a practical audition. This audition will consist of different types of copy that the announcer will be required to read. The announcer must be flexible in his style so the audition will consist of disc jockey and obituaries, of announcements addressed to children and news programs.

This project consists of students judging the auditions of their classmates, using the talk-back equipment when it is available. The students should build a file of audition evaluations for all in the class so that the producer can select from the cards his announcers. Figure 98 is the audition analysis used by C.B.S.

	Rating:							
Sample:	1	2	3	F	Comments:	Make-Up:	Comments:
Ad Lib.						Voice	
News						Pronunciation	
Music Serious						Enunciation	
Music Dance						Style	
Music Misc.						Tempo	
Spl. Annct.						Personality	
Speaker						Imagination	
Com'l. Gen.						Variety	
Drama 1:						Color	
Drama 2:						Pace	
Com'l. Inst.						Delivery	

Columbia Broadcasting System, Inc.
ANNOUNCER AUDITION ANALYSIS
F199-8-16-44
Name:
Address:
Telephone:
Classification:
General:
Date: Heard By: Original Classification:

FIG. 98. Announcer's audition analysis.

Types of copy to be used in these auditions follow. Read the whole thing, not only the parts that are obviously announcer's copy.

This is _____, speaking.

Announcers on the _____ station _____ are called upon to exercise their talents in a variety of ways. An announcer may be required to narrate a children's story, deliver an ad-lib commentary on convocation or graduation, read news, and assume the responsibilities of a master of ceremonies on a classical music program. For instance, here is a sample of the news he may be asked to read:

Good morning. This is John MacVane in the N.B.C. newsroom in New York with your World News Roundup. The Communist espionage hunt continues in Washington and New York—concentrating on secret papers taken from government files. Secretary of State Marshall is recovering from a major operation—and may give up his post soon.

The United Nations postpones debate on the Italian Colonies—regarded as a favorable move for Italy. This morning we expect to hear from Washington, from Berlin, Rome, and Buenos Aires. Now your announcer.

First spot   8.0115–8.0315

In both New York and Washington, investigations of alleged Communist espionage in the Government are being pressed forward rapidly this morning.

The New York inquiry is being conducted by a Federal Grand Jury and the United States Attorney behind closed doors. For two days the Grand Jury has been listening to testimony by the two chief figures in the case, Whittaker Chambers and Alger Hiss. But little has been made public. United States

Attorney McGoey will only say that the grand jury is turning up some real evidence and the investigation is closer than ever before to a real conclusion.

It is being said at the New York Federal Courthouse that every effort is being made to obtain quick indictments. When the indictments are returned and the matter comes to open court, there will probably be no lack of news.

In the meantime, the Un-American Activities Committee of the House of Representatives is conducting its own investigation in Washington. The Committee suffers from no inhibitions about publicity and conducts its proceedings accordingly.

Today, for instance, the Committee says it is hunting for two unnamed men accused of taking secret papers from Government files and hopes to have them testify this morning. The Committee is also after a third for later questioning. All three—it is said—were mentioned in New York on Monday by Whittaker Chambers, the ex-Communist journalist who produced the microfilms of documents abstracted from the State and Navy Departments.

Yesterday's most spectacular development was the fact that Assistant Secretary of State Peurifoy identified the documents as most secret and said the fact they were taken out of the State Department ten years ago meant American Government codes were being read by foreign nations during that period.

Mr. Sumner Welles, who was Undersecretary of State during 1937 and 1938, also testified that possession of the documents—along with the originals in code—would have permitted the code to be deciphered. Both Peurifoy and Welles cautioned the Un-American Activities Committee against making the papers public on the ground that national security might be endangered and this country be embarrassed in its relations with another. The Committee— with such a warning before it—apparently agreed not to publicize the documents.

There is other important news in the Capital today—and to give it—Lief Eid in Washington.

(off at 0315)

Second spot   8.0445–8.0630

Washington has had its doubts about the future of the Congressional Un-American Activities Committee. It has been accused of making spectacular charges that it never backed up—accusing people without giving them a chance of reply. The chairman of the Committee at the moment, Representative J. Parnell Thomas, is under indictment on charges of defrauding the Government.

The Committee and its staff may believe that the Committee's future existence may depend on its present investigation.

Today a bishop declared that the Un-American Activities group is itself un-American for trying to pin a Communist label on some church men and church grounds.

Bishop G. Bromley Oxnam of the Methodist Church said the business of naming and calling men Communist or any other label without first giving the person a chance to answer the accusations is in itself un-American. He spoke of recent statements by the Committee that Communists have infiltrated the nation's churches. The Bishop said the Methodist Council of Bishops rejects Communism—but will not remain silent when confronted by practices at once un-American and a threat to a free church and a free society.

And for our news from abroad today—in Paris, the United Nations General Assembly today voted to postpone debate on the question of the former Italian Colonies until the Assembly reconvenes in New York on April first. The Assembly defeated by 31 to 11 a proposal to discuss the question before the UN adjourns this week end. The big five countries split on the vote. Russia and Britain wanted to take up the matter now—the United States, France, and China wanted the delay.

The United Nations Security Council won't delay its activities until April. It remains in permanent session and will be back in New York in January, still trying to do something about the Russian-American dispute on Berlin.

For a direct report from that city now—we'll hear Ed Haaker in Berlin.

(to Haaker at 8.0630)

Third spot   8.1130–.1230

From China today comes a report that some units of a Chinese Nationalist Army group trapped and surrounded by Communists between Suchow and Nanking have been able to break out southward.

The report was not confirmed by the Government's military news agency, but it was said the units that broke through the ring had made contact with other Nationalist Units advancing northward.

The Army group concerned in the reported breakout was the Twelfth Army group which has been encircled for two weeks in a small pocket and has been running short of food and ammunition.

But three more Chinese Nationalist Army groups—the bulk of the divisions that garrisoned Suchow—are still encircled by Communist forces. The Communists are reported to be strengthening their hold on these three Army groups of Chiang Kai Shek. If the Communists destroy them, the major defense of Nanking will be gone.

There were hysterical rumors in Shanghai that American Marines would be landed to protect the city. American officials immediately denied the rumor.

More news in a moment. In the meantime, your announcer.

End Spot   8.1330—.1425

The Jugoslav Communists of Marshal Tito are admitting today that much of the aid their country receives comes from the United States. Until Tito's disagreement with Moscow, the tendency in Belgrade was to conceal and minimize what the West had done for Jugoslavia.

The Jugoslav Communist paper, Borba, today asserts that the huge bulk of money and supplies reaching Jugoslavia from outside comes from American residents and organizations—a total of fifteen and a half million dollars' worth in the last three years.

In Australia today—the UN Economic Commission for Asia today admitted the Indonesian Republic as an associate member. Holland does not admit the

Republic has the right to act as an independent unit in international affairs and the Dutch delegation walked out of the UN Commission in protest. The Dutch said the UN group's action affects delicate negotiations between Holland and the Indonesian Republic.

And that's your World News Roundup. This is John MacVane saying goodbye from the N.B.C. newsroom in New York.

A short time later, the same announcer will conduct a program of popular music with a format as follows:

Yes, it's Campus Varieties, a full half hour of your favorite transcribed music, both old and new. Featuring the Campus Varieties orchestra, the Golden Gate Quartet, Johnny Guarnieri at the piano, the beautiful voices of Louise Carlyle and Willard Young and the barbershop harmony of the Knickerbacker Four Quartet, all under the direction of Norman Cloutier. (*Pause.*)

And so the curtain rings down on our Campus Varieties Stage for this afternoon. All the gang (Norman Cloutier and the Campus Varieties Orchestra, the Golden Gate Quartet, Johnny Guarnieri, Willard Young, Louise Carlyle, and the Knickerbacker Four Quartet) is going to be back with us tomorrow at 3 o'clock with more of your favorite transcribed music both old and new. Until tomorrow then, this is _____, reminding you to stay tuned now for Concert Highlights which follows immediately.

Within half an hour or so, our typical announcer will work with a classical music script. He should be familiar with the pronunciation of composers' names: Wagner, Shostakovich, Debussy, César Franck, Albeniz, Ibert, Mascagni, Buxtehude, and many others. He should be familiar with a variety of musical terms, such as: *un poco moderato,* allegro, coloratura, viola, pianist, and recitative. He may be called upon to announce *Die Götterdämmerung, Une Vision Fugitive,* or an aria from *I Pagliacci,* or discuss the respective merits of singers like Ezio Pinza, Tagliavinni, and Enrico Caruso.

From a classical music program our versatile announcer will turn to a children's story. His introduction will probably go something like this:

Say there, boys and girls, do you like to hear music? You do—Oh, but what kind you say! Well, I'll bet we've got just the kind of music you'd like to hear. Yes, but what—well, say, you just want to know everything, don't you? Well. I'll tell you just what music we've got for you for the next fifteen minutes. You know Frank Luther, don't you? Why sure! Well, Frank has a few records that he's made, and we're going to play them for you. Sounds pretty swell, doesn't it? He's got some nursery rhymes, and some of those swell Winnie the Pooh songs. Might tell you the names of a few of them—remember the Buckingham Palace, or Hoppity, or maybe the King's Breakfast? Well, here they are just for you to listen to. So Frank, suppose you just get up to the microphone and sing them.

From time to time all announcers find themselves obliged to ad-lib in order to fill time between programs, describe local color at a football game, or interview visiting celebrities. For instance, when asked to describe the studio in which he is sitting and all that is visible to his eye, he might say something like this:

AD-LIB FOR ONE MINUTE

If the applicant is seeking a position with a commercial station he will be tested with various types of commercial copy.

FIRST AID for cold discomfort—Alka-Seltzer! FIRST AID for acid indigestion—Alka-Seltzer! FIRST AID for headache—Alka-Seltzer! Yes, this is *one* product *so* good for *so* many common ailments that you'll never want to be without it. Alka-Seltzer can give you really fast, really effective relief from headache, acid indigestion and cold discomfort. That's why I want to suggest that you keep an ample supply of Alka-Seltzer on hand—at home always, and where you *work*, as well. Then if a headache should come along, if something you have to eat or drink brings on acid indigestion, or if you're troubled with the discomfort of a cold, Alka-Seltzer can help you feel better *FAST!* Alka-Seltzer's alkalizing properties can settle the upset of acid indigestion, and its analgesic—sodium acetyl salicylate—offers pleasant, fast relief from headache and the ache-all-over feverish misery of a cold! Yes, keep prepared with Alka-Seltzer. Buy TWO packages instead of one—for an extra package on the side keeps a family well supplied. An extra package of Alka-Seltzer!

The applicant should be prepared to be a lively emcee on a give-away program.

KING: Is there a student in the house?

AUD: YES!

KING: Well, let's all study about CINDERELLA WEEKEND.

Applause

KING: Hi, everybody, this is Johnny King. . . .

ZIM: and Dave Zimmerman . . . Your quizzing coachmen welcoming you to another CINDERELLA WEEKEND program. Someone here today enjoying PUMPKIN luck may be the very lady who will win a complete new outfit and a grand all-expenses-paid weekend vacation in New York for two. Each day we find a new CINDERELLA and on Friday the four winners battle it out to decide which of them will get to town on that wonderful CINDERELLA WEEKEND.

SIGN OFF

WUOM, the University of Michigan, Ann Arbor, now leaves the air until _____ o'clock tomorrow (Sunday). WUOM, owned and operated by the Regents of the University of Michigan, operates on an assigned frequency of 91.7 megacycles, channel 219, with an effective power of 115,000 watts. KQA—61, the studio-transmitter link operates on 950 megacycles. WUOM and KQA–61, with studios in the Administration Building and transmitter at Peach Mountain, are licensed by the Federal Communications Commission. On behalf of the entire staff, this is _____ bidding you a very pleasant good evening.

The more auditions you take before you take *the* audition the better you will do. Don't worry about the station audition. Those you have in the classroom are more tricky than the professional ones, but grades are easier to get than jobs. The station will not be impressed by what you were in college but only by what you can do. Leave your Phi Beta Kappa key at home. Study the station before the station studies you. You can't tell the station what you are; you have to prove it.

PROJECT IV

AUDITIONS—ACTORS

Mr. James Schiavone, former production director, WUOM, built up a comprehensive audition for those being considered for dramatic parts. Each piece of copy was selected by him to bring out one distinct emotion or re-action, intensity, trait, interpretation, or age level from the auditionee. Most of the copy is flexible to the extent that the age range may be variable as necessary. Most of the scenes are long, so that if the director wants to hear a particular auditionee attempt to develop a characterization fully, he may hear it through; otherwise, he may stop the scene at any point short of the end. Mr. Schiavone feels that this rather inclusive dramatic audition includes every-thing which is usable in disclosing any specialized talent. In many cases, audi-tionees may do a satisfactory job with monologue type of material and yet prove unsatisfactory in actual dramatic scenes working with others because of their lack of "contact," poor technique of picking up cues, motivating natural ad-libs not indicated in the script. Of course, the person taking the audition must be briefed about the character he is to create—age, physical condition, background, education, social environment, etc.

NARRATIVE (MALE) STRAIGHT

NARR: I am not mad—and I am not dreaming. Tomorrow I die, so today I must unburden my soul. My purpose is to place before the world—plainly and without comment—a series of events. Events which have terrified—tor-tured—destroyed me. I will not attempt to explain them. To me they have presented only horror—to others they may seem less terrible. Perhaps someone less excitable than I will find in them nothing but a succession of natural causes and effects.

From my infancy I have been known for my quiet, unexcitable disposition. I was especially fond of animals, and was allowed by my parents to keep a large variety of pets. I spent most of my boyhood with them, and was never so happy as when feeding and petting them. This peculiarity in my character grew with my body, and after I had grown to manhood, my animals were my principal source of pleasure. To those who have known the affection of a faithful dog, I need hardly explain this feeling. There is something in the unselfish and self-sacrificing love of an animal that goes far beyond the thing that men call friendship. I married early, and was happy to find in my wife a disposition like my own. She shared my liking for domestic pets. We had birds, goldfish, a fine dog, rabbits, and a small monkey. One day my wife came into my study, and standing in the doorway (*Fades*), spoke to me as I turned.

NARRATIVE (MALE) INTENSE–FEAR

NARR: Someone was following me. Someone was following me as I walked through the woods to my friends' house. I was sure of it, though it was so dark I saw nothing when I looked around. But I could hear. And I'd been hearing new, strange sounds ever since I left the avenue and struck out over the short cut to Harrison Street. Why had I taken the short cut . . . when I knew . . . the papers were full of it . . . that the convict who'd escaped from State's prison—a few miles away—was still at large. I'd taken this short cut many times . . . but never before had I heard that odd crackling noise behind me.

There! I heard it again. And it stopped again. As though someone stepped on a branch in his path . . . and then waited for the sound to die away. I hurried. But I was afraid to run. The woods ahead were too black. If I should stumble and fall . . . or if whoever was following me should see me run and run after me . . . faster than I . . . reach me before I came to the stretch of treeless flat ground between the woods and Harrison Street . . . I hurried, silently. Behind me came the crackling noise again . . . and it sounded to me as though whoever was following had begun to hurry, too. I walked faster . . . knocking against a tree and scratching my arm . . . feeling the lash of a swinging branch against my face . . . stubbing my foot on a twisted root . . . and all the time hearing that noise more clearly behind me. And then I began to run. I couldn't help it . . . it was foolish . . . but I couldn't be caught there . . . robbed . . . slugged . . . maybe killed. I ran (*Panting*) and the thing happened that I knew would happen . . . I ran against a rock and fell over it and lay breathless on the damp earth . . . I lay there on the ground, listening. My ankle throbbed. I didn't know for a moment whether I had sprained it or only turned it, but it didn't matter. The noise behind me was gone.

NARRATIVE (FEMALE) PLAINTIVE TO BUILD

JANE: I believe I was already half in love with him then. In the weeks that followed, when evening after evening I sat with him by the fire in the library, I came to love him deeply and miserably. Miserably, because I knew I was to him only the paid governess to his ward. Each night, after I left him, I tossed sleeplessly on my bed, telling myself that I should go from Thornfield now, before I made myself foolish with my love. It was on one of those wakeful nights that I heard . . .

MRS. ROCHESTER: (*Wild laugh off mike*)

JANE: (*Continuing without pause*) . . . Grace Poole laughing close to my door, and more wildly than I had ever heard her. So wildly that I was frightened. I sat up in bed. The laughter faded away down the hall. The house was quiet then. I slipped on my robe and walked to my door to make sure it was locked. When I reached the door, I smelled smoke. I opened the door quickly. Smoke poured in from the hallway . . . smoke that came from Mr. Rochester's room. I ran down the hall, into his room, seized a pitcher of water, and drenched the bed and Mr. Rochester with it . . . (*Calling*) Wake, Mr. Rochester! Wake!

DIALOGUE (ONE MALE, TWO FEMALES) STRAIGHT

MRS. BENNET: I, for one, though it was a lovely ball, Elizabeth, and I saw nothing out of the way in anything Mr. Collins said last night.

ELIZABETH: He was ridiculous.

MR. BENNET: It's his nose. It wriggles when he speaks.

ELIZABETH: If it were only that, father. But he took it upon himself to address the whole party and explain why he, a parson, finds no harm in balls.

MR. BENNET: Very kind of him.

MRS. BENNET: He's an excellent young man, and quite right, and I do think, Elizabeth, you might cease making fun of a guest in our house. It isn't polite, and besides he might come in here any minute, and furthermore, under the circumstances, it isn't proper in you.

ELIZABETH: What circumstances?

MR. BENNET: He invited himself here. And besides he's walking in the garden, and furthermore—furthermore, Mrs. Bennet, I thought you, yourself, disliked him heartily.

MRS. BENNET: I do—I did—but now—. Oh, Elizabeth, my dear daughter—

ELIZABETH: You're not being very clear, mother.

MRS. BENNET: Oh, please have pity on my nerves! Why shouldn't I dislike a man who's going to turn us all out of house and home?

MR. BENNET: Well, since it won't be before my death, I should think Elizabeth could make fun of him until then.

MRS. BENNET: Mr. Bennet! Have you no perception? Oh, to be married to a man who encourages his daughter to mock the very man who'll inherit his estate . . . who jokes about the time his wife and daughters will live in want . . .

MR. BENNET: It may be some years yet, my dear. I'm still in tolerably good health. Which I'll try to keep now, by spending a quiet morning in my study. (*Fading*) Excuse me, my dears.

Sound: Door open and close, slightly off mike

ELIZABETH: (*With sound*) I think I'll go to my room now, too, mother.

MRS. BENNET: Oh, no, you mustn't. You must stay here in the drawing room with me, Elizabeth. I don't want to sit alone.

ELIZABETH: You won't. Mr. Collins has just turned in from the garden and is coming this way.

MRS. BENNET: Precisely why . . . Elizabeth! Come back!

ELIZABETH: (*Fading slightly*) But I don't care to see Mr. Collins . . .

MRS. BENNET: Elizabeth! I command you.

ELIZABETH: (*Slightly off mike*) What difference . . .
(*Fading on*) Oh, dear, there's no escaping now. Here he comes.

MRS. BENNET: (*Raising voice*) Mr. Collins? Do come in the drawing room and sit with us. (*Low*) Look civil, Elizabeth.

DIALOGUE (TWO FEMALES) CHARACTER

MRS. BENTON: Put that one over there, Maggie. Pack it down good and tight. . . . Not too tight though.

MAGGIE: Whew! I'm tired, Mama. Can't we rest a while?

MRS. BENTON: We're almost through now. We'd better get done before it gets too dark to see.

MAGGIE: My back's almost broke in two from bending over so long.

MRS. BENTON: Well all right. Set down an' rest then. I'll finish 'em up.

MAGGIE: Look Mama! There she is!

MRS. BENTON: What, who?

MAGGIE: That woman in mourning. The one who's been putting flowers on Bill Anderson's grave.

MRS. BENTON: Yes, I see her now. Poor soul. I wonder who she is. Bill Anderson didn't have no relatives that I ever heard of.

MAGGIE: Maybe it's his widow.

MRS. BENTON: His widow? Why, Maggie Benton, you know as well as I do, Bill Anderson was a bachelor.

MAGGIE: Maybe she was his secret wife, like in the books sometimes, an' she was rich an' he was a poor orphan an' they couldn't let her folks know, an'—

MRS. BENTON: Maggie! I declare, I'll have to set my foot down on them trashy love stories you been readin'. Such ideas!

MAGGIE: (*Stubbornly*) Well, it could happen like that an' who else would be puttin' flowers on Bill Anderson's grave?

MRS. BENTON: That I don't know. But we'll find out in God's good time.

MAGGIE: Couldn't we ask her?

MRS. BENTON: H-m-m. Well, it might be neighborly to go over and speak to her. Yes. I could take her some of my rose cuttings.

MAGGIE: Let's take these. They're the best.

MRS. BENTON: The poor woman must be lonely. In a strange place too. (*Fading out*) Watch your step there—be sure you don't step on any graves (etc.) . . .

DIALOGUE (TWO FEMALES) INTENSE

MARLENE: Paula, listen, do you hear a strange sound?

PAULA: What sort of a sound?

MARLENE: A sound like a woman moaning?

PAULA: No!

MARLENE: I heard it distinctly. You listen!

PAULA: You drink this tea and forget about such things.

MARLENE: Please, Paula! Quiet!

MOTHER: (*Moaning off*)

MARLENE: Now, do you hear?

PAULA: Heavens!

MARLENE: You do hear it?

PAULA: Some unusual sound.

MARLENE: Where is it coming from?

PAULA: I don't know.

MOTHER: (*Moaning*)

MARLENE: There it is again.

PAULA: Yes . . . it sort of seems to be coming from these walls of the music room!

MARLENE: That's it!

PAULA: Or from out on the terrace!

MARLENE: It's nearer than that!

MOTHER: (*Moaning*)

PAULA: Here . . . in this wall behind the piano.

MARLENE: Yes.

PAULA: Mmmmm.

MARLENE: Why are you feeling of the walls?

PAULA: This panel here . . . look!

MARLENE: It's. . . . It's. . . .

Sound: Spring clicks . . . panel sliding open

MARLENE: Why it's a panel that opens. I've lived here all my life and I never knew of it before!

PAULA: An inner room in here!

MOTHER: (*Moaning closer*)

MARLENE: And you can hear the moaning from here much closer.

PAULA: Marlene, get the candle from the piano. I'm going to look around in here!

MARLENE: Yes. (*Pause*) Here, Paula!

Sound: Lighting match.

PAULA: This passage in here must lead to another room in the house!

MARLENE: I'm coming with you.

Sound: (Now muffled voices as if in tunnel)

PAULA: The moaning we heard was from someone in the adjoining room from here!

MOTHER: (*Moan . . . close . . . but muffled*)

MARLENE: Paula, wait, here, look!

PAULA: What is it?

MARLENE: This enormous chest. Listen!

MOTHER: (*Moaning*)

MARLENE: Quick! There's someone inside this chest!

PAULA: I believe you're right!

MARLENE: Hurry, they'll smother to death!

PAULA: It's locked!

MARLENE: LOCKED! Someone has been pushed into this chest then and it's been locked against them. Hurry, can't you break it open?

PAULA: I'm going to try!

Sound: Pounding against chest

PAULA: No use. I'll have to go to the garage for tools.

MARLENE: Hurry, Paula, O, please hurry!

Organ: Comes in. Hold for scene transition. Fade for:

Sound: Pounding chest with hammer

PAULA: Did you hear the moaning while I was gone?

MARLENE: No, it stopped. Whoever is inside must have fainted or died. Are you getting it?

DIALOGUE (TWO MALES) STRAIGHT, LOW

HALL: Keep your eye on the Major.

HAWKINS: You know what I been thinking all this week?

HALL: He's gettin' pretty snappy with his orders.

HAWKINS: I been thinkin' this is the sweetest life a man ever knew.

HALL: You mean just coastin' downstream?

HAWKINS: Look at us go, slickin' by that bank. Water smooth as a kitten's purr. Good food. Duck soup and roasted ribs every night. Biscuit.

HALL: You're a fine cook, Billy.

HAWKINS: Except it's always so quiet. Take like now—what're we whispering for?

HALL: Well, we could talk loud.

HAWKINS: You want to talk loud?

HALL: Not particular. Do you?

HAWKINS: I don't mind whisperin'.

HALL: Me too. Saves the voice.

HAWKINS: I guess the Major figured 'cause you an' me was boys they'd put us in the last boat 'cause we didn't count so much.

HALL: It's all right by me.

HAWKINS: Me too. That way we're together.

HALL: That's all right too.

HAWKINS: Sure. That way we're in the same boat.

DIALOGUE (TWO MALES) CHARACTER, OLDER

WEBB: A mighty fine ceegar, Mr. President. My compliments on your taste.

CLEVELAND: Thank you, thank you. Uh—haven't noticed you dancing with my wife this evening, Mr. Webb—you were paying her pretty close attention last time you were here.

WEBB: Well, I'll tell you, sir. She is *so* surrounded by attentive young gentlemen. . . . And if you don't mind my sayin' so—she'd better kinda watch her step.

CLEVELAND: I *do* mind your saying so. What do you mean?

WEBB: The talk, Mr. President. You know how people *love* to talk.

CLEVELAND: And what about? My wife enjoys her social life—being surrounded by friends. I wouldn't have it any other way.

WEBB: But when it gets around that she's makin' political promises that she can't keep—that's a different horse of another color, Mr. President!

CLEVELAND: I don't believe that . . .

WEBB: You may be sure—them as wants to get you outa the White House will believe it.

CLEVELAND: You wouldn't be hoping for that happy day yourself, would you, Mr. Webb?

WEBB: Me? To be perfectly honest, I'm willin' to work my head off for your re-election . . . long as I know where I stand—on m'home ground, that is, with no Indians on it.

CLEVELAND: In other words, if I'll oppose the Indian Emancipation Act, you'll play ball with me. . . . No, it's all settled, all settled. Sorry . . .

WEBB: Mr. President, it may turn out that you *really* will be *sorry*.

DIALOGUE (TWO MALES) RESTRAINT, OLD AND YOUNG

HENRY: You've been a good son to me Peter.

PETER: I've tried.

HENRY: I appreciate your taking care of me. . . . Keeps you home all the time too.

PETER: I don't mind, father. It's just that Matt . . .

HENRY: What about Matt?

PETER: Matt's shirked all of his responsibilities. He's gone off on his own . . . enjoying himself, seeing the world.

HENRY: He's fighting for his country.

PETER: (*Bitterly*) Yes, fighting. The first time he ever got any fighting blood was when he was afraid he'd get tied down here.

HENRY: Peter!

PETER: Matt's disgraced this family—showed the whole neighborhood what he thinks of us. And you! You won't even make a will showing that dirty spalpeen what you think of his going off and leaving you to die alone!

HENRY: The money and property should be divided between you fairly.

PETER: Was he fair to you? Was he fair to me? No! He always thought of himself first! Please, make your will!

HENRY: The money will be divided between you fairly.

DIALOGUE (MALE, FEMALE) STRAIGHT, FATHER–DAUGHTER

JOAN: Shall we go any further?

BARRETT: Oh, I think so, daughter. . . . Not tired, are you?

JOAN: No, no, I'm not tired.

BARRETT: You can talk about Norman if you want to.

JOAN: I want to . . . but not now.

BARRETT: Perhaps you would rather we didn't talk at all . . . want me to shut up?

JOAN: No, father . . .

BARRETT: I suppose you think I'm a cruel parent to ask you to do this—drive this canoe along the same paths that you and Norman traveled.

JOAN: I don't pretend to like it . . .

BARRETT: Didn't think you would . . .

JOAN: Father, we have talked about this a good many times before, but all of a sudden it has come over me again.

BARRETT: What has, daughter?

JOAN: It's a tough job being a father, isn't it?

BARRETT: It's a wonderful job . . . seems kind of easy when you think of it. . . . Consists mostly of loving a lot . . .

JOAN: And thinking a lot . . .

BARRETT: Yes, thinking a lot. . . . That's not hard to do. Comes pretty easy somehow. You get up in the morning and take a bath, start to shave, and probably say to yourself—and you laugh a little when you say it—"I bet Joan wouldn't like to scrape her face like this!"

JOAN: Father, did you ever really say that to yourself?

BARRETT: Lots of times. . . . Of course I have. Comes kind of natural. Sometimes I feel kind of sorry for you, Joan, thinking you're not going to be anybody's father . . .

JOAN: I'm afraid I'm not even going to be anybody's mother, father . . .

BARRETT: Daughter, I wouldn't count on that too much if I were you . . .

JOAN: But, father—

BARRETT: Now, wait a minute, daughter. You're in a pretty mean jam now, but you're young, you're strong and healthy, you're not going to feel like this always.

JOAN: But, father—I love Norman. . . . I'm frantic with anxiety about him. . . . He's been missing more than two weeks. I don't know whether he's living or whether he's dead. I don't know how I can go on from here.

BARRETT: Joan, you're drifting a little, dear. . . . Put your paddle in the water and give the boat a push. . . .

DIALOGUE (MALE, FEMALE) MALE CHARACTER, AGE 45; FEMALE SOPHISTICATED

COLLINS: Your modesty, Miss Elizabeth, adds to your perfections.

ELIZABETH: You mistake me, Mr. Collins.

COLLINS: Allow me to assure you that I have your mother's permission for what I am about to say. And I would presume that she has not left you totally unprepared for my address.

ELIZABETH: And I assure you, Mr. Collins, that I have no notion of what you may be about to say.

COLLINS: Dear Miss Elizabeth! You have natural delicacy! Have you not known that almost from the moment I entered this house I singled you out as the companion of my future life?

ELIZABETH: Mr. Collins!

COLLINS: I believe firmly that every clergyman should marry. I believe marriage would add greatly to my happiness. And I feel it my responsibility, nay, my duty, since I am to inherit this estate, to choose my wife from among your father's daughters.

ELIZABETH: (*Growing angry*) You're too kind, Mr. Collins.

COLLINS: Not at all, Miss Elizabeth. Never in all our years together will a single reproach pass my lips concerning the smallness of the dowry you will be given. . . . I am aware that your father and mother have no great fortune. It is perhaps even better so, since you are then accustomed to making yourself useful and will fit the modest, though respectable, position of a parson's wife.

ELIZABETH: Please, Mr. Collins . . . before you go on. . . . Accept my thanks for the compliment, but understand that I must decline your proposal. There is no need for you to take pity on any of us.

COLLINS: If you had not interrupted me, Miss Elizabeth, I would have continued to tell you of the violence of my affections for you. Duty led me to this house, yes. But your amiable disposition and bright manner have done much to encourage my stay.

ELIZABETH: Mr. Collins, by proposing to me you have discharged your duty to our family. I thank you again, but believe me, I am not the woman for you, and I cannot marry you.

COLLINS: I understand that it's customary for young ladies to refuse a man on his first proposal, and so I'm by no means discouraged, dear Elizabeth.

ELIZABETH: If I had any intention of accepting you, I should do so now, and not risk a change of heart in you. Believe me I cannot and never will marry you.

COLLINS: When I do myself the honor of speaking to you again on this subject, Miss Elizabeth, I will expect a more favorable answer.

DIALOGUE (MALE, FEMALE) INTENSE

WIFE: He likes you.

NARRATOR: (*Angrily*) He doesn't like me. He throws himself in my way to torment me. He doesn't want me to forget how I killed Pluto. He keeps taunting me—daring me to kill him. Well—I will kill him! I hate him—I despise him—I loathe him!

WIFE: What are you going to do?

NARRATOR: Where's the axe?

WIFE: You're not going to kill him!

NARRATOR: Oh, yes I am! You see this glistening steel? It will cut through his skull and rid me of him forever. Look at him jeering at me—accusing me. I'll close that glaring eye of his.

WIFE: Oh, no, you mustn't—I won't let you. Go away from him!

NARRATOR: And don't you try to stop me. You're as bad as he is!

WIFE: You'll not touch that cat. He's done nothing but give you his affection.

NARRATOR: I'll get rid of him here and now.

WIFE: No! No!

NARRATOR: Don't try to stop me.

WIFE: I will stop you.

NARRATOR: I warned you once before not to interfere. I told you I'd kill you if you did (*Fading. Insane rage*) I'll kill you—I will kill you—I will kill you—

WIFE: (*Screams off mike*)

DIALOGUE (KIDS)

BILL: Yeh?

SAM: You heard me.

BILL: Sammy's got a case on Miss Florence . . . yah . . . yah . . . yah . . .

SAM: That's a lie.

BILL: Yah . . . yah . . . I thought you were going to do something about it.

SAM: I am. Take that.

Sound: A few whacks, followed by "Ow." It's a kids' fight.

BILL: Thought you were going to fix me. . . . (*Panting*) . . . You'll be sorry. . . . Hey, look out for that bank . . .

SAM: Ohhhhhhhhhhhhh. (*Falling about fifteen feet*)

BILL: (*Climbing down, panting and sobbing*) Sammy, are you all right? Sammy! Sammy, I didn't mean to knock you off the bank. . . . We wuz fightin' so hard . . .

SAM: I guess I'm all right. . . . My leg hurts awful though . . .

BILL: Here, I'll help you up. Gee, Sammy, I'm sorry . . .

SAM: (*As he's getting on his foot*) I guess I'm all right . . . Ohhhh, my leg, it hurts awful. I can't walk, Billy. You better get someone.

BILL: Dad's not home, he went into Romsey today.

SAM: Well, get someone, quick. My leg . . .

BILL: Sure, I'll have to get someone . . . (*Fading*) . . . Gee, Sammy, I'm sorry.

DIALECT, FRENCH (TWO MALES)

JEAN: Parlez-vous français?

GOVERNOR: I would rather speak English.

JEAN: My name, Jean Poquelin.

GOVERNOR: How can I serve you, Mr. Poquelin?

JEAN: Zat swamp behind my house belong to me.

GOVERNOR: Yes, sir.

JEAN: To me, Jean Poquelin; I hown 'im meself.

GOVERNOR: Well, sir?

JEAN: He don't belong to you; I get 'im from my father.

GOVERNOR: That is perfectly true, Mr. Poquelin, as far as I am aware.

JEAN: They want to make strit pass yond; but strit can't pass dare!

GOVERNOR: But, why, Mr. Poquelin?

JEAN: I tell you zat land belong to me!

GOVERNOR: Of course, realize you will be indemnified for any loss you suffer. (*Pause*) You will get PAID, you understand?

JEAN: I don't want money, I want my land!

GOVERNOR: Well, Mr. Poquelin, I can do nothing. You will have to see the municipal authorities.

JEAN: (*Slowly*) Pardon, Monsieur, you is not Le Governeur?

GOVERNOR: Yes.

JEAN: Yes, you har Le Governeur—yes. Veh-well, I come to you. I tell you, strit can't pass at me 'ouse.

GOVERNOR: But you will have to see—

JEAN: I come to you. You is Le Governeur! I know not the new land. I am a F-r-r-renchman! F-r-r-renchman have something go wrong—he come to his Governeur. I come. I want you do something for me, eh?

GOVERNOR: (*Patiently*) What is it?

JEAN: I want you tell Monsieur le Président strit–can't–pass–at me house.

GOVERNOR: Why, Mr. Poquelin?

JEAN: I tell you zat is my house, my land. You mus' not let them touch it!

GOVERNOR: You go to see the municipal authorities. I'll be glad to ask them to help you out.

JEAN: (*Dejectedly*) All right. I go.

GOVERNOR: One moment, Mr. Poquelin. (*Slowly*) You will possibly be called upon to make some explanation—you realize the Creole citizens tell some very odd stories about your house.

JEAN: (*With deep feeling*) I am Jean Poquelin. I mine my own bizness. Zat all right? (*Pause*) I go. Adieu.

PROJECT V

TV BRETZ BOX

A very valuable exercise is to have each member of a class construct a Bretz box. Instructions may be found on pages 75 and 76 of *Techniques of Television Production* by Rudy Bretz, published by McGraw-Hill. Lens angles may also be found on page 60 of the same book.

I suggest that openings be included for the 50-millimeter, 90-millimeter, 135-millimeter, and 8½-inch lenses. A 35-millimeter and a 13-inch lens may be added if desired.

A few additional suggestions as to how to proceed with the making of the Bretz box will prove useful. Using a common apex, lay out all the desired angles on one card with a protractor. Run the lines from the apex to the edge of the card. Next, using the edge of this card mark off one angle on each of the other cards. Use two sets of dots, one below the other. You now have the dimensions for the horizontal angle. Connect the two sets of dots from one edge of the card to the other. Measure this dimension, take three-fourths of it and you have the vertical dimension. Locate the center of the card. Go half the vertical dimension above the center and half below. Connect these points to the lines marking the horizontal dimension. You now have the size of the window to be cut out. It is best to assemble the box with masking tape. It is very helpful to paint the inside surfaces black.

It doesn't matter which opening is opposite to any given window. The window that defines the picture for a particular lens is the one away from your eye. The cube shape of the box forces you to hold this window at a fixed distance from the eye. Thus, when looking through the finished box, hold it right up against the eye. If only four lenses are desired you must, of course, put the two windowless sides opposite each other. For most purposes, the four common lens sizes will serve.

Using a Bretz box in conjunction with Project VI, it is possible to simulate many of the most important problems in television directing and production. No beginner can get too much of this kind of practice.

MATERIALS REQUIRED: 6 pieces of 6-by-6 poster board
                     protractor
                     1-inch masking tape
                     good ruler
                     pencil
                     black poster paint

PROJECT VI

PLOTTING THE TV SHOW

Next to actually doing television programs in a studio, the most valuable experience is to plot a show, as completely as possible, on paper. Many of the problems of staging and camera coverage will become immediately apparent in the course of such an exercise.

Original shows may be planned and written, or scripts available in published books may be used. Each student should have a copy of the script, so the easiest thing is to duplicate them by the ditto or mimeograph process. I suggest that the class start with a short script. The scripts should be typed in television form with ample space left on the pages for writing in camera cues, etc.

The students should start by analyzing the show and writing up an analysis of the characters, purposes, and important values in the show. Next, draw a ground plan for the set, or sets, on graph paper. The most usable scale is ¼ inch equals 1 foot. Graph paper with ¼-inch squares can be obtained in any store that sells art or engineering supplies. Draw everything to scale. Check such things as pianos, desks, etc., so that they will be in proper scale. Now, work out all of the action and movements and indicate them in the script. Using a Bretz plotter, put in the camera positions, angles, and lenses to be used. (Bretz plotters can be obtained by ordering directly from Rudy Bretz, Croton-on-Hudson, New York. They cost $2.50 each. It is not necessary for every student to have one. If a class has enough to allow the work to proceed it is satisfactory. One plotter for each five students would be ample.) In addition to the camera information, it is possible to put in the mike boom by using the plotter. It is also helpful to draw sketches of the key shots. Draw a small rectangle in the 3:4 proportion. Sketch in the figures and objects to be included. Simple stick drawings will suffice for this purpose. This helps to make clear the kind of shot desired. Enter all of the camera cues and instructions in the script, clearly indicating where the cuts are to be made. Add audio cues, special effects, and all other cues.

When the script has been worked over in every possible detail, scenes, or all of it, may be staged. The staging and planned camera coverage can be checked with the Bretz box. This exercise provides a quite realistic experience in the planning of a TV show. Students should be aware that the things covered in this project are the important ones. The trappings such as scenery, lights, costumes, etc., are far less important, and much less of a problem.

MATERIALS REQUIRED: television script
Bretz plotter
¼-inch squared paper
architect's scale (or ruler)
pencils (different colors are helpful)
T-square and triangles (helpful but not necessary)

PROJECT VII

A MIRROR CAMERA

A one-way mirror can be used to advantage for training students in acting, announcing, speaking, etc., for television. The student performs before the mirror side of the glass and observes his own performance as well as possible. The instructor, and other students, watch from the other side of the mirror. A more realistic view is obtained of the performance by viewing at least a portion of it through a Bretz box.

For at least part of the exercises done in this manner the performing student should know whether he is being seen in a close-up, a long shot, or a medium shot. The gestures and expressions used should be worked out for the appropriate shot.

I strongly suggest that class discussion and criticism follow such performances. Many aspects of the performance and its effect on an audience are apt to come out of such discussions. Furthermore, the ability to analyze the work of others is a big step toward improvement in the performance fields.

SUGGESTED CLASS ASSIGNMENTS

These exercises correspond roughly with the material in the chapters which bear the corresponding numbers. They are loosely arranged in order of increasing difficulty, so that instructors on various scholastic levels can select quickly the exercises which best correspond to the abilities of their classes. It is urged that these exercises should be considered only as suggestions, and should be used as the basis for others that the instructor can devise.

Chapter I

FUNDAMENTALS OF RADIO—AMPLITUDE MODULATION

1. Refer to Project 1.

2. Unscrew the mouthpiece of a telephone, remove the diaphragm, and you will observe the principle of an old carbon microphone. The ear unit of the telephone is similar to a condenser receiver.

3. Make a dial chart of all stations that may be heard regularly in your area.

4. Visit the local station to observe the acoustic treatment of the studios.

5. Visit the transmitter of your local station. Report to the class your observations. Draw the type of antenna used.

6. By using an oscillator, or a buzzer that has a constant volume output of sound, plot the exact pattern of the beams of the microphones at your disposal.

7. Purchase an outline map of your state. Mark the location of each radio station in the state with its call letters. Mark the coverage areas of state stations. For 100-watt stations use a radius of 15 miles; for a station of 500 watts, use a radius of 20 miles; for 1000 watts, 30 miles; 5000 watts, 40 miles; 10,000 watts, 50 miles; 25,000 watts, 60 miles; 50,000 watts, 70 miles.

8. Many electronic supply houses sell inexpensive kits, costing under $10, which enable you to "broadcast" through your electric record player, or to build a crystal receiver. The circuits are simple, the directions are easy to follow, no technical experience is necessary.

Chapter II

FUNDAMENTALS OF RADIO—VERY HIGH FREQUENCIES

1. Write to Zenith Radio Corporation for their fine map showing AM and FM coverage in the United States.

2. Write to the United States Office of Education, Federal Security Agency, which will send you a pamphlet on *FM for Education* by Franklin Dunham, and to General Electric for its pamphlet on *How to Plan an FM Station.*

3. Get all the information you can concerning the low-power station. Both General Electric, Electronic Department, Syracuse 1, New York, and Collins Radio Company, Cedar Rapids, Iowa, will provide information concerning transmitters and low-powered stations. Over thirty-six educational institutions operated low-power stations in 1955.

4. Can you discover if there are any differences in the number of educational programs that FM stations and AM stations are scheduling in your area?

5. Why has FM failed to become commercially successful?

Chapter III

FUNDAMENTALS OF TELEVISION

1. Have available for reference the F.C.C.'s *Sixth Report and Order,* April, 1952, or any later documents relating to TV frequency and channel allocations. These documents may be secured by writing to the Superintendent of Documents, U.S. Government Printing Office, Washington 25, D.C.

2. Other government documents which should be available for class use are: *The Communications Act of 1934* and *Public Service Responsibilities of Broadcast Licensees.*

3. Have available the latest television station and network status map. These are published by *Television Digest with Electronic Reports,* 611 Wyatt Building, Washington 5, D.C. They cost $1. It would also be useful to have the latest *Television Factbook,* published by the same concern.

4. Contact your nearest R.C.A., G.E., G.P.L., and Du Mont sales offices and ask for any pamphlets, brochures, etc., they may have on television in general, and on color television.

5. Read the pertinent sections of *Television Broadcasting* by Howard Chinn, published by McGraw-Hill. This book is more understandable to a nonengineer than most engineering texts. It would be helpful to make use of an engineer, a physics teacher, or a science teacher to cover this subject, if you can find one who can translate the essential information into plain language.

6. The following is an outline of the major points that need to be covered to provide an elementary understanding of how TV works:

    a. The radio spectrum.

    b. Persistence of vision.

    c. Mechanics of motion pictures.

        (1) The frame.

        (2) Intermittent projection, pull-down mechanism, and shutter.

    d. The essential characteristics of light.

    e. The scanning process in television. (Iconoscope and image-orthicon.) (Conversion of light energy into electrical energy.)

f. The transmitting process.

g. The kinescope and the reconstruction of the picture in the receiver.

7. Make use of the pictures in this handbook to clarify the function of each piece of equipment in the system: the camera, the pickup tube, the power supply, the camera-control unit, the sync generator, the transmitter, and the receiver.

8. Analyze with the class the problems of VHF vs. UHF television channels. What are the implications of the existing dilemma?

Chapter IV

RADIO AND TELEVISION PROGRAMMING

1. Among the programs that you listen to regularly, choose the one you consider best from the standpoint of program building. Justify your choice.

2. Prepare for the class a schedule of your radio listening for the coming week. Why have you selected the programs that you indicate?

3. Check up on the programs from your local station. In what way and to what extent does the station conform to the ruling of the F.C.C. that it must serve "public interest, convenience, and necessity"?

4. Compare the program schedules of a network station and an independent station located in your area. Which serves the community better?

5. Referring to the listing of the radio and TV programs of your location stations for a single day, analyze the programs:

a. Network program:
Sponsored.
Sustaining.

b. Programs originating in the local stations:
Sponsored.
Sustaining.

c. Make a comparative evaluation of like programs.

6. Radio and TV stations make surveys to determine the popularity of their programs. See if you can induce your local station to assign some survey to the members of your class. Such a survey should be useful to the station and instructive to the students who make it.

7. If public-address equipment is available, organize the class into a broadcasting-station staff. Operate or present an abbreviated day of broadcasting which will run for 3 hours. During the first hour present shortened and typical morning programs, during the second hour broadcast afternoon types, and during the third period present typical evening programs. Students should write all copy and direct, rehearse, and produce programs. No program period should be over 15 minutes in length. Maintain a rigid time schedule. Observe rules for station breaks. Emulate programs that are on the air. Present all types of programs that are popular during the 3-hour period.

If TV equipment is available, repeat this exercise assuming a hypothetical TV station.

8. Have the following available for reference:
   a. *Public Service Responsibilities of Broadcast Licensees,* U.S. Government Printing Office.
   b. *Radio, Television, and Society,* Charles A. Siepmann, Oxford University Press.
   c. Television Code, National Association of Radio and Television Broadcasters.
   d. *Broadcasting-Telecasting Magazine.* 1735 DeSales Street N.W., Washington 6, D.C.
   e. *Television* magazine. 600 Madison Avenue, New York 22, New York.

9. Ask the manager, the program director, or the sales manager of a local TV station to address the class on the problems of programming a station.

10. Have members of the class view selected TV programs which are representative of different types. It is very important that this viewing be done with a specific organized purpose. To this end, it is suggested that students be required to keep a form similar to the one shown at the end of this section. The forms can be dittoed or mimeographed.

11. Have some members of the class analyze the program schedule of a local station and report as to the percentage of programs which are live and which are filmed. What trends can be seen in the ratio of film to live? What are the implications?

12. Have members of the class analyze a TV station's programs in terms of intended audience and time of day. For example: early morning programs, what audience? late morning, what audience? noontime, what audience? etc., through the day. Do this for both weekdays and for Saturday and Sunday.

13. Have a committee of the class check back and report to the class on the popularity of the top network programs over the past six months. Does the national rating information agree with the ratings in your local area? (You can check this with the local station.) If it is different, why? Is there any local program in your area that exceeds or favorably competes with the top network programs? Why?

PROGRAM ANALYSIS

Student's name_____Date_____

Program title_____Channel and/or network_____

Type of program_____Day and time_____

Sponsor_____Type of product_____

Does this program use same cast each week?_____ If not, what kind of device is used to give succeeding programs continuity?_____

_____

_____

Opening:

   Type of opening_____

   Describe elements of opening_____

_____

   Length of opening_____

Program segments:

　Give content and running time of each segment of the program.

1. _____

2. _____

3. _____

4. _____

5. _____

6. _____

7. _____

8. _____

9. _____

10. _____

(Use reverse side of sheet if more space is needed.)

Closing:

　Type of closing_____

　Describe elements of closing_____

_____Time_____

　What kind of time cushion was used?_____

Chapter V

RADIO AND TELEVISION ANNOUNCING

1. Participate in Project III.

2. Who is your favorite radio/TV commercial announcer? Why?

3. Practice sight-reading commercial copy prepared by another student.

4. To get a comparison of your performance with that of a professional speaker, record an outstanding newscaster on a tape, then record one of your own readings of news. Compare the two. This exercise should be done not for purposes of imitation, but to evaluate your own performance in terms of professional standards.

5. Get some used transcribed commercial programs from your local station. Copy the commercials on those transcriptions; then read the copy to a tape or wire recorder. Compare your delivery with that of the announcer on the transcription.

6. Listen to your best radio station and compare the commercial with the noncommercial announcements. Is there a difference in the style of delivery?

7. Listen to and evaluate various professional announcers. Compare the merits of those upon the local station with those of the network.

8. Note the emphasis that is placed upon certain words by experienced announcers, and try to determine why these words are emphasized.

　　a. Is accent used more effectively than a change of pitch?

　　b. Is it advisable to emphasize a word by lowering the pitch or by raising it?

9. Radio stations are generally very willing to give auditions. Take one of these auditions and ask for criticisms that you can report to the class. What

type of material was given to you to read? How long did the audition last? What instructions were given to you before the audition? What criticism was made? What type of job application did you fill in?

10. Pick out the station where you would like to be employed after graduation. Listen to the style of its announcers and try to emulate them. Take down some of the commercials used on that station and try to give them in the same style.

11. Obtain some commercial slides and write commercials to accompany them. Have members of the class read the commercial to the slides. An ordinary slide projector and screen will serve for this purpose.

12. It is frequently possible to obtain out-of-date film commercials from stations, advertising agencies, or advertisers. Have copy written to go with such films and have the class read against the film, stressing the need to adjust timing to fit the film. Any 16-millimeter sound projector will do the job.

13. Have members of the class practice delivering commercials straight to a "camera" with the copy memorized. Try the same thing with demonstration-type commercials. Try both of these using an idiot board. The use of a one-way mirror, Bretz box, and other simulated equipment will make such exercises more realistic. In all cases have something to represent cameras and some method of indicating to which camera the announcer should speak.

Chapter VI

RADIO AND TELEVISION SPEAKING

1. One of the first things to do in training the radio announcer or speaker is to create within him the feeling that he is reading to a small audience when he is addressing the microphone. With this in mind, one method of obtaining the necessary directness and intimacy is to place the radio speaker with his copy at a table with the microphone before him and a listener on the opposite side of the table and try to get the speaker to read his material as if he were talking to the person who is opposite him. His auditor in this case must show by facial expressions he understands what is going on. After the speaker becomes accustomed to the microphone and to reading in such a way that what he is reading sounds conversational, allow the auditor to remain in the room with the speaker while he is addressing the microphone. It is not until after the novice has become accustomed to the microphone that a visible auditor is taken away.

2. Have various members of the class deliver the same 3-minute talk to the class. Determine to what extent listening interest is due to the manner of speaking.

3. Using a stop watch, check the number of words (or typed lines) you read in 1 minute.

4. Record a 1-minute news story at the beginning of the semester. Record the same story about three-quarters of the way through the semester and play both back to determine if there has been any improvement in communication.

5. By listening to many samples of radio and television speaking try to discover the speakers' methods of achieving and renewing audience contact by changes in attitude, style, emphasis, word color, rate, inflection, etc.

6. Practice various kinds of speeches as they might be given over television. Try some memorized, some from an idiot board, and some extemporaneously from an outline. Again, be sure to simulate cameras and other studio equipment. The speaker should be able to tell at all times which "camera" is on. Part of the technique a speaker on TV needs is the ability to shift smoothly from camera to camera. Have other members of the class observe these speeches through Bretz boxes so that they may criticize body positions, gestures, etc.

Chapter VII

PRONUNCIATION

1. Are there examples of sectional or regional speech to be heard over stations in your locality? What is the public reaction to such speech?

2. Compare the pronunciations of foreign names and titles as given by announcers with pronunciations of these same names and titles as given in a pronouncing dictionary. Which are the more understandable? Do your findings prove or disprove the idea that foreign names should be Anglicized for American listeners?

3. Using one of the pronouncing aids mentioned in the text, practice the correct pronunciations of at least five words each day. Select words that are frequently heard over the radio.

4. Select 10 words with disputed pronunciations and discover the pronunciation preferred by educated people in your locality.

5. Look up the "proper" pronunciation of such common names as Tschaikowsky, Stokowski, Bizet, Berlioz, Debussy, for example, to determine if the "book" pronunciation is that which is in general use in your area.

6. Write to the G. & C. Merriam Company, 10 Broadway, Springfield, Massachusetts, for a pronunciation test. Enough copies of this will be sent to an instructor for the entire class. Make it the basis of an announcer's test over the public-address system. It will be admittedly poor radio copy but is good practice in pronunciation.

7. Different state organizations in the various states issue pronunciation guides for names of places in their states. Write for these—particularly in your own state.

Chapter VIII

ARTICULATION, INTONATION, RHYTHM

1. Practice the common tongue twisters to loosen the articulation.

2. Send to Dr. W. P. Halstead, Department of Speech, University of Michigan, Ann Arbor, Michigan, for a copy of his *Voice Drills* for practice in articulation, intonation, and rhythm.

3. Listen to the speech of your classmates to determine if their articulation is at high standard. For example, do they say "een" for "ing," "d" for "t" in such words as "Italy"?

Chapter IX

NEWS PROGRAMS

1. Practice the news audition in Project III.

2. Prepare a 5-minute summary of world news for broadcast. Use the local newspaper as your source.

3. Select items from a newspaper which you would use in a news broadcast. Arrange them in the order in which you would present them. Justify the selection and arrangement.

4. Have a student obtain from the local newspaper a strip of A.P., U.P., or I.N.S. news. Rewrite this strip for radio presentation.

5. Try preparing scripts for different types of news broadcasts, such as women in the news, youth makes news, science in the news.

6. Develop a different type of news commentating—backwoods philosopher —a Will Rogers type—feature stories of the day—brighter side of the news, etc.

7. Those students who are interested both in broadcasting and in journalism may be organized into a news-dissemination service for the university. Their copy should embrace material of an educational nature designed to inform the public accurately concerning the scholastic news of university life. Classroom news, advances in educational methods, and the value and extent of research as presented by such news broadcasts will give to the public an insight into college life different from that afforded by newspaper items. Accuracy, methods of unifying the news, transitions from one item to another, and the development of an individual style are matters to be stressed in addition to journalistic principles.

8. Listen to four newscasters in one day, keeping notes on the content of each program. Which news items are given the most important emphasis and which are omitted altogether? Can you tell if a newscaster is simply reading the copy as it comes off the teletype machine or if he has rewritten it in his own style?

9. After the class has developed some skill in the assembling, writing, and reading of news, have them prepare some TV news programs. Pictures from newspapers and magazines, photographs, maps, charts, graphs, and other visuals should be used. If a 35-millimeter still camera is available, 2- by 2-inch slides can be made. Occasionally, 16-millimeter film can be obtained. All of the visual material should be carefully integrated into the show and the newscaster should be able to use it smoothly throughout the newscast. It is recommended that TV newscasts be short in the beginning.

10. Have members of the class view both network and local TV newscasts. Evaluate their effectiveness. How are visuals used? What kinds of visuals are the most effective? Compare the effectiveness of TV and radio newscasts.

Chapter X

SPORTS PROGRAMS

1. Make a compilation of the slang terms used by sportscasters on radio and television.

2. List the adjectives which are used in newspaper stories on sports. How does this newspaper usage compare with the practice of sportscasters on radio and television?

3. To illustrate the principles of selection, attend a sports event with a portable radio. Listen to the announcer describe the plays and compare his description with the actual event.

4. Make a sports announcer's spotter board. (See Fig. 26.)

5. Read the rule books and sports sections of newspapers for various major sports and report to the class on those rules which the sportscaster must know.

6. After attending a sports event (football, basketball, baseball, etc.), write a résumé of the game for radio presentation.

7. Prepare the filler to be used by the sports announcer for a sports broadcast.

8. The athletic department of nearly every college takes motion pictures of its football games to be used for analysis by the coaches and players. Borrow some of these films and run them slowly in the classroom and try to give a running account of the game.

9. Using one of the above silent films, announce the game as the television sportscaster would. Your classmates will see the picture on the screen just as they would see it in television.

10. Watch the telecast of a sports event which is also being broadcast on radio. Does the radio announcer present an accurate representation of what you see?

11. Using a portable tape recorder, cover a school or campus sporting event for playback and evaluation in class.

12. Using a scale-plan drawing and a Bretz plotter, plan the camera coverage for football, basketball, and baseball from your local fields and gym. Make a detailed analysis of the kind of coverage you would use if you had two cameras, then three cameras.

13. Watch the TV coverage of various sports events and write up a summary of the number of cameras used, their locations, and just how the event is televised.

Chapter XI

UNWRITTEN TALK PROGRAMS

1. Make a list of subjects on which you could talk or carry on an intelligent interview, with little or no preparation.

2. Conduct a 15-minute round table, using a stop watch. Arrange it so that those participating in the discussion are invisible to the balance of the class.

Have the other members criticize the presentation from the standpoint of human interests, unity, sequence, delivery, and summary.

3. Prepare quiz programs for your various classes, bearing in mind that the material presented must be interesting, entertaining, and test the knowledge not only of those participating but also of the radio and TV audience. Have quiz programs in civics, English literature, political science, botany, history, etc., both as radio and as TV shows. There are many question-and-answer books (a complete list can be obtained from the Library of Congress, Department of Bibliographies). Using these, build a classroom quiz program. Here are a few recommended books:

GOLENPAUL, DAN, ed.: *Information, Please!*, Simon and Schuster, Inc., New York.

Live Them Again [the *Time* Quiz Book and Memory Jogger]. Prepared by *Time, the Weekly News Magazine*. Simon and Schuster, Inc., New York.

SMITH, DON: *Peculiarities of the Presidents*, 4th ed., Don Smith, Van Wert, Ohio.

STIMPSON, GEORGE WILLIAM, *Book about American History*, Harper & Brothers, New York.

———— *Book about American Politics*, Harper & Brothers, New York.

4. A small, domestic, motion-picture projector can be used to throw a silent picture on a screen which can be seen through a window in the announcer's booth. The student announcer will be required to describe the action vividly and clearly so that the rest of the class, who cannot see the picture, will be able to visualize it by listening to him. This will require vocabulary control by the announcer and concentration upon his task. Another student who has previously seen the picture can blend the necessary sound effects from recordings to make the audition realistic. Such auditions should start with simple types of motion pictures. Comedies and parades should be practiced.

Chapter XII

PREPARING THE BROADCAST ADDRESS

1. Select a descriptive sentence from some article and rewrite it in such a way that the description is addressed to an individual. Use the second-person pronoun.

2. What visual material, slides, photos, models, specimens, and motion pictures can be used to make a selected radio talk into a TV show?

3. Force yourself to listen to a dull radio talk (such as might occur under the title "Meet Your Governor"). Try to determine why the talk was uninteresting. What could the speaker have done to hold your interest? Could TV have made it more interesting?

4. Copy several complex sentences from a printed article and then rewrite them, incorporating the fundamentals of proper radio sentence structure.

5. Watch a talk on television, such as one given by Bishop Fulton J. Sheen, to observe how variety is achieved in content, delivery, and technical production.

6. Criticize a radio address upon the following points:
   a. Conversational style of the speaker.
   b. His choice of words.
   c. Sentence structure.

7. Write to the broadcasting services of some universities which broadcast programs, requesting copies of radio talks. Criticize these.

8. Write and record what seems to you to be a screamingly funny 4-minute talk, using no audience. Record the same talk using a live audience. How has the audience affected the delivery? What timing problems arise in the second reading?

9. Practice television speeches which are prepared in outline form for extemporaneous delivery. What are the problems in timing? Does this method result in a more natural style than reading from a manuscript?

Chapter XIII

BROADCASTING IN THE PUBLIC SERVICE

1. Evaluate the programs that are broadcast to appeal to the community to determine whether they are entertaining as well as instructive. If they are uot, suggest methods by which the audience appeal may be increased.

2. Listen to and watch the local radio and television stations and report upon all community and public-service programs.
   a. Are they presented during the morning, afternoon, or evening?
   b. Are they prepared, presented, and conceived by the station or by local groups or individuals?

3. Originate and plan additional programs to serve the local audience. Submit these to the local station manager. Report upon his reaction to your suggestions.

4. By personal interviews determine the influence of the local station upon the community.

5. Present a radio drama version of a medical fact; then present a straight talk on the same topic. Which method of presentation results in the more lasting impression upon the audience? Dr. Bauer of the American Medical Association, 535 North Dearborn Street, Chicago, has a great number of scripts on medical subjects. It is possible to obtain from him mimeographed copies of some of these scripts and various instructions and informative papers on different phases of medical radio programs. Also, ask for the *Radio Handbook* of the Bureau of Health Information.

6. At the University of Michigan I have found that my students in writing courses are offered outside opportunity to practice the preparation of radio skits. The Bar Association of the state was eager to have a series of programs prepared to familiarize the public with the service rendered by the lawyer. The legal group furnished facts to be used in the preparation of such programs, which combined the dramatic with discussion; and the students prepared the continuity, which was then submitted to the committee of lawyers

before it was put on the air. Another group that appealed to the university was the Forty-Plus Club, which requested that the students prepare dramatic programs for these men over forty, who are seeking employment. Such programs offered problems that had to be met by those in the writing class. Historical groups, medical societies, and other organizations need aid in preparing their programs which may be obtained through the writing class and the workshop.

7. List some of the significant public-service programs that might be done in any community as television remotes. Include such things as meetings of the city council, school boards, etc. Why isn't this kind of program done more often? What are the economic factors involved?

Chapter XIV

MUSIC PROGRAMS

1. Prepare a musical program which is understandable to children and of interest to them. Write the continuity to be included in the program. Make the program lively, entertaining, and instructive.

2. Arrange a half-hour program of dance music. How would you unify the program? How will your announcer contribute interest to the program?

3. Write to WQXR, 730 Fifth Avenue, New York, for a sample of its program schedule and study the musical programming. The Zenith FM station in Chicago also does a fine job.

4. You will hear a great deal about A.S.C.A.P. Write to the American Society for Composers, Authors, and Publishers, 30 Rockefeller Plaza, New York, for *The ASCAP Story.*

5. Write up an abbreviated disc jockey show. To save time, it is suggested that each disc be played as follows: Begin at the beginning of the disc and fade it down and out after about thirty seconds. Place the needle about a quarter of an inch from the end of the recording and fade it back up to normal volume to close. This will give the proper effect of a recording without taking time to play the whole piece.

6. View the "Hit Parade" for at least three successive weeks. Make a careful analysis of the factors that make this a successful show. Estimate the number of man-hours involved for each week's show.

7. Plan a program of serious music for television. Stage it in some specific place, and plan the camera coverage, mike placement, and general scheme for the broadcast. What are the major problems involved?

Chapter XV

THE PREPARATION OF PROGRAMS FOR CHILDREN

1. Prepare a program of poetry that will interest children.

2. Listen to and watch various types of children's programs to determine the age level at which the program is aimed. What are the factors of the pro-

gram that make this apparent? Write to the producers of these programs to find out what ages they believe their audience to be.

3. Of what value is the child audience to the radio advertiser?

4. Many children's plays require the dramatization of such characters as frogs, fishes, dolls, dogs, etc. Attempt to evolve speech modes that might be used by these characters—for instance, how would a frog talk?

5. Get some of the albums of recorded children's stories and observe how they are done: music, sound effect, voices, etc.

6. Listen to or watch a program and criticize it from the standpoint of:

    a. Clarity for child comprehension.

    b. Interest for the listener.

    c. Plot.

    d. Personality and voice of performer.

    e. Percentage of commercial copy.

7. Select an historical incident that may be used as the plot for a play arranged for children. It must be interesting, informative, accurate, and have plenty of action.

8. Choose a successful radio play for children and adapt it for television.

9. If your school has a film library, check over the films that would make good TV shows for children.

10. What moral responsibilities do producers of children's programs have to assume?

11. To produce a simple television show for children, the following format is suggested. A storyteller sitting in an armchair reads the story while it is acted out in silhouette through a "picture frame" in the wall. Actors perform before a large cloth lighted from behind. If they are 15 to 20 feet from the opening in the storyteller's wall, they seem to be 6 to 10 inches high. The camera merely looks "at the picture on the wall" as the storyteller reads.

12. Watch all of the children's programs offered by one of your local television stations. Tabulate your findings by type, noting any common characteristics such as subject matter, style, treatment, etc.

Chapter XVI

BROADCASTS TO SCHOOLS

1. Prepare visual aids to be used in conjunction with a program to be received in the classroom.

2. Talk to a teacher who uses radio or television in her classroom and find out what her problems are in using the programs.

3. Talk to a teacher of the same subject who does not use radio or television, and find out why she does not.

4. Visit a classroom in which an educational program is being received. Report on the visual aids used, student attention, teacher attitude, reception, the program itself, and what the class retained from the program.

5. What sponsored programs may justly be considered educational? How do they compare in value and presentation with sustaining educational programs?

6. Write to the various boards of education in cities (Cleveland—WBOE, Detroit—WDTR, Chicago—WBEZ, Ohio State University—WOSU) where school broadcasting is extensive and obtain from them sample scripts and other informative material.

7. Report to the class on the use of radio and television by your local school system. Classify the broadcasts into direct-teaching, supplementary-instruction, and workshop programs.

Chapter XVII

WRITING THE RADIO AND TELEVISION PLAY

1. Listen to radio dramas to determine if all the characters are clearly drawn. How could their characters be better delineated?

2. Listen to and analyze a radio play.
   a. Type of plot.
   b. How much of the program time is devoted to the play?
   c. Number of main characters.
   d. How are characters identified?
   e. Is there a contrast of voices?
   f. How is the scene set?
   g. How are the transitions or scene changes made?
   h. What are the sound effects?
   i. Were they essential?
   j. How important to the play was the announcer or narrator?

3. Dramatize and cut for a 10-minute radio play a story by O. Henry, Bret Harte, Morgan Robertson, or some other short-story writer.

4. Write a brief skit using the same plot for a radio presentation and for a TV presentation. Present the radio version to one group of students and the TV presentation to another group, and try to ascertain which group got more out of the presentation.

5. Creative writers occasionally hit periods of stagnation in which stories and plot lines perversely refuse to take shape. The same difficulty afflicts students and professionals alike. The wellspring of creation seems to have run dry. Now what?

Scores of mechanisms have been developed to relieve this state of intellectual drought, so the following should not be taken as the only panacea. However, it can act as a lever to start the creative process moving.

Divide a page into six columns. In the first, jot down the most colorful adjectives you can dream up. In column two, list various occupations and character descriptions. Active verbs go into column three, and another group of characters into column four. In columns five and six list climactic verbs. Let's jot down some examples:

I	II	III	IV	V	VI
Glamorous	Chorus girl	Scares	Detective	Elopes	Escapes
Hunted	Flyer	Pursues	Moonshiner	Quarrels	Marries
Miserly	Minister	Cheats	Spy	Slanders	Jilts
Shrewd	Neighbor	Gambles	Salesman	Tempts	Rewards

Now you're all set to go (though, of course, you should have several more examples of your own under each category). Combine one word from each of the categories into a skeletal plot statement. Use dice if you want random selection. How about: hunted . . . chorus girl . . . cheats . . . spy . . . quarrels . . . escapes. Can't you begin to see a story there? As an exercise, list a dozen words under each category and make up 20 plot outlines. Playing with these six categories can be fun. Some have even turned it into a parlor game. Best of all, it is one way of stimulating your creative talent when you sit down to write a story.

6. By viewing and listening, and reading scripts, analyze the differences between radio drama and television drama. Compare the importance of the dialogue in each. Just what does the visual aspect of television add?

7. Experiment with various forms for TV scripts. Inspect scripts available from published collections or other sources and note the good and bad features of various script forms.

Chapter XVIII

WRITING THE RADIO AND TELEVISION SERIAL

1. Listen to four or five radio serials, noting how many characters appear in each episode. Compare with a television serial.

2. Check these serials to see the exact apportionment of time among the various elements of the programs: commercials, announcer's recap of the plot, the drama itself, announcer's teaser after the action.

3. Analyze a radio serial which is presented five days a week. How much advance is made in plot development during the week? Is plot or characterization more important? Do the same for a TV serial.

4. The series of radio skits is very much like a comic strip in a newspaper. Frequently the cartoonist will use a strip to summarize the action of the past month. Write a summarizing program for a series of radio skits.

5. At the University of Michigan, we took the report of a trial and from that transcript we started a serial—first the facts in an auto accident, then the selection of a jury, the testimony of witnesses, the charge to the jury, and finally the decision of the jury. The program became an interesting and informative serial. Try something like that. Write it for either radio or television.

Chapter XIX

DIRECTING THE RADIO PLAY AND THE ACTOR

1. What vocal qualities among the members of your class seem to type them for particular kinds of roles? Why? Could these people play the same kinds of roles in television drama?

2. Record three versions of a 5-minute radio drama (directed by three different people with three different casts, working independently). Play back all three to see how the characters are interpreted differently by different actors. Which interpretations do you feel more completely realize the intentions of the authors?

3. Problem in sound perspective: Place a door in an off-mike position near a microphone. On the same mike, move a speaking actor back from an on-mike to an off-mike position until the perspectives of door and actor are the same. Record the process for playback to the actor, so he can hear the perspectives come into the proper relationship.

Chapter XX

SOUND EFFECTS

1. Play a series of sound records for the class, asking each student to identify the sound with no clues but the sound itself. From this experiment, reach conclusions regarding (1) which recorded sound effects are self-identifying and which are not, (2) the importance of introducing a sound orally.

2. Devise dramatic situations, each requiring knocking on a door—demanding, stealthy, timid, etc. Demonstrate the different knocks and see if the class can determine your attitude.

3. Tell the story of a wakeful night with sounds of movement in the house. The sound effects should tell a story themselves. Rehearse these routines and present them for the class. For instance: a man drives up in an automobile, gets out, walks across the sidewalk and up some stairs, undresses, and goes to bed.

Chapter XXI

DIRECTING THE TELEVISION PLAY

1. Have the class read a variety of dramatic scripts and carefully analyze them. Stress the fact that an analysis of a script is not a rehash of the plot. Emphasize the dramatic values of the play: character, dialogue, comedy, tragedy, sentiment, suspense, etc. From what are these values to be derived? It is impossible to direct a dramatic show unless the director understands the script, knows what effects can be achieved with it, and how these effects can be gotten onto the TV screen.

2. Spend some time blocking the action for different scripts on paper. This requires the use of an accurate scale ground plan. Check the results by marking off the ground plan on the floor with chalk and having actors move according to the planned action. With sufficient practice the director can have the action quite accurately blocked before he ever meets with the cast.

3. View some dramatic shows with the class, pointing out how the blocking can emphasize and delineate character relationships. Stress that groupings, movement patterns, and business have an artistic purpose as well as a mechanical one.

4. Have each member of the class write a detailed analysis of the characters in a script. Then proceed to have them cast the show with known actors, and then with members of the class.

5. Have the members of the class stage some scenes from dramatic scripts. The scenes need not be long to demonstrate the problems of staging, and the difficult task of coaching actors.

Chapter XXII

THE TELEVISION ACTOR

1. Coach members of the class in a wide variety of dramatic scenes. Remember that for TV all scripts must be memorized! For TV the coach (or director) must work close to the actors so that you get the effect of close-ups. Work on gestures, facial expressions, and the other subtle techniques that can be used.

2. When a scene is ready, stage it as though it were on camera. Use a floor manager who will give signals, time cues, etc. When appropriate, be certain that the actors know which camera is on them.

3. Stage a scene as it would be done for a stage performance and then restage it for TV. Emphasize the limited space used in TV, the absence of need to play to the "front," the lack of need to project for the back row, and the differences in blocking.

4. Remember above all that acting is learned by acting. If you have students who want to learn to act, provide every possible opportunity for them to act on any medium. Once the student has learned something about acting it is relatively easy for him to adapt these skills to TV.

Chapter XXIII

TELEVISION PRODUCTION

1. If your school does not have a television studio, arrange to take your class to one of the local stations. Try to see the crew set up a show, and watch a rehearsal and the broadcast. Have each member of the class write a report on the visit.

2. Go through all of the studio and control-room jobs with the class. Be certain they understand each position and why each is important.

3. Select some representative TV shows and have the class analyze the production elements including settings, lighting, costumes, and the smoothness of the production as a whole.

4. Give strong emphasis to the photographic character of television. Go through the material on lenses and their properties with care. Read the pertinent chapters in *Techniques of Television Production* by Rudy Bretz. This is an extremely important phase of the medium to understand, and one that persons not accustomed to a visual medium find difficult to grasp. The construction and use of Bretz boxes, 35-millimeter still cameras, and other simulated devices will help.

Chapter XXIV

TELEVISION CAMERA DIRECTING

1. Using the Bretz plotter, plan the camera coverage for various kinds of shows. This requires the use of a ground plan drawn to ¼-inch scale. While this exercise might seem tedious at first, it is in many ways the best means of learning about the problems of planning what to do with TV cameras. Insist upon the maximum accuracy.

2. Make certain that the class understands how typical TV switching systems work and what they can do. Clarify the uses of the cut, the dissolve, and the fade. Observe how these transitions are used in various kinds of shows.

3. By staging scenes, planning the camera coverage with a plotter, and checking with a Bretz box, explore the relationship between blocking, camera positions, and choice of lenses.

4. If no equipment is available for actual practice, make every effort to observe a show being done from the control room. Note carefully how the director operates the cameras and the switcher, and coordinates the many production elements. Note the standard instructions and cues given.

5. Much can be learned about skillful use of cameras by watching the better live TV shows. Note how many cameras are used, from what positions, and with what effects.

Chapter XXV

AUDIO AND VIDEO RECORDING

1. Working with your control operator, learn how to spot a record.

2. Use your tape recorder to make sound recordings of traffic, thunderstorms, crowds, etc.

3. Arrange with distributors in your locality for demonstrations at your school of tape and disc recording equipment.

4. Obtain such literature as is available on kinescope and magnetic TV recording.

Chapter XXVI

THE BUSINESS OF RADIO AND TV ADVERTISING

1. Analyze a number of commercial programs. How much time is devoted in each to straight advertising? What proportion of the program period?

2. Ask your local station for a "rate card" which shows the cost of air time. Why does one segment of time cost more than another segment at a different hour?

3. Make a survey of local merchants.

    a. Interview those who are advertising by radio and television. Are they satisfied with the results?

    b. Interview those who are not advertising by radio and television. Why aren't they?

4. You are preparing to approach a merchant with the idea of selling him time upon the local station. Prepare a prospectus showing station coverage, the cost, the advantages, the tie-in campaign, and the program to be presented.

5. The manufacturer of Ironclad Overalls has decided to broadcast a series of 5-minute advertising programs.

    a. Decide upon a name for the series.

    b. Decide upon a time for presentation.

    c. Will the programs be given by transcriptions, or by spot programs?

    d. Create a distinctive idea for such a series.

    e. Plan and write continuity for the first program.

        (1) To what extent will music be used? For what purpose? What selections?

        (2) Will the program be in the form of skits, talks, or dialogues?

        (3) How will the advertising material be tied into the program material?

        (4) Number of actors required. Types.

    f. Outline the remainder of the series.

Chapter XXVII

WRITING COMMERCIAL CONTINUITY

1. Count the number of times that the sponsor's name (or the product name) is used in a 1-hour radio or TV program.

2. Make a comparison of the commercial copy used over the radio to advertise a product with the copy printed in magazines to advertise the same product, and with television copy used.

3. Analyze an advertisement in a national magazine. Write three 30-second commercials from the copy for radio, and three for television.

4. Go to your local station and obtain copies of its used commercial continuity for class examination. Endeavor to emulate the copy for the same product.

5. Write a series of commercial continuity slanted toward:

    a. Human interest.

    b. Economy.

    c. Hospitality.

    d. Personal appearance.

6. Radio sells ideas but not products. Therefore, the advertiser cannot put a product into your hands, but must be content to put an idea for *need* for his product in your mind. What are some of the ideas that he sells you which are designed to make you take the next step and buy his product?

7. Prepare the script for a television commercial, first as a live commercial and then as a film commercial. What are the desirable features of each form?

Chapter XXVIII

THE LAW AS IT AFFECTS BROADCASTING

1. Discuss the terms "public interest," "convenience," and "necessity." What types of programs come under each category?

Chapter XXIX

RADIO AND TELEVISION AS VOCATIONS

1. Check with your local station on the qualifications required of different employees.

2. Induce members of the staff of the local station to appear before the class and be interviewed concerning their work.

3. Go to an audition session as an observer (if you are too petrified to go as a participant) and report to the class on the procedure.

4. File an application for a particular position in a radio or TV station, stating your qualifications.

BIBLIOGRAPHY

RADIO—GENERAL

Beckoff, Samuel: *Radio and Television,* Oxford Book Company, Inc., New York, 1952.

Ewbank, H. L., and S. P. Lawton: *Broadcasting: Radio and Television,* Harper & Brothers, New York, 1952.

Gorham, Maurice: *Training for Radio,* U.N.E.S.C.O., Paris, 1949.

Head, Sidney: *Broadcasting in America,* Houghton Mifflin Company, Boston, 1956.

Joels, Merrin E.: *How to Get into Radio and Television,* Hastings House, Publishers, Inc., New York, 1955.

Jones, Charles R.: *Your Career in Motion Pictures, Television, Radio,* Sheridan House, New York, 1949.

Levenson, William B., and Edward Stasheff: *Teaching Through Radio and Television,* rev. college ed., Rinehart & Company, Inc., New York, 1952.

Lindsley, Charles F.: *Radio and Television Communication,* McGraw-Hill Book Company, Inc., New York, 1952.

Meyer, J. S.: *Picture Book of Radio and Television and How They Work,* Lothrop, Lee & Shepard Co., New York, 1951.

Phillips, David C., John M. Grogan, and Earl H. Ryan: *Introduction to Radio and Television,* The Ronald Press Company, New York, 1954.

Ranson, Jo, and Richard Pack: *Opportunities in Radio,* Vocational Guidance Manuals, Inc., New York, 1949.

Reinsch, J. Leonard: *Radio Station Management,* Harper & Brothers, New York, 1950.

Schramm, Wilbur: *Mass Communications,* University of Illinois Press, Urbana, Ill., 1949.

Skornia, Harry Jay, Robert H. Lee, and Fred A. Brewer: *Creative Broadcasting,* Prentice-Hall, Inc., Englewood Cliffs, N. J., 1950.

Warner, Harry P.: *Radio and Television Rights,* Matthew Bender & Co., New York, 1953.

RADIO ADVERTISING

EVANS, JACOB A.: *Selling and Promoting Radio and Television*, Printer's Ink, New York, 1954. (Periodical).

MIDGLEY, NED: *The Advertising and Business Side of Radio*, Prentice-Hall, Inc., Englewood Cliffs, N. J., 1952.

SEEHAFER, EUGENE F., and J. W. LAEMMAR: *Successful Radio and Television Advertising*, McGraw-Hill Book Company, Inc., New York, 1951.

RADIO PRODUCTION AND DIRECTION

BARNHART, LYLE D.: *Radio and Television Announcing*, Prentice-Hall, Inc., Englewood Cliffs, N. J., 1953.

————: *Problems in Announcing for Radio and Television*, Student Book Exchange, Evanston, Ill., 1950.

BARNOUW, ERIC: *Handbook of Radio Production*, Little, Brown & Company, Boston, 1949.

CREWS, A. R.: *Radio Production-Directing*, college ed., Houghton Mifflin Company, Boston, 1944.

DIMOND, SIDNEY A., and DONALD M. ANDERSSON: *Radio and Television Workshop Manual*, Prentice-Hall, Inc., Englewood Cliffs, N. J., 1952.

DUERR, EDWIN: *Radio and Television Acting*, Rinehart & Company, Inc., New York, 1950.

GILMORE, ART, and GLENN Y. MIDDLETON: *Television and Radio Announcing*, Radio Publishers, Hollywood, 1949.

GOULD, SAMUEL B.: *Training the Local Announcer*, Longmans, Green & Co., Inc., New York, 1950.

KINGSON, WALTER KRULEVITCH, and ROME COWGILL: *Radio Drama Acting and Production: A Handbook*, college ed., Rinehart & Company, Inc., New York, 1950.

TURNBULL, ROBERT B.: *Radio and Television Sound Effects*, college ed., Rinehart & Company, Inc., New York, 1951.

WHITE, MELVIN R.: *Beginning Radio Production*, Northwestern Press, Minneapolis, 1950.

————: *Microphone Technique for Radio Actors*, Northwestern Press, Minneapolis, 1950.

RADIO WRITING

CAMPBELL, LAURENCE R., HARRY E. HEATH, and RAY V. JOHNSON: *A Guide to Radio-TV Writing*, Iowa State College Press, Ames, 1950.

COWGILL, ROME: *Fundamentals of Writing for Radio*, college ed., Rinehart & Company, Inc., New York, 1949.

FLETON, FELIX: *The Radio Play: Its Techniques and Possibilities*, Transatlantic Arts, New York, 1949.

KAPLAN, MILTON ALLEN: *Radio and Poetry*, Columbia University Press, New York, 1949.

MACKEY, D. R.: *Drama on the Air*, Prentice-Hall, Inc., Englewood Cliffs, N. J., 1951.

MALONEY, MARTIN: *The Radio Play*, Student Book Exchange, Evanston, Ill., 1949.

McCANN, DOROTHY B.: *Do's and Don'ts of Radio Writing*, McCann-Erickson Advertising Agency, New York, 1951.

MILLER, JUSTIN: *The Profession of Radio Farm Broadcasting*, National Association of Radio and Television Broadcasters, Washington, D.C., 1949.

WYLIE, MAX: *Radio and Television Writing*, college ed., Rinehart & Company, Inc., New York, 1950.

TELEVISION—GENERAL

ALDRICH, LOUISE D.: *Censorship of Television*, National Association of Radio and Television Broadcasters, Washington, D.C., 1951.

BENDICK, JEANNE, and ROBERT BENDICK: *Television Works Like This*, McGraw-Hill Book Company, Inc., New York, 1954.

BETTINGER, HOYLAND: *Television Techniques*, new rev. college ed., Harper & Brothers, New York, 1955.

BOLEN, MURRAY: *Fundamentals for Television*, Radio Publishers, Hollywood, 1950.

CALLAHAN, JENNIE W.: *Television in School, College and Community*, McGraw-Hill Book Company, Inc., New York, 1953.

CHESTER, GIRAUD, and GARNET R. GARRISON: *Television and Radio*, 2d ed., Appleton-Century-Crofts, Inc., New York, 1956.

CHINN, HOWARD A.: *Television Broadcasting*, McGraw-Hill Book Company, Inc., New York, 1953.

CUMMING, WILLIAM K.: *This Is Educational Television*, The Author, Lansing, Mich., 1954.

DENMAN, FRANK: *Television, the Magic Window*, The Macmillan Company, New York, 1952.

ENNES, HAROLD E.: *Principles and Practices of Telecasting Operations*, Howard W. Sams, Indianapolis, 1953.

FLOHERTY, JOHN JOSEPH: *Television Story*, J. B. Lippincott Company, Philadelphia, 1951.

GABLE, LUTHER S. H.: *The Miracle of Television*, Wilcox & Follett Co., Chicago, 1949.

HARRINGTON, RUTH LEE: *Your Opportunities in Television*, Medill McBride Co., New York, 1949.

HEAD, SIDNEY: *Broadcasting in America*, Houghton Mifflin Company, Boston, 1956.

HODAPP, WILLIAM: *The Television Manual*, Farrar, Straus & Young, Inc., New York, 1953.

KAUFMAN, WILLIAM IRVING: *Your Career in Television,* Merlin Press, New York, 1950.

KIVER, MILTON E.: *Television Simplified,* 4th ed., D. Van Nostrand Company, Inc., Princeton, N. J., 1954.

RANSON, JO: *Opportunities in Television,* Vocational Guidance Manuals, Inc., New York, 1950.

STASHEFF, EDWARD, and RUDY BRETZ: *The Television Program, Its Writing, Direction and Production,* new rev. ed., Hill and Wang, Inc., New York, 1956.

TOOLEY, HOWARD: *The Television Workshop,* The Northwestern Press, Minneapolis, 1953.

VAN VOLKENBURG, J. L.: *The Structure of Television,* Columbia Broadcasting System, New York, 1949.

WARNER, HARRY P.: *Radio and Television Law,* Matthew Bender & Co., New York, 1948.

TELEVISION ADVERTISING

SETTEL, IRVING: *Television Advertising and Promotion Handbook,* Thomas Y. Crowell Company, New York, 1953.

SEEHAFER, EUGENE F., and J. W. LAEMMAR: *Successful Radio and Television Advertising,* McGraw-Hill Book Company, Inc., New York, 1951.

TELEVISION PRODUCTION AND DIRECTION

ADAMS, CHARLES: *Producing and Directing for Television,* Henry Holt and Company, Inc., New York, 1953.

BRETZ, RUDY: *Techniques of Television Production,* McGraw-Hill Book Company, Inc., New York, 1953.

HUBBELL, RICHARD: *Television Programming and Production,* rev. college ed., Rinehart & Company, Inc., New York, 1950.

KAUFMAN, WILLIAM I.: *How to Direct for Television,* Hastings House, Publishers, Inc., New York, 1955.

O'MEARA, CARROLL: *Television Program Production,* college ed., The Ronald Press Company, New York, 1955.

REISZ, KAREL: *The Technique of Film Editing: Basic Principles for TV,* Farrar, Straus & Young, Inc., New York, 1953.

WADE, R. J.: *Designing for TV,* Pellegrini & Cudahy, New York, 1952.

WHITE, MELVIN R.: *Beginning Television Production,* college ed., Burgess Publishing Co., Minneapolis, 1953.

TELEVISION WRITING

BRETZ, RUDY, and EDWARD STASHEFF: *Television Scripts for Staging and Study,* Hill and Wang, Inc., New York, 1953.

CAMPBELL, L., HARRY HEATH, and R. JOHNSON: *A Guide to Radio-TV Writing,* Iowa State College Press, Ames, 1950.

DRISCOLL, WILLIAM C.: *Editing Television News,* Strauss Publications, Philadelphia, 1950.

GREENE, ROBERT: *Television Writing,* college ed., Harper & Brothers, New York, 1952.

HEATH, ERIC: *Writing for Television,* rev. ed., Research Publishing Co., Los Angeles, 1953.

KAUFMAN, WILLIAM I.: *How to Write for Television,* Hastings House, Publishers, Inc., New York, 1955.

MOSSE, BASKETT, and FRED WHITING: *Television News Handbook,* Northwestern University Press, Evanston, Ill., 1953.

ROBERTS, EDWARD BARRY: *Television Writing and Selling,* The Writer, Inc., Boston, 1954.

WEISS, M. R.: *The TV Writer's Guide,* Pellegrini & Cudahy, New York, 1952.

WYLIE, MAX: *Radio and Television Writing,* rev. college ed., Rinehart & Company, Inc., New York, 1950.

INDEX

521

DATE DUE

APR 2 6 1994	
NOV 2 2 1998	
MAR 1 8 1999	

DEMCO, INC. 38-2931